DISCOVER INTRANETS

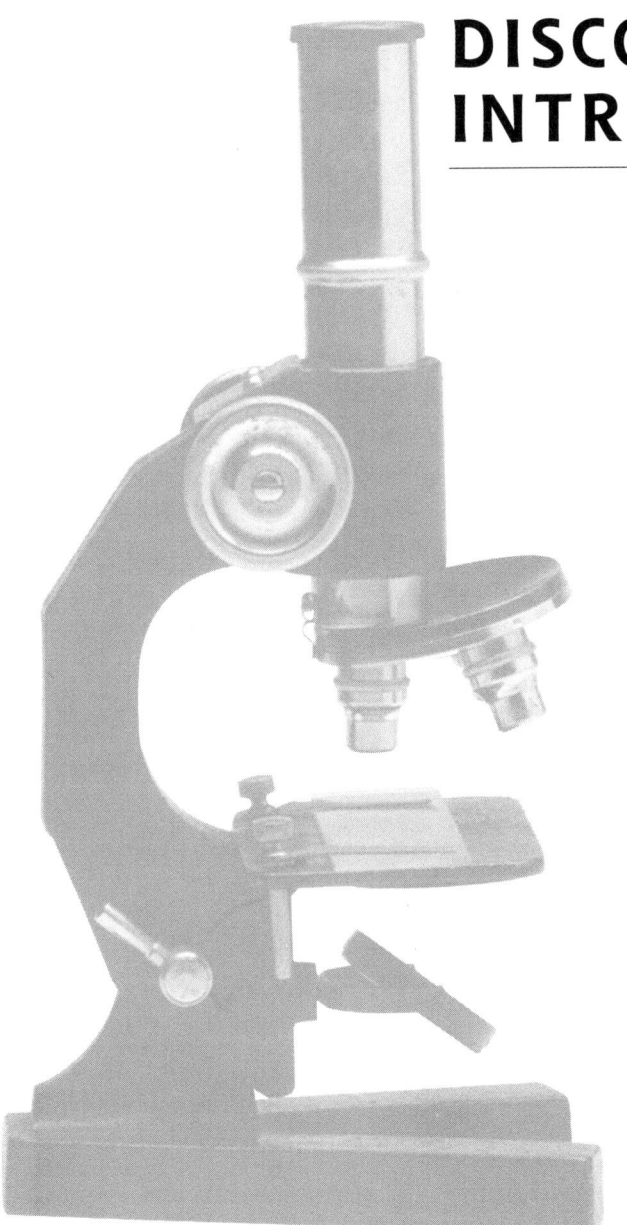

DISCOVER
INTRANETS

BY SUZANNE VAN CLEVE
AND MIKE BRITTON

IDG BOOKS WORLDWIDE, INC.

AN INTERNATIONAL
DATA GROUP COMPANY

FOSTER CITY, CA • CHICAGO, IL •
INDIANAPOLIS, IN • SOUTHLAKE, TX

Discover Intranets

Published by
IDG Books Worldwide, Inc.
An International Data Group Company
919 E. Hillsdale Blvd., Suite 400
Foster City, CA 94404

`http://www.idgbooks.com` (IDG Books Worldwide Web site)

Copyright © 1997 IDG Books Worldwide, Inc. All rights reserved. No part of this book, including interior design, cover design, and icons, may be reproduced or transmitted in any form, by any means (electronic, photocopying, recording, or otherwise) without the prior written permission of the publisher.

Library of Congress Catalog Card No.: 97-70950

ISBN: 0-7645-4020-3

Printed in the United States of America

10 9 8 7 6 5 4 3 2 1

1B/SR/QU/ZX/FC

Distributed in the United States by IDG Books Worldwide, Inc.

Distributed by Macmillan Canada for Canada; by Contemporanea de Ediciones for Venezuela; by Distribuidora Cuspide for Argentina; by CITEC for Brazil; by Ediciones ZETA S.C.R. Ltda. for Peru; by Editorial Limusa SA for Mexico; by Transworld Publishers Limited in the United Kingdom and Europe; by Academic Bookshop for Egypt; by Levant Distributors S.A.R.L. for Lebanon; by Al Jassim for Saudi Arabia; by Simron Pty. Ltd. for South Africa; by Pustak Mahal for India; by The Computer Bookshop for India; by Toppan Company Ltd. for Japan; by Addison Wesley Publishing Company for Korea; by Longman Singapore Publishers Ltd. for Singapore, Malaysia, Thailand, and Indonesia; by Unalis Corporation for Taiwan; by WS Computer Publishing Company, Inc. for the Philippines; by WoodsLane Pty. Ltd. for Australia; by WoodsLane Enterprises Ltd. for New Zealand. Authorized Sales Agent: Anthony Rudkin Associates for the Middle East and North Africa.

For general information on IDG Books Worldwide's books in the U.S., please call our Consumer Customer Service department at 800-762-2974. For reseller information, including discounts and premium sales, please call our Reseller Customer Service department at 800-434-3422.

For information on where to purchase IDG Books Worldwide's books outside the U.S., please contact our International Sales department at 415-655-3172 or fax 415-655-3295.

For information on foreign language translations, please contact our Foreign & Subsidiary Rights department at 415-655-3021 or fax 415-655-3281.

For sales inquiries and special prices for bulk quantities, please contact our Sales department at 415-655-3200 or write to the address above.

For information on using IDG Books Worldwide's books in the classroom or for ordering examination copies, please contact our Educational Sales department at 800-434-2086 or fax 817-251-8174.

For press review copies, author interviews, or other publicity information, please contact our Public Relations department at 415-655-3000 or fax 415-655-3299.

For authorization to photocopy items for corporate, personal, or educational use, please contact Copyright Clearance Center, 222 Rosewood Drive, Danvers, MA 01923, or fax 508-750-4470.

LIMIT OF LIABILITY/DISCLAIMER OF WARRANTY: AUTHOR AND PUBLISHER HAVE USED THEIR BEST EFFORTS IN PREPARING THIS BOOK. IDG BOOKS WORLDWIDE, INC., AND AUTHOR MAKE NO REPRESENTATIONS OR WARRANTIES WITH RESPECT TO THE ACCURACY OR COMPLETENESS OF THE CONTENTS OF THIS BOOK AND SPECIFICALLY DISCLAIM ANY IMPLIED WARRANTIES OF MERCHANTABILITY OR FITNESS FOR A PARTICULAR PURPOSE. THERE ARE NO WARRANTIES WHICH EXTEND BEYOND THE DESCRIPTIONS CONTAINED IN THIS PARAGRAPH. NO WARRANTY MAY BE CREATED OR EXTENDED BY SALES REPRESENTATIVES OR WRITTEN SALES MATERIALS. THE ACCURACY AND COMPLETENESS OF THE INFORMATION PROVIDED HEREIN AND THE OPINIONS STATED HEREIN ARE NOT GUARANTEED OR WARRANTED TO PRODUCE ANY PARTICULAR RESULTS, AND THE ADVICE AND STRATEGIES CONTAINED HEREIN MAY NOT BE SUITABLE FOR EVERY INDIVIDUAL. NEITHER IDG BOOKS WORLDWIDE, INC., NOR AUTHOR SHALL BE LIABLE FOR ANY LOSS OF PROFIT OR ANY OTHER COMMERCIAL DAMAGES, INCLUDING BUT NOT LIMITED TO SPECIAL, INCIDENTAL, CONSEQUENTIAL, OR OTHER DAMAGES.

TRADEMARKS: ALL BRAND NAMES AND PRODUCT NAMES USED IN THIS BOOK ARE TRADE NAMES, SERVICE MARKS, TRADEMARKS, OR REGISTERED TRADEMARKS OF THEIR RESPECTIVE OWNERS. IDG BOOKS WORLDWIDE IS NOT ASSOCIATED WITH ANY PRODUCT OR VENDOR MENTIONED IN THIS BOOK.

IDG BOOKS WORLDWIDE is a trademark under exclusive license to IDG Books Worldwide, Inc., from International Data Group, Inc.

ABOUT IDG BOOKS WORLDWIDE

Welcome to the world of IDG Books Worldwide.

IDG Books Worldwide, Inc., is a subsidiary of International Data Group, the world's largest publisher of computer-related information and the leading global provider of information services on information technology. IDG was founded more than 25 years ago and now employs more than 8,500 people worldwide. IDG publishes more than 275 computer publications in over 75 countries (see listing below). More than 60 million people read one or more IDG publications each month.

Launched in 1990, IDG Books Worldwide is today the #1 publisher of best-selling computer books in the United States. We are proud to have received eight awards from the Computer Press Association in recognition of editorial excellence and three from *Computer Currents*' First Annual Readers' Choice Awards. Our best-selling ...For Dummies® series has more than 30 million copies in print with translations in 30 languages. IDG Books Worldwide, through a joint venture with IDG's Hi-Tech Beijing, became the first U.S. publisher to publish a computer book in the People's Republic of China. In record time, IDG Books Worldwide has become the first choice for millions of readers around the world who want to learn how to better manage their businesses.

Our mission is simple: Every one of our books is designed to bring extra value and skill-building instructions to the reader. Our books are written by experts who understand and care about our readers. The knowledge base of our editorial staff comes from years of experience in publishing, education, and journalism — experience we use to produce books for the '90s. In short, we care about books, so we attract the best people. We devote special attention to details such as audience, interior design, use of icons, and illustrations. And because we use an efficient process of authoring, editing, and desktop publishing our books electronically, we can spend more time ensuring superior content and spend less time on the technicalities of making books.

You can count on our commitment to deliver high-quality books at competitive prices on topics you want to read about. At IDG Books Worldwide, we continue in the IDG tradition of delivering quality for more than 25 years. You'll find no better book on a subject than one from IDG Books Worldwide.

John Kilcullen
CEO
IDG Books Worldwide, Inc.

Eighth Annual Computer Press Awards ≥1992

Ninth Annual Computer Press Awards ≥1993

Tenth Annual Computer Press Awards ≥1994

Eleventh Annual Computer Press Awards ≥1995

IDG Books Worldwide, Inc., is a subsidiary of International Data Group, the world's largest publisher of computer-related information and the leading global provider of information services on information technology. International Data Group publishes over 275 computer publications in over 75 countries. Sixty million people read one or more International Data Group publications each month. International Data Group's publications include: **ARGENTINA:** Buyer's Guide, Computerworld Argentina, PC World Argentina; **AUSTRALIA:** Australian Macworld, Australian PC World, Australian Reseller News, Computerworld, IT Casebook, Network World, Publish, Webmaster; **AUSTRIA:** Computerwelt Osterreich, Networks Austria, PC Tip Austria; **BANGLADESH:** PC World Bangladesh; **BELARUS:** PC World Belarus; **BELGIUM:** Data News; **BRAZIL:** Annuário de Informática, Computerworld, Connections, Macworld, PC Player, PC World, Publish, Reseller News, Supergamepower; **BULGARIA:** Computerworld Bulgaria, Network World Bulgaria, PC & MacWorld Bulgaria; **CANADA:** CIO Canada, Client/Server World, ComputerWorld Canada, InfoWorld Canada, NetworkWorld Canada, WebWorld; **CHILE:** Computerworld Chile, PC World Chile; **COLOMBIA:** Computerworld Colombia, PC World Colombia; **COSTA RICA:** PC World Centro America; **THE CZECH AND SLOVAK REPUBLICS:** Computerworld Czechoslovakia, Macworld Czech Republic, PC World Czechoslovakia; **DENMARK:** Communications World Danmark, Computerworld Danmark, Macworld Danmark, PC World Danmark, Techworld Denmark; **DOMINICAN REPUBLIC:** PC World Republica Dominicana; **ECUADOR:** PC World Ecuador; **EGYPT:** Computerworld Middle East, PC World Middle East; **EL SALVADOR:** PC World Centro America; **FINLAND:** MikroPC, Tietoverkko, Tietoviikko; **FRANCE:** Distributique, Hebdo, Info PC, Le Monde Informatique, Macworld, Reseaux & Telecoms, WebMaster France; **GERMANY:** Computer Partner, Computerwoche, Computerwoche Extra, Computerwoche FOCUS, Global Online, Macwelt, PC Welt; **GREECE:** Amiga Computing, GamePro Greece, Multimedia World; **GUATEMALA:** PC World Centro America; **HONDURAS:** PC World Centro America; **HONG KONG:** Computerworld Hong Kong, PC World Hong Kong, Publish in Asia; **HUNGARY:** ABCD CD-ROM, Computerworld Szamitastechnika, Internetto online Magazine, PC World Hungary, PC-X Magazin Hungary; **ICELAND:** Tolvuheimur PC World Island; **INDIA:** Information Communications World, Information Systems Computerworld, PC World India, Publish in Asia; **INDONESIA:** InfoKomputer PC World, Komputek Computerworld, Publish in Asia; **IRELAND:** ComputerScope, PC Live!; **ISRAEL:** Macworld Israel, People & Computers/Computerworld; **ITALY:** Computerworld Italia, Macworld Italia, Networking Italia, PC World Italia; **JAPAN:** DTP World, Macworld Japan, Nikkei Personal Computing, OS/2 World Japan, SunWorld Japan, Windows NT World, Windows World Japan; **KENYA:** PC World East African; **KOREA:** Hi-Tech Information, Macworld Korea, PC World Korea; **MACEDONIA:** PC World Macedonia; **MALAYSIA:** Computerworld Malaysia, PC World Malaysia, Publish in Asia; **MALTA:** PC World Malta; **MEXICO:** Computerworld Mexico, PC World Mexico; **MYANMAR:** PC World Myanmar; **NETHERLANDS:** Computer! Totaal, LAN Internetworking Magazine, LAN World Buyers Guide, Macworld Netherlands, Net, WebWereld; **NEW ZEALAND:** Absolute Beginners Guide and Plain & Simple Series, Computer Buyer, Computer Industry Directory, Computerworld New Zealand, MTB, Network World, PC World New Zealand; **NICARAGUA:** PC World Centro America; **NORWAY:** Computerworld Norge, CW Rapport, Datamagasinet, Financial Rapport, Kursguide Norge, Macworld Norge, Multimediaworld Norge, PC World Ekspress Norge, PC World Nettverk, PC World Norge, PC World ProduktGuide Norge; **PAKISTAN:** Computerworld Pakistan; **PANAMA:** PC World Panama; **PEOPLE'S REPUBLIC OF CHINA:** China Computer Users, China Computerworld, China InfoWorld, China Telecom World Weekly, Computer & Communication, Electronic Design China, Electronics Today, Electronics Weekly, Game Software, PC World China, Popular Computer Week, Software Weekly, Software World, Telecom World; **PERU:** Computerworld Peru, PC World Profesional Peru, PC World SoHo Peru; **PHILIPPINES:** Click!, Computerworld Philippines, PC World Philippines, Publish in Asia; **POLAND:** Computerworld Poland, Computerworld Special Report Poland, Cyber, Macworld Poland, Networld Poland, PC World Komputer; **PORTUGAL:** Cerebro/PC World, Computerworld/Correio Informático, Dealer World Portugal, Mac*In/PC*In Portugal, Multimedia World; **PUERTO RICO:** PC World Puerto Rico; **ROMANIA:** Computerworld Romania, PC World Romania, Telecom Romania; **RUSSIA:** Computerworld Russia, Mir PK, Publish, Seti; **SINGAPORE:** Computerworld Singapore, PC World Singapore, Publish in Asia; **SLOVENIA:** Monitor; **SOUTH AFRICA:** Computing SA, Network World SA, Software World SA; **SPAIN:** Communicaciones World España, Computerworld España, Dealer World España, Macworld España, PC World España; **SRI LANKA:** Infolink PC World; **SWEDEN:** CAP&Design, Computer Sweden, Corporate Computing Sweden, Internetworld Sweden, it.branschen, Macworld Sweden, MaxiData Sweden, MikroDatorn, Nätverk & Kommunikation, PC World Sweden, PCaktiv, Windows World Sweden; **SWITZERLAND:** Computerworld Schweiz, Macworld Schweiz, PCtip; **TAIWAN:** Computerworld Taiwan, Macworld Taiwan, NEW ViSiON/Publish, PC World Taiwan, Windows World Taiwan; **THAILAND:** Publish in Asia, Thai Computerworld; **TURKEY:** Computerworld Turkiye, Macworld Turkiye, Network World Turkiye, PC World Turkiye; **UKRAINE:** Computerworld Kiev, Multimedia World Ukraine, PC World Ukraine; **UNITED KINGDOM:** Acorn User UK, Amiga Action UK, Amiga Computing UK, Apple Talk UK, Computing, Macworld, Parents and Computers UK, PC Advisor, PC Home, PSX Pro, The WEB; **UNITED STATES:** Cable in the Classroom, CIO Magazine, Computerworld, DOS World, Federal Computer Week, GamePro Magazine, InfoWorld, I-Way, Macworld, Network World, PC Games, PC World, Publish, Video Event, THE WEB Magazine, and WebMaster; online webzines: JavaWorld, NetscapeWorld, and SunWorld Online; **URUGUAY:** InfoWorld Uruguay; **VENEZUELA:** Computerworld Venezuela, PC World Venezuela; and **VIETNAM:** PC World Vietnam. 2/14/97

Welcome to the Discover Series

Do you want to discover the best and most efficient ways to use your computer and learn about technology? Books in the Discover series teach you the essentials of technology with a friendly, confident approach. You'll find a Discover book on almost any subject — from the Internet to intranets, from Web design and programming to the business programs that make your life easier.

We've provided valuable, real-world examples that help you relate to topics faster. Discover books begin by introducing you to the main features of programs, so you start by doing something *immediately*. The focus is to teach you how to perform tasks that are useful and meaningful in your day-to-day work. You might create a document or graphic, explore your computer, surf the Web, or write a program. Whatever the task, you learn the most commonly used features, and focus on the best tips and techniques for doing your work. You'll get results quickly, and discover the best ways to use software and technology in your everyday life.

You may find the following elements and features in this book:

Discovery Central: This tear-out card is a handy quick reference to important tasks or ideas covered in the book.

Quick Tour: The Quick Tour gets you started working with the book right away.

Real-Life Vignettes: Throughout the book you'll see one-page scenarios illustrating a real-life application of a topic covered.

Goals: Each chapter opens with a list of goals you can achieve by reading the chapter.

Side Trips: These asides include additional information about alternative or advanced ways to approach the topic covered.

Bonuses: Time-saving tips and more advanced techniques are covered in each chapter.

Discovery Center: This guide illustrates key procedures covered throughout the book.

Visual Index: You'll find real-world documents in the Visual Index, with page numbers pointing you to where you should turn to achieve the effects shown.

Throughout the book, you'll also notice some special icons and formatting:

FEATURE FOCUS — A Feature Focus icon highlights new features in the software's latest release, and points out significant differences between it and the previous version.

WEB PATH — Web Paths refer you to Web sites that provide additional information about the topic.

TIP — Tips offer timesaving shortcuts, expert advice, quick techniques, or brief reminders.

X-REF — The X-Ref icon refers you to other chapters or sections for more information.

> **Pull Quotes emphasize important ideas that are covered in the chapter.**

NOTE — Notes provide additional information or highlight special points of interest about a topic.

CAUTION — The Caution icon alerts you to potential problems you should watch out for.

The Discover series delivers interesting, insightful, and inspiring information about technology to help you learn faster and retain more. So the next time you want to find answers to your technology questions, reach for a Discover book. We hope the entertaining, easy-to-read style puts you at ease and makes learning fun.

Credits

ACQUISITIONS EDITOR
Nancy Dunn

DEVELOPMENT EDITOR
Susannah Davidson

COPY EDITOR
Tracy Brown

TECHNICAL EDITOR
Rehan Zaidi

PROJECT COORDINATOR
Katy German

QUALITY CONTROL SPECIALIST
Mick Arellano

GRAPHICS AND PRODUCTION SPECIALISTS
Dina F Quan
Ed Penslien

PROOFREADERS
Melissa Buddendeck

INDEXER
David Heiret

BOOK DESIGN
Seventeenth Street Studios
Phyllis Beaty
Kurt Krames

About the Authors

Suzanne Van Cleve and **Michael R. Britton** are the principals of Van Cleve Britton Publishing, Ltd., providing authoring, editorial, design, and production services to publishers.

Van Cleve and Britton have coauthored several books for IDG Books Worldwide. They have developed computer book titles for IDG Books and Adobe Press. Van Cleve and Britton manage the marketing, sales, production, and manufacturing for ICS Press.

Van Cleve and Britton have over 30 years of expertise in the publishing industry, developing comprehensive information management and production systems for HarperCollins, Random House, Macmillan, Adobe Press, and Standard Publishing.

For more information, visit their Web site at:

http://www.vcbweb.com

or they can be reached via e-mail at:

suzannevan@earthlink.net

FOR MY MOM, THE WIND BENEATH MY WINGS.
—SVC

PREFACE

Why Is This Book Different?

As authors, we take a manager's perspective first, and a technologist's perspective second. While we've successfully integrated both sides in our careers as publishing professionals, we know that content is still king, whether it comes on dead trees or bits and bytes.

We began creating intranets several years ago, focusing on the content first and using some really rudimentary tools to get the job done. Today, there are a host of incredibly powerful tools are available, and intranet capabilities and ease of use improve continually. You don't have to be a digithead to create an intranet. What you do need is a clear head, the ability to categorize and prioritize information, and a willingness to explore the digital world.

> **TIP** Who are the digitheads? They are the Digerati: People who dig into the nuts and bolts of technology and often speak in code and other technical jargon. They are infinitely useful when building the technical side your intranet — just keep a glossary handy!

Who Should Read This Book?

As corporations downsize to survive tough economic conditions and dwindling profitability, smart professionals are recognizing that efficiencies and effective information management can translate into success.

This book is designed for both nontechnical managers who want an overview of the emerging technology and IT professionals who want to learn more about the content side of the digital world. This isn't a book about hardware platforms or custom coding solutions; there are other great titles on that subject.

> **TIP** What is the IT? IT at your company probably refers to the Information Technology department, are also known as: Systems, MIS (Management Information Systems), and IS (sort of short for MIS). They are generally the folks who find code and other technical details to be quite fascinating.

For a searchable database on many detailed technical books, visit the IDG Books Worldwide Web site at:

`http://www.idgbooks.com`

Emerging intranet technologies empower managers to run offices with technology performing the most routine and administrative tasks. Properly used, an intranet can redefine your internal operations dramatically, as well as improve your communication with the outside world.

How This Book Is Organized

In Part I, "Are You Ready for an Intranet," we help you to evaluate what should be included, and tell you what issues to anticipate in designing and implementing an intranet. We'll give you some tips on justifying both the time and money resources required to implement system and meet your objectives.

In Part II, "How to Create and Maintain an Intranet," we dive into the nuts and bolts of *how* to implement your intranet. We use conventional office filing techniques to illustrate similar (but better!) functionality with a digital solution. We explain the technical side and explore implementation issues.

Finally, in Part Three, "Advanced Intranet Features," we talk about advanced features and how to keep your intranet from getting musty. We also bring out our crystal ball and share some projections about where this evolution is headed and how you can utilize technology to keep your organization on the cutting edge of information management.

Where Do You Go from Here?

Think about weaving these new technology tools into your current work. And then contemplate the possibilities for your future business, letting technology be the catalyst for your success.

Keep this book handy as a reference. Conasider it a compass, and refer to it whenever you think integrating a new feature into your intranet might help you to be more efficient.

Enough said. Come along for the ride as we explore how to create dynamic digital information within an organization.

ACKNOWLEDGMENTS

We'd like to thank Bradford Foltz for his intranet designs and the juggling-balls metaphor used throughout Chapter 4. We'd also like to thank Jerry Lazar for his contributions on networking and security.

CONTENTS AT A GLANCE

Preface, xi
Acknowledgments, xiii

QUICK TOUR   1

PART ONE—ARE YOU READY FOR AN INTRANET?

1   INTRODUCTION TO INTRANETS   9
2   ASSESSING CONTENT, CREATING A PROCESS   25
3   JUSTIFYING YOUR INTRANET   35
4   EFFECTIVE DESIGN FOR EASY ACCESS   51

PART TWO—HOW TO CREATE AND MAINTAIN AN INTRANET

5   SETTING A COMMON DENOMINATOR   71
6   TOOLS TO CREATE INTRANET PAGES   87
7   ALL ABOUT BROWSERS   115
8   TOOLS FOR SITE MANAGEMENT   125
9   TOOLS FOR SEARCHING YOUR INTRANET   139
10   HARDWARE NEEDS AND NETWORK STRATEGIES   155
11   INTRANET SECURITY ISSUES   169

PART THREE—ADVANCED INTRANET FEATURES

12 TRAINING AND SUPPORT   187

13 INTEGRATING ADDITIONAL SERVICES   201

14 AUDIO AND VIDEO CONFERENCING   225

15 EXPANDING YOUR INTRANET TOOLBOX   237

16 MAKING YOUR INTRANET ORGANIC   255

Discovery Center, 265
Visual Index, 291
Appendix A, 297
Index, 311

CONTENTS

Preface, xi

Acknowledgments, xiii

QUICK TOUR, 1

PART ONE—ARE YOU READY FOR AN INTRANET? 7

1 INTRODUCTION TO INTRANETS, 9

What Is an Intranet?, 10

The Rise of the Full-Service Intranet, 12
  Bridges to Proprietary Systems, 13
  Full Integration of All Digital Information Needs, 14

Benefits: Access to a World of Information, 15
  Easy Access, 15
  Effectively Managed and Accessible Content, 17
  Productivity Gains, 19

Sacrifices, 20
  Network Dependence, 20
  Resource Requirements, 21
  Process Issues, 21

Does Your Boss Get It?, 21

Managing Your Expectations, 22
  Your Staff's Use of Information, 22
  Technology Tools, 22

Quiz: Are You Ready for an Intranet?, 23

Summary, 24

2 ASSESSING CONTENT, CREATING A PROCESS, 25

Understanding the Power of Information, 25

What Are All Those Documents for, Anyway?, 26
  Assessing Your Content, 26
  Managing Your Content, 27

The Joys of Process Mapping, 29

Leaders of the Pack, 32

Electronic Flowcharting Tools, 33

Summary, 34

3 JUSTIFYING YOUR INTRANET, 35

The Art of the Plan, 35
- Purposes of Your Plan, 36
- Elements of Your Plan, 36

Owning Your Stuff, 38
- It's a New Ballgame, 39
- Setting Up a Team Meeting, 43

Technical Issues, 43

Financial Issues, 43
- Estimating Your Costs, 44
- Potential Savings, 44
- Cost and Savings Projecting, 44

Preparing a Schedule, 47

Look Out for Feature Creep, 48

Return on Investment, 49
- ROI, 49
- Payback Period, 50

Summary, 50

4 EFFECTIVE DESIGN FOR EASY ACCESS, 51

Designing Your Intranet, 51

Design and Structure, 52

HTML Basics, 53
- HTML Resources, 55

Metaphors as an Understandable Road Map, 55
- Icons, 58
- Backgrounds, 59

Working with Type, 60

Creating Tables, 61

Managing Graphics, 61
- File Formats, 62
- Creating Image Maps, 63

Color Management, 64

Design Elements, 65
    Keeping Your Look Fresh, 65

Seven Rules for Effective Design, 66

Summary, 67

PART TWO—HOW TO CREATE AND MAINTAIN AN INTRANET, 69

5 SETTING A COMMON DENOMINATOR, 71

Getting Paperless, 72
    Scanning Paper: Physical Aspects, 72
    Scanners, 72
    Scanning Software, 75
    What Is OCR?, 76

You Can Use all the Stuff Piled on Your Hard Drive, 78
    Creating a PDF File using Acrobat Exchange, 79
    Converting Office Documents to HTML, 82

Bridging to the Homegrown Systems, 84

Summary, 85

6 TOOLS TO CREATE INTRANET PAGES, 87

Alphabet Soup Wars: HTML versus WYSIWYG Tools, 88

Do It with Pictures, 89
    Basics of Graphic-Oriented Tools, 90
    Editing, 91
    Navigation Ease of Graphic-Oriented Tools, 92
    Importing Graphics, 92
    Frames, 93
    Multimedia, 93
    HTML Source Code Editing, 94
    Forms, 94
    CGI, 94

The Tools, 95
    Microsoft FrontPage 97, 95
    Adobe PageMill, 96
    DeltaPoint QuickSite, 98
    Netscape Navigator Gold, 98
    NetObjects Fusion, 98

Creating Intranet Pages, 99
    Using Wizards, 99
    Importing Images, 103

Importing and Formatting Text, 104
Adding Sound and Video, 104
Changing Backgrounds and Colors, 104
Adding Tables, 104
Adding Frames, 106
Inserting Forms, 106
Adding Pages for Specific Tasks, 107
Adding Links, 109
Editing HTML Code, 109
Publishing Pages, 110

One-Stop Intranet Building with NetObjects Intranet Module, 111

Summary, 113

7   ALL ABOUT BROWSERS, 115

Browsers: Tools for Viewing Your Pages, 116
Performance, 116
Navigation, 116
Bookmarks/Favorites, 118
Finding Information, 119
E-mail and Attachments, 119
Plug-ins, 121

How to Customize Browsers, 122

Summary, 124

8   TOOLS FOR SITE MANAGEMENT, 125

What Do You Need to Manage, Anyway?, 125
File Management, 126
Maintaining Links, 127
Updating Material, 128
Multiple Locations for Your Business, 128

Site Management 101: The Tools, 129
Key Features of Site Management Tools, 129
Microsoft FrontPage Explorer, 131
DeltaPoint QuickSite, 134
NetObjects Fusion, 134
Adobe SiteMill, 136

Tips for Managing Intranet Sites, 137

Summary, 137

9   TOOLS FOR SEARCHING YOUR INTRANET, 139

Getting Around: Navigating Your Intranet, 139
Using a Table of Contents, 140

Bookmarks, 140
  Frames, 141
  Keywords, 142
  Indexes, 143

Sifting for Gold: Basic Search Principles, 143
  Using Search Tools, 144
  Simple Queries, 145

Get Out Your Magnifying Glass: Advanced Searching Techniques, 146

Intranet Search Tools, 148
  Verity SEARCH '97 Intranet Spider, 148
  Adobe Acrobat Search for PDF Collections, 148
  CompassWare InfoMagnet, 150
  Quarterdeck WebCompass, 152

Test-Driving the Internet Search Engines, 152

Summary, 153

10 HARDWARE NEEDS AND NETWORK STRATEGIES, 155

Gizmos, Gadgets, Hardware, and More, 157

Service with a Smile, 158
  Server Needs, 158
  Choosing the Speed of Your Server, 159
  Server Memory Requirements, 159

Picking Your NOS, 160

Choosing Your Desktop Weapons, 161

Okay, Speed Is of the Essence, 163
  LAN Speed, 163
  WAN Speed, 164

Talk Is Cheap, 165

Copy Cats, 166

What You'll Need for an Intranet, 167

Summary, 168

11 INTRANET SECURITY ISSUES, 169

Safe and Secure?, 169

Blanket Security, 170
  Elements of Intranet Security, 170
  The Secret Word Is SwOrDfIsH, 171

Back to Backups, 173
How to Back Up Your Intranet, 173
Backup Storage Media Compared, 174

Enter the Internet, 174
Fighting Fire with Firewalls, 176
Checkpoint Charlie, 177
Data Encryption, 178

Don't Bug Me!, 178

On the Road Again, 181

Keep up with Hackers, Viruses, and Other Foes, 182
Publications, 182
Web Sites, 182
Usenet Groups, 183

Summary, 184

PART THREE—ADVANCED INTRANET FEATURES, 185

12 TRAINING AND SUPPORT, 187

Training for Your Intranet, 187

Computers as Teachers, 188
Training for Use of the Intranet, 189
Training for Other Aspects of Your Operation, 191

It's Quiz Time, 191

Intranets 101, 192
Books, Video, CD-ROMs, 193
Online Instruction, 193
Classroom Instruction, 194

Intranets 201, 195

Creating Your Rescue Squad, 197

Top Five Skills Your Staff Needs, 197

Summary, 199

13 INTEGRATING ADDITIONAL SERVICES, 201

Groupware Everywhere, 202

E-Mail: It's Worse Than Snail Mail, 212

Digging up Your Data, 214

Extranets: Turning Your Intranet Inside Out, 216

News Distribution, 216
   PointCast and IntraExpress, 217

Windows NT Peer Web Service: A Virtually Instant Intranet for a Small Workgroup, 222

Summary, 223

14 AUDIO AND VIDEO CONFERENCING, 225

Concept of Audio and Video Conferencing, 226

See It, Hear It, 226
   Travel Savings, 226
   Time Savings, 227
   Retrieving Lost Opportunities, 227
   Telecommuting, 227

Overview of Microsoft NetMeeting, 228
   NetMeeting Main Window, 228
   A Tour of NetMeeting's Features, 230

Making an Audio and Video Call in NetMeeting, 233

Getting a Camera, 235

Summary, 236

15 EXPANDING YOUR INTRANET TOOLBOX, 237

Perk up Your Intranet with Some Java, 238

Tiptoe into Programming with ActiveX, 240

Wake Them up with Shockwave, 241

Creating Animations for Your Intranet, 242
   GIF Animations, 242
   Getting Animated with GIF Construciton Set, 243

It's Getting Better All the Time, 252
   Templates, 252
   Style Sheets, 252
   Frames, 253

3-D: The Interface on the Horizon, 254

Summary, 254

16 MAKING YOUR INTRANET ORGANIC, 255

Ask Them What They Think . . . and Brace Yourself, 256
   Writing Style, 257
   Content, 258

Structure, 258
Performance, 259

Energize Your Intranet, 259

A Online Quiz for Your Users, 260
Intranet Quiz: The Basics, 261

Summary, 263

Discovery Center, 265

Visual Index, 291

Appendix A, 297

Index, 311

INTRANETS QUICK TOUR

PRACTICE USING THESE SKILLS

ASSESSING YOUR CONTENT   PAGE 1

USING ICONS AND BACKGROUNDS   PAGE 3

SETTING UP YOUR INTRANET USING WIZARDS
   PAGE 4

CREATING BOOKMARKS   PAGE 5

MANAGING YOUR SITE PAGE EFFECTIVELY   PAGE 5

This Quick Tour gives you a brief overview of what you will learn from this book. It describes the processes involved in creating an intranet. Read it before the rest of the book, and as a refresher in between. Afterward, use it as a reference to give you new ideas for your intranet.

How to Assess Your Content

The first step in creating an intranet is assessing your content. Follow these steps to get started:

1. Start by gathering paper-based materials that you use on a regular basis, in the form they presently exist — whether it's 8 ½"-×-11" paper, multipart forms, odd-sized slips, or whatever. Take paper files and sort them using the tools you know: paper folders, hanging folders, file cabinets, and so on. This is a visual and tangible method that will be familiar to everyone.

2. Gather your historical paper documents (contracts, old reports and letters, completed projects). Categorize and file them.

3. Copy your electronic files into one location, regardless of the application used. (Keep the original files in a safe place in case you need to refer to them.) Use the folder hierarchies of Windows to create a structure, using the same theory of folders and file cabinets as noted above. Think carefully about the labels you use for hierarchies, and you'll have the beginnings of your process, discussed later in this chapter.

4. Gather your historical electronic documents and evaluate what can be archived offline and what needs to be accessible live on your intranet.

5. Clean house while you're at it. Look for duplicate forms and functions, and other outdated materials. Decide on a time frame that you consider the useful life of a document for your business, and discard anything older.

6. Decide which documents can be combined and improved. Decide who in your organization is best equipped to do so.

7. Create a wish list of materials that you don't currently have but would like to add in an intranet. Again, think about who's best situated to create the new materials.

8. Actively solicit input from the future users of the intranet for potential content and ways they want to use information. You will be surprised what you'll hear that you haven't considered.

Questions to Ask Your Users

After assessing your content, next you will want to solicit feedback from your users.

* How do they categorize the information they use? Do they think of information by project, by department, or something else?
* What fields of information would they search for? For example, would they search by product number or name, due dates, projects for which they're responsible, subject, or other fields?
* How often does this information change? Would it help to have more frequent updates?
* How do they manage information now? Find out what manual tools they use, what electronic tools they have, and what they'd like to have at their fingertips.

* How do they think an intranet can make them more productive? Can they project how much time and money can be saved by having information more accessible?

Design Issues to Address

Now you're ready to address design issues. Think about the following needs that you many have:

* **Interactive or published pages.** Will your users need to enter information or sort on the information presented? Or, will your users be more recipients of published information?
* **Complex or simple.** Do your users want just the facts, and how much data are you going to be handling? Will you need a lot of tables for posting details?
* **Searchable or directory oriented.** Should your home page include clickable elements to other pages to get users to subsections quickly, or are they going to enter keywords to search your site? Or, do you want both?
* **Cross-referencing or hierarchy.** Do your users need a lot of pointers within your intranet to get around? You'll always want to point them back to your home page, but you might want links between pages, too.
* **Digital and paper formats.** Will your users print out some segments of your intranet onto paper? Whether it's reports for group meetings, or forms to be taken off-site, you'll need to plan your page dimensions to be suitable for online and paper.

Effectively Use Icons and Backgrounds

Start thinking about icons and backgrounds for your intranet pages.

* How your intranet looks is as important as what it says; like it or not, it's got to be pretty to be read.
* Metaphors quicken the learning curve, and they don't necessarily need to be bells and whistles to succeed. The most successful intranets have a distinguished look without being overpowering.
* Try to create enough variety to keep your site intriguing and fun, but don't tease your visitors with "under construction" signs, dead links, or demands for user feedback.

How to Set Up Your Intranet Using Wizards

Now that you've thought about the basic elements that go into your intranet, pull it all together by creating a complete intranet site. This section will tell you a little about *wizards* (automated programs) you can use to set up your intranet. Here's an example, using Microsoft FrontPage 97.

Follow these steps:

1. When you launch FrontPage, choose Create a New FrontPage Web From a Wizard or Template. Unless otherwise specified here, use the default check boxes, and click OK to get to the next dialog box.

2. Choose the Corporate Presence Wizard. You can modify the pages for an intranet.

3. You'll be prompted for a location to which you want to save your Web site; name it something logical and remember where you're storing it. You'll publish it to a central Web server later.

4. You're now into the wizard, where you'll be asked a series of questions about your business. Choose all the pages on each screen. You can edit the pages later for the specifics of your intranet.

5. On the wizard page for Feedback Form, choose the information you want to know about your users. On the next screen, choose the tab-delimited format for reviewing your feedback in a database.

6. On the wizard for Table of Contents, check Show pages not linked into Web in addition to the other defaults.

7. On the wizard page for choosing a presentation style, pick one that fits your organization. You'll get a preview in the box on the left.

8. On the next wizard page defining colors, you'll select colors for your Web page. Remember to keep high contrast between the background and the text, even though it's tempting to use a really wild background. You'll be able to modify your colors later by editing the page titled Web Colors.

9. Enter your company information as prompted on the next three screens. Then check the Show To Do List on the last screen. Choose Finish and the skeleton of your intranet site will be generated, as well as the To Do List.

How to Create and Use Bookmarks

Once you have the basic elements of your intranet in place, you should bookmark important pages in your intranet for future reference. We'll use Microsoft Internet Explorer as an example here.

1. Open the page to which you want to attach a bookmark.
2. Choose Add to Favorites from the Favorites menu.
3. Modify the name of the page so it's logical to you. The name will default to the name of the page on your intranet.
4. Choose the appropriate folder in which to put the bookmark in, or create a new folder using the button. You can have as many folders as you need to easily access your bookmarks. File them in the same pattern that you'd set up a conventional paper-based file system.
5. From the Favorites menu, or the Favorites button, select the bookmark of the page to which you want to go. If you use the same browser for your Internet and intranet searching, you can access all of your bookmarks from one location, and use the folder hierarchy to keep them sorted out.

Tips for Managing Your Site

When you have your site up and running, you'll need to manage it effectively.

- Make sure everyone uses the consistent naming conventions for your Web page's title and filenames.
- Keep the file extension (the characters after the period) to identify the file format (generally .htm or .html).
- Establish a method for tracking revisions.
- Keep the filenames the same.
- Use the document header information to track dates of modification and creation, and comments.
- Require the submitter to provide the file header information, including:
  - Author
  - Date
  - Subject
  - Keywords

- Decide who will be responsible for reviewing updated material, and establish approval procedures if necessary.
- Put the approved files on your intranet and archive old files immediately.

Using Desktop Video Conferencing

One fun and useful thing you can do with your intranet is to provide audio and video conferencing for employees who telecommute or work in remote offices. The main features of desktop video conferencing are:

Feature	Description
THE INTERNET PHONE	Talk over the Internet.
APPLICATION SHARING	Share a program with a group of people.
SHARED CLIPBOARD	Copy and paste information across the intranet.
FILE TRANSFERS	Send files to one or a group of people.
WHITEBOARDS	Use graphics to communicate your message.
CHATTING	"Speak" using a text-based method.
VIDEO CONFERENCING	Send and receive live video communications.

Now that you've seen the elements involved in creating an intranet, turn to Chapter 1 to start learning about the specifics.

PART ONE

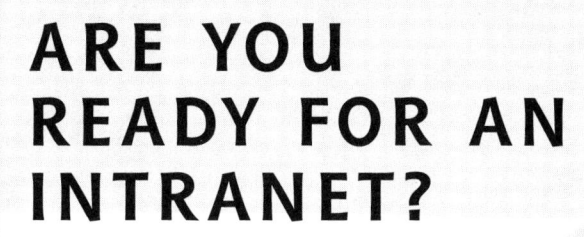

ARE YOU READY FOR AN INTRANET?

THIS PART CONTAINS THE FOLLOWING CHAPTERS

CHAPTER **1** INTRODUCTION TO INTRANETS

CHAPTER **2** ASSESSING CONTENT, CREATING A PROCESS

CHAPTER **3** JUSTIFYING YOUR INTRANET

CHAPTER **4** EFFECTIVE DESIGN FOR EASY ACCESS

Intranets are quickly becoming standard fare in organizations that need to manage diverse information effectively. Whether you're part of a large corporation, a midsized business, or any other type of organization, an intranet can help you find, modify, route, deliver, approve, store, and archive just about any piece of information, regardless of the source.

This part will introduce intranets, help you assess your content and create a process for managing information in a digital environment, help you justify the time and cost of your intranet, and provide some design guidelines.

SPREADING THE NEWS ABOUT INTRANETS

For Inform Interactive, intranets are a business as well as a tool. The company, based in Toronto, works with clients to consult on their information needs, design functional intranets, and implement solutions.

Educating its clients on the potential uses of an intranet is a critical part of its business. To facilitate the learning process, Inform Interactive built a demonstration intranet for customers as an interactive environment, with plenty of explanations of the functional areas.

"We want to provide the tools and training to our clients for building an intranet, transferring as much of our knowledge as possible," says Rob Hollingsworth, VP of Sales and Business Development. "We also want them to see that they can leverage existing skills, such as word processing and spreadsheets, into the common environment of the intranet."

Inform Interactive's demonstration intranet features a fictitious company, RedTraktor, to illustrate a range of information management features for departments, including the following:

* Human resources: employee database, organizational chart, job postings, policies, and procedures.
* Sales: Discussion area and document sharing.
* Marketing: Collaborative workspace and product information.
* Engineering: Project management systems, events/conferences, and test results.
* Finance: Annual reports and financial statements
* Information Systems: FAQs, technical glossary, and HTML tutorial

The RedTraktor site is also a testing ground for emerging technologies that Inform Interactive is considering for use with its clients. Keep an eye on the site for new tools from third-party vendors. Check out RedTraktor at:

`http://www.redtraktor.com`

But Inform Interactive doesn't stop there. The company uses its own intranet to manage client projects. This is the ideal way for a number of people to collaborate effectively from different locations. And the next frontier, extranets, is already under way — the idea of allowing its clients to tap into the Inform Interactive intranet to participate in pro-ject discus-sions or to check on work in progress.

Screen shots from the RedTraktor intranet can be seen in Chapter 1.

CHAPTER ONE

INTRODUCTION TO INTRANETS

IN THIS CHAPTER YOU LEARN THESE KEY SKILLS

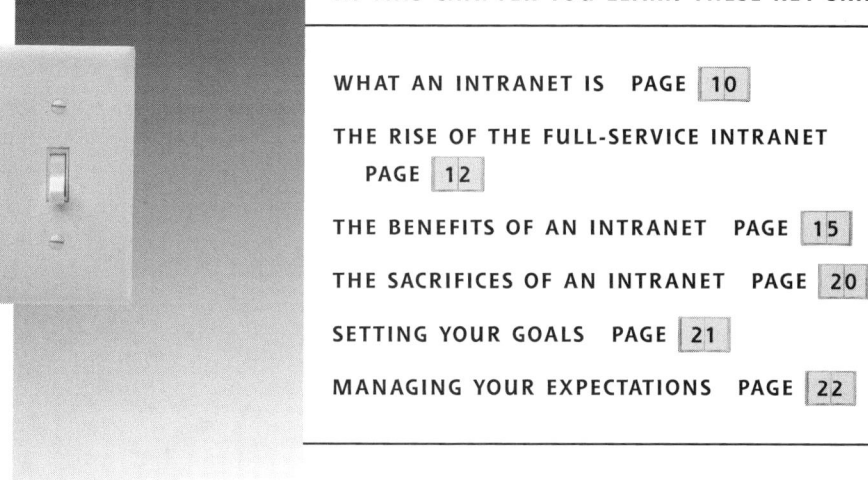

WHAT AN INTRANET IS   PAGE 10

THE RISE OF THE FULL-SERVICE INTRANET   PAGE 12

THE BENEFITS OF AN INTRANET   PAGE 15

THE SACRIFICES OF AN INTRANET   PAGE 20

SETTING YOUR GOALS   PAGE 21

MANAGING YOUR EXPECTATIONS   PAGE 22

Do you dream of quick and easy access to your core corporate information, such as phone books, sales office locations, or employee benefit forms? Do you long for the day when you can access the schedules of three colleagues instantly, regardless of the calendar program they use? Do you ponder a more efficient way of routing materials for approval? Do you hope to improve the environment for your kids by reducing the amount of paper you use everyday?

Imagine a simple, central source for the following:

* Employee manuals and benefit information
* Product information and current pricing
* Project status reports
* Company news
* Personal information (announcements, classified ads, and so on)
* Document management
* Routing and approvals
* Help desk functions

- Corporate training programs
- Reusing information across divisions

All of the above is possible, with the advent of the World Wide Web as an intracompany tool. Intranets are exploding across many types of organizations, providing a common denominator of sorts for everyone to share information. Whether it's paper, mainstream applications (such as the Microsoft Office suite), proprietary systems, or harnessing the wealth of digital data on the Internet — it can all be accessed via an intranet.

That doesn't mean that intranets are a catch-all solution; in fact, you may already have an intranet installed and find yourself wondering what on earth it's doing for you and your staff. You might think it's a gateway to information that's as useful to you as a pile of C code. Or you might just be seeking ways to actually link this technology to the information you'd really like to see.

What Is an Intranet?

An *intranet* is literally a network within a corporation; it can be used to manage information, including creation of content, routing and approval, publishing, using, and archiving.

In comparison, the *Internet* is a series of interconnected networks providing global links to information. It encompasses e-mail, the World Wide Web, FTP (File Transfer Protocol) sites, Gophers, and more.

The World Wide Web is seen through the graphic-oriented user interface of a browser, with graphics and page design to enhance the information. It's based widely on *hyperlinks,* which are connections between files for easy navigation and cross-referencing.

FTP is a way of moving files, using what now seems to be rather rudimentary file hierarchies and folder-management schemes. FTP is used most often with files downloaded directly from Web sites.

Gophers are somewhat dated, but you'll still hear the term from the old guard of the Internet. *Gophers* were the precursors of today's more sophisticated infobots, or search agents, that go out on the Net searching for your queries.

Intranets can fulfill many information management needs, primarily the following:

- Document collaboration, such as a digital bulletin board, including routing and approval functions.
- Links to corporate systems, providing easier access to proprietary systems such as sales information.
- Links to company information, such as human resource handbooks, forms, and phone directories.

* Support for mobile workers, and the creation of an environment for future telecommuting.

But an intranet has many other functions. The ways in which an intranet can be used grow rapidly as the tools improve in power and ease of use. Consider an intranet for any task, including the following:

* Reduce cycle time.
* Reduce paper costs for circulating information.
* Improve communication among staff.
* Eliminate the confusion of old and new versions of policies, guidelines, standards, and other changing information.

Finally, you can permit outsiders to view and interact with segments of your intranet. This can include access to electronic brochures and product information, access to discussion groups or important product/service updates, customer service functions, ordering functions, and so on. At some point, the line between inside and outside becomes blurred, which requires solid security measures (see figure 1-1).

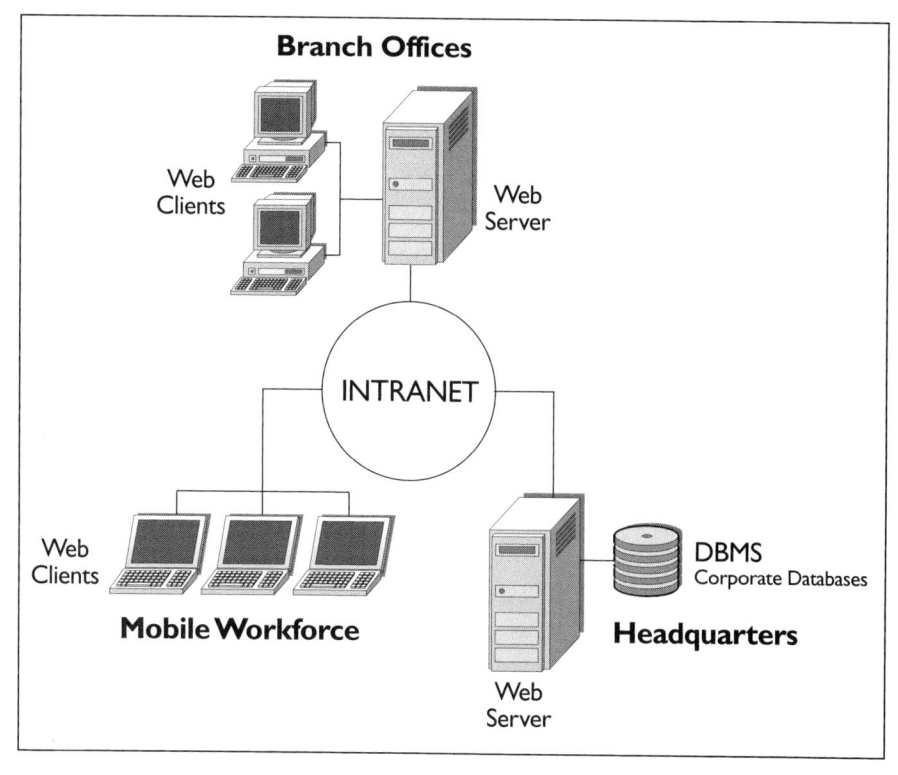

Figure 1-1 Your intranet can include any information that you define on the Web within your company.

INTRODUCTION TO INTRANETS 11

X-REF For details on intranet security issues, see Chapter 11.

The Rise of the Full-Service Intranet

Intranets are relatively young beasts, but they're growing at an exponential rate in both content and capability. Depending on the source you read, a third of companies in this country have some sort of intranet in place, and another third say they're committed to doing so by 1998. That's a lot of people making dramatic changes to the way they manage their information.

Intranets put the power of information management back into the hands of the authors, or publishers, of the information. It's a change that is likely to threaten the existing balance between operating departments, product departments, and the systems department. For a manager who needs to improve information management, reduce costs, or speed up operations, an intranet can be a tremendous help. For a systems person, an intranet can be threatening, both in terms of job stability and the quality of applications developed for an intranet by novices outside of the IS department. An intranet can be a very scary proposition for the end users, for its perceived complexity and for the changes it creates in job duties, such as managing and publishing information.

At first, intranets were used to publish static information from virtually any electronic or paper source, but now they've become full-service systems with interactive and frequently updated information.

The best way to understand an intranet's potential is to visit one. Inform Interactive has posted its demonstration intranet on the Internet for people to visit and experience firsthand, and several figures of the site will be shown in this chapter to illustrate key points. Figure 1-2 shows the home page of the fictitious company RedTraktor, with a comprehensive overview of information available on its intranet site.

WEB PATH The entire RedTraktor site is available at:

http:///www.redtraktor.com/

There are also many useful sites to explore when evaluating an intranet for your company. The information is updated regularly so you'll have current facts. Check out the following sites for a comprehensive listing of articles on intranets:

http://www.lochnet.com/client/smart/intranet.htm

For links to the Microsoft, Lotus, and Netscape white papers on intranets, as well as other articles, visit:

http://webcompare.iworld.com/intranet.html

For a searchable site and a good beginner's FAQ (Frequently Asked Questions), visit:

http://www.innergy.com/

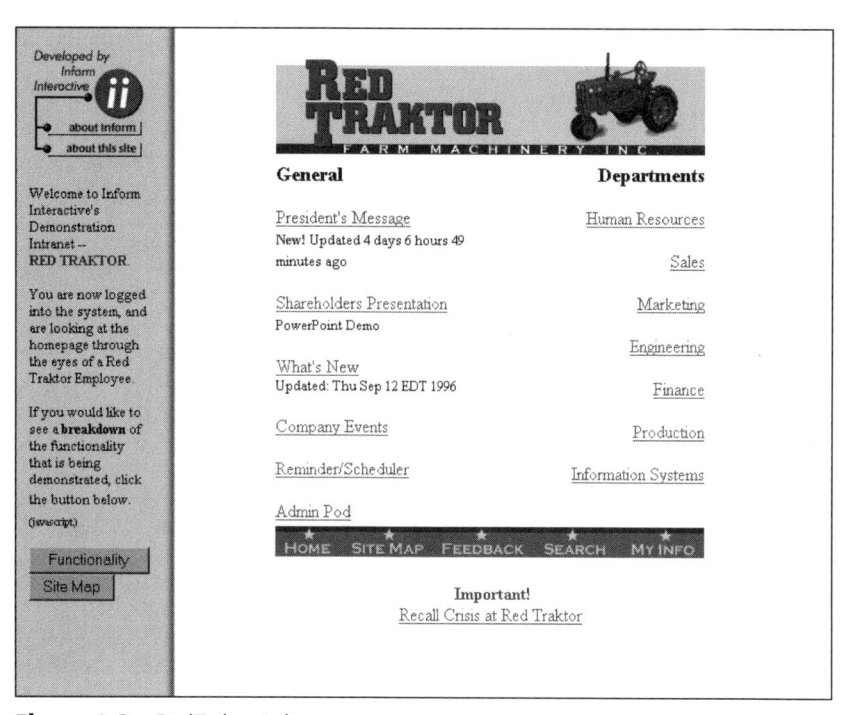

Figure 1-2 RedTraktor's home page
Copyright 1996 Inform Interactive Inc. All rights reserved.

Bridges to Proprietary Systems

Intranets come with open standards, which means just about anybody can write miniprograms that link to any part of an intranet. Regardless of the tools you use to build your intranet, you can hire consultants to customize the functionality to suit your business. You can also use multiple products from multiple vendors; many plug-ins will work with both of the leading browsers.

Plug-ins are miniapplications that extend the functionality of another application. They are much like those extra components on your vacuum cleaner — the ones that enable you to clean corners or vacuum your fish tank. The vacuum works just fine without them, but it's great to have those add-on tools.

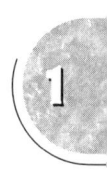

The good news is you can still utilize most of your current IS proprietary systems, meaning the applications that have been developed specifically for your company by your IS staff or hired consultants. These systems are not available in a shrink-wrapped box at the local computer store. You can access proprietary systems through direct links that update information constantly, or through the regular publishing of data to your intranet. It's the ideal way to build on your existing infrastructure, with minimal costs for substantial improvements for end users to get and use vital information.

The intranet can be utilized by your IS department to distribute and update information about all systems, proprietary, intranet, and desktop applications, such as Microsoft Office. Figure 1-3 shows RedTraktor's information systems page.

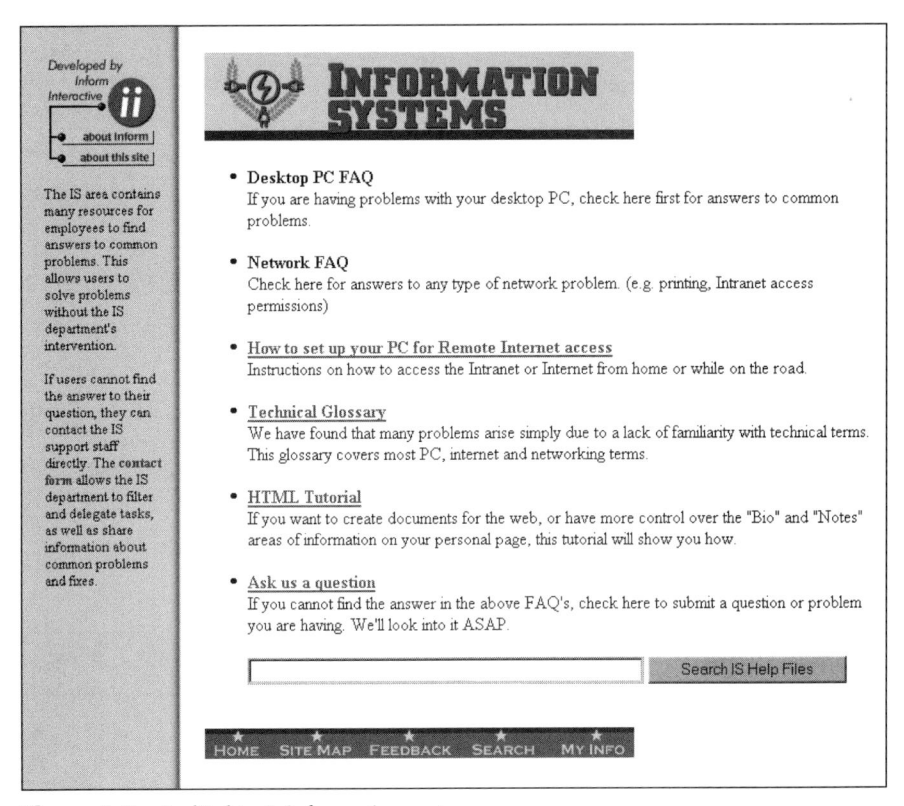

Figure 1-3 RedTraktor's information systems page

> **X-REF** For a detailed review of the technology tools, see Chapter 6 for page-building tools, Chapter 7 for browsers for your users, and Chapter 8 for site-management tools.

Full Integration of All Digital Information Needs

The functionality of intranets is expanding rapidly beyond a common repository for static information. Your intranet can include any elements that are appropriate for your business needs, and can be developed and implemented in phases to suit your budget, product cycles, staff training, and adjustment needs.

Intranets can include interactive tasks, including:

* **E-mail:** You can use the e-mail that's compatible with your browser, or link any other mail application.

* **Groupware:** Groupware applications enable users to collaborate on many things, including review of documents and discussions. Lotus Notes was the first product of this genre, but was complicated to implement, expensive, and difficult for users to understand. Several software developers have launched products in this area, and the features sets continue to get richer with each update of the software.
* **Database Access:** You can link to any database using your intranet as a consistent front end.
* **Conferencing:** This emerging technology holds much promise for reducing travel time, cutting expenses, and getting through meetings faster. Features such as audio and video connections make you feel like you are all in the same room.

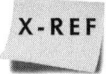

X-REF For the detailed review of e-mail, groupware, and database access, see Chapter 13. For conferencing, see Chapter 14.

Benefits: Access to a World of Information

There are many benefits to an intranet, including easy access, effective information management, and productivity gains. It takes an investment to create an intranet, but the rewards are substantial.

Easy Access

Like the Internet itself, an intranet provides a common interface between a variety of data sources. The good news is that everyone involved can continue using their tool of choice to create and manage information (including software and computer platforms — PC, Mac, Unix). But when it comes to sharing with others, the intranet simplifies things by providing a common source of information.

Intranets can be digital warehouses for information that only existed previously on paper. Paper files can be scanned and stored as fixed images (like a photocopy) or as fully searchable files (like a word processing document). Electronic files created by any software package can be translated easily into one common format. And all information created in the future can be created using intranet tools, if desired.

The intranet is available to anyone connected to your company network, whether at the local site, in another office location, or remotely (say, in a hotel room) by direct dial-up or via the Internet. Security measures ensure the safety of company information from unauthorized eyes.

Unlike most corporate departments, the intranet should be accessible 24 hours a day, 7 days a week. It can be updated anytime, by everyone or by designated people. For example, your human resources information could be available all the time, so you can get that pesky medical form or check out the job postings. Figure 1-4 shows RedTraktor's human resources page.

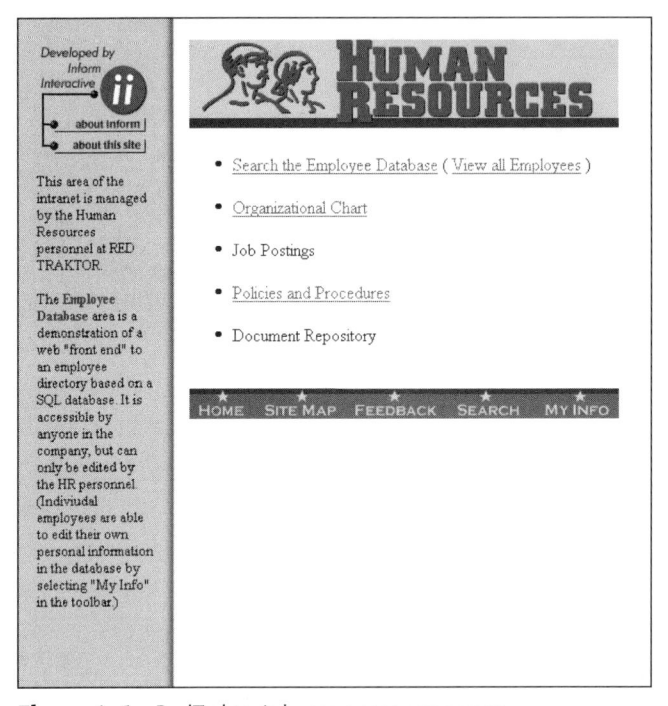

Figure 1-4   RedTraktor's human resources page

The cost of an intranet is reasonable, and is far less than that of proprietary information systems or off-the-shelf groupware solutions. If your company has Internet access, you probably have a Web browser already. Netscape is available as a site license for a reasonable price; Explorer is shipping with all PCs configured with Windows 95.

> **SIDE TRIP**
>
> ## How to Experience an Intranet on the Internet
>
> If your company doesn't have Internet access, you can visit RedTraktor or Netscape's Virtual Intranet through an online service such as America Online or CompuServe, or go directly to an IPO such as Earthlink or NetCom. Either route requires a computer and a modem, and both have relatively easy setup requirements. Spend some time on the Internet and see firsthand what all the fuss is about. You will be amazed how many ideas you'll get from visiting sites, especially those of industries different from yours.

SIDE TRIP

Online services: Considered the Internet on training wheels, online services act as assistants sorting your inbox. You can access the World Wide Web, and get unique, members-only features. The prices and hours of usage are changing rapidly, and can range from $9.95 for 5 hours of access to $19.95 for 20 hours — in some cases, connect time is unlimited.

The leading online services are America Online, CompuServe, and Prodigy, each boasting several million members. It's easy to get connected through all of them, and it's a great way to get started with the online extravaganza.

ISPs: Internet Service Providers are an on-ramp to the Internet, with limited features available to subscribers. Some ISPs will sort through the Internet for you, offering news and features, technical guidelines, and Web-searching tips.

ISPs focus on providing fast access, and most people now connect via a browser such as Netscape or Explorer. ISPs offer unlimited connect time for a set fee per month.

Effectively Managed and Accessible Content

What's the greatest advantage of an intranet? The information inside. That's why you need to evaluate your content carefully, contemplate your structure, and get the involvement of the people who will use the system. If you simply digitize all your paper and convert all your electronic documents, you may create a digital dump site that everyone avoids.

In the digital age, we no longer view information in a linear fashion. That is, authors can write and publish without technical constraints, but they no longer dictate the start, the finish, and the in-between. Visitors control the flow of information, and can dive right in to topics that interest them the most. Thus, design becomes a critical navigation tool that must be contemplated before launching an intranet.

On the RedTraktor site, users can navigate directly to the information they want. Figure 1-5 shows a site view and the links between pages. By simply clicking a link, the user can immediately go to that page. Users can also use a search feature, shown in Figure 1-6, to find any word or phrase in the intranet.

X-REF Chapter 2 provides guidelines for evaluating the worth and importance of your content.

Chapter 4 helps you survey how your users want the information, with pointers to creating an effective design framework that can grow with your intranet.

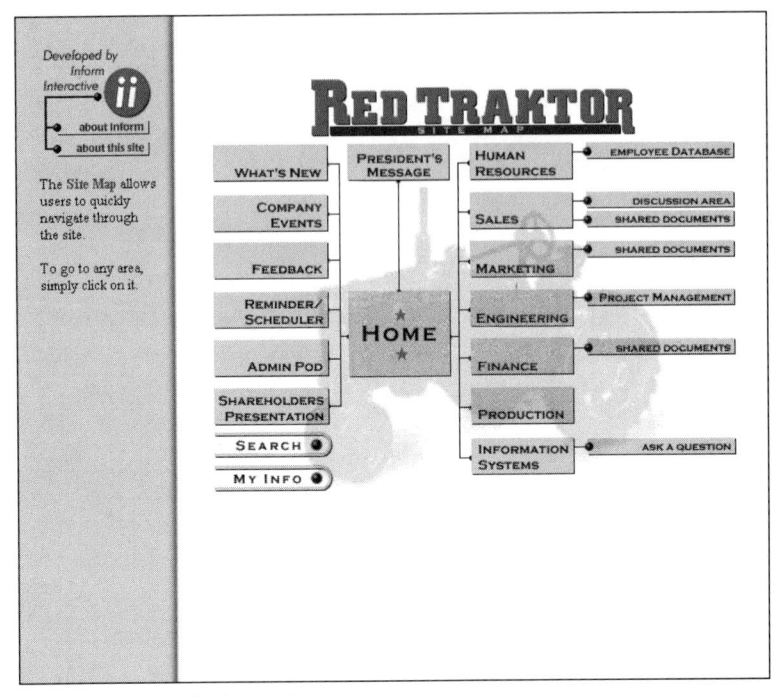

Figure 1-5 RedTraktor's site map

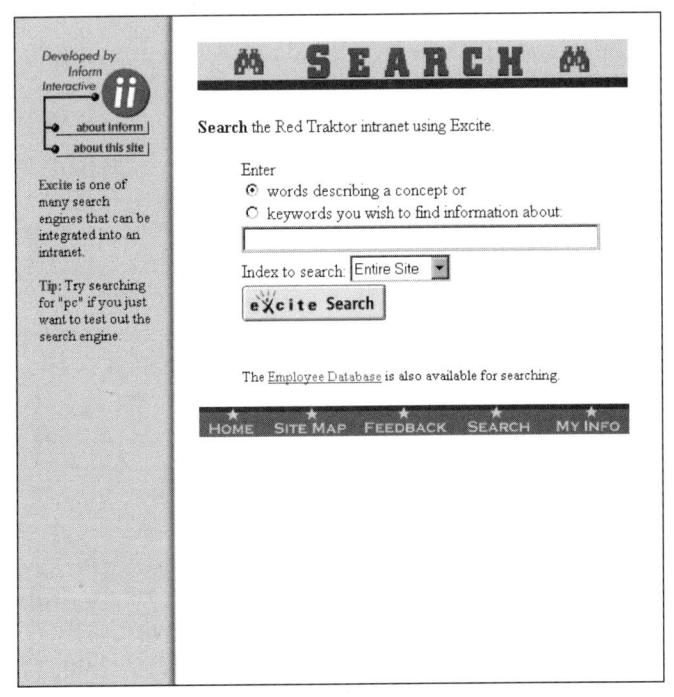

Figure 1-6 RedTraktor's search page
Copyright 1996 Inform Interactive Inc. All rights reserved.

18 ARE YOU READY FOR AN INTRANET?

TIP It's never too early to start cleaning your file cabinet. You can probably dump something you haven't used in a year, unless it pertains to legal matters that require original signatures. When in doubt, check with your corporate legal department.

Productivity Gains

An intranet offers substantial productivity gains if implemented in sync with your business needs. Measuring these gains isn't always quantitative, so you'll need to consider the potential benefits in qualitative terms, such as improved decision making.

NEEDS-BASED PUBLISHING

An intranet enables needs-based publishing, rather than limit you to creating and distributing information within some artificial schedule such as printer deadlines.

Consider a human resources manual. It's full of important detailed information that your employees will need periodically. It's also full of information that changes quickly — whether it's updates to your 401K plan, a personnel phone directory, or a calendar of events. By publishing your human resources material on an intranet, you can update it as information changes and distribute it for little cost (compared to reprinting an entire manual).

RAPID DEVELOPMENT

On the systems side, development time on an intranet can be very fast, with a technical person and a business or operations person working side by side. Using intranet development tools, the systems expert can create prototypes of the intranet for quick testing by representative users, and can quickly refocus any features that don't improve productivity or the quality of information.

Intranets are considered scaleable and extensible, meaning you can start small and grow over time. You should carefully develop a strategic plan for your overall intranet picture as soon as possible, even if you can only forecast your information needs for the next year. But, you can test-drive the effectiveness of your intranet by implementing either one function or department, and then roll out from there. You'll learn as you go, getting smarter with each implementation.

DISTRIBUTED INFORMATION AND SYSTEMS

The days of centralized information controlled by your systems department are over. You can deploy intranet servers throughout your organization, whether it's in one location or spread throughout the world. You can link them together as you wish, like the Web. You can control access privileges for adding, changing, and deleting information or features.

Distributed systems are closer to the users, and thus more likely to contain the tools for accessing information that can improve productivity.

Sacrifices

Intranets also have their downsides, potentially putting a strain on both your computer infrastructure and your staff. It's important to consider the following issues when building or expanding your intranet.

Network Dependence

Dependency is something you can't avoid in the corporate setting. If you have a weak network infrastructure presently, it's only going to get worse with an intranet. Then again, approaching the head of IS about such sensitive subjects can be an unpleasant experience, unless you're educated in the basics. Try talking to IS in its language and you're likely to at least get its respect, and maybe its cooperation. After all, you're all on the same team, right?

IS people are the key resource for your network infrastructure and core systems support. However, we've often found a gap between that technical expertise and the needs of the business itself. For a successful intranet, you must have an intranet champion with the strategic perspective to determine business needs first and technology solutions second. It's a delicate balancing act between IS and line managers who will manage content. It's another area in which you should enlist their support, and get them involved throughout the development. But you should always remember who has final accountability for the costs and benefits of the intranet.

The positive side is that the expensive infrastructure already exists, and for many companies, growing pains have been an educational experience. If your intranet is well developed and executed, you're likely to increase network traffic substantially, so at least consult IS on your implementation plan. Scalability via an implementation in several phases will help manage the growth of your intranet. For example, you might want to launch your intranet with basic human resources information, such as a phone directory, policies, and so on. Then you might want to add discussion groups to collaborate on projects. You might want to add links to your sales data that resides on another computer system. Each phase makes your intranet more powerful, and enables your users to adjust to the new world of digital information in bite-sized pieces.

X-REF Chapter 10 will provide checklists to help you evaluate your network needs.

Resource Requirements

Don't be fooled; an intranet is not free. You'll need to allocate some funds for hardware and software, depending on what's installed already. You'll need to designate the right people for the right tasks, and get their commitment to the project. But most of all, you'll need a mandate from management to make the intranet the *replacement*, not a complement, to the existing information management process.

> **X-REF** In Chapter 3, we'll give you a template to help you estimate your needs and consider several scenarios of resources to benefits.

Process Issues

If the term *reengineering* makes you shriek, take a deep breath and stick with us. A recent study cited that 70 percent of reengineering efforts were determined failures; half of those were attributed to inadequate computer system support, while another third was attributed to a lack of staff training. It was not the process of change itself, but the support aspects that failed.

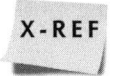

> **X-REF** In Chapter 2, we'll explore process issues and try to keep it as painless as possible.

Does Your Boss Get It?

Let's face it, the projections for future growth of intranets are enormous. But what about 6–12 months after launching your intranet, the time when you've got to start showing some tangible results to upper management? What happens when you have to go back for more resources, money, and staffing to effectively maintain or even expand your intranet?

Come budget season, the effectiveness of your intranet will likely be scrutinized. If you're the champion, you're carrying the burden of helping your top management understand the value of your intranet, which may not immediately be measurable in dollars or time saved.

> **X-REF** For roles and responsibilities of people building the intranet, see Chapter 2.

The best way to get management to understand the value of the intranet is to create a firsthand experience for them. Make sure your intranet contains some functionality that is vital to decisions they make, and show it to them.

For example, your company might have sales reporting information distributed weekly on heaps of computer printouts because it's still running on a centralized mainframe or minicomputer. It is easy to make this information accessible in a published electronic form on your intranet. Your executives can search the information with a few keystrokes instead of wading through paper, and it's even better if they're traveling and can get to the information electronically.

X-REF **Resource allocations for intranets will become increasingly competitive as corporations continue to carefully assess costs, risks, benefits, and opportunities for any investment. See Chapter 3 for details on justifying your intranet.**

Managing Your Expectations

So let's say you're on your way to becoming an intranet champion for your department, your branch, or your entire company. What can you realistically expect from the tools, your staff, and your systems support over the next months?

Your Staff's Use of Information

We keep saying that content is king (or queen, depending on your orientation), so let's first consider what the people using your intranet need to know. You'll want to get their philosophical support as early in the process as possible. Invite them to participate in the planning and development of the content of your intranet. Their acceptance of the intranet and interest in maintaining, updating, and expanding the content is critical. If you make information access easy and provide adequate training, you're likely to get support from some of your staff. Some people will reject a new way of managing information, and you'll have to decide if this affects their job performance.

Technology Tools

The tools for creating and managing an intranet keep getting better and better. The costs of software are quite reasonable compared to what you're spending now on either proprietary systems or paper-based information distribution. Hardware prices also continue to drop, while performance continues to increase. New functionality is added monthly, so high expectations for the technology can be realized quickly.

BONUS

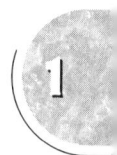

Quiz: Are You Ready for an Intranet?

Aside from expanding your technical intranets vocabulary for dazzling cocktail party conversation, what are your goals? An intranet can be a lot of work during preconstruction, implementation, and ongoing maintenance. Take time out to set your goals — it's a worthwhile investment. It will also help at the justification stage, when you'll need to equate costs with benefits, whether they're quantitative or qualitative. Try the following worksheet: Identify which goals coincide with yours, and tally up your points. The total will give you a rough idea of how well an intranet solution fits your needs.

The Intranet Quiz

Goal	Check If Goal Applies to Your Organization
Publishing information about company matters (news, employee phone directories, and so on)	
For internal use	❏
For external use (customers)	❏
Publishing information about products and pricing	
For internal use	❏
For external use (customers)	❏
Routing and approval of documents	❏
Posting and revising company standards (operations manuals, production guidelines, and so on)	❏
Archiving company documents	❏
Sharing calendars	❏
Posting project schedule information	❏
Viewing information in legacy/proprietary systems	❏
Interactive links to legacy/proprietary systems	❏
Help desk support	❏

(continued)

The Intranet Quiz (continued)

Goal	Check If Goal Applies to Your Organization
Company training programs, both computer and other subjects	❏
Publishing employee information (announcements, classifieds, and so on)	❏
Providing audio/video conferencing capabilities	❏
Providing an open forum for idea sharing	❏
Total	____

If you checked more than eight items, develop your intranet now!

If you checked between two and eight items, start planning for implementation within six months.

If you checked less than two items, you may not need an intranet.

TIP

Keep your goals visible and refer to them often. With projects of this complexity, it's easy to get offtrack, and, perhaps, forget where you were heading in the first place.

Summary

Embarking on an intranet is a challenging endeavor, with issues of content, your business structure, and technology all affecting your potential for success.

Intranets are an evolving cost-effective solution for growing demands for digital information in all types of businesses and organizations.

Intranets can encompass: document collaboration, links to corporate systems, links to company information, and support for mobile workers.

Intranets can: reduce cycle time, reduce paper costs and associated distribution, improve communication among staff, and reduce outdated information.

CHAPTER TWO

ASSESSING CONTENT, CREATING A PROCESS

IN THIS CHAPTER YOU LEARN THESE KEY SKILLS

THE POLITICS OF INFORMATION   PAGE 25

MAPPING OUT YOUR CONTENT   PAGE 26

THE JOYS OF PROCESS MAPPING   PAGE 29

APPOINTING CHAMPIONS AND SHEPHERDS   PAGE 32

Understanding the Power of Information

If information is indeed power, then putting the spotlight on information use and management in your organization is likely to make many people uncomfortable. Illuminating tasks and procedures across organizational boundaries can improve your business and quality of work life. There's little point in blindly digitizing your existing documents and procedures; you'll potentially wind up with an electronic mirror of your present operation. You're going to be making a substantial investment, and you'll need to prove that an intranet is *better* than your current method of managing information.

The tools available for publishing and distributing information electronically blur the lines of information producers and receivers. The production cycles for creating, routing, approving, publishing, and archiving are much shorter, and virtually anyone can get their opinions and ideas heard. You'll need to consider where to draw the lines, if you wish, or at least be aware of the potentially massive amounts of information that will need sorting.

What Are All Those Documents for, Anyway?

Before you even think about *how* to set up your information, you'll need to identify *what* to include in your intranet. Remember, we're in an era of information overload and people are bombarded with voice mail, faxes, e-mail, express mail, and snail mail on a daily basis. And the digital tools available to create and distribute content are making it even worse with the onslaught of multimedia features that have quick temporary appeal but little staying power.

Assessing Your Content

To start with, you'll need to figure out exactly what content you have already. The following steps explain how to begin assessing your content:

1. Start by gathering paper-based materials that you use on a regular basis in the form they presently exist, whether it's 8 ½- × 11-inch paper, multipart forms, odd-size slips, or whatever. Take paper files and sort them using the tools you know: paper folders, hanging folders, file cabinets, and so on. This is a visual and tangible method that will be familiar to everyone.

2. Gather your historic paper documents (contracts, old reports, letters, and completed projects). Categorize and file the documents.

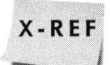

> **X-REF** See Chapter 5 for details on converting paper documents into digital form and putting all your digital files into an accessible format.

3. Gather your electronic files in one location, regardless of the application used. The folder hierarchies of Windows, shown in Figure 2-1, can be used to create a structure using the same theory of folders and file cabinets as noted previously. Think carefully about the labels you use for hierarchies and you'll have the beginnings of your process, discussed later in this chapter.

4. Gather your historical electronic documents and evaluate what can be archived offline and what needs to be accessible live on your intranet.

5. Clean house while you're at it. Look for duplicate forms and functions and outdated materials. Decide on a time frame that you consider the useful life of a document for your business and discard anything else.

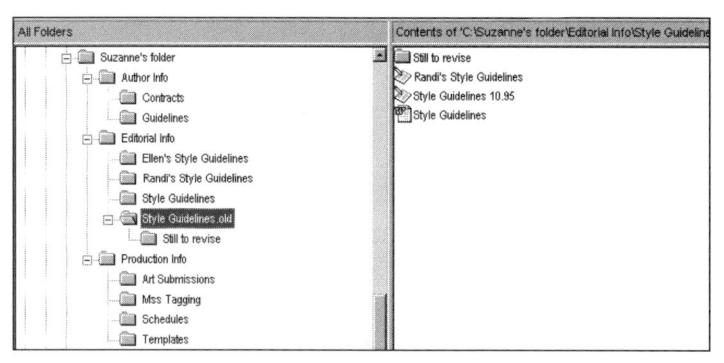

Figure 2-1 Folder hierarchies of Windows 95 used to sort out documents destined for an intranet

> **CAUTION:** Consult your legal department about the specific length of time you must keep contracts or other legally-binding materials.

6. Decide which documents can be combined and improved. Decide who in your organization is best equipped to do so.

7. Create a wish list of materials that you don't currently have but would like to add in an intranet. Again, think about who is best situated to create the new materials.

8. Actively solicit input from the future users of the intranet for potential content and ways they want to use information. You will be surprised by what you hear that you haven't thought of yet.

Managing Your Content

To begin managing the contents of your intranet, create a tracking sheet to follow the stages of each element. An element can be either a single-page document, a 20-page manual, or a specific report. Use whatever tool is easiest for you: a word processing table (as shown in Figure 2-2), a spreadsheet, a database, or a project management application.

ASSESSING CONTENT, CREATING A PROCESS

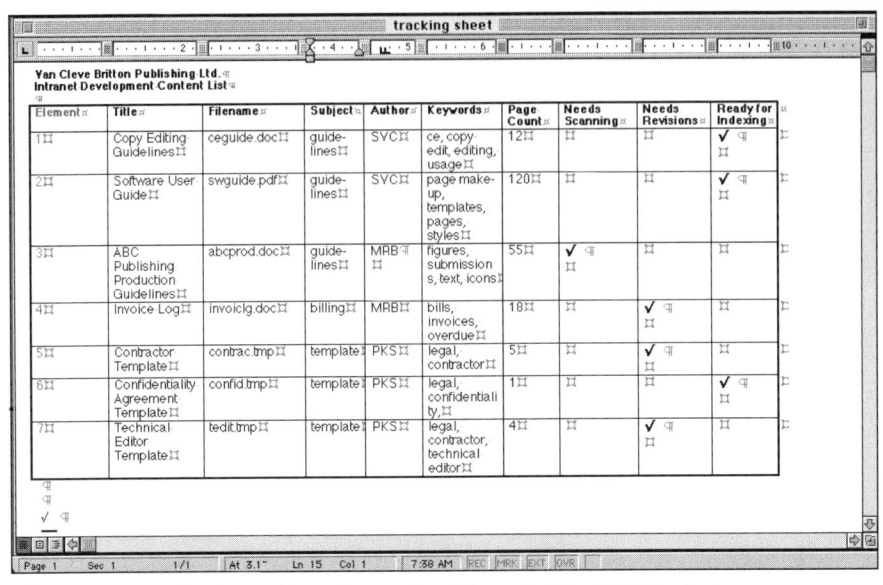

Figure 2-2 A simple tracking sheet using Microsoft Word's Table feature

All but word processing tables can be set up to automatically revise dates. Include the following about each element:

* **Title:** Include the filename for digital documents, too. Even though Windows 95 supports 32-character filenames, many indexing applications and search engines don't. Be safe and use the old 8.3 (eight-letter title, three-letter document extension) standard, such as *filename.doc* for a Word file.

* **Author:** The author is the person responsible for approving the content of that element.

* **Subject:** The subject is the category for the element, such as Human Resources, Sales Information, or Training Materials.

* **Keywords:** What terms might someone think of when hunting for this information? You can use as many as you like, but keep your thinking mainstream for future users.

* **Page length or file size:** Alert readers about the length or size of the document.

Dedicated project management applications, such as Microsoft Project or FastTrack Schedule, are very powerful. They are, however, difficult to learn, and can be very frustrating to set up for the first time. If your needs are modest and the size of your project is manageable (say 100 elements or less through 5 stages or less for starters), a table, spreadsheet, or database that you already know will work.

SIDE TRIP

DIVIDE AND CONQUER: WINNING THE PAPER BATTLE

At a leading book publisher, a production team had 100 paper-based forms and guidelines used by editors and authors across the country. Materials were continually updated, and paper replacements for a conventional binder were mailed biweekly. During the early stages of creating an intranet, the team pulled all the paper forms, separated them into folders labeled with categories, and designated an entire file cabinet to hold the documents.

Once all the forms were sorted, the team divided the folders by stages of the process, and set out to eliminate redundant, outdated, and purposeless forms.

The entire procedure may sound rather old-fashioned, but it worked. The very visualization of the piles of paper, duplicated effort of the staff created a lot of support for building the intranet.

Now you're beginning to get a better idea of the content for your intranet, and structuring in a way that's ready for digital delivery. The time you spend now will pay off handsomely when you launch your intranet.

The Joys of Process Mapping

Process mapping, the idea of visually tracking all the steps required to do a particular task or project, is one of those necessary evils on the road to understanding how your organization uses information. Once you've drawn the road map, you'll quickly see areas for improvement. You will probably see redundant tasks, between people and/or departments, and you're bound to find steps that are totally unnecessary to helping your business run.

What you do need, most of all, is an open mind and the willingness to improve the status quo. Admitting that you're inefficient is a tough thing, but building an intranet based on a dysfunctional process is a project destined for failure.

Here are a few things to keep in mind before you begin:

* Designate a team to evaluate a process, and get input from members at all levels.
* Make it impersonal: Take *people* out of the equation and focus on the tasks and results.
* Remember that you're looking for efficiencies (doing things right). But even more important, you're looking for your organization's effectiveness (doing the right things).

ASSESSING CONTENT, CREATING A PROCESS

* Establish guidelines and time frames for project completion. Associate values with every stage of your process, whether it's time or money. Make sure a stage has substantial enough value to warrant the time and money you'll invest in mapping and analyzing it.

Process mapping can be done in a conventional sense, using a pad of sticky notes and a flip chart. Simply write down the inputs and outputs on separate sticky notes, and place them on a flip chart. Draw lines and arrows between them to show workflow and relationships. If you need to jot down the process quickly so you and your staff can visualize what you need to design your intranet, take the casual sticky note approach.

If you need to mass-distribute the results of your process mapping, electronic tools make sense to capture and assess your process. You can create simple flowcharts as shown in Figure 2-3, or complex drawings as shown in Figure 2-4. (See the Bonus section at the end of this chapter for an overview of software tools that you can use to create flowcharts.)

CAUTION

Process mapping can take on a life of its own, especially if you've got detail-oriented perfectionists on the project. We've seen organizations process-map thousands of steps, many of which were redundant tasks performed solely to fuel the bureaucracy. However, without a mandate for streamlining operations, process mapping alone won't resolve any process problems or create a successful intranet.

SIDE TRIP

BENCHMARKING: COMPARING YOUR OPERATION TO OTHERS

Benchmarking is another tool for assessing the efficiency and effectiveness of your process. It's the idea of comparing your process to that of someone else, whether it's another department or company.

Benchmarking is the practice of being humble enough to admit that someone else is better at something, and being wise enough to learn how to match and even surpass them. Benchmarking studies are often done by consulting organizations, including the nonprofit American Productivity & Quality Center (APQC). Such consulting companies audit and track performance in just about any area and publish the resulting studies for purchase. They'll also come to your site, for a fee, to assess any process and make recommendations for improvement, whether you're looking to decrease the time it takes to get a product to market, reduce your production costs, or other matters.

WEB PATH For details on benchmarking, including freely downloadable reports, visit the APQC site at:

http://www.apqc.org

ARE YOU READY FOR AN INTRANET?

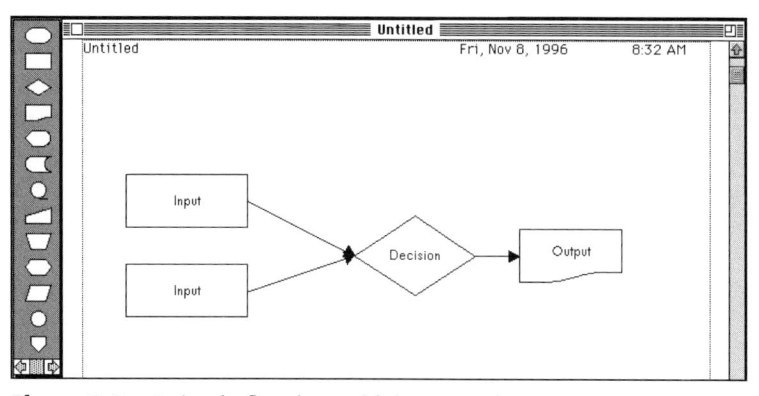

Figure 2-3 A simple flowchart with inputs and outputs

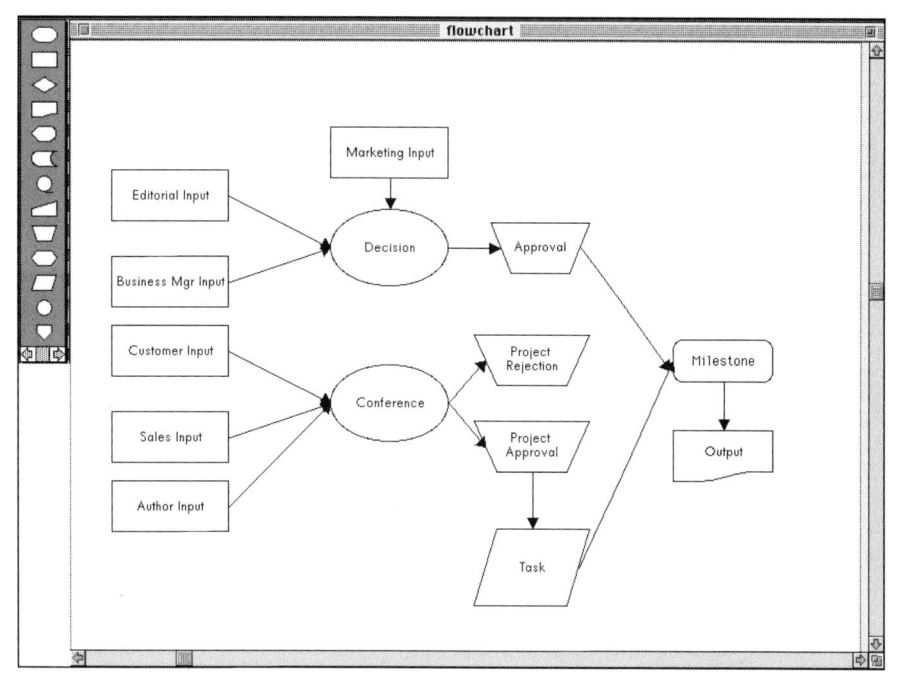

Figure 2-4 A more complex flowchart, including numerous steps and decisions

To give you and your team a quick idea of process mapping, take a simple task and map it. For example, use making a cup of coffee or changing a tire. If one of your staff shouts, "Send out for Starbucks" or "Call AAA," give them credit for creativity and willingness to consider outsourcing!

Consider your current process in conjunction with what you'll need to create and maintain your intranet, including the following:

Inputs and Outputs: What are all the components that will go into your intranet, and what do you get out of it? Include the things that don't seem important. You'll want to ask yourself why you're doing them.

Routing and Approval: Who needs to see material that will be included in the intranet, and who has final approval?

Publishing: How will materials get from their native source (paper, spreadsheet/word processor/database document, proprietary system) into a format accessible on your intranet? What mechanism can you build to make this an automated task?

Revising: How will materials be revised and who will be the gatekeeper? Will it vary according to content?

Archiving: When will materials be removed from your intranet and how will they be archived? How long will you need to keep an index of archive contents?

WEB PATH Many consulting companies are publishing useful information about process mapping and benchmarking on the Web, but the sites change frequently. Your best bet to find current information on these topics is to point your browser to one of the big search sites and search for *processing* and *mapping*. Our favorite sites to begin our Web searches are:

```
http://www.lycos.com
http://www.yahoo.com
http://www.webcrawler.com
```

Leaders of the Pack

When you're thinking about staff, immediately separate the tasks of content from technology. It is extremely rare to find one person who has both the technical expertise to create your intranet and the business savvy to understand the implications of it to your company. And finally, don't think that the Webmaster running your Internet site can simply manage your intranet in his or her spare time.

To build a successful intranet, you need three people in the following categories. Call them by whatever title you want, but the responsibilities should be similar.

- **Champion:** The champion has ultimate responsibility for designing the content and structure of your intranet. You can have different champions in different areas (like departments), but he or she needs to be accountable and authorized to make changes to both information use and overall operations. Although we wish that a business could be run as a democracy, truth is it can't be; you're better off if the champion has formal authority over the future users of the intranet.

* **Shepherd:** The shepherd is responsible for the creation and management of the content of the intranet. He or she must be an excellent trafficker and something of a diplomat when it comes to keeping everyone on schedule. There are terrific technical tools to help track and manage materials, but it will be the person who makes it happen.
* **Webmaster:** The Webmaster is the technical wizard who can put all the pieces together to meet the information demands of the user. This may be a straightforward server setup and maintenance, or as complex as creating and implementing links to other systems in the way of scripts and other programming.

All three must work together to create, test, modify, implement, refine, upgrade, and maintain your intranet.

BONUS

Electronic Flowcharting Tools

A flowchart and an organization chart are pretty similar in nature; they are both based on hierarchies. Any flowcharting or organization charting software can help you visualize the structure of your Web site because you can simply drag icons representing your pages to promote or demote pages on your intranet.

The tools you can use include:

* **OrgPlus,** by Broderbund, which is indeed an org chart tool marketed for designing Web and intranet sites. It's simple but effective for charting how information flows through your organization. Visit its Web site at: http://www.broderbund.com
* **ABC FlowCharter,** by Micrografx, is more sophisticated with a full set of customization features for setting shapes, rules, and alignment of objects. This application includes some very useful templates (we're all for minimizing your effort when possible!) on which you can simply build. If you're really game, you can get into reporting and data analysis, too; but we think basic flowcharting is what's really important for building an intranet. Visit its Web site at: http://www.micrografx.com

* **FlowCharting PDQ,** by Patton & Patton, is designed for easy use and includes the basic features you need for flowcharting. Visit its Web site at:

    `http:www.patton-patton.com`

The tools vary substantially in complexity, but most organizations just need a realistic look at what they're doing. Becoming a process mapping expert won't make your intranet successful; understanding the flow of information will. As long as you can create new elements, easily draw the relationships between them, and easily cut, paste, and move elements, you've got a tool that will accomplish your process mapping needs for designing an intranet.

X-REF There are even more sophisticated tools designed specifically for intranet workflow management, including version control, access rights, and file locations. See Chapter 8 for details.

Summary

This chapter explored the importance of assessing your content before building an intranet, including the following:

Assessing your content using a combination of conventional and electronic tools

Using the idea of process mapping to help you understand how and why information flows through your company as it does

Appointing the right people to the project, including a shepherd to watch over your content and a Webmaster who can use the technology to implement your system

CHAPTER THREE

JUSTIFYING YOUR INTRANET

IN THIS CHAPTER YOU LEARN THESE KEY SKILLS

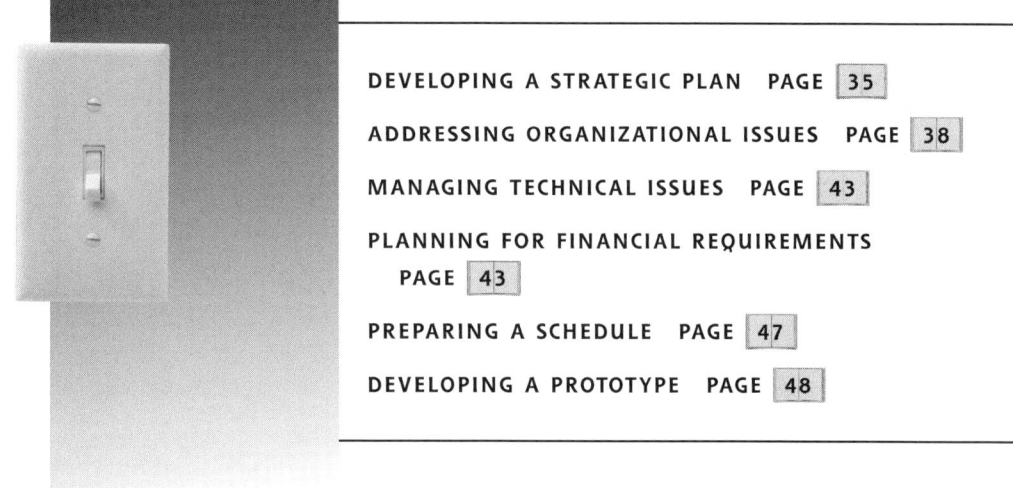

DEVELOPING A STRATEGIC PLAN   PAGE 35

ADDRESSING ORGANIZATIONAL ISSUES   PAGE 38

MANAGING TECHNICAL ISSUES   PAGE 43

PLANNING FOR FINANCIAL REQUIREMENTS
   PAGE 43

PREPARING A SCHEDULE   PAGE 47

DEVELOPING A PROTOTYPE   PAGE 48

Justifying your intranet can be a major challenge. It's a unique hybrid to your organization that will require you to wrestle with organizational, technical, and financial issues, all while sitting in the spotlight. You've got to do it right — the first time. Just ask anyone who's had an intranet more than a year. Right now they're at the juncture where someone holding the budget strings asks, "Just what are we getting for this?" This chapter will prepare you to have those answers available in a mouse click.

The Art of the Plan

While everything around you is moving fast and furious, the most important step in planning an intranet is to stop and get out of the frenzy. It's the only way you'll see the big picture — taking a time-out is something computer industry execs such as Bill Gates do religiously. Gates now reportedly takes two "think weeks" a year, going off alone with no interruptions to contemplate where the technology world is headed.

Purposes of Your Plan

A good plan serves several purposes:

- **Organization:** The task of structuring your plan for presentation to others in your company will force you to logically assess your goals, resources, and methodology.
- **Multiple angles:** You can assess the financial, marketing, operational, and cultural aspects of your intranet, hopefully with a bird's-eye view. You'll be more critical about your judgments if you put all this in writing.
- **Marketing:** A well conceived plan will help sell your intranet to the organization. Accounting for potential problems, including critical issues, being practical about what's achievable, and projecting realistic time frames, will all contribute to the credibility of your intranet. Think of it as a start-up business plan — the more comprehensive your analysis, the more likely you are to get the resources you need from your organization.

Elements of Your Plan

Your plan needs a few essential ingredients for best results. We recommend that you follow these steps:

1. Create a one-page executive summary. Include all the pertinent elements, especially a cost/benefit summary.
2. Use headings and bullets to make your plan easy to read. Remember, most people will skim the bulk of it but focus in on the segments that matter to them. Make it easy for people to find what they want.
3. Discuss the business strategy, costs, and benefits of your intranet. Use both quantitative and qualitative assessments. Include how you'll measure both aspects.
4. Propose your intranet team. Include the potential team members and their responsibilities.
5. Define your content. Outline update strategies, both timing and responsibility.
6. Cover technical infrastructure and applications. Detail what existing technology can be migrated to the intranet.
7. Plan the implementation; be sure to accommodate your business cycles in the schedule.

SIDE TRIP

MAKING THE MOST OF STYLE SHEETS

Use your word processor's style sheets to make formatting easy. In Microsoft Word, for example, use one of the built-in Report templates to create an easy-to-read hierarchy of headings and formatting. The Heading 1 style is bigger than the Heading 2 style, the Bullet style sheet includes all the indents and bullet symbols, and so on. The following figure shows Word's Report template in action.

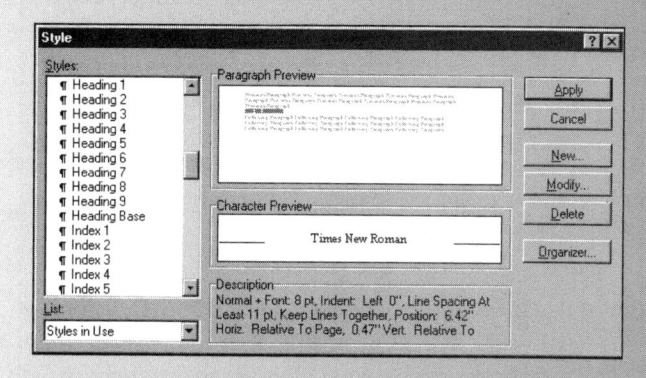

If you prefer to format after the fact, use Word's AutoFormat feature (Format → AutoFormat → Options) to apply styles to headings, clean up your lists, and other formatting. Depending on how consistently you entered your report (for example, if you always tab after a bullet), you may get decent results. Word can also AutoFormat as you type, but that drives us mad when we're trying to focus on content rather than appearance. The following figure shows how AutoFormat can clean your work.

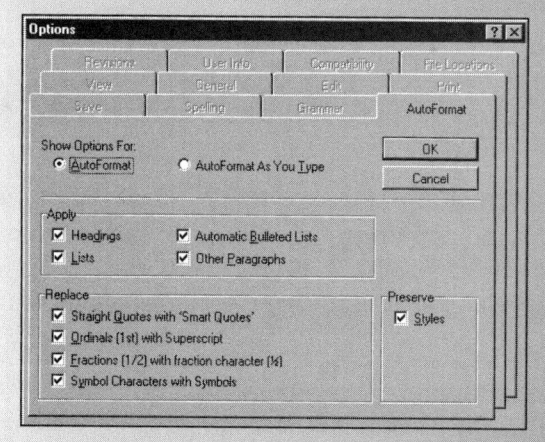

The bottom line: Get in the habit of using style sheets.

8. Outline the ongoing maintenance plan.

9. Project future growth plans for your intranet.

X-REF For quick and easy details on using Microsoft Word, see *Discover Word 97* by Shelley O'Hara (1997, IDG Books Worldwide).

TIP You'll be walking a fine line, balancing expectations with the reality of limited resources. It's the basic premise of "underpromise and overdeliver." Involving people early in the process and getting their support and approval for your plan will help immensely.

Owning Your Stuff

We all have an innate desire for ownership of our *stuff*. Whether it's a toy to be kept from a sibling or a piece or corporate information to be used to our advantage, it's all the same underlying philosophy. So although implementing a system designed to enable everyone to share everything may be technically achievable, your staff may resist the idea.

You must nurture an intranet culture, so to speak, to as many people as possible who are in sync with the new ways of information sharing and workgroup collaboration. You'll need some common sense, smart management, and, quite frankly, quite a bit of politicking for your cause. Here are a few ideas to nurture your culture:

1. Get as many people as you can involved in the intranet, even if some people will have to share a workstation at first — that's okay. Your intranet will never become the de facto company bulletin board and communication vehicle if everyone can't get to it.

2. Market your intranet with the same flair as you do your products. Remember, you're making dramatic changes to how people will work, and it's going to get pretty territorial. Explain it, demo it, and reassure your staff that it's all about improving the quality of work life and business operations.

3. Be radical in the revamping your organization to fit the new information paradigm. This means changing your compensation system for contributions to parallel rewards. If you can offer bonuses for participants on your intranet team, do so. Rewards don't always need to be financial; many of your early adopters will be thrilled with more technology toys, additional intranet responsibilities, or public recognition of their contribution.

4. Put role models in the limelight. Whether it's a department or an individual, promote successes large and small. Illustrate the benefits with some tangible applications of the technology. And invite others to come along for the technology ride.

5. Get support from top management and promote it. The rank and file are likely to dismiss a lot of executive propaganda, but do it anyway. Silence is the worst approach, and you'll get some staff support this way.

Culture change is one of the toughest obstacles in business today, so don't expect it to happen overnight. Consider that the last technological innovation to have a dramatic effect on communication was the telephone, and realize that it may take some people awhile to warm up to the idea of using an intranet.

It's a New Ballgame

Because business is undergoing rapid-fire change with this new access to information, remind your staff that it takes a team effort to make an intranet succeed. You'll need to create a team that represents a cross section of your organization or department that's first targeted for an intranet. Some people can cover more than one area of responsibility, but no one can do it all. Take a look at your staff and consider current work level, talent, interest, and enthusiasm. You'll need to find someone on your team to cover each of the following functional areas.

> **TIP** Make the intranet team a high profile entity in your organization, and make membership a privilege, not a chore.

WRITING/EDITING

Everybody can write, but not everyone can write well. You'll be soliciting contributions from people in many areas of the company, each with a different level of writing ability, and you'll need to designate a writer/editor. Consistency in structure and good writing will keep your users interested and informed. Microsoft Word includes a spell checker, grammar checker, and thesaurus (see Figure 3-1) to improve material before putting it into your intranet.

> **TIP** People read less onscreen. Reports say that people read 25 percent slower in the electronic medium than on paper. You need to write 25-50 percent less than you would on a paper report.

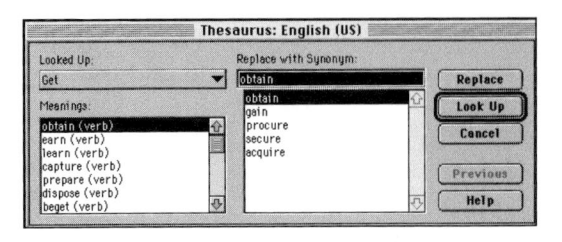

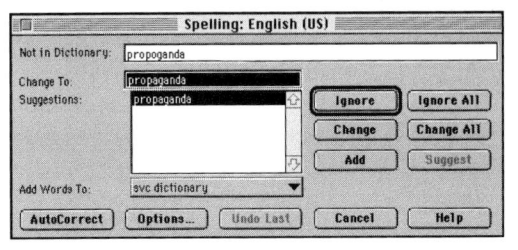

Figure 3-1 Word's thesaurus and spell checker can improve your accuracy.

COORDINATION

An intranet can quickly become an unwieldy project because of the vast number of elements involved. Assign an organized and structured person to the task. You need someone who can track the stages of many elements, prod people who are behind schedule, and identify problems while there's still time to fix them. Project management tools, such as Microsoft Schedule and FastTrack Schedule, are ideal for tracking elements, due dates, percentage completion, and providing an audit trail of due dates achieved and projects overdue.

DESIGN

With an intranet, how the written word *looks* is fast becoming as important as what it *says*. Much of the structure and navigation of your intranet will be conveyed via the design. You'll need someone who can create a look and feel that is both speedy and compelling. The person responsible for this task should have design expertise as well as technical savvy — beautiful pages that load too slowly won't get used.

How the written word looks on your intranet is as important as what it says. Your intranet's structure and navigation should be conveyed via the design.

There are many tools available for the design component of an intranet. You can use a traditional page makeup tool, such as PageMaker (see Figure 3-2) and export the files to HTML to be used on the intranet. PageMaker 6.5 does this easily; expect other desktop publishing tools to catch up soon. Or, you can create pages with tools designed specifically for Web authoring, such as Microsoft FrontPage, Adobe PageMill, Claris HomePage, and others.

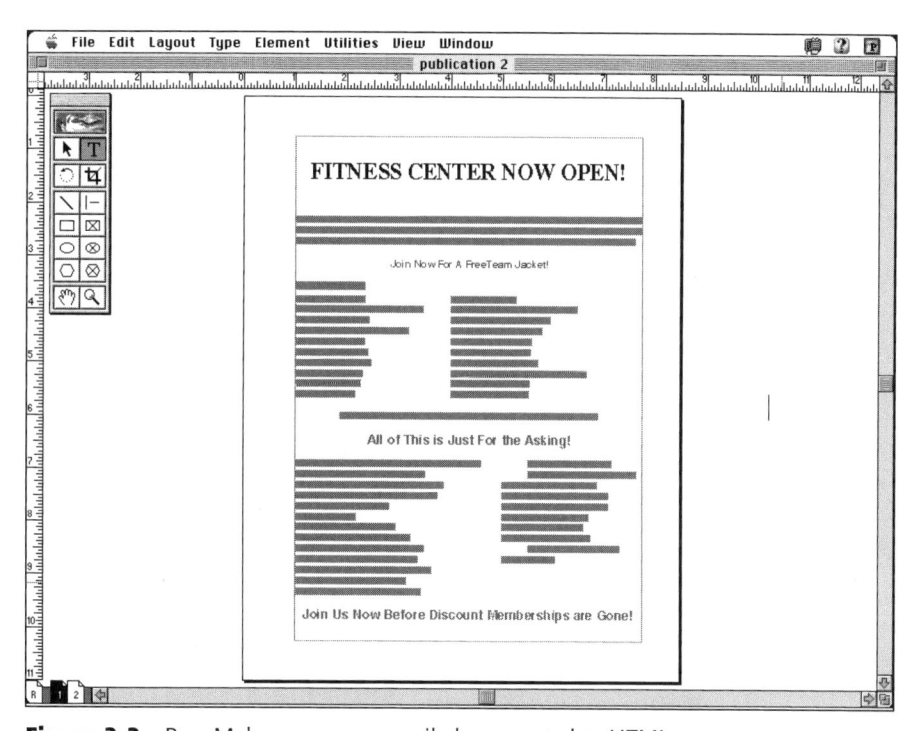

Figure 3-2 PageMaker pages can easily be exported to HTML.

TECHNICAL DEVELOPMENT

You need one expert technologist on the team who can build, or in many cases duplicate, a bridge that links all the components of your intranet. In addition, you might want to build additional functionality that requires some programming, such as miniapplications to complete rote tasks and queries to external databases. Tools such as NetObjects' Fusion and Borland's IntraBuilder are two multifunctional applications for creating Web sites.

NetObjects Fusion includes templates such as this to get your intranet jumpstarted.

> **WEB PATH** NetObjects Fusion includes free page and site templates to get you started. Visit its Web site at:
> http://www.netobjects.com/

TESTING

You'll need beta testers to put your intranet to the test for both technical performance and content accessibility. This means getting representation from each area to test-drive your intranet and make constructive comments before you roll it out to the general community. Pick your beta testers carefully, because the early word on the company grapevine will establish the reputation of your intranet. This is an opportunity to stack the jury in your favor.

On the technical side, all Web page creation and site management applications enable page previewing and link testing. You'll need to test links separately among applications or other custom modules.

PRODUCTION

Depending on the volume of material in your intranet and the frequency of updates, you may need to designate someone to oversee the production of information from its original source to intranet-ready format. Much of the transition can be automated, but you still need a production manager to review the clarity of resulting pages.

> **X-REF** See Chapter 6 for details on processing large amounts of paper documents or converting digital documents.

SITE ADMINISTRATION

Your site administrator can be the same person who did the development, although that's not a mandate. The site administrator should monitor usage, check integrity of links and contact between multiple sites, and add and delete pages and content sections as directed by content providers. Microsoft FrontPage, Adobe PageMill (shown in Figure 3-3) and DeltaPoint QuickSite are a few programs for managing Web sites.

Figure 3-3 Adobe PageMill provides the basic necessity of managing a Web site: tracking links to and from pages.

Setting Up a Team Meeting

Once you've designated your team, hold a kick-off meeting to give them a jump start. Introduce everyone and reconfirm the importance of their contribution and the mission of the team. Solicit ideas, but consider carefully the benefits and costs of any new aspects of the project.

Technical Issues

There are two parts to the technology: the underlying infrastructure and the functional applications. The infrastructure is generally managed by your Information Systems (IS) department, and includes the backbone for your intranet. If you're a line manager focused on the use of information in the intranet, your best bet is to consult with IS on what the current infrastructure can support and what new elements will be necessary. Try to get as much detail as you can on the cost — of both equipment and personnel. Intracompany chargebacks for staff time are common these days and you'll need to include that cost in your plan.

On the application side, it is easier to define requirements specifically for your intranet. You'll need to include the cost of at least Web server software and a browser for each workstation. (Although Microsoft now offers Internet Explorer free, you'll still have to pay a per-seat charge for Netscape's Navigator and any add-on applications you need.)

Outsourcing the startup phase of an intranet is popular for several reasons. With outsourcing, you're paying someone who's already gone through the learning curve so you can get your intranet implemented faster. You don't have any ongoing commitment or expense, and you can get several people working on the project at once, all with differing areas of expertise.

The downside of outsourcing is the potentially higher cost and the possibility of cultural backlash. Your in-house team may feel neglected, overlooked, or threatened, and be less cooperative when it comes to their contributions of content and ongoing support and maintenance.

But make sure that your in-house team is up to speed before the outsourced workers finish their work. The transfer of knowledge and experience is critical to continuing the smooth operation of the intranet. (The involvement may also reduce some of the possible cultural backlash.)

Financial Issues

When justifying your intranet, you'll need to examine both the costs and benefits of the project. This includes money and time spent developing and managing the project.

Estimating Your Costs

When considering your costs, hardware and software are only part of the equation. You've also got to estimate the cost of the people resource — both the one-time application development and the ongoing costs of support and maintenance to the system. The good news is training costs are lower than in the past for two reasons: Browsers are easier to use with graphical user interfaces, and an intranet has a consistent interface that makes multiple applications intuitive for the user.

Improved productivity is going to affect your organization's bottom line, but measuring it can be a challenge. You'll need to solicit assistance from your staff to approximate the time savings on particular tasks, and then multiply that by the associate personnel cost.

Potential Savings

Surveys on the financial benefits of intranets abound; estimates of Return on Investment (what you get in return for what you invest) range as high as 1,000 percent — much higher than usually found with technology. Payback Periods (the length of time required to repay what you've invested in the intranet) are also much shorter than previous technology implementations, especially if you're old enough to remember the days of the multiyear mainframe implementation.

> **WEB PATH** Studies on the financial benefits of intranets are constantly being conducted; the best source for keeping current is to visit online reports. For summaries by Forrester Research, one of the leading authorities on online data, visit:
> http://www.forrester.com/
> You'll have to subscribe to its service if you want the full report, but you'll get an idea of what's available for free.

Cost and Savings Projecting

The cost of your intranet will vary depending on the scope and contents, spread over the following areas: content management, personnel (creation and maintenance, internal staff or outsourced), hardware, software, and training. You may be surprised that hardware and software cost less than you expect, but with constant innovation and improvements, the costs are dropping while the functionality increases.

Figures 3-4 and 3-5 are Microsoft Excel spreadsheets that can help you assess and manage your costs. A clear and simple presentation of projections is the most effective way to get approval for your projects; Excel does it easily.

Figure 3-4 An Excel worksheet for projecting costs of building an intranet

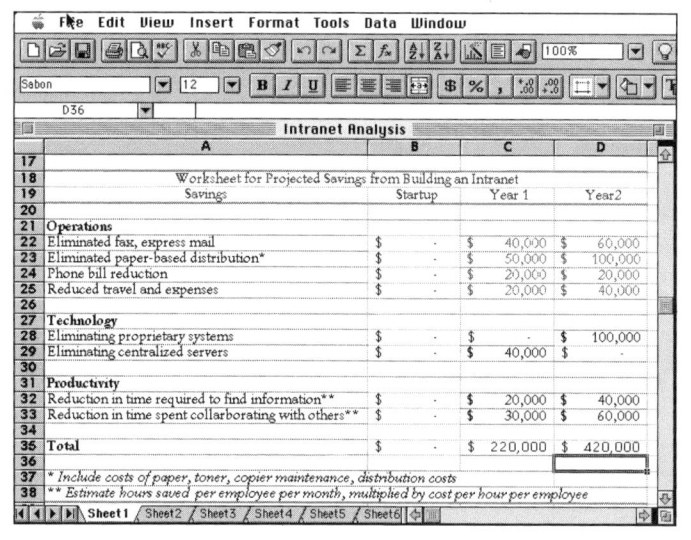

Figure 3-5 An Excel worksheet for projected savings from an intranet

> **TIP** Use Excel's Format → AutoFormat... features to select from predefined templates that will improve the appearance and clarity of your figures.

Your costs and savings will vary based on the tasks you're fulfilling with your intranet. Don't write off anything until you've evaluated its potential merit; you'll be surprised where savings can come from.

> **X-REF** Financial managers often want an assessment of Return on Investment and Payback Periods. See the Bonus section in this chapter for details.

JUSTIFYING YOUR INTRANET   **45**

SIDE TRIP

Some Specifics on Hardware and Software Costs

To implement and maintain a midsized active site that's worth the investment, hardware costs can range from $150K–$200K for the first year. Off-the-shelf software can cost $10K–$50K, including your browser and server software.

Most desktop operating systems include TCP/IP, an intranet prerequisite. Presuming your users are connected by a LAN to a server, creating a basic intranet is fairly inexpensive. You'll also need the following:

- **TCP/IP router:** About $1,000
- **Web server:** Microsoft's Internet Information Server, free; software: Netscape servers, $295 and up; O'Reilly & Associates' WebSite, $499; Spry's Web Server for Windows NT, $495
- **Browsers:** Netscape Navigator 3.0, $49; the Netscape Navigator Power Plus Bundle, $39.95; Microsoft Internet Explorer, free
- **HTML editor:** HoTMetaL Pro 2.0, $195; HotDog Professional, $99.95

ESTIMATING THE PEOPLE RESOURCE

Support and maintenance for a year can cost $180K to $200K, but you can divvy that up in a variety of ways. You can allocate a portion of personnel time based on projections of time dedicated to the intranet. Or, you can create new full-time positions devoted entirely to the intranet to keep your costs separate. Finally, you can outsource all or some of the functions; some companies find it effective to outsource the development and implementation, and then use existing personnel for the maintenance and support.

IS YOUR BUDGET FIXED, OR NEGOTIABLE?

Are you designated a budget based on previous spending or other criteria, or will the content and functionality of your intranet drive your allocation? Here's where your diplomacy skills and careful projections will serve you best. Arguably, we're in a rough new world of information accessibility — some projections are realistically quantifiable (express mail cost reductions) while others are somewhat ambiguous (productivity improvements and their relative dollar value). You'll have to make your best guess, back it with detail, and dive into it.

TIP Build a hearty intranet that carries enough functionality to justify the cost of implementation. For example, the savings for one department alone may not justify the expense of installing a T1 line, but it might be a smart financial move if the cost is spread across five departments.

Try associating costs with potential future savings whenever possible. It will help you focus on the areas for maximum results first, when so many people are watching.

Preparing a Schedule

Setting a schedule is vital to your project's success. Time overruns can cost you money and credibility, not to mention fraying everyone's nerves and decreasing quality. Depending on the complexity of your project, you can use a simple spreadsheet to set dates (using Date formatting and formulas), or you can jump into more robust and full-featured project management applications, such as Microsoft Project (shown in Figure 3-6).

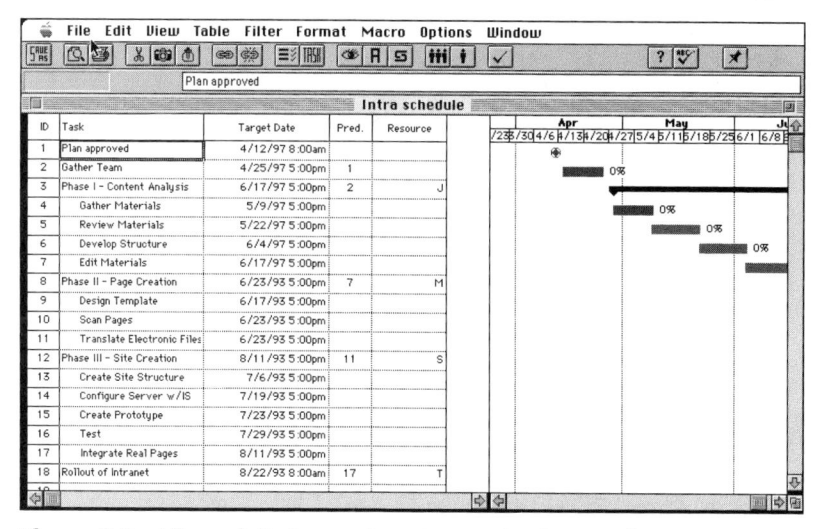

Figure 3-6   Microsoft Project tracks tasks, people, dates, and more.

Make your schedule as detailed as your Web team needs; using tools such as Microsoft Project, you can allocate tasks to individuals (and create a to-do list for each team member), and sort by task name, due date, or any of the fields in the schedule. Milestone dates are helpful for measuring progress at visible points along the way, and you'll also want to track what's called a critical path — linear elements that absolutely must be completed before taking the next step.

Most project schedules enable you to create tasks, assign durations, link tasks in the order they need to happen, and then automatically generate a schedule. You can also track projected dates versus actual, and, if you're really compulsive, you can do all types of statistics. Generally, however, all the stats in the world won't motivate your team as much as honest support and your involvement and commitment to the project.

Look Out for Feature Creep

The final part of your plan is a prototype. A visual and tangible demonstration of a slice of your intranet will convey more than anything else. Intranet prototyping is rather easy with tools such as Microsoft FrontPage and Adobe PageMill, shown in Figure 3-7. You can set up dummy pages, add links, add additional functions using plug-in applications, and have something to demo when presenting your plan.

Figure 3-7   PageMill, with a home page in editing mode

At the planning stage, the most important thing to control in prototyping is something known as *feature creep*. These are additional functions about which many people seeing the prototype will ask, ignorant of the additional cost of time and money. Be clear about what their request will cost, and find out if they'll help you get the resources to do it. Otherwise, note it for a possible future implementation.

X-REF   For details on the Web page creation tools, see Chapter 7.

TIP Don't hesitate to use a good old paper-based prototype. Take a stack of 3 × 5 cards representing the types of information you use. Sort the cards in a way that makes sense to you. You'll probably see some obvious categories of information, and begin to assess ways that you'll use them, and how often.

BONUS

Return on Investment

So what is Return on Investment (ROI)? It's how much money a project such as an intranet returns to a company for every dollar spent. Then there's something called the Payback Period, which defines how long it takes your company to return the money. Both are used as barometers of success, and it's valuable to understand the basics for justifying your intranet.

ROI

You may find yourself wondering about the scope of your project relative to these financial measures. For example, should you ask for a million dollars and return that million plus a hundred thousand, or should you go small scale and ask for $100,000 and return $120,000? One is more dollars (and a much bigger project to manage, with more room for problems) and the other is a higher percentage return. Take a look at the following table for a comparison.

Table 3-1 Return on Investment

	Project 1	Project 2
Cost	$1M	$100,000
Return	$1.1M	$120,000
ROI	10%	20%

When you're in budget season, your project is likely to be evaluated based on ROI, compared to other projects or even compared to the company making outside investments. So, your ROI has to at least beat the current interest rate to pass the scrutiny of your Chief Financial Officer or other money manager. Most will easily approve projects that promise an ROI of 20 percent or more.

Tracking your costs and savings will be critical, both for your career longevity and for future funding. Use the tables in this chapter to help you.

Payback Period

Payback Period is the amount of time before you can "pay back" the corporation for the money invested in the project. Your project could pay back a large portion of the up-front cost very quickly, if, for example, you eliminate some paper-based task or dramatically cut travel expenses by sharing information on your intranet. Or, your project may not pay back the bulk of funding for a year or more while you run parallel systems in the transition to fully using your intranet. Talk to your financial manager to find out what your company's financial goals are for the coming year; fair or not, your project's funding may be driven by other projects, market conditions, or simply management preference.

Summary

Planning for your intranet is critical for success. You need to:

- Create a comprehensive plan that's easy to read
- Address the cultural issues that may arise
- Understand and plan for the technical aspects of your intranet
- Assess the financial costs and benefits
- Set a schedule and track progress
- Create a prototype to illustrate your vision

CHAPTER FOUR

EFFECTIVE DESIGN FOR EASY ACCESS

IN THIS CHAPTER YOU LEARN THESE KEY SKILLS

DESIGNING YOUR INTRANET   PAGE 51
SETTING A DESIGN AND STRUCTURE   PAGE 52
LEARNING THE BASICS OF HTML   PAGE 53
CREATING USABLE METAPHORS   PAGE 55
WORKING WITH TEXT   PAGE 60
CREATING TABLES   PAGE 61
MANAGING GRAPHICS   PAGE 61
MANAGING COLOR   PAGE 64
ESTABLISHING DESIGN ELEMENTS   PAGE 65

Designing Your Intranet

When designing your intranet, remember that less is more. For a variety of reasons, people tend to have a much shorter attention span when reading material online than they have when reading on paper. Your intranet users will be more demanding and more critical of your digital knowledge base than they are of the piles of paper dumped on them daily.

Fair? Maybe not. The aesthetics of your intranet will set the tone and credibility of the information it contains. With a clear and inviting design, a usable metaphor or guideposts, logical elements and fast download times, your intranet will be off to a strong start with your user community.

Rather than guess what your users want, ask them. They'll tell you what works with their current information tools and what doesn't. If you listen carefully, you'll hear what they actually use, and what they do that looks good to their boss. You can gather information informally by talking to your users, setting up structured focus groups to collect feedback systematically, or taking the more anonymous approach of surveying. The route you take depends on the scope of your intranet and the culture of your organization.

Here are some questions to ask your users:

* How do they categorize the information they use? Do they think of information by project, by department, or by something else?
* For what fields of information do they search? For example, do they search by product number or name, due dates, projects for which they are responsible, subject, or other fields?
* How often does this information change? Would it help to have more frequent updates?
* How do they manage information now? Find out what manual tools they use, what electronic tools they have, and what they'd like to have at their fingertips.
* How do they think an intranet makes them more productive? Can they project how much time and money can be saved by having information more accessible?

Your intranet can accommodate a greater breadth of requests than you might think by providing different views on and better access to information.

Design and Structure

You'll need to make a few decisions upfront before starting your design. Think about the following points:

* **Interactive or published pages:** Will your users need to enter information or sort the information presented? Or, will your users be recipients of published information?
* **Complex or simple:** Do your users want only the facts? How much data will you be handling? Will you need a lot of tables for posting details?
* **Searchable and directory oriented:** Should your home page include clickable elements to get users to subsections quickly, or are they more likely to enter keywords to search your site? Do you want to make both routes easily accessible?

- **Cross-referencing or hierarchy:** Do your users need a lot of pointers within your intranet to get around? You'll always want to point them back to your home page, and you'll want links between pages, too.
- **Digital and paper formats:** Will your users print out some segments of your intranet? Whether it's reports for group meetings, or forms to be taken off-site, you'll need to plan your page dimension to either fit the screen or be scrollable.
- **Standardized layout or flexible design:** Layout standards are familiar to users, and enable faster production. Flexible designs encourage artistic variety and personality. Decide which is a better fit for your organization.

TIP Users don't like to scroll, but a screen is a pretty small space in which to cram important information. A good design puts all the important elements on one screen as much as possible, and includes links to additional detail, whether it's on the same scrollable page or a separate page.

HTML Basics

HTML (HyperText Markup Language) is the basis of the pages you create for your intranet. You may not need to dabble in the raw code, but it's helpful to understand the basics before getting into more detail about page design. HTML is essentially a collection of styles, determined by what are called *tags,* that define elements of Internet and intranet pages. HTML is platform independent, which means that it works on PC, Mac, Unix, and other types of computer operating systems.

HTML documents are plain text files that can be edited with any text editor, such as Notepad, Microsoft Word, and so on. Web authoring tools, such as Microsoft FrontPage, Adobe PageMill, NetObjects Fusion, and DeltaPoint QuickSite, use the HTML language to create your intranet pages. (A similar relationship is that of PostScript to desktop publishing applications such as QuarkXPress, Adobe PageMaker, CorelDraw, and so on.)

If you're working in raw HTML, use the tags to denote elements such as heads, tables, paragraphs, and lists. Tags surround the element you want to change (for example, making text bold or italic), and consist of an open bracket (<), the tag (such as B for bold), and a close bracket (>). Often, there's an open tag (such as <B>) to begin the element and a close tag indicated with a slash (/) to signal the end of that element (such as </B>). For example, text marked as bold would appear in HTML as follows:

```
<B>Bold Text Here </B>
```

When viewed in a browser, the code would be translated into bold text, and look something like the following:

Bold Text Here

Note that HTML is not case sensitive, so it doesn't matter if your tags are upper- or lowercase.

> **CAUTION** Not all HTML tags are supported by all browsers. Some are proprietary tags that only work on Netscape Navigator or Microsoft Internet Explorer. Check the tag with your organization's browser before integrating it into your intranet.

You can nest tags within others for additional attributes. Done properly, you can establish a logical hierarchy of your information that will make it easier for your intranet users to find what they want. The following sample HTML shows a very basic document. See Figure 4-1 for how this code looks when viewed in a browser.

```
<html>
<body>
<h1>Headline #1, Biggest</h1>
<p>This P tag indicates the beginning of a paragraph, and the next
   tag indicates the end of a paragraph.</p>
</body>
</html>
```

Headline #1, Biggest

This P tag indicates the beginning of a paragraph, and the next tag indicates the end of a paragraph.

Figure 4-1 Your browser formats the HTML tags to create heading and paragraph styles.

In addition to the simple tags above, HTML tags can be instructions for the following:

* Addresses — usually referring to the author of the document
* Background graphics and color
* Forced line breaks to control how text wraps
* Forms
* Hyperlinks between pages and locations on pages
* Image attributes, including relative size and alignment
* Lists, unnumbered and numbered, definition lists, nested lists
* Quotations
* References to external images, sounds, and animations

- Rules
- Tables — captions, rows, headers, and attributes
- Type sizes and formats
- URLs (Uniform Resource Locators) to link to files on servers other than your intranet

TIP Imitation is flattery! If you're surfing the Internet and see elements you like, choose View Source (or the equivalent) from your browser to view the HTML code. It will show you how to implement similar features in your intranet. Don't copy graphics or images, though — that's plagiarism.

HTML Resources

Web authoring tools will do a lot of the HTML creation for you, but if you want to dig in to the HTML yourself, try the following online resources:

- *NCSA Beginner's Guide to HTML,* From the NCSA, this is a great introduction to HTML. Visit:

    http://www.ncsa.uiuc.edu/General/Internet/WWW/HTMLPrimer.html

- *WWW Style Manual,* From the smart folks at Yale, this intermediate manual digs into interface, page, and site design using HTML. Visit:

    http://info.med.yale.edu/caim/StyleManual_Top.HTML

The following books are also good sources for more information on HTML:

- *HTML For Dummies,* by Steven N. James and Ed Tittel (IDG Books Worldwide, 1996)
- *HTML For Dummies Quick Reference,* by Deborah S. Ray and Eric Ray (IDG Books Worldwide, 1996)
- *HTML: For the World Wide Web, Visual Quick Start Guide,* by Elisabeth Castro (Peachpit Press, 1996)

Metaphors As an Understandable Road Map

A metaphor can give your intranet personality, but it has to be something familiar to your audience and you've got to implement it consistently. A metaphor has to be logical and intuitive so your users can find their way around without having to learn something new — that's the whole idea of using a metaphor. Figure 4-2 shows the metaphor of juggling balls, suitable for organizations with a lot of projects or issues in the air all the time. Each of the balls can be labeled with departments, tasks, projects, or other logical areas.

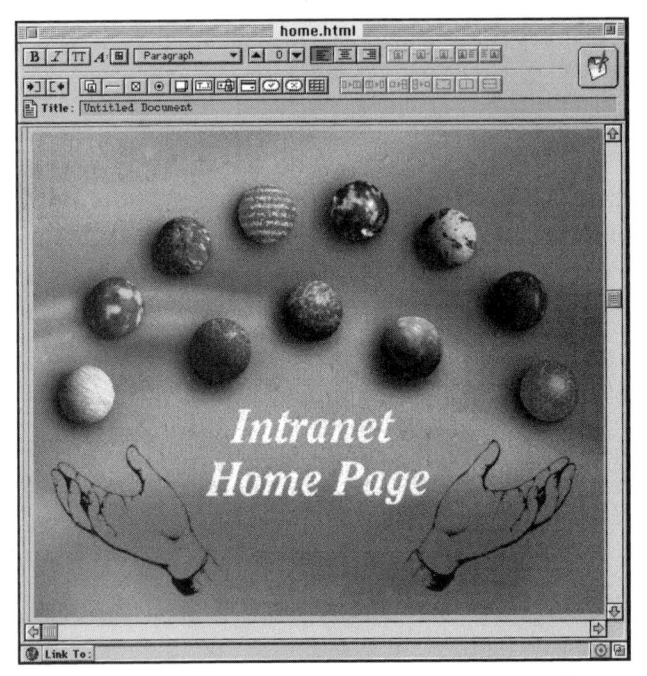

Figure 4-2 The metaphor of a juggler can lead to a fun intranet home page.

SIDE TRIP

JUGGLING METAPHOR

For one company, the intranet project manager sat down with the production department to find out how they worked with information, and what look and feel would work for their intranet. She and the site designer kept hearing terms such as *overloaded, juggling,* and *balancing act* from the staff.

The designer also observed some apprehension from the more senior staff members who were reluctant to give up their paper-based reports in favor of an electronic solution. For the production department's home page, he created the juggling metaphor as shown in Figure 4-2. In addition to the balls, which all lead to other pages on the intranet, he kept the warmer feel of woodcut hands to link the old and new worlds.

Common metaphors for intranets include: magazines, file cabinets, buildings, cities, and maps. Some intranets use familiar things, such as pull tabs and buttons, to illustrate hierarchy and structure. Calendars or clocks can lead to schedules; cash registers or dollar signs can lead to price lists; envelopes can lead to mail; maps can lead to locations, and so on. Use a metaphor when it helps convey content or structure, but don't overdo it. Figure 4-3 shows the people page of an intranet with eyes to give the page a personal feel, and images pertinent to the topics of building facts, phone numbers, company guidelines, and coffee break information. Figure 4-4 is a reference page of an intranet, using the metaphor of a card catalog in front of a collage of paper materials. Each card leads to additional information on manuals, forms, checklists, and product life cycles.

TIP Surf the Web for ideas. Don't limit your search to organizations in similar fields. Visit places that you normally would not; you'll be surprised at the ideas you'll come up with by just looking around.

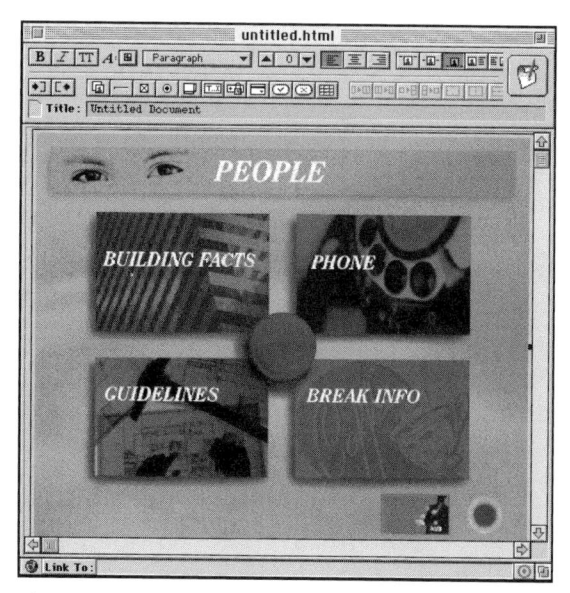

Figure 4-3 The people page of an intranet, with photos pertinent to each subject area

EFFECTIVE DESIGN FOR EASY ACCESS

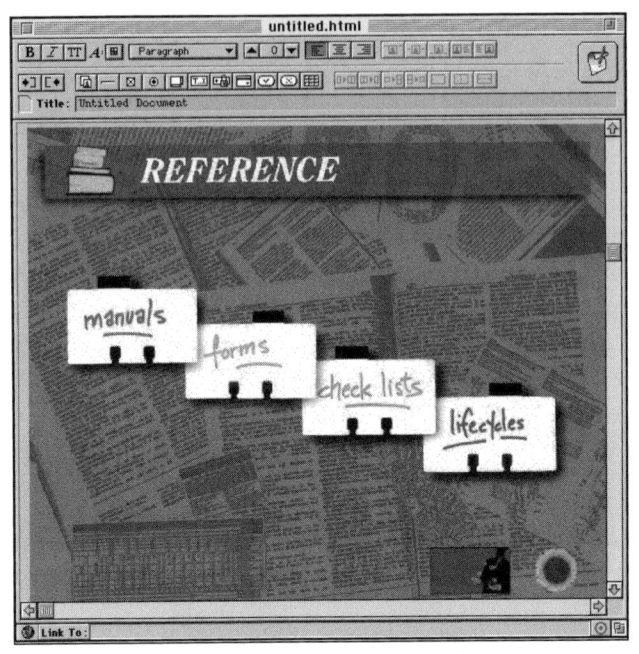

Figure 4-4 The reference page of an intranet, with a card catalog metaphor

Icons

Icons can also lead the user through your intranet — the simpler images, the better. Use images that have an easily definable click area, or put borders around them. Again, think about your business and what's a good fit. Figure 4-5 shows the procedures page of an intranet with a hand icon, clickable for more information on procedures in general. The two icons in the lower-right corner serve as navigation tools to the top of the section and back to the home page.

TIP Talk to your training liaison about building in a guided tour, including an icon to follow. Create something fun, such as *follow the purple spotted hyena*, to get your users to explore new pages.

There are many CDs available full of royalty-free icons and images that you can use on your intranet, provided you're not reselling the resulting material. Be sure to check the small print outlining their usage requirements before you develop an entire intranet based on their images. They are a great solution for the artistically-challenged who want to build a pretty site.

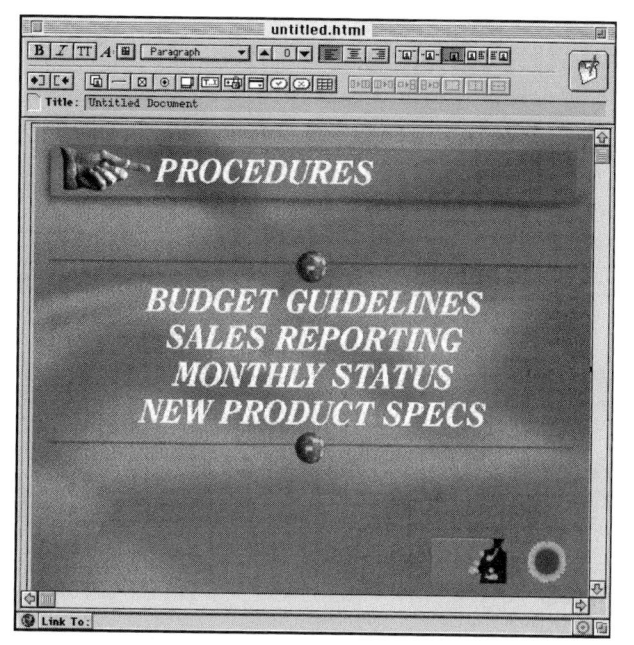

Figure 4-5 The procedures page of an intranet, using icons for navigation aids

Backgrounds

Backgrounds are an easy way to add a professional and polished look to your site. Use backgrounds that complement both the colors and type used on your Web page. It's tempting to use a really complex background, but restrain yourself. If the page can't be read, it won't be used. Figure 4-6 shows a schedule page from an intranet, with clocks used as the images to click for more detail. The shadowed clock gears in the background add dimension and color to the page.

Backgrounds are easy to add in most applications that create Web pages; just be careful that you're using files in the JPEG (Joint Photographic Experts Group) or GIF (Graphics Interchange Format) format to keep the file sizes to a minimum. Use an image that will tile well because it will be duplicated across your page, and you usually can't control where the start point is and how often it will duplicate. Backgrounds are like wallpaper.

TIP A background color, rather than a pattern, can also be added to your Web page. Colors eliminate the problem of slow loading of backgrounds due to file size, because the color takes up no file space. It can be inserted into your HTML source code using the <BODY BGCOLOR=*hexadecimal color*> tag.

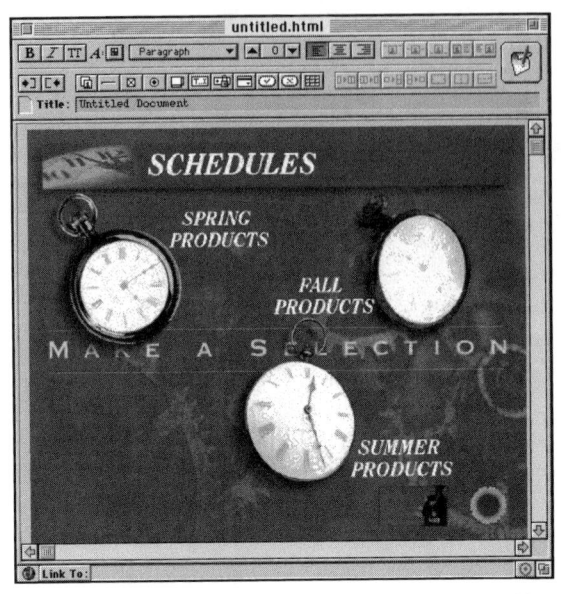

Figure 4-6 The schedule page of an intranet, with clock gears in the background

Working with Type

Type handling on an intranet is tricky; your users' browsers will control the default typeface and size in which your text appears. You can recommend the relative type size (for example, Small, Smaller, Smallest) for best viewing of the site, and depending on the browser you use and the consistency of its installation with your users, you may be able to designate type font and precise size. To control how text breaks, you have to use HTML tags. If you don't control line breaks, you can have problems such as proper names or numbers split on different lines.

> **TIP** To create a line break in HTML source code, use the HTML `<BR>` tag. The `<P>` tag inserts a paragraph break. If you don't want a line to break, use the `<NOBR>` tag. Finally, if you want to force a break in a `<NOBR>` line, use the `<WBR>` tag.

Web page creation applications, such as Microsoft FrontPage and Adobe PageMill, offer limited typographic control, but capabilities are expanding with each new version. Text tools can generally format the following:

* **Paragraphs:** Indent Left and Indent Right
* **Headings:** Smallest, Smaller, Small, Large, Larger, Largest
* **Lists:** Bullet, Directory, Menu, Numbered, Definition, Term

You can set the color of the text when creating your pages. You can also set the colors for links to other pages, read and unread.

If you have text that must appear in its original typeface, such as a company logo, you'll want to import it as a fixed image. If you use special characters, such as mathematical symbols, you'll also need to use them as images.

TIP You might think page creation tools are pretty limited, but consider that desktop publishing has only been around since 1985. Back then, there were 11 typefaces and 1 page composition program, PageMaker. Now we have thousands of typefaces, and hundreds of applications to design publications electronically. The Web and intranets are both infants in technological years.

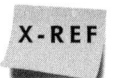

X-REF For details on using Web page creation tools, see Chapter 6. For details on setting type preferences in a browser, see Chapter 7.

Creating Tables

On an intranet, tables are critical design tools for aligning text and images on a page. Large amounts of data can be presented in tables so that users can scan information quickly. You can create cells, columns, and rows for your table using most Web page creation tools — just as you'd see on a spreadsheet. Cells can contain text, numbers, links, lists, forms, images, sounds, and movies. When you're done creating your table, you can also use your Web page creation tool to include captions for your tables.

Tables usually include a visible frame, as shown in Figure 4-7. Some designers say leaving the frames visible is a sin; others think it helps readers to see division between the data. Depending on your Web authoring tool, you can turn off the borders by looking at the properties of the table.

Item	Rental Cost
Boots	$5
Skis	$15
Poles	$5

Figure 4-7 A table created in FrontPage

Managing Graphics

There are a few things you need to know about managing graphics. You should keep an eye on file formats and file sizes, and you can create useful effects using image maps.

File Formats

When you use graphics editing programs, you're able to save your files in a number of different formats. But when creating images for your Web pages, you should be aware of a few important points. The only formats you can use for your pages are GIF and JPEG. And, for your images, strive for smaller file sizes — they translate into faster downloading time.

Intranet pages and Internet pages can include both GIF (Graphics Interchange Format) and GIF89a graphics. GIF89a graphics include new features, such as transparency and animation, and are now somewhat of an industry standard. When you're on the Web, you'll notice two types of images: those that come up blank with an icon in their place until it imports, and those that import in a few passes with a fuzzy image to begin and a clearer image on each pass. The latter is in a format called *interlaced,* which is generally more interesting for your users. It's usually a check box in whatever software you're using to create or edit your images. *Antialiasing* is another feature that will improve the appearance of your images by reducing the jagged edges; it's also usually an option when saving from your image editing software.

And if that's not enough, you can link multiple GIFs together to make an animated GIF, using shareware programs available on the Internet. Blinking logos and waving hands seem to be the most frequent application of this; spare your organization from this boredom! Save the blink for new items that really deserve attention.

JPEG (Joint Photographic Experts Group) files are the best way to compress large photos. There's a lot of overhead to writing a JPEG file, which results in larger files, so you won't want to use this format for images for buttons and other small graphics. Unlike GIF, which retains all of the information in the file, JPEG is a lossy compression format, meaning that as the file gets smaller, the quality of your image is reduced. JPEG can provide more exact color, so if you need to show precisely the shade of red on your company T-shirt, then JPEG is worth using.

TIP Use the smallest files you can. If your image software gives you quality options, choose the lowest quality and work your way to the best. See how each looks on your screen. You'll be surprised what's good enough for online viewing.

What application do you need to edit images? Adobe Photoshop set the standards for sophisticated photo manipulation, but it's the high-end in both price and learning curve. Other simpler applications may suffice for your intranet, including Illuminatus3 by Digital Workshop, and Paintshop Pro by JASC.

Creating Image Maps

Image maps are single images that contain multiple links. When you click different parts of the image, called *hotspots,* you move to different pages or sections of your intranet. You can use any GIF or JPEG image to create an image map, but it should contain logical separate elements, such as the juggling ball metaphor earlier in this chapter. Your Web authoring application will have tools to create various shapes of hotspots to designate the region on which your users will click to activate the link.

TIP Remember, office lighting is usually nasty yellow-green fluorescent, and looks awful in a digital image. If you can, set up a place to shoot staff pictures where you can control the lighting for more favorable results.

SIDE TRIP

DIGITAL CAMERAS TO SHOOT YOUR STAFF

Digital cameras have become affordable (less than $1,200) and the quality has improved dramatically since their debut a few years ago. It's a great solution for getting images of your staff into the employee directory of your intranet site. Imagine never forgetting a new VP's name again!

Admittedly, the quality of a digital image still can't compete with good ol' Kodak film, but for a fraction of the cost and immediate turnaround time, it's a good alternative for screen viewing. The cameras work just like the film-based ones except there's no mechanical motion because it's saving to disk. (The early ones made no sound either, confusing users who kept taking photos over and over. The new ones make a click sound like a camera shutter, even though there is no physical shutter!)

You shoot photos as you would with a conventional camera, and when you're done you connect the camera to your PC using a cable and the camera's own software. Files can be copied to disk, where you can use an image editing program to adjust for light or other flaws. (Photo retouching is also an option, at your own risk!) The number of images you'll get per "roll" will vary depending on quality, but expect at least 24 images per shoot. After you've copied the images to your disk, you can erase the camera's disk and you're ready to roll with the next department.

Two cameras lead the pack consistently: The Canon PowerShot and the Kodak DC line. If possible, see examples of quality before you buy.

Color Management

Your intranet pages will be seen on a vast range of monitor types and sizes, as well as on a vast range of operating systems. There are only 216 colors visible via a browser; you can either work within that color space or allow the browser to change your color to fit within the limit.

How important is precise color? If you're promoting your company store on the intranet and want to make sure your softball jackets are exactly Coca-Cola red, you'll need tools to ensure color accuracy. Keep in mind that the number of colors in the real world (millions) far exceed those visible in printed documents (hundreds of thousands) on your basic office computer monitor (216).

However, if you simply need to use color to highlight due dates, jazz up some buttons, or present basic images (even staff photos will look okay), 216 colors will work.

> **SIDE TRIP**
>
> ### LOADING THE WEB COLOR SPACE INTO PHOTOSHOP
>
> If your designer is fussy about color, he or she will want to work within the 216 colors visible on a standard computer monitor. That's not very hard if you follow these steps:
>
> 1. Find an image of the color space on the Web. Try either of the Web sites listed below:
>
>    ```
>    http://www.killersites.com/
>    http://www.lynda.com/
>    ```
>
> 2. Save a copy of the color space to your hard disk.
>
> 3. Launch Photoshop.
>
> 4. Select `Mode` → `Color Table`. Save the image as Browser Colors, or something else that you'll remember.
>
> 5. From the Color Swatch palette, choose Load Swatches and pick the file you just saved. You're on your way to true Web color.
>
> Be sure to work in RGB color mode, which represents the Red-Green-Blue color space of video, as in computer monitors. You're likely to get dithered images (mixed colors that are pointillist in appearance) if you work in CMYK, the Cyan-Magenta-Yellow-Black color space of the ink-on-paper world.
>
> If your designer is still griping, and/or color accuracy is critical to your intranet, you'll need a product such as Pantone's ColorWeb. It's a comprehensive system of color pickers to ensure color consistency for both creators and viewers.

Design Elements

When creating your design, you'll need to plan for the following elements:

- **Home page:** The core of your intranet and launching point for all major sections.
- **Major section pages:** The major sections, which can include departments, product lines, tasks, and so on.
- **Minor section pages:** The details on any of the major sections, including file attachments where needed.
- **Intranet links:** Live links to other locations on the intranet. Blue underline is the browser default for links the user has not visited; red underline is the browser default for links the user has visited — you may confuse your users if you modify those colors.
- **Internet links:** Live links out onto the Web. Colors are the same as intranet links unless you specify otherwise. Your users should be warned that it's an Internet link in the text; using an icon is a good indicator.
- **Buttons:** A frame or dimension, along with an appropriate label, prompts users that the button is live.
- **Navigation icons:** Create an icon to return to the home page, and possibly arrows for navigation between pages.

Keeping Your Look Fresh

Change is good. Realize that your intranet is going to be an organic entity; once you get it launched you'll already be working on the next iteration. If your first pages are linear in nature and structured, you'll probably loosen up the design as your users and content evolve and become more comfortable with the new medium.

BONUS

Seven Rules for Effective Design

These tips will point you toward quality intranet design:

* Change your look regularly. Even if you're just modifying backgrounds and colors, your users will sense something new.
* Make sure your type is legible, both the color of it and the background under it.
* Don't overdesign your pages trying to implement all the nifty new things you're learning. Phase them in over time. It will keep you and your users stimulated.
* Create a palette of the 216 colors that Web browsers recognize, and use them.
* Make graphics as small as possible, using GIF format whenever you can and antialiasing to avoid the jaggies. Use graphics for a reason, not just because they look pretty.
* Try to put material on one screen to avoid the need to scroll. Add links to additional pages if necessary.
* Create a set of buttons and icons to make your intranet look and feel like one synergistic package.

WEB PATH → **For an informal but great list of beginning tips on designing Web pages and managing your graphics, visit:**

http://www.unplug.com/great/

Summary

In this chapter you learned how to:

- Design your intranet
- Establish a design and structure
- HTML basics
- Create usable metaphors
- Establish design elements
- Manage graphics
- Manage text
- Manage color

PART TWO

HOW TO CREATE AND MAINTAIN AN INTRANET

THIS PART CONTAINS THE FOLLOWING CHAPTERS

CHAPTER 5 SETTING A COMMON DENOMINATOR

CHAPTER 6 TOOLS TO CREATE INTRANET PAGES

CHAPTER 7 ALL ABOUT BROWSERS

CHAPTER 8 TOOLS FOR SITE MANAGEMENT

CHAPTER 9 TOOLS FOR SEARCHING YOUR INTRANET

CHAPTER 10 HARDWARE NEEDS AND NETWORK STRATEGIES

CHAPTER 11 INTRANET SECURITY ISSUES

The next stage of an intranet is building the site itself and deciding how it will be managed (and by whom) on a regular basis.

This part will cover getting your paper documents on the intranet, the tools you can use to create intranet pages, a comparison of the leading browsers, the technical tools for managing your site, tools for searching on your intranet, networking/hardware needs, and security.

ON THE ROAD — TO GOOD METAPHORS

For freelance designer Adam Rogers, designing a good metaphor is what comes naturally. As the designer of an intranet for a New York-based media company, Adam was called upon to infuse the intranet with a dose of the familiar. The project included dealing with a committee that was, in Adam's playful words, "design challenged" and "philosophically diverse."

After an initial round of brainstorming meetings, Adam felt a bit adrift about the direction of the intranet. "They were all over the map, so to speak, following a blind mandate from management to 'digitize all their information' and improve productivity. I knew if their intranet wasn't focused, and if they hadn't carefully thought through the structure, my designs would never have the chance to live on an intranet."

After taking a time-out to reassess the project, the intranet team created a more structured map of the site, including functional areas. "From there I was able to see their vision of the site, and the design began to flow as a logical integration of information and delivery form," says Adam.

For the opening page, Adam used a metaphor of juggling balls as the opener to each functional area, including human resources, schedules, budgets, seminar registration, product development procedures, and document collaboration and sharing. Then, in the different areas of the intranet, Adam created animated clocks to liven the schedule pages, inserted Rolodexes to bring familiarity to the company phone book, sprinkled dollar signs throughout finance pages, and displayed file cabinets that "held" and "sorted" shared documents.

Adam limited his designs to the 216 color palette that's available on both Mac and PC because the company was evenly divided by platform. The images were created in Adobe Photoshop, and were used throughout the intranet as image maps. Later, page frames were added to expedite navigation, at the request of the users who asked for a quicker way to drill down into information.

Adam says that blending the familiar into a sometimes intimidating new medium, such as an intranet, helps to bridge the gap between the paper and digital worlds.

CHAPTER FIVE

SETTING A COMMON DENOMINATOR

IN THIS CHAPTER YOU LEARN THESE KEY SKILLS

SCANNING PAPER-BASED DOCUMENTS PAGE 72

CONVERTING DOCUMENTS IN ELECTRONIC FORMAT FOR YOUR INTRANET PAGE 78

ORGANIZING NEW DOCUMENTS FOR YOUR INTRANET PAGE 84

Moving from a paper-based world to a digital one is a major task, but with the right software and hardware tools, you can digitize the information that you need for your intranet. You'll also want to include information that resides currently in an electronic format, even though your staff might be using different applications for the same task. For example, it's quite common for the general office staff to use Excel for numeric tasks if they purchase the Microsoft Office bundle with that application. But the accounting department may still use Lotus because all its macros and formulas are written for that application.

And then you've got proprietary systems and other types of file formats that you users can't open on their desktops. With some straightforward conversion methods, you can get all your information into one common denominator, accessible to all.

Getting Paperless

You've probably got more paper lying around than you can stand to think about, and a lot of that information needs to get into your intranet. Start by gathering your paper files and taking a close look at what you have. Time spent preparing paper files is a good investment.

Scanning Paper: Physical Aspects

The biggest challenge when dealing with paper documents is the physical condition of the incoming material. Look at the paper you need to scan:

1. Is it orderly, with logical structure in file folders or paper clips?
2. Is the paper itself flat and clean? Are staples removed? Is the paper punched for a binder?
3. Is the paper free of handwritten notations?
4. Is there enough contrast between the paper and the text?

If you can answer yes to most of these questions, you're ready to start scanning. But most organizations have problems with one or more of the criteria, which will complicate the scanning process.

To get your paper ready to scan, follow these steps:

1. Get the paper organized in sync with the structure of your intranet.
2. Remove all staples and flatten out any holes in the paper.
3. Remove any handwritten notations that you don't want scanned.
4. Sort anything on color paper or with poor image quality. You'll want to deal with those files separately by tweaking the adjustments on your scanner software.

TIP For an excellent reference to digitizing, organizing, and searching on your documents, read *Paper to Web*, by Tony McKinley (Adobe Press, 1997). Tony's company, Intelligent Imaging, can also be visited at: `http://onix.com/tonymck/ocrlab.htm`

Scanners

There are many types of scanners on the market, and it's important to select the one that fits your needs. Consider the following criteria:

* What size paper will you be scanning? This will determine the size of the image bed on the scanner.

* How much paper will you be scanning initially to create your intranet, and how many pages per month do you expect of new material? This will determine if you need an automatic document feeder.
* Do you need color or will black and white suffice?
* Will you only be reading the files electronically, or will you also need to print them? If you need to print to paper, you'll need to scan your paper files at a high resolution.

TIP If you have a massive amount of paper to scan before launching your intranet, but modest scanning needs on an ongoing basis, consider outsourcing the task. The cost per page to scan, OCR (Optical Character Recognition), keyword, and link the text is about $2 per page.

There are several important measures to consider when buying a scanner. Resolution is measured in dots per inch (dpi), and represents the number of ink dots within a one-inch square. Resolution determines the quality of the resulting image. Each scanner has an actual optical resolution and a resolution that's enhanced by software interpolation to fill in the missing data.

You need input resolution equal to half of the output resolution. For example, if you want a nice clean printout from your 600 dpi laser printer, the scanned image would need to be at least 300 dpi. A general rule of thumb is that a personal scanner is going to be good enough to read, a desktop scanner would be good enough to give to a customer, and a high-end scanner is good enough for professional publishing tasks.

Another variable is color range, measured in number of colors, shades of gray, or bits. For standard office documentation, 256 shades of gray will suffice — 16.7 million colors is ridiculous unless color accuracy is your business, as in textiles or high-quality publishing.

Finally, for high volume jobs, you'll need to buy a document feeder so you don't have to pay staff to sit there and feed each sheet into the scanner manually.

Table 5-1 compares the important criteria for scanners.

Table 5-1 Scanners Compared

Feature	Personal Scanners	Desktop Scanners	High-End Scanners
RESOLUTION	200, enhanced to 400	300, enhanced to 1200	600 enhanced to 2400
GRAYS	Black and white	256 shades of gray	256 shades of gray
COLOR	256 shades of gray	16.7 million colors	16.7 million colors
PRICE RANGE	$200	$500	$900
PAGE FEEDER	none	none	$500

SIDE TRIP

A Personal Scanner on Every Desk

For personal scanners, Visioneer pioneered the way in 1995 with the Paperport, first released on the Macintosh and then on the PC. Hewlett-Packard introduced the ScanJet 4S in 1996, and a host of other personal scanners came to market, including a scanner and keyboard combination device.

Personal scanners are great for individual workstations, and situations in which the incoming paper can be in a variety of sizes and formats. You simply feed the item into the scanner, which fits comfortably on top of most monitors. The scanner will automatically "wake up," scan the paper, and open the application to view it, print it, fax it, or convert it into a Word document. The accompanying figure shows the Paperport scanning desktop. Personal scanners are presently limited to black-and-white or gray scale images, but look for color soon.

WEB PATH ➡ To check out the latest models of personal scanners, visit Visioneer at:

http://www.visioneer.com/

or Hewlett-Packard at:

http://www.hp.com/ computing/main.html

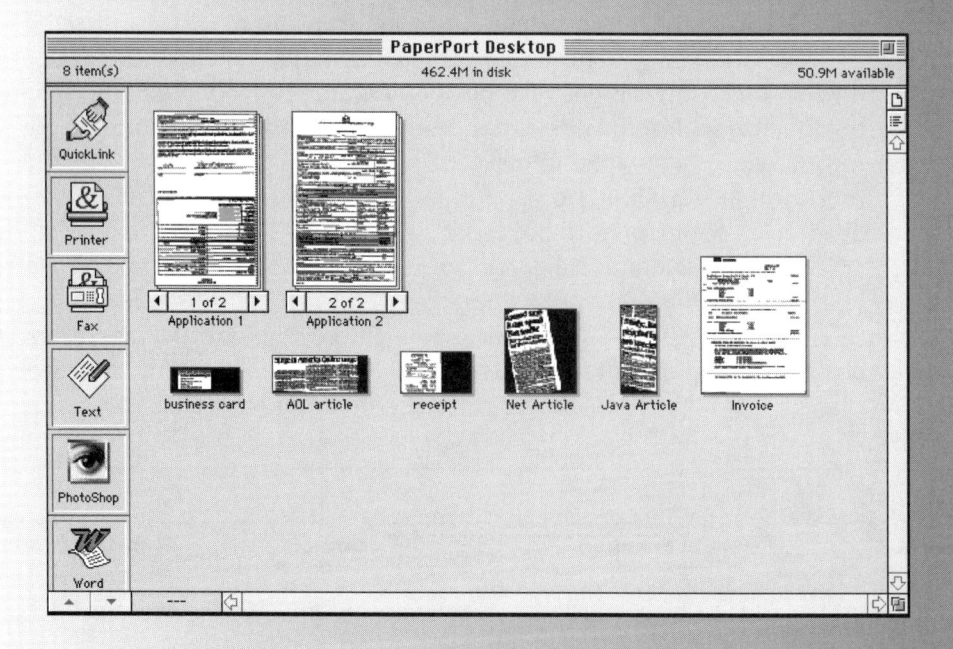

74   HOW TO CREATE AND MAINTAIN AN INTRANET

> **TIP** Agfa, a leader in high-end imaging solutions, publishes a terrific scanning guide that's quite useful for beginners, even though it also contains a lot of high-end color scanning detail. For a copy of the guide, for a mere $1.99, call Publishing Perfection at 1-800-782-5974.

Scanning Software

Scanning software serves two primary functions. It will digitize your paper files and convert the files into the format you want. You need to first decide if you want your scans to be fixed-image files or searchable by character. If you want a library of fixed documents that will never have to be altered, then image files will be okay. If you need to edit the documents, or want to do a search on any of the words in the document, then you'll need to run the scan through an OCR application to convert it from an image to individual characters.

Caere Corporation's OmniPage Pro has been the leader in OCR software for years. It set the standards for image recognition. The other prominent application is Adobe Acrobat Capture, which set the standards for document-recognition programs, not just scanning for characters. That means that Capture, now with a simplified version bundled as a plug-in to Adobe's Acrobat Exchange, recognizes the structure of the page in addition to the characters. Thus, if you're scanning straight text documents, such as the legal contract shown in Figure 5-1, a simple character recognition program will do the job. But if you're scanning a multicolumn newsletter with graphics, as shown in Figure 5-2, you'll want to use a document recognition application. Xerox publishes TextBridge Pro, which also recognizes document structure and graphics, and has been praised for its performance in high-volume projects.

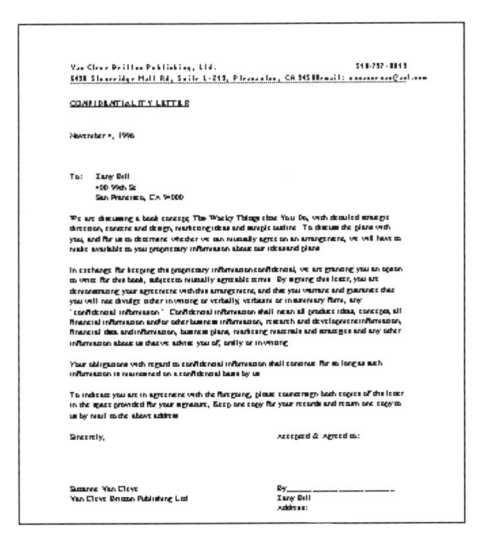

Figure 5-1 A straight text document for scanning

SETTING A COMMON DENOMINATOR **75**

What Is OCR?

OCR is the process of taking a paper-based document and converting it into editable text. During the OCR process, software such as OmniPage Pro, Capture, and TextBridge Pro analyzes the series of scanned characters to identify the appropriate characters. Each application checks against logic algorithms, dictionaries, and grammar rules to determine what characters and words should logically appear.

The second generation of OCR products, known as document recognition programs, can now recognize graphics (such as photos, line art, and logos), some text formatting (such as bold and italic), and some page formatting (such as number of columns and headlines).

Your results can be 95–99 percent accurate, depending on your software settings and the quality of the material you're scanning into the system. If accuracy of the documents is critical, you'll want to have it proofread by a human eye — only a person can make the final logical judgment call about the content.

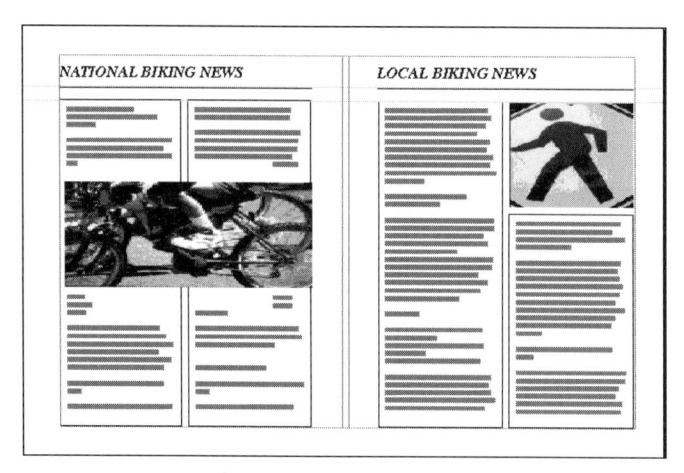

Figure 5-2 A multicolumn newsletter for scanning

Your scanning results can be 95–99 percent accurate, depending on your software settings and the quality of the material you're scanning into the system.

OCR is relatively easy to do, but you'll have to experiment with your software settings to get the best results. Remember, OCR is never 100 percent accurate.

Follow these basic steps to use OCR software:

1. Set your preferences for resolution. You'll need a minimum of 150 dpi for rough results and 300 dpi minimum for character recognition. 600 dpi is preferred, or 1200 dpi if you have the luxury of a lot of storage space.

2. Set your accuracy level. Remember that high accuracy will be slower and create bigger files.

3. Set your compression standards, again considering your quality needs and your storage capacity.

4. Do a quick preview scan to get the document into your OCR software.

5. Create zones to identify what areas of your document you want scanned for text recognition and what areas are graphics.

6. Straighten the paper if the scan is not aligned.

7. Scan again, this time at the actual resolution you want.

8. Clean the document as your software enables; remove edges, spots, and other smudges that might get caught in the OCR scan.

9. Run the OCR module to scan in the text, and then check spelling and grammar. Edit it as you wish.

10. Adjust images as your application allows.

11. If you're using Acrobat, save as a PDF file. Or, export the document to the appropriate application, which is what you'll have to do from OmniPage or TextBridge. If it's mostly text, use a word processor. If it's intensive page design, such as a newsletter, use a desktop PageMaker or any other publishing application.

WEB PATH

For scanning software details, visit the Caere site at:

http://www.caere.com/

Adobe at:

http://www.adobe.com

and Xerox at:

http://www.xerox.com/

WHAT ABOUT FORMS?

Forms can now be captured and used with scanning software such as OmniForm. You can either scan or fax forms into your PC, and the software will convert it into an editable document. Visioneer also includes software to manage forms — it's a really handy tool for registration forms and other materials that become tedious tasks when they're stuck on paper.

Adobe's Acrobat Exchange can add form functions to any PDF document, as shown in Figure 5-3. You select options to define Field Properties, including text options, appearance, and the actions the field will perform. It's an easy way for nontechnical people to add functionality quickly to digital documents.

GETTING YOUR PAPER TO THE INTRANET

Consider the implications of converting your paper-based documents to documents on your intranet. You can take just about anything and "publish" it instantaneously over your intranet. Several of the OCR packages include an export-to-HTML feature if you want to present your information as Web pages. Otherwise, you can use Adobe's PDF (Portable Document Format) for distribution as hyperlinked files. The benefit of using PDF is that your users can save the file to their local hard drive and retain all the formatting, regardless of the fonts on their system, what platform they're using, or what images are included. The PDF files can now be viewed in the Acrobat Reader, which launches within your Web browser.

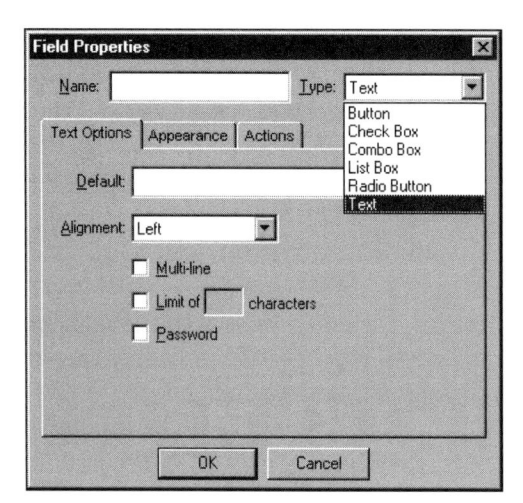

Figure 5-3 Adding a form function in a PDF document

X-REF For details on indexing collections of Adobe PDF files, see Chapter 9.

You Can Use All the Stuff Piled on Your Hard Drive

What if you've already got your documents in an electronic format? With a few conversion steps, you can make all your electronic files compatible with your intranet. You've got two choices: tools designed specifically for file conversions and enhancements for online delivery, and plug-in tools for mainstream applications, such as the Microsoft Office suite.

Creating a PDF File using Acrobat Exchange

You can easily convert any electronic document into a common file format such as Adobe Acrobat PDF or even into HTML. Acrobat Exchange works like a print driver — you're essentially "printing" to a file instead of paper.

Follow these steps to use Adobe Acrobat Exchange to create common digital files:

1. Choose Adobe PDFWriter from the Print dialog box in Acrobat Exchange. Figure 5-4 shows the Print dialog box from Microsoft Word as an example.

2. Set the page range and other document setup features, such as page size, as you would when printing to paper.

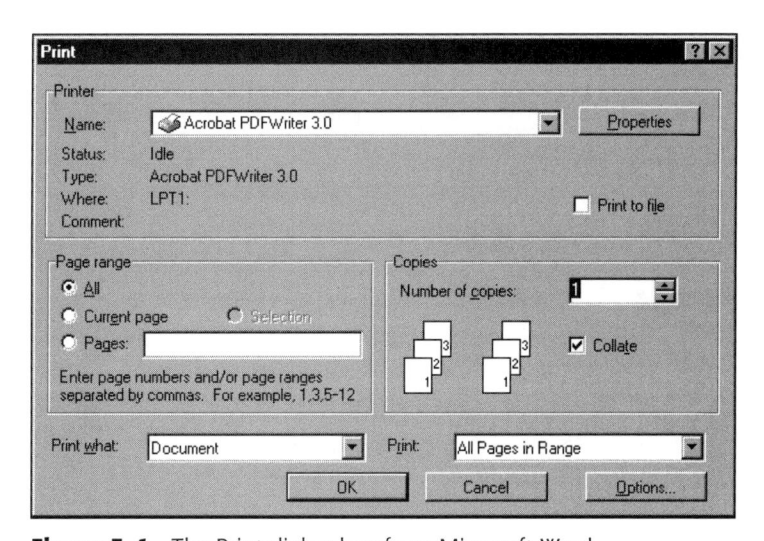

Figure 5-4 The Print dialog box from Microsoft Word

3. Choose the Options button. Select the option for Summary Document Information and choose Print.

4. Choose a file location for the PDF document.

5. At the Document Information dialog box as shown in Figure 5-5, enter Title, Subject, and Keywords information that will help you and your users find the file.

6. Choose OK and the PDF file will be created, as shown in Figure 5-6.

X-REF For details on keywording and search tips, see Chapter 9.

Figure 5-5 The Document Information dialog box

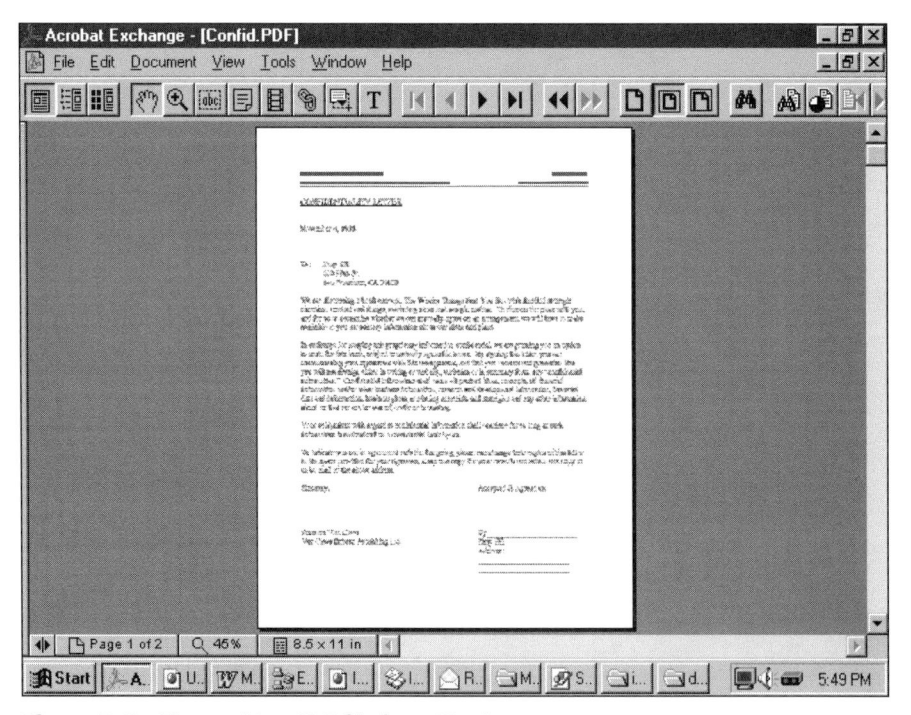

Figure 5-6 The resulting PDF file from Word

Converting complex documents, such as a newsletter created in Adobe PageMaker, takes a few more settings because of the complex graphics and type involved. For example, you can directly export to Acrobat PDF from PageMaker using Export → Adobe PDF menu to get to the dialog box shown Figure 5-7. The resulting PDF file is shown in Figure 5-8.

Figure 5-7 The Acrobat PDF dialog box in PageMaker

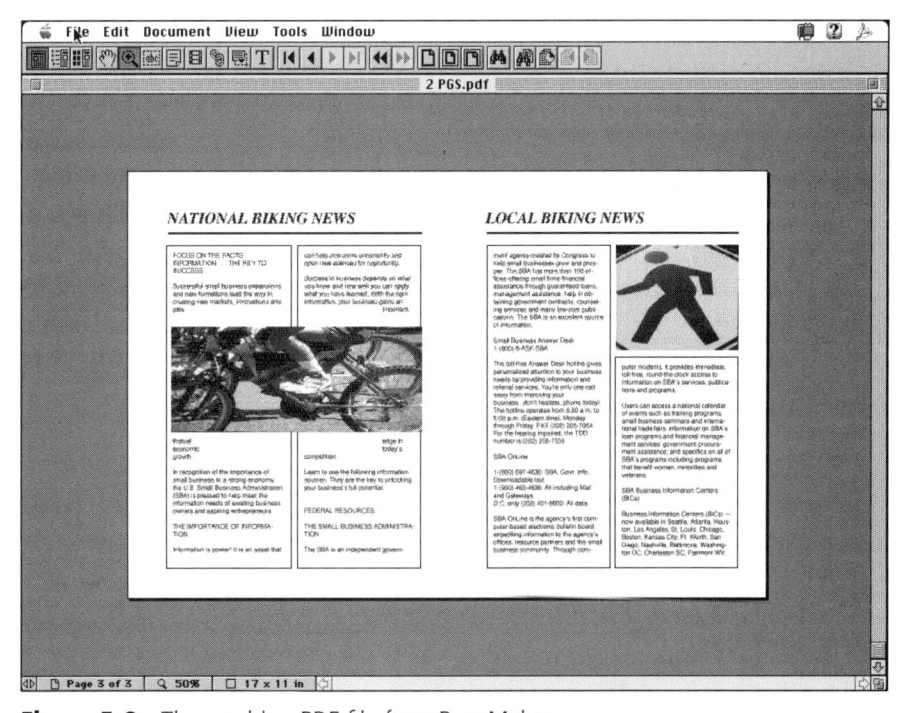

Figure 5-8 The resulting PDF file from PageMaker

Software that converts files into HTML format operate in about the same way. You can use tools that convert files into HTML and then import those files into Web page-creation applications. Or, you can import many file formats directly into the Web page-creation application.

SETTING A COMMON DENOMINATOR

WEB PATH → For a free copy of the Acrobat Reader, which you need to view Acrobat files, visit Adobe at:

http://www.adobe.com/

Converting Office Documents to HTML

Many mainstream applications now include filters to export your files directly onto the Web or an intranet. For example, every application in the Microsoft Office Suite now has Internet Assistants that enable you to export to HTML, preview the file in your browser, and add hyperlinks between documents, to an intranet, or out onto the Web. That means you can easily connect word processing documents, spreadsheets, databases, and schedules all into one common accessible format on your intranet.

It's easy to use the Internet Assistants to make a file intranet ready.

Follow these steps to use the Internet Assistant in Microsoft Word:

1. Download the Internet Assistant from the Microsoft Web site at:
   http://www.microsoft.com

   Follow the installation guidelines.

2. Open a Word file. To insert a hyperlink, which is done in Word's normal editing mode, choose **Insert** → **Hyperlink** to get the dialog box as shown in Figure 6-9. Browse to look through your hard drive or the Web for the location to which you wish to link. Set Bookmarks to the location if you wish.

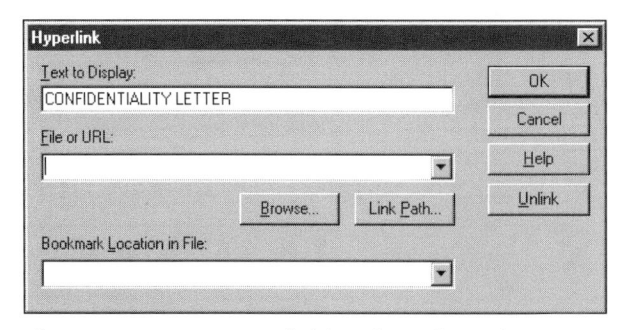

Figure 5-9 Insert Hyperlink in Microsoft Word

3. Switch to Web Browse view by clicking the eyeglasses button, as shown in Figure 5-10.

Eyeglasses button

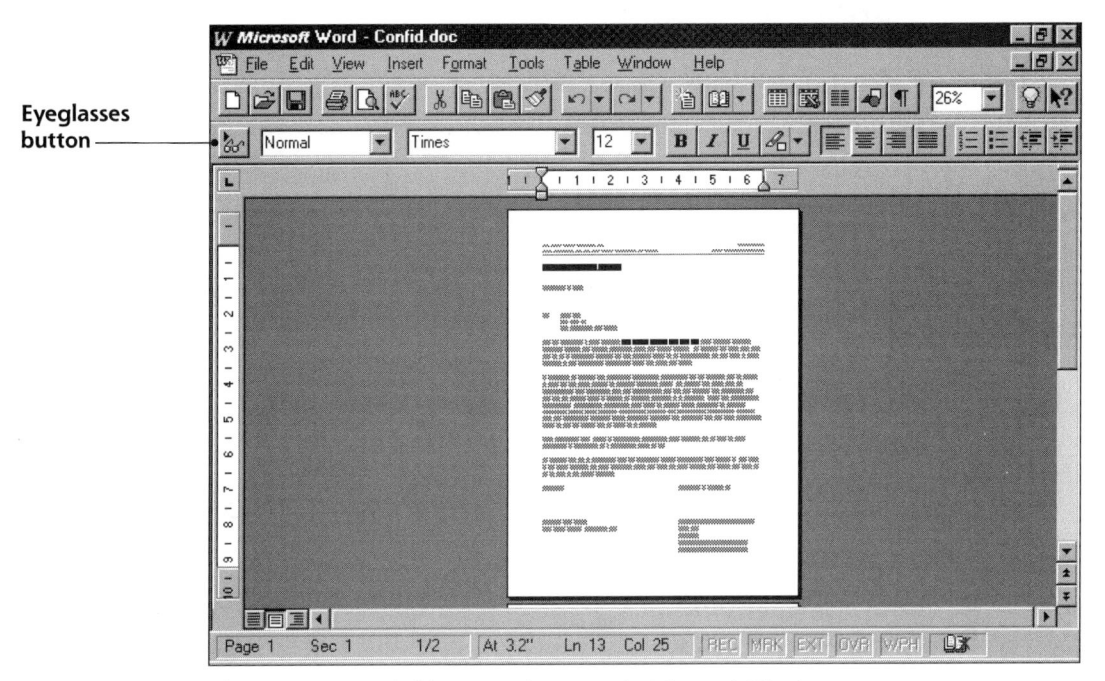

Figure 5-10 Switching to Web Browse in Microsoft Word

4. Your toolbar now looks like Figure 5-11, and your menus include HTML and Web-authoring tools.

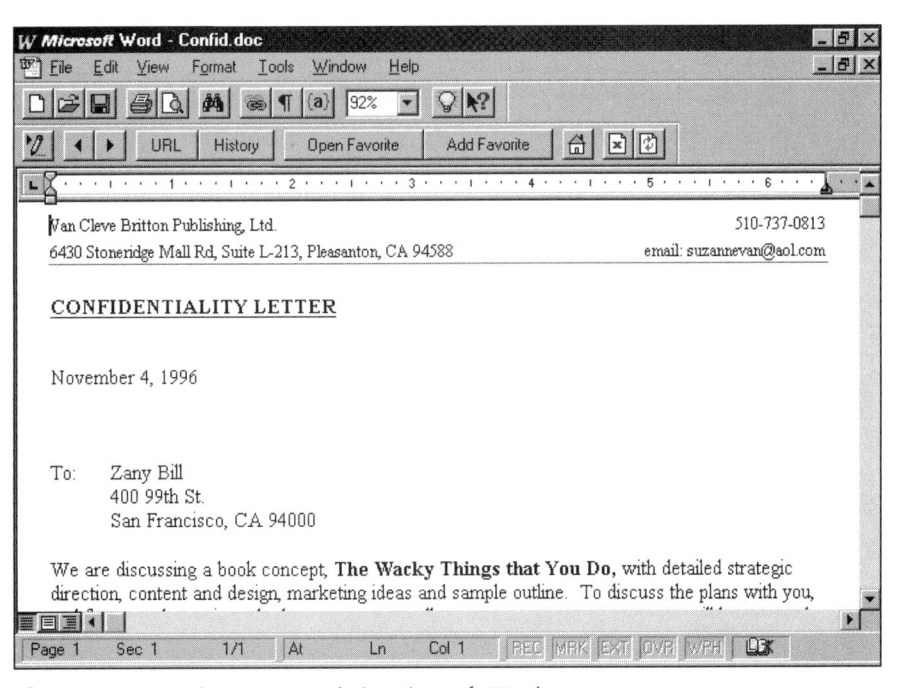

Figure 5-11 Web Browse mode in Microsoft Word

SETTING A COMMON DENOMINATOR

5. Your hyperlink appears in blue underline, indicating that it's linked. If you're in Browse mode you can test the link by clicking it.

Internet Assistants will also convert Excel spreadsheets, Access databases, PowerPoint presentations, and calendars in Schedule to HTML.

BONUS

Bridging to the Homegrown Systems

Finding a common denominator to proprietary information systems has been especially difficult because applications were complex, inconsistently coded by many different IS staff people, and poorly documented. Many companies have wrestled with critical information — such as sales statistics, budget reports, and inventory levels — being locked away in formats that are virtually impossible to reach. Combine that with a mobile staff and multilocation offices, and you can see the nightmare that unfolds.

With an intranet, and common file formats such as PDF or HTML, it is possible to publish information from your proprietary IS system. You can use the tools discussed in this chapter to convert anything you can access electronically, provided you can print the document to paper. And you can do it yourself, on your desktop, with writing proposals, negotiating priority for your application enhancement, or arguing with programmers. It is a short-term fix — the real solution is to overhaul your IS systems, but realistically the price will be astronomical and the time frame too long for your business to survive.

So get access to your information now. PDF it or HTML it and post it on the intranet. Then begin the process of sitting down with IS for a long-term solution.

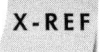

X-REF For details on automated conversions of proprietary system data, see Chapter 13.

Summary

In this chapter you learned:

Scanning techniques for paper-based documents

How to choose a scanner based on your needs

How to use OCR software

Ways to convert electronic documents for your intranet

CHAPTER SIX

TOOLS TO CREATE INTRANET PAGES

IN THIS CHAPTER YOU LEARN THESE KEY SKILLS

THE BASIC FEATURES OF TOOLS FOR CREATING
INTRANET PAGES   PAGE 88

A SUMMARY OF EACH OF THE LEADING
WEB-AUTHORING APPLICATIONS   PAGE 95

CREATING PAGES FOR YOUR INTRANET   PAGE 99

TIPS FOR CREATING INTRANET PAGES USING OTHER
APPLICATIONS   PAGE 111

There are many applications out there to help you build Web pages for your intranet. Which you choose depends on the type of pages you want to create, your technical savvy and/or interest in emerging technology, and of course, your budget. Some tools hide the underlying HTML (HyperText Markup Language) and rely on WYSIWYG (What You See Is What You Get) tools to build pages, while others expose the HTML tags for editing. Both types of Web-authoring tools offer similar features, and the WYSIWYG tools will enable you to open the hood and poke around in the HTML if you wish. This chapter focuses on WYSIWYG tools, on the premise that content matters most, and page creation should be an easy form of online delivery.

Alphabet Soup Wars: HTML versus WYSIWYG Tools

The language of the Web is HTML, whether you see the code directly or not. HTML tags were developed in the early days of the Internet, long before anyone conceived the design-intense pages you see on the Web and on intranets today. Thus, HTML is quite limited in its design capabilities. For example, HTML can support twenty-some *style sheets* (such as Large Head, Larger Head, Largest Head), while sophisticated page-makeup applications can support 256 or more. If you have to simplify your design to 10 percent of the variation of the original, you'll realize you're sacrificing a lot of aesthetics. With new tools, such as PageMaker 6.5, you can convert documents from the page makeup application (with a lot of design features) to HTML with one mouse click.

There are two distinct tools for creating Web pages for your intranet: the source code modifying HTML editors and WYSIWYG tools. Raw HTML editors enable you to modify HTML code yourself, a sample of which is shown in Figure 6-1 in a simple word processor. Editing the HTML files directly gives you more control over the look of your document, but it takes much more time to edit the codes within brackets. The WYSIWYG tools translate the HTML code into visible editable objects, such as the headers, text formatting, buttons, and rules shown in Figure 6-2.

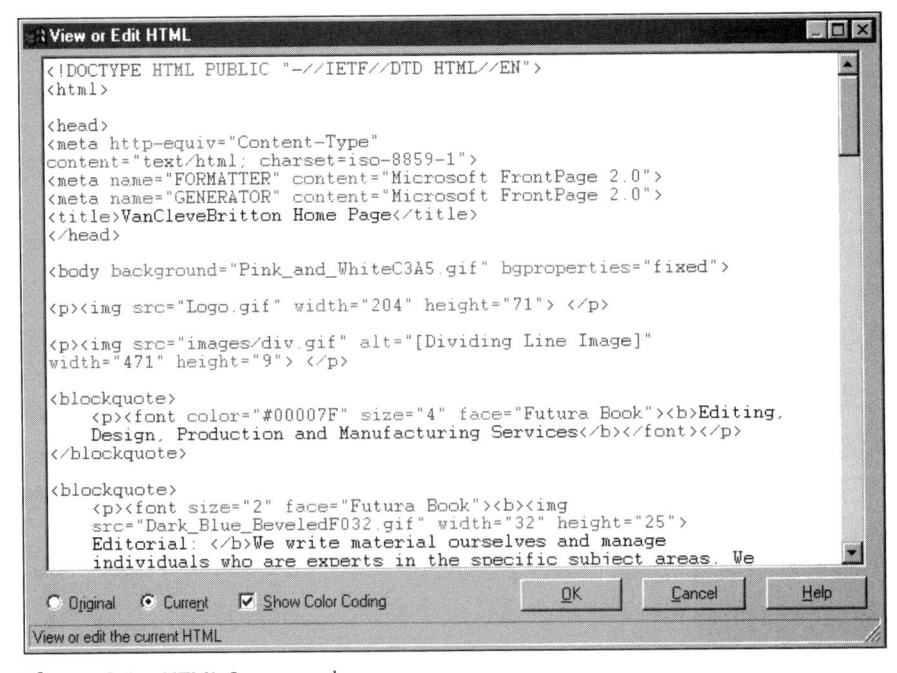

Figure 6-1   HTML Source code

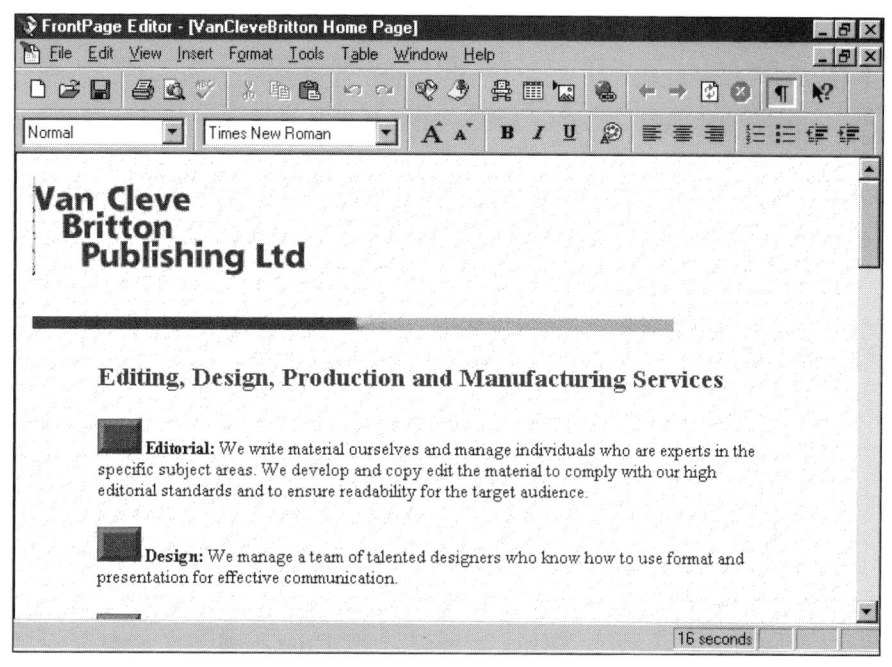

Figure 6-2   The same code viewed in a WYSIWYG tool, FrontPage 97

Our goal is to present the capabilities of this WYSYWIG genre of tools to give you an idea of what you can do. For easier reference, we'll call them *graphic-oriented tools* instead of dealing with that lengthy acronym. You can always view the HTML source code from any of these graphic-oriented tools if you want to make changes or add features not available with the tool you use. For the specifics on using any of the products, you'll need to experiment with the tool(s) that you choose to build your intranet.

Do It with Pictures

This section covers the features available in graphic-oriented tools. Decide which capabilities you need, consider the complexity of the application, and think about who will be doing your authoring. You might choose the easier tools for general use by your staff if you're largely distributing the task of creating intranet pages. Then, you might use the more complex tools for integrating more advanced features, such as frames, forms, and interfaces to other applications outside of your intranet. All tools discussed here are available for both Windows and Macintosh; many of the companies are working on versions for Windows NT. Check the applicable product's Web site for details.

SIDE TRIP

RAW HTML EDITING TOOLS TO CONSIDER

If you want to explore the nuances of HTML Editing on a Macintosh, check out BBEdit by Bare Bones Software. It includes HTML coding aids in a palette that is easy to use. It's a minimalist program, which reduces the clutter and learning curve. You can insert HTML tags, but you won't be able to do any visual formatting of text and graphic elements. BBEdit has two other useful features, spell checking and searching throughout files, which are helpful if you realize after coding an entire page that you've made a spelling error.

The tool palette validates links, checks that you've got start and end tags for each element, and check the syntax of your code for errors in logic.

Another highly rated HTML editing tool is Rick Giles's HTML Editor. It's a shareware application, which means you can download it and then pay the author a $25 shareware fee if you decide to keep the application. HTML Editor has HTML tags that are easy to read, as well as some formatting capabilities that other tools do not offer. Text is displayed in relative sizes, and links and image tags are color coded.

If you're game for learning more about HTML tags, take a look at the following from IDG Books Worldwide: *Creating Cool HTML 3.2 Web Pages* by Dave Taylor, or *HTML For Dummies* by Deborah and Eric Ray, both from IDG Books Worldwide.

Sound complicated? If all this sounds a bit too geeky for you, stick to the graphic-oriented tools discussed in the rest of this chapter.

WEB PATH You can get more info on BBEdit at:

http://www.barebones.com/

Basics of Graphic-Oriented Tools

An intranet page will generally have three elements: text, graphics, and hyperlinks to other pages in the intranet or the World Wide Web. All the products discussed in this chapter include tools to get you started quickly, whether it's page templates or set-up wizards. A template is helpful if you can find one that is close to the scope of your intranet, or at least segments of it. Set-up wizards get you started quickly, helping you insert consistent design elements for a uniform look throughout your intranet, default links between pages, e-mail and contact information, formatting, and more. You can edit anything in the templates, or by using wizards, copying and pasting your own text information and graphics. You can edit links and design elements.

After creating the page, preview it using your Web browser. The authoring tools enable you to designate which browser you're using.

It's important to understand the distinction between the tool used to create a page and the one used to view it, especially when product names are so close. Netscape Navigator Gold creates pages it can view; Netscape Navigator just views them. Microsoft FrontPage Editor creates pages; Microsoft Internet Explorer views them. There's Microsoft FrontPage Explorer, which is used to manage an intranet or Web site. Finally, there's the Windows Explorer for Windows 95. Write to Microsoft and complain! If only everyone could be as obvious as Adobe, whose PageMill helps you create pages and SiteMill helps you manage sites. (They don't publish a browser, but if they did, would it be BrowserMill?)

Editing

Most Web-authoring tools contain toolbars and command menus to help you edit text and graphics to your needs. You can import text from other applications, but the amount of formatting support varies; most support Rich Text Format (RTF) at a minimum. Microsoft FrontPage 97, of course, supports the file formats of all its Office suite applications, so you can import formatting from Word, Excel, PowerPoint, and Access files into HTML.

To format text, select it and choose from a toolbar or menu to set its relative size, as shown in Figure 6-3. Remember, you can't designate fonts because that depends entirely on the fonts available on your user's computer. Or, you can dictate company standard fonts, and use the <FONT> tag in HTML to specify their use.

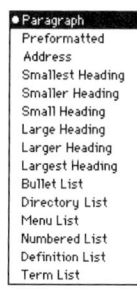

Figure 6-3 Formatting text from a toolbar in PageMill

Most applications now include ScreenTips, so if the toolbar icons seem obscure, drag your mouse over them and pause for a moment. A description of the icon appears either directly next to your cursor or in a separate location on the page, as shown in PageMill in Figure 6-4.

You want HTML editing to be easy, whether your staff is working in another application such as Word and importing the results, or making editing changes right on the page in the graphic-oriented tool. What's important is that your tool makes it simple to keep the information on your intranet current and lively.

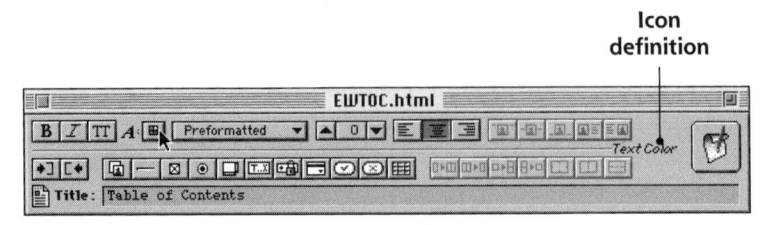

Figure 6-4 A PageMill icon definition

Navigation Ease of Graphic-Oriented Tools

An important criteria when choosing a graphic-oriented tool is how easily you can import objects, move them around, resize them, or delete them. Adobe PageMill and NetObjects Fusion are the most desktop publishing-like applications of the available graphic-oriented tools. You also need the ability to add links for moving around the page, going back to your home page, or moving to other sections of your intranet. You want to be able to add buttons or other elements that your users can recognize easily.

You can link from text or graphics by simply selecting the item and then choosing the link feature in your Web-authoring tool. Text will default to being blue and underlined, which will trigger your staff that clicking will lead them somewhere else. Images will not visibly change; you might want to add visible frames or a directive to "click here to see . . ."

It should be intuitive for your intranet development staff to create links where they see logical connections between the information in your intranet.

Importing Graphics

Some HTML editing applications convert any readable graphic format into a GIF or JPEG file format for your intranet. Others require that you convert your graphic files to GIF or JPEG format first. Some Web-authoring applications enable you to resize and move your images. In addition, some graphic-oriented tools enable you to set the background of your graphics to transparent, which is helpful if you've imported a logo and want to see the background through it, rather than a white square around the image.

Graphics help liven up your intranet and make logical navigation paths.

TIP Many paint and image manipulation applications provide the Save As option for various file formats. Whenever possible, save your graphics as GIF files for easiest use on your intranet. They are smaller and will download faster than JPEG files.

X-REF For details on using graphics, formats, and redrawing speeds, see Chapter 4.

Frames

Frames, shown in Figure 6-5, enable you to format your pages in multiple columns, using scroll bars if your page is longer than one screen and giving your users more control over how they move around your intranet. Frames can contain text and images, can be visible or hidden. Frames are really the first step to providing more graphic control in page creation; expect the functionality in this area to continue improving.

Frames can help organize the information on your intranet and improve its structure to make information more accessible.

WEB PATH For an example of a site that uses frames effectively, visit:
http://www.cnn.com

Figure 6-5 An example of frames

Multimedia

This new generation of authoring tools generally supports one-click imports of animated multimedia objects. This includes animated GIF files, which may seem cute and harmless because they're just a sequence of single images that play when clicked. For example, it's become quite popular to make your company logo blink using an animated GIF. Shockwave objects are Macromedia Director movies that are compressed for distribution on Web pages. Java applets are miniprograms created using the Java programming language, and can usually be stopped and started by the user once inserted into a Web page.

X-REF For more information on Java applets, see Chapter 15.

Don't forget sound formats, such as a clip of the CEO at a recent press conference or a quick update that you really want to emphasize. Use AU files for cross-platform compatibility, or WAV format for strictly PC distribution.

When building an intranet, sounds and video are not only fun, they also add to the learning experience.

WEB PATH To experience a Shockwave and download a free copy of the player plug-in, visit Macromedia at:

http://www.macromedia.com/

CAUTION Remember, your browser must recognize the file format of the multimedia object, and thus all your users need to have the right plug-ins to extend the functionality of your browser. These plug-ins need to be updated, and while it's easy to e-mail updates, it's hard to get everyone to take the few moments to do the installation.

HTML Source Code Editing

All of the graphic-oriented tools have the capability to edit the HTML directly by choosing the Show Source Code command in your authoring tool. Most authoring tools now show the HTML with color coding to indicate links, comments, and other instructions.

How much HTML source code editing do you need for an intranet? If you're going to start with a simple intranet, you can probably avoid getting your hands dirty with HTML. As you expand the functions of your intranet, you may need to do some hands-on editing of the source code.

Forms

Some Web-authoring tools provide templates for tabulating your results. You can create text fields for data entry, pop-up menus to restrict choices, radio buttons, and buttons to submit and reset the form.

Forms are great for collecting feedback from your users on the content, structure, and effectiveness of your site. Forms are also good for registering people for training and other matters.

CGI

CGI (Common Gateway Interface) enables communication between a Web browser and a Web server. A script or program can be run through CGI and return the results to the user, as in a query to a large database. You can make a call to CGI from text or an image, but complex scripting should be done by your technology experts.

CGI is a great way to link your intranet to other proprietary databases and systems in your company. This means your intranet can be the launching point for *all* of your organization's needs, through one common looking glass: a Web browser.

X-REF For details on using CGI, see Chapter 13.

The Tools

Picking a graphic-oriented Web-authoring tool that's right for your organization is important, but you'll probably settle on more than one depending on the people involved and the content they'll be creating and managing. The following overview looks at the leading graphic-oriented tools from the perspective of building your first intranet.

X-REF The line between Web-page authoring tools and site management tools is blurring, and most products here do both. For details on their site management features, see Chapter 8.

Microsoft FrontPage 97

FrontPage is relatively easy to use once you understand the difference between the FrontPage Explorer, which shows you the overall site and FrontPage Editor, which enables you to manipulate page elements.

FrontPage wizards, step-by-step instructions that guide you through a task, enable you to establish your pages and site structure quickly. Comment tags prompt you on where to customize your pages. FrontPage has a unique To Do List to keep track of elements that need editing, items that need importing, and links that need to be fixed or added.

For advanced functions, FrontPage includes *WebBots,* prepackaged tools that add interactive features to your intranet. WebBots can be used to add forms, discussion groups, add navigation bars to your pages, and time and date stamp items. You can insert Java applets and multimedia sound and video easily. Microsoft is adding more data-publishing support to improve connectivity to other databases in your organization. As an added touch, FrontPage 97 includes the Microsoft Image Composer, as shown in Figure 6-6, which is a useful image editor for modifying your graphics.

Figure 6-6 Microsoft Image Composer can be used to edit artwork for your intranet.

FrontPage has strong server-supported capabilities for your intranet, including interactive discussion groups and processing forms. You can publish to your Web server right from FrontPage; you can even create you own personal Web server right on your PC.

FrontPage is a good page building tool for your intranet if your operation uses the Microsoft Office suite, server integration is important, you like the Wizard and template approach, and you want an integrated site management tool.

WEB PATH To download a trial version of FrontPage, visit Microsoft at:

http://www.microsoft.com/

Adobe PageMill

Adobe's PageMill was the first graphic-oriented Web-authoring tool, and it functions more like a desktop publishing tool than any of the other applications. With roots on the Mac platform, PageMill enables you to click and drag elements around the page as shown in Figure 6-7. You can spell check, and search on text, graphics, sound, and video. You can create tables easier with more formatting than with most Web-authoring tools, drop objects into cells, and have the table reformat automatically to make everything fit.

Selection handles

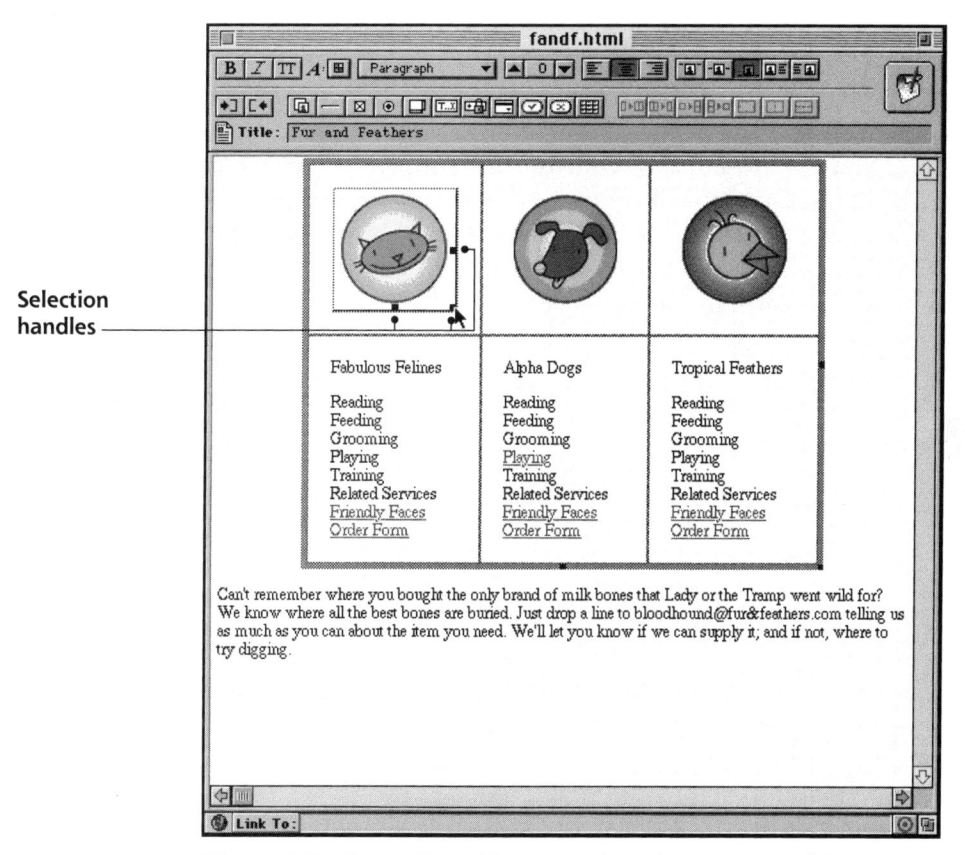

Figure 6-7 PageMill enables you to drag elements around the page.

You can insert frames easily, embed Shockwave elements, QuickTime Movies, and Adobe PDF files. PageMill enables you to view and edit HTML source code.

Because testing your intranet pages is critical and time-consuming, PageMill's toggle button between editing mode and previewing mode is very useful. You don't need to switch applications to see the results of your work.

> **CAUTION**
> If you're using QuickTime movies, a format native to Macintosh but now available for Windows, your users will have to have the QuickTime plug-in installed on their PCs.

If you're choosing a tool for staff accustomed to working with PageMaker, QuarkXPress, FrameMaker, or other desktop publishing tools, PageMill will be the most intuitive tool.

WEB PATH For information on PageMill, visit Adobe at:
http://www.adobe.com/

TOOLS TO CREATE INTRANET PAGES

DeltaPoint QuickSite

DeltaPoint QuickSite is the only application included here that isn't really an graphic-oriented page creation tool. It does, however, include wizards that expedite creating the structure of your intranet pages. You can create a consistent look and feel by working through the wizards, and set up links automatically. You get a spreadsheet-like overview of all the elements, how they're linked, and the names of the pages, but you can't *see* how the site will connect together. The same visual void applies to pages: You can flip through dialog boxes that contain the text and tags for images, but you can't actually *see* how the page will look until you launch your browser.

QuickSite is a good tool for intranets if the content of your pages is simple and quick site management is paramount.

WEB PATH ➡ To download a trial version of QuickSite, visit DeltaPoint at:
http://www.deltapoint.com/

Netscape Navigator Gold

Netscape Navigator Gold has an easy-to-use interface, especially if you're familiar with the Navigator browser. For those who need help in design, Navigator includes the Gold Rush Tool Chest: graphics, templates, color themes, and JavaScript to add some pizzazz to your pages.

Netscape Navigator Gold integrates a page creation tool, a Web browser, newsgroup access, e-mail, discussion groups, and file transfer all in one package. Because Netscape has been the precedent setter in Web browsers, it has set the standards for plug-ins to support audio, video, 3D, and animation. It also includes search capabilities, bookmark features, and a customizable user interface.

Netscape and Microsoft continue to attempt setting standards such as HTML-based style sheets and other components that would improve consistency with creating and viewing pages.

If you're using Netscape Navigator to view your intranet, and the idea of having one tool for Web page creation, news management and mail is appealing, then Navigator Gold would be a good tool for your intranet.

WEB PATH ➡ For information on Navigator Gold, visit Netscape at:
http://www.netscape.com/

NetObjects Fusion

NetObjects Fusion is a powerful site management tool that also has strong page design tools. It's more like a desktop publishing application, with click-and-drag capabilities to position elements. NetObjects Fusion uses style sheets to enable tagging of elements and global changing of formatting. This means you can label text Heading 1 consistently, and designate the same formatting for all the text tagged Heading 1. That way, if you change your mind and want to make all the Heading 1 text bigger, you only make that change once. You can drag and drop Java, ActiveX, and Shockwave applets onto your intranet pages, and audio and video streaming plug-ins are supported. You can generate pages separately, and then link them together for the global intranet with links and navigation automatically generated.

Fusion costs more than FrontPage, PageMill, or QuickSite ($500 compared to $149 or so for the others). Fusion is a powerful tool that includes sophisticated database import tools. The AutoSites templates aren't just pretty layouts, they are well thought-out site building tools, including Fusion's intranet template. The template includes prebuilt pages that will get you started quickly. For example, take the employee directory page and import your own data. Elements are placed (substitute your logo for theirs), text is formatted, links are set to the home page, and so on. Or you can use the human resources page and link your organization's handbook, calendar, and other information. FrontPage includes some intranet page templates, but no overall site template. Expect to see more templates from other developers soon.

WEB PATH To download a trial version of Fusion, visit NetObjects at:

http://www.netobjects.com/

Creating Intranet Pages

Each application creates pages for your intranet similarly, but for precise details you need to use the specific tool. In this section, we'll walk through creating a basic intranet. When we reach specific steps, we'll use Microsoft FrontPage to demonstrate. The theory and approach will be the same regardless of the tool you choose; what's important is that you get an idea of the capabilities.

We'll use the FrontPage Wizards to get started, and then modify our intranet to accommodate some of the basic subject areas that you may want to include. Later in this chapter, we'll look at tools that include specific modules for building intranets; first we want you to understand the building blocks.

Using Wizards

For the technically advanced, wizards have been an annoying set of training wheels that limited what you could do with an application, and were mediocre tools for the newbie page builder. No more! Wizards (some applications may call them something else, but the industry is heading toward *wizards* as a generic term) are full-powered, flexible assistants that prompt you to include basic information and a lot of valuable core structure. Plus, you'll be learning the application as you go.

Remember the distinction between FrontPage Explorer (the site view) and FrontPage Editor (the page creation or authoring tool). After you set up the pages using wizards, you'll toggle between the two to see the site and edit the pages. Finally, you'll preview how they will look on your intranet using a browser such as Explorer.

Throughout this example, we'll create an intranet with the following sections:

- Company News
- Meeting Schedules and Agendas
- Employee Directory
- Human Resources: Information, Forms and Employment Opportunities
- Intranet Feedback Form
- Search Page
- Seminar Registration Form
- Discussion Groups

To set up your intranet using the FrontPage wizards, follow these steps:

1. When you launch FrontPage, choose Create a New FrontPage Web From a Wizard or Template. Unless otherwise specified here, use the default check boxes, and click OK to get to the next dialog box.

2. Choose the Corporate Presence Wizard. You can modify the pages for an intranet.

3. You'll be prompted for a location to which you want to save your intranet site; name it something logical and remember where you are storing it. You'll publish it to a central intranet server later.

4. You're now into the wizard, where you'll be asked a series of questions about your business. Choose all the pages on each screen of the wizard. You can edit the pages later for the specifics of your intranet.

5. On the wizard page for Feedback Form, choose the information you want about your users. On the next screen, choose the tab-delimited format for reviewing your feedback in a database.

6. On the wizard for Table of Contents, check the Show pages not linked into Web box in addition to the other defaults.

7. On the wizard page for choosing a presentation style, pick one that fits your organization. You'll get a preview in the box on the left.

8. On the next wizard page defining colors, you'll select colors for your Web page. Remember to keep high contrast between the background and the text, even though it's tempting to use a really wild background. You'll be able to modify your colors later by editing the page titled Web Colors.

TIP Don't change the default colors of text. It will confuse anyone accustomed to the default palette of hyperlinks and the Web.

9. Enter your company information as prompted on the next three screens. Then check the Show To Do List on the last screen. Choose Finish and the skeleton of your intranet site will be generated as shown in Figure 6-8, and a To Do List as shown in Figure 6-9.

WEB PATH Keep your eyes on the Microsoft Site Builder Web pages for continually updated tools for building Web pages. Visit:

http://www.microsoft.com/

X-REF For more detail on creating pages and sites with FrontPage, see *Discover FrontPage 97*, by Peter Kent (IDG Books Worldwide, 1997).

You've now got a skeleton for your intranet site. If you double-click on your home page, FrontPage Editor will launch so you can add and edit pages. You'll see your home page, as shown in Figure 6-10.

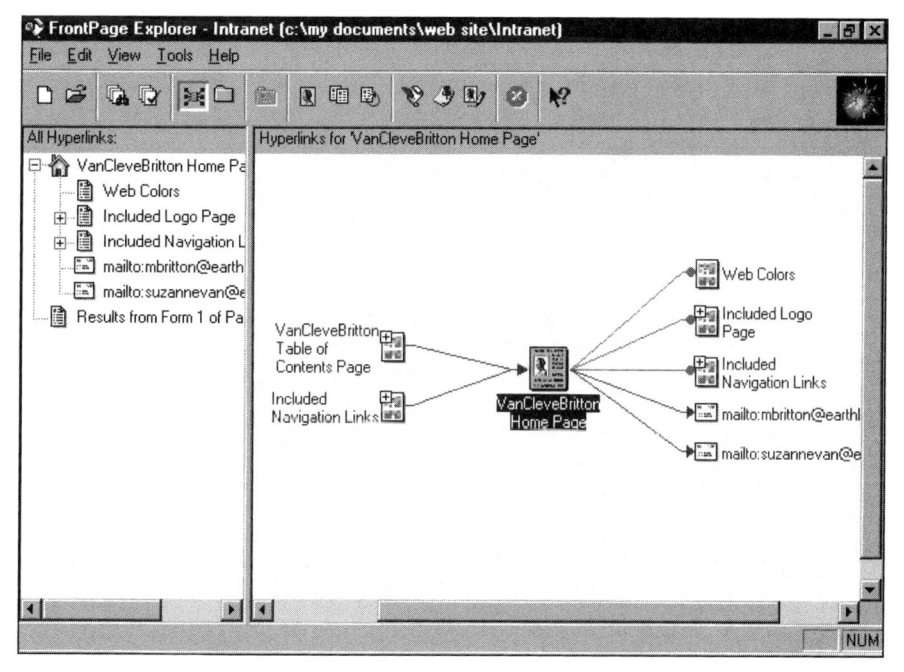

Figure 6-8 A site view

TOOLS TO CREATE INTRANET PAGES

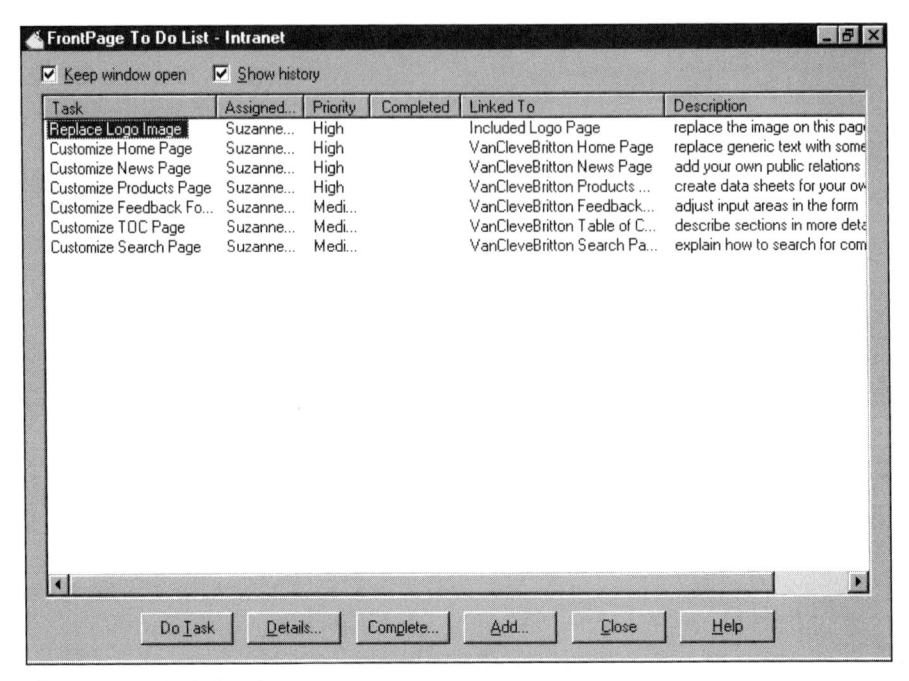

Figure 6-9 A To Do List

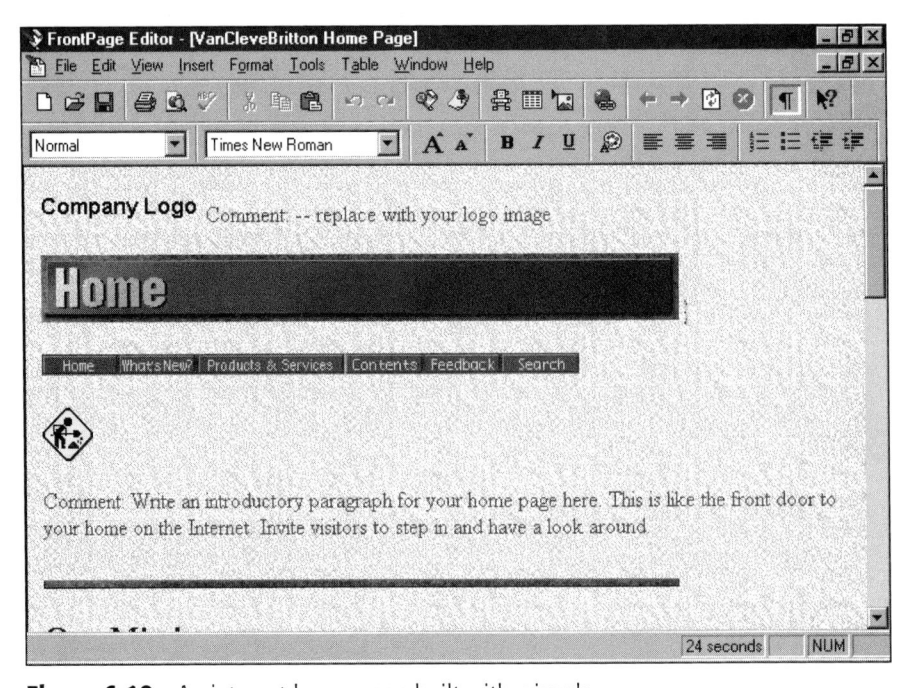

Figure 6-10 An intranet home page built with wizards

Importing Images

Images, such as your company logo, need to be imported. Remember, your page is going to look for the source image, so keep your files in one directory; don't move them around or change their names. It's like importing art into Word or another word processor in that you use the cursor as an insertion point. You can also set your image background to be transparent if you're getting a white background around your logo.

TIP The To Do List is very helpful for tracking tasks. You can also delegate To Do Lists to others on your team, and track the overall progress of a project.

Use an image editing tool such as Microsoft Image Composer or Photoshop to edit artwork, or use the included templates. Add elements, such as the bullets shown in Figure 6-11, for each of the subject areas in your intranet.

X-REF Logo stuck on paper? See Chapter 4 for details on scanners and getting paper-based documents into the digital world.

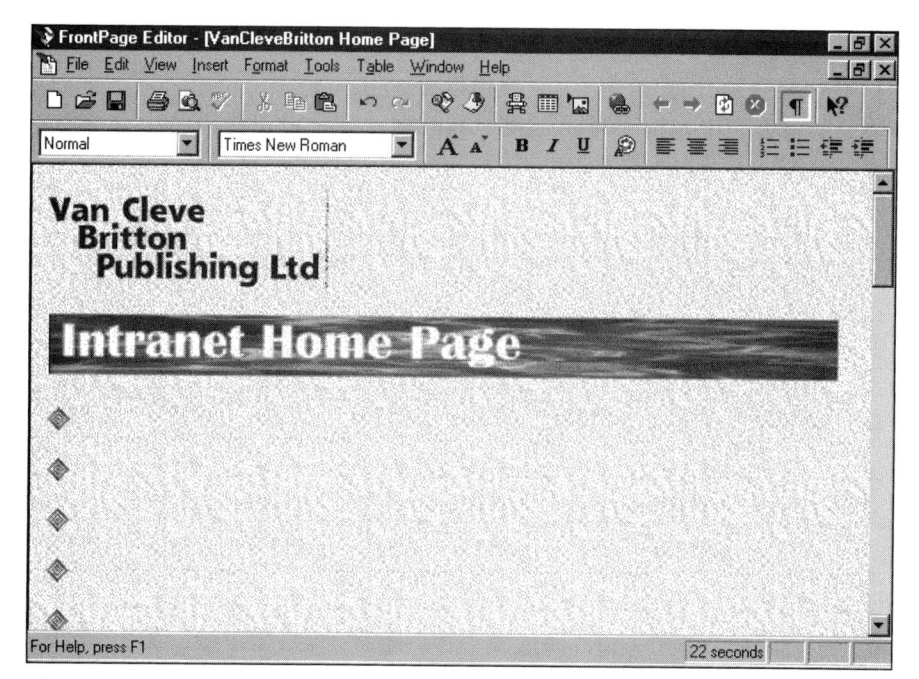

Figure 6-11 Bullets can help flag different elements for your users.

TOOLS TO CREATE INTRANET PAGES

Importing and Formatting Text

If you want stylized text, such as the logo or intranet home page bar in the previous figure, you'll need to create it as artwork. Remember, it's the user's computer that determines available fonts, so for ordinary text you're pretty much limited to Arial/Helvetica and Times/Times New Roman.

To add text to your home page, click the insertion point and type. Your options for size are relative, so you'll be selecting Big, Bigger, Biggest variables instead of a specific point size as you would in a word processor.

You can also import text from your word processor; most authoring tools include filters to save your text formatting as well.

Adding Sound and Video

Sound and video are imported just like images, but remember that your users will need the plug-ins to use them. Most developers of sound and video creation tools include free player plug-ins; that means you buy the application to create of sounds and videos while your staff can hear and watch them for free.

Changing Backgrounds and Colors

You can modify backgrounds and default colors globally in most authoring tools by finding the Web Colors page (usually located within the folder containing the files for your site) and making changes to it. It works like a document template in a word processor, or a master page template in a desktop publishing program. The next generation of Web-authoring tools promises the same functionality of style sheets for character and paragraph formatting.

Adding Tables

Inserting tables adds structure to your pages, and is useful for keeping key information on one screen. The Insert Table command in HTML editing programs works like Tables in a word processor, as shown in Figure 6-12. You can set the number of rows and columns, and whether you want to include visible borders and other spacing options. Edit table size, columns, and rows by selecting the table to return to the dialog box. Some authoring tools, such as PageMill, dynamically resize the table based on elements that you cut and paste into it. Others will require some handwork.

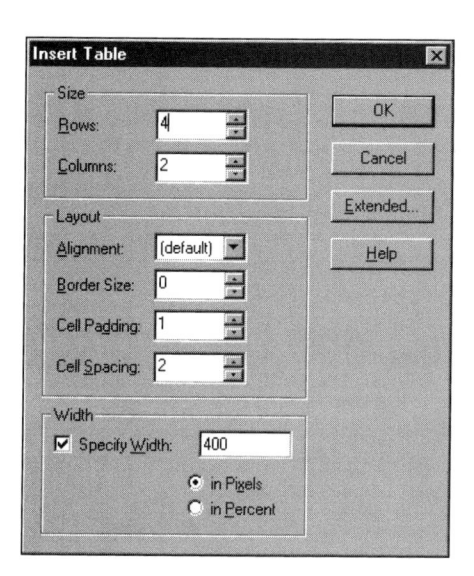

Figure 6-12 The Insert Table dialog box in FrontPage

Tables can quickly set a structure for information or navigation around your intranet, as shown in Figure 6-13.

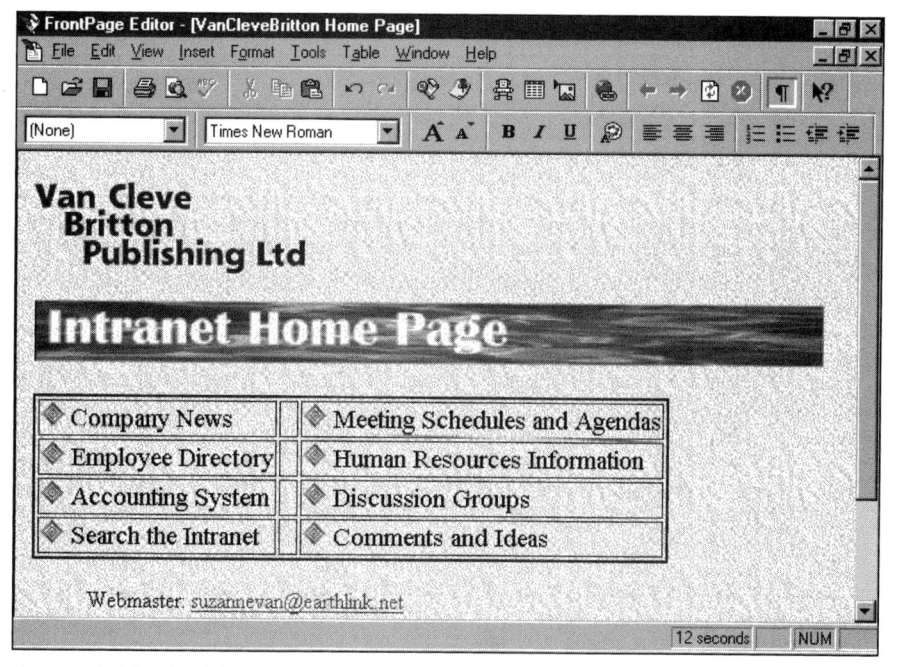

Figure 6-13 A table inserted on the home page

TOOLS TO CREATE INTRANET PAGES **105**

Adding Frames

Frames divide the Web page's display into separate windows, each of which can have a different scrollable page. Each frame is a separate element, so you can modify one frame while keeping the others the same. A collection of frames can make up one full page to be seen by your users.

The easiest way to create a frame set is to use a wizard such as those in FrontPage, shown in Figure 6-14.

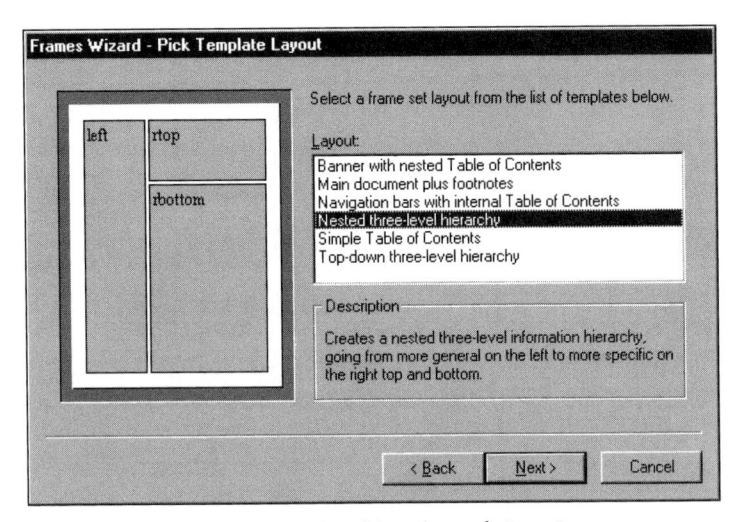

Figure 6-14 The Frames Wizard in Microsoft FrontPage

WEB PATH To see good examples of the use of frames, visit the following sites. Keep in mind the content they're sorting and presenting by using frames. See the Lycos search engine site at:

http://www.lycos.com/

or the CNN site at:

http://www.CNN.com/

Inserting Forms

Forms are a great way to collect feedback from your users, and the basic structure can be created again using a wizard (shown in Figure 6-15). You can customize the field labels, the field content, the order of the fields, and so on. After finishing with the wizard, you can modify the page as you wish. Your final form will look professional and help you gather the information you need — and everyone will think you've been coding for days! Figure 6-16 shows a form created with a wizard.

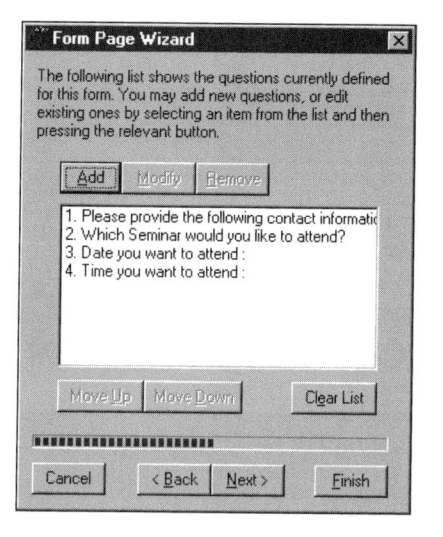

Figure 6-15 The Form Page Wizard in FrontPage

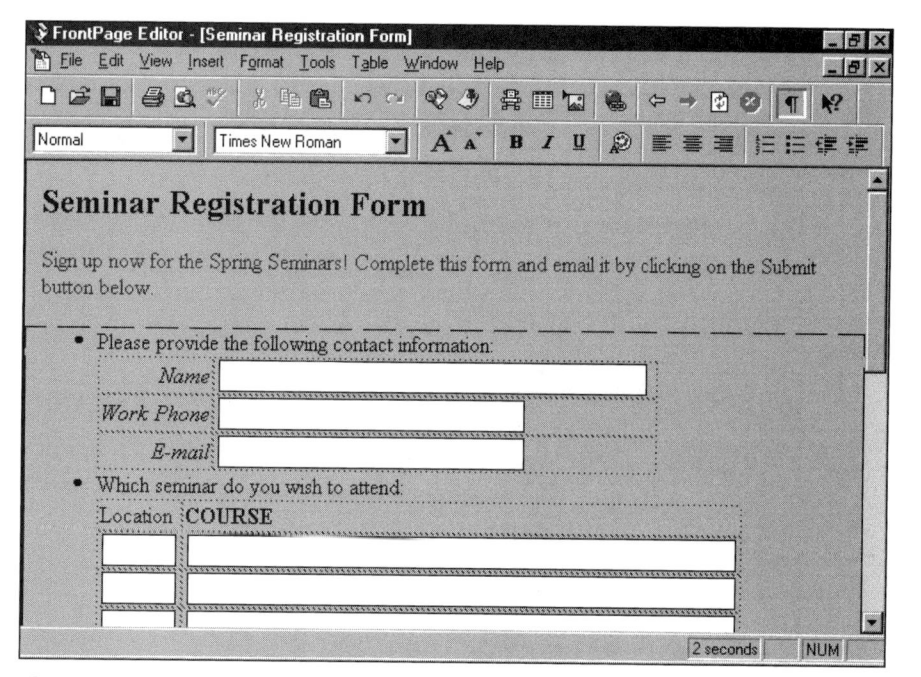

Figure 6-16 A form created with a FrontPage Wizard

Adding Pages for Specific Tasks

You can add custom pages for each function on your intranet, choosing New from the File menu and selecting from the wizards to set up your page. For example, you can add a page for the Employee Directory using the FrontPage template. Depending on the size of your organization, you may want to list all names at the top as shown in Figure 6-17, and link to details as shown in Figure 6-18.

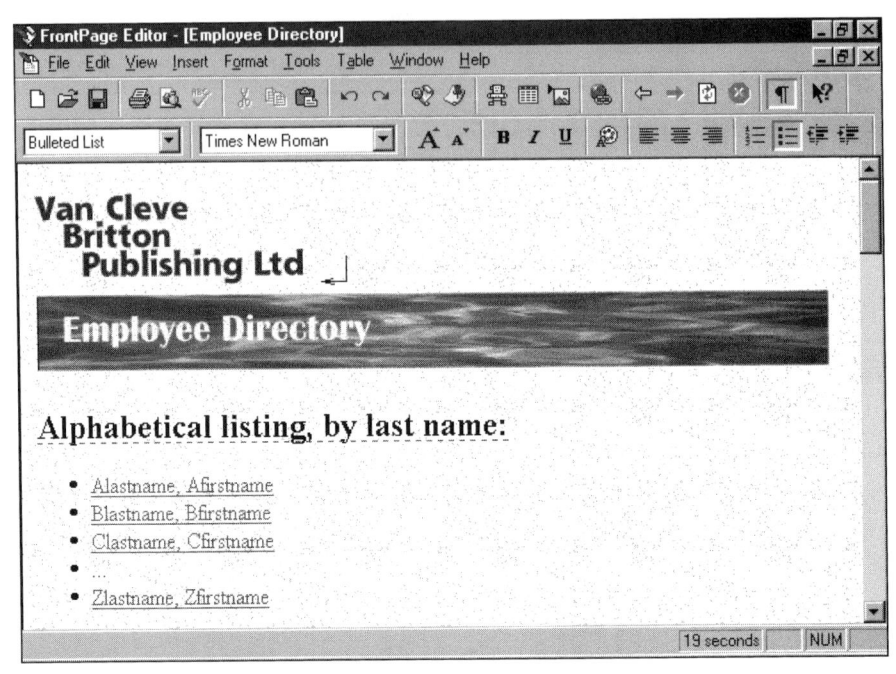

Figure 6-17 An employee directory with all names listed up top

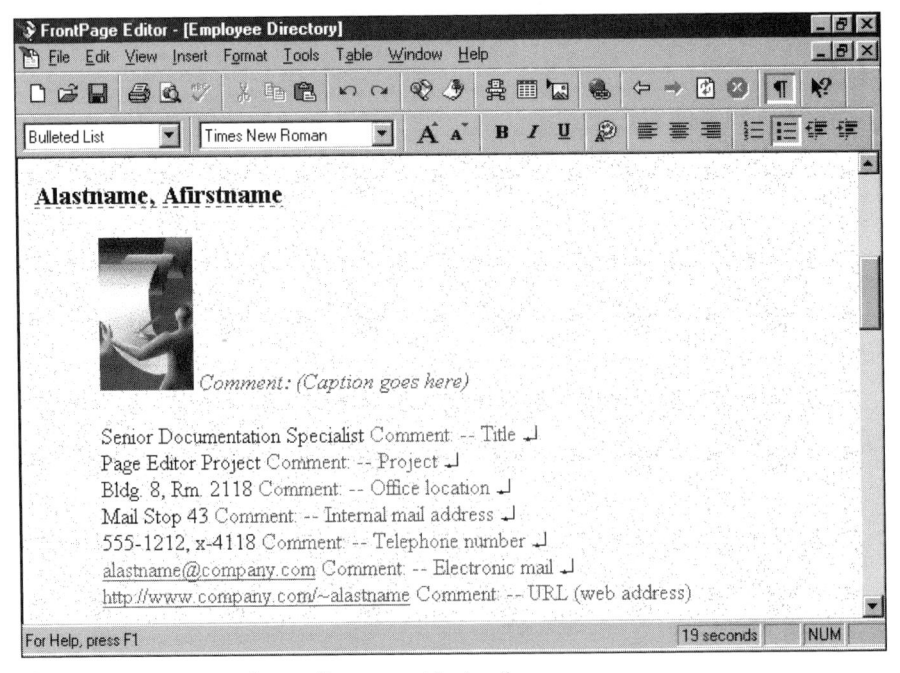

Figure 6-18 An employee directory with details

You can import your employee directory from a variety of sources, including a database or a word file. You can place it on your intranet as text, rich text with formatting, or as HTML.

Adding Links

It's easy to add links to pages on your intranet. To link from text, select the text, choose insert Hyperlink under the Insert menu, and navigate to the page you want. Your linked text will appear in blue with an underline to indicate that it's now clickable, as shown in Figure 6-19.

You can also add your e-mail address in the same fashion.

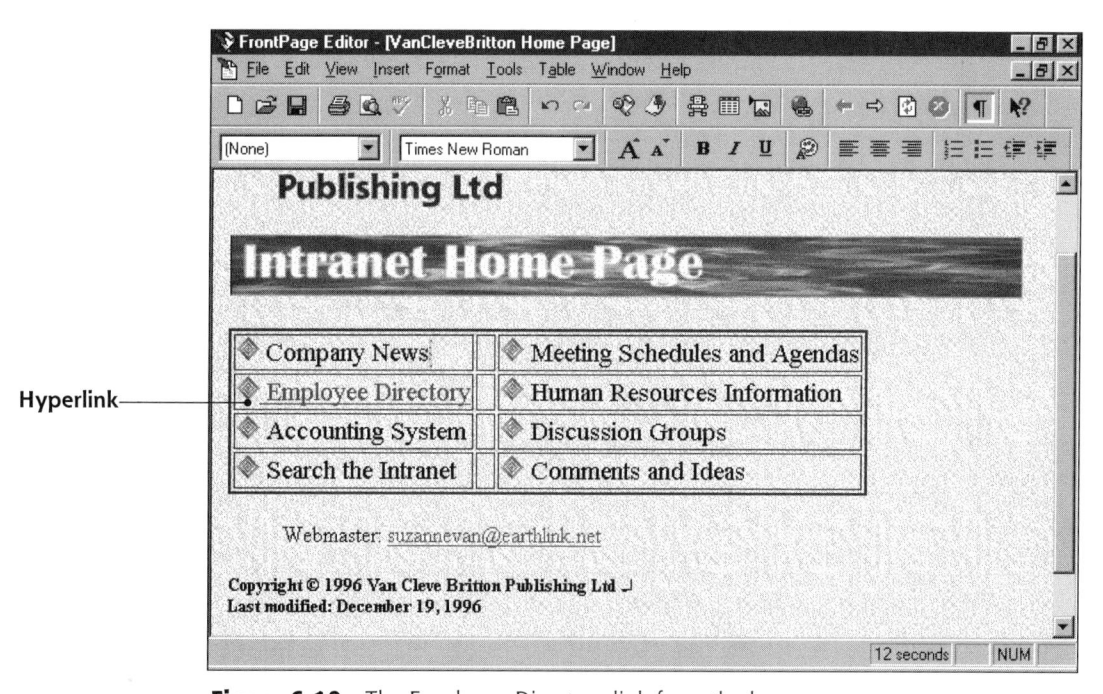

Figure 6-19 The Employee Directory link from the home page

Editing HTML Code

If you want to customize your pages beyond the capabilities of your Web-authoring tool, you can show the source code and edit the HTML directly. Your Web-authoring tool will either launch Notepad or another word processor so you can edit the code. FrontPage enables you to add HTML coding at numerous points with an Extended button and prompts for what HTML code may be appropriate for specific functions, as shown in Figure 6-20.

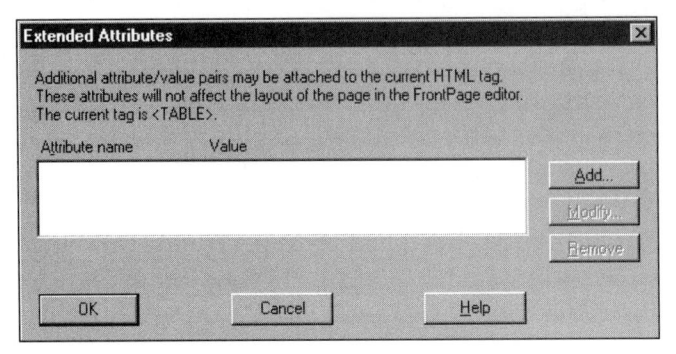

Figure 6-20 Extended Attributes to add HTML codes in FrontPage

Publishing Pages

Once you add and edit your new pages, you need to return to the site management tool to publish all your pages on your intranet. In Front Page, this is the Explorer application, which will show you the entire site with links that can be edited.

To publish your intranet to the server and make it a live, clickable entity that your users can access, choose the Publish function. You need to select a destination folder and click OK. You should then preview your intranet in the browser you and your company's employees will be using to ensure that links are working and any special features are functioning.

> **CAUTION** Smart file naming and management is critical! Misplacing pages is one of the biggest frustrations of new Web page builders. Keep all your work nested in the same directory, and watch the default prompts from your Web-authoring tool. Think carefully before changing the destination, and try not to move pages after you've linked and published them. Leave a forwarding notice at the old location so users can find the page's new address.

That's what it takes to build a basic intranet. As you get more comfortable with the technology, you can add new features. Test features carefully before releasing them to your users. Watch the Web page-creation tool developers' Web sites for emerging tools that keep getting more powerful and easier to use. Most of all, keep an eye on the content and listen to your users. They'll tell you what's working and what needs improvement.

> **TIP** Another important issue in creating Web pages is making sure that the pages work for the users. Because of the differences between Microsoft Internet Explorer and Netscape Navigator, what looks right on one browser may not in another. Sometimes the result is surprisingly disappointing. It's not really enough to create a page in a WYSIWYG tool and verify it there. If possible, check it in as many variations of the browsers with which the users may be working.

BONUS

One-Stop Intranet Building with NetObjects Intranet Module

If you want one-stop shopping, you may prefer one tool with a template to build your intranet. Using tools such as NetObjects with the intranet site module will build you a site quickly, but you'll have much less flexibility than with working through the development of your intranet yourself. An example of a site created by NetObjects is shown in Figure 6-21.

The intranet site module includes templates for: human resources, sales, marketing, and R&D. The human resources core page is shown in Figure 6-22, and uses frames and links to manage information effectively.

You can modify these department descriptions to fit your organization, and you can edit pages to contain your content. One very nice feature of Fusion that no other product has is a zoom tool — it's terrific to be able to see your entire page or site from a bird's-eye view.

Fusion includes both a site manager and a page builder, but again, features are limited. You can download a 30-day trial version from:

```
http://www.netobjects.com
```

and decide if an instant intranet might work for you.

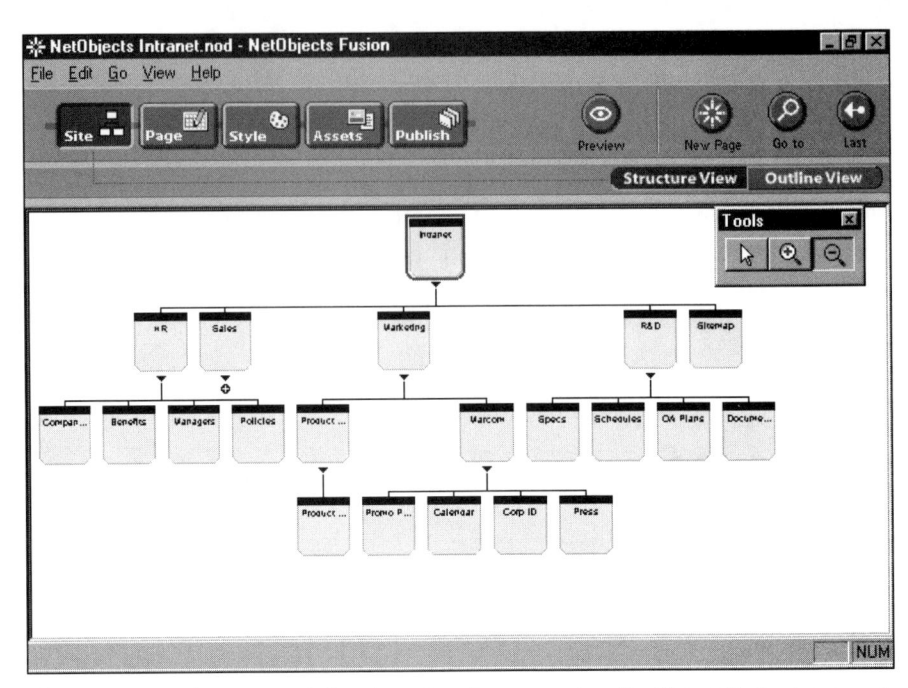

Figure 6-21 The structural site view of an intranet using NetObject Fusion's Intranet AutoSite

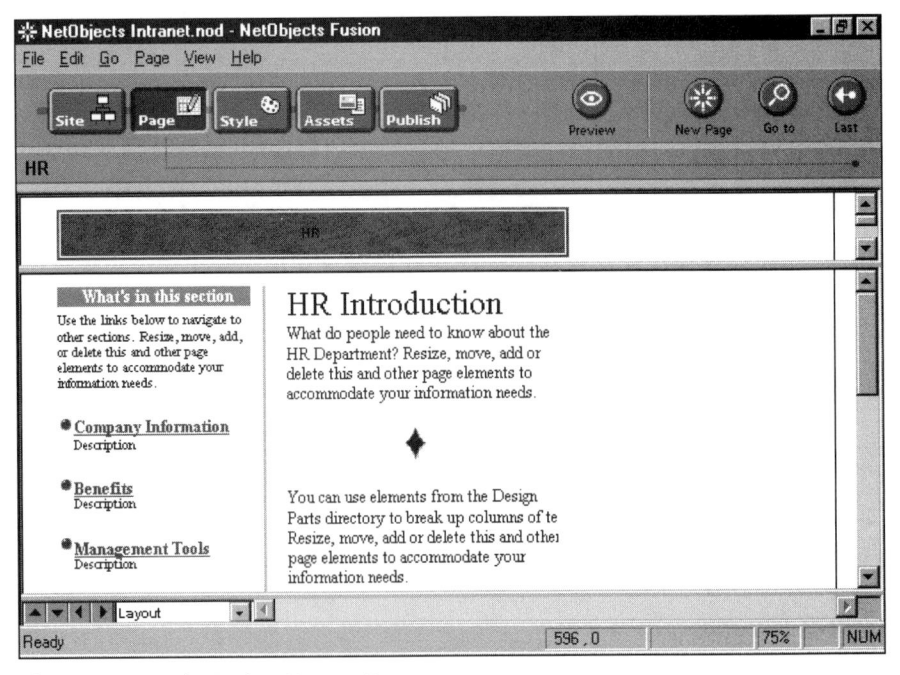

Figure 6-22 The Fusion Human Resources core page

Summary

In this chapter, you learned:

- What tools you can use for creating Web pages
- Important features in Web-authoring applications
- An overview of how to create an intranet site with wizards and/or templates

CHAPTER SEVEN

ALL ABOUT BROWSERS

IN THIS CHAPTER YOU LEARN THESE KEY SKILLS

BROWSER PERFORMANCE PAGE 116

BROWSER NAVIGATION PAGE 116

USING BOOKMARKS PAGE 118

FINDING INFORMATION PAGE 118

USING E-MAIL PAGE 119

USING PLUG-INS PAGE 121

The browser war between Microsoft's Internet Explorer and Netscape Navigator won't soon be over, and you need to select one for your team to access your intranet. The two products have similar features, and if one doesn't have a specific feature now, it will. Yes, there are a few other browsers that are still available, but if you're interested in a long-term solution for your organization, these are the two players to consider.

This chapter reviews the features of browsers and provides criteria for making your decision.

The features of both Internet Explorer and Navigator continue to expand, and they continue to mirror each other with each upgrade. One of the most compelling criteria for selecting a browser is price: Internet Explorer is available free from Microsoft, while Navigator carries a retail price tag of about $40 — less if you're licensing an entire site. Both charge fees up to thousands of dollars for their server applications and supporting programs, so the browser cost alone isn't the complete financial picture. But psychologically, it's tough to cough up $40 for something you can get free.

Browser Performance

In terms of performance, browsers differ in these areas: platforms supported (for example, Internet Explorer only recently created browsers for Macintosh, Windows 3.1, and Windows NT), ActiveX and Java support, scripting capabilities including CGI and JavaScript, support for HTML style tags, and emerging new tools, such as telephony and shared whiteboards. Again, both applications are rapidly moving toward supporting all areas.

CAUTION If you're going to be doing a lot of CGI links to other programs and networks, consult your IS department before selecting a browser.

WEB PATH To keep up with the frantic pace of change, visit the sites of both Microsoft and Netscape to find out what features are now available (and possibly free for downloading) and what's coming in the future. Both companies are working on browsers that will be integral parts of operating systems. Visit their sites at:

http://www.microsoft.com

and:

http://www.netscape.com

The more "user sensitive" matters, such as navigation, bookmarks, plug-ins, and e-mail handling, are more of a preference issue than a technical one. But the feel of the browser, and subsequently the feel of your intranet, can figure highly in the usability perception of your intranet.

Browser Navigation

Both browsers use toolbar buttons to navigate around pages in your intranet. Both enable you to go Back, Forward, Home; both Reload/Refresh the image if needed to complete the page transmission; and Stop if you just want to give up on downloading a big page. But, of course, you read Chapter 4 and know all about keeping files small, so your users won't need this, right?

Netscape's toolbar buttons, as shown in Figure 7-1, include an Open button to find pages manually, a Print button to print the page to paper or a common file format such as Acrobat, and a Find button to search the page, site, or other directories. The Directory buttons, located underneath the Location address, are useful for Internet surfing to Netscape's home page. For your intranet, you can disable them using Options → Show Directory Buttons to get a cleaner look and a bit more page space, as shown in Figure 7-2. This change can be done by your individual users.

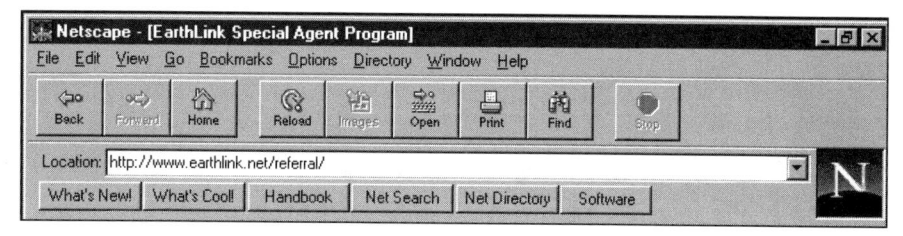

Figure 7-1 Netscape's navigation buttons

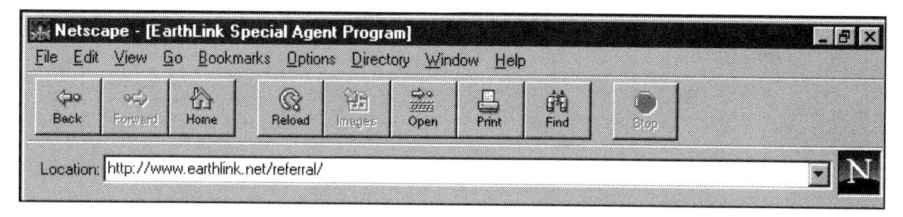

Figure 7-2 Netscape's navigation buttons with Directory buttons hidden

Internet Explorer's toolbar buttons, as shown in Figure 7-3, include Search to find words in a predesignated range of pages, such as your entire intranet, or a smaller subsection. Explorer puts Favorites — pages you visit often — as a drop-down menu (see Figure 7-4); Navigator puts Bookmarks as a menu or a separate window. Internet Explorer enables you to adjust the default font and access mail from buttons, while Netscape uses menus for both.

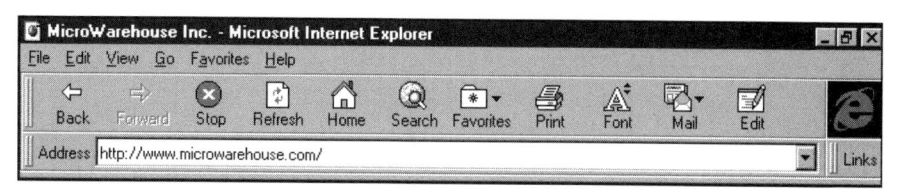

Figure 7-3 Internet Explorer's Navigation buttons

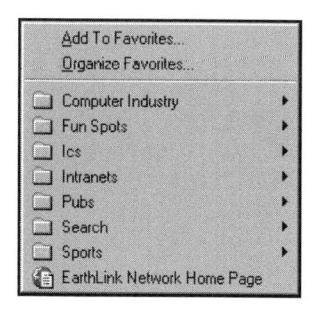

Figure 7-4 Internet Explorer Favorites

ALL ABOUT BROWSERS **117**

Both browsers are solid performers in terms of navigation ease. The biggest difference for your intranet is that Explorer's elements are easier to use, while Navigator's are easier to create and file.

Using Bookmarks and Favorites

Internet Explorer's Favorites work just like all the other Favorites on the Windows 95 platform. Whenever your users are on a page they want to revisit, they choose Add to Favorites to mark the spot, as shown in Figure 7-5. It's best to file them right away according to subject area rather than letting them run amuck. You'll then have subfolders by topic, accessible from the Favorites button or the menu.

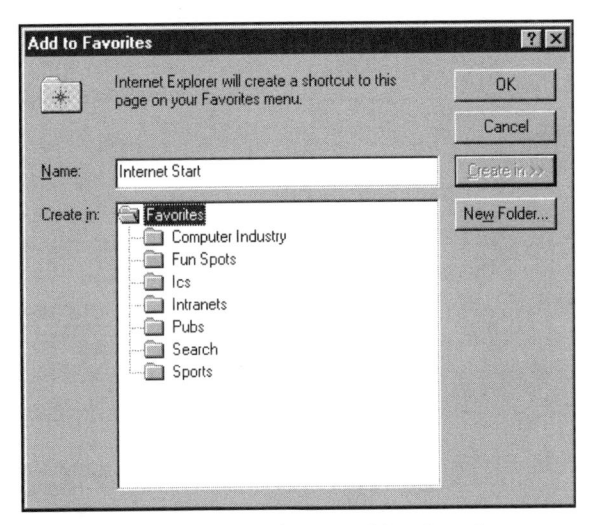

Figure 7-5   Internet Explorer's Add to Favorites

In Navigator, you can open your Bookmarks as a separate window, if you have the monitor space to spare. Your users can file and rename bookmarks as it makes sense to them, rather than having to use the actual page name. You can create Bookmark folders, too, and drag the current URL to any particular place in the bookmarks to add it.

Finding Information

Easy searching is critical for users of your intranet, and realistically you'll create your own search mechanism. Rather than using the menus or buttons built into the browser, you'll probably have your own search fields and buttons somewhere on your home page and possibly other locations.

TIP A nifty feature of Internet Explorer is that you can type **? something** into the address location, and the browser will launch a search for *something.* It's one simple option for users.

X-REF For details on search engines, see Chapter 10.

Using E-mail and Attachments

E-mail interfaces vary among the browsers and other e-mail software your users are likely to have experienced. Thus, there's not much intuitive about e-mail interfaces, and a crash course for your users on opening, sorting, saving, and archiving mail is a worthwhile investment. (Of course, that blows your excuse about never getting that e-mail about yesterday's meeting!)

The Netscape e-mail program, shown in Figure 7-6, relies on a lot of buttons and pull-down menus for opening, replying to, and saving mail. The Address Book, handy for keeping e-mail addresses of frequent contacts, can add the e-mail address of a message sender automatically by clicking the Add User to Address Book button.

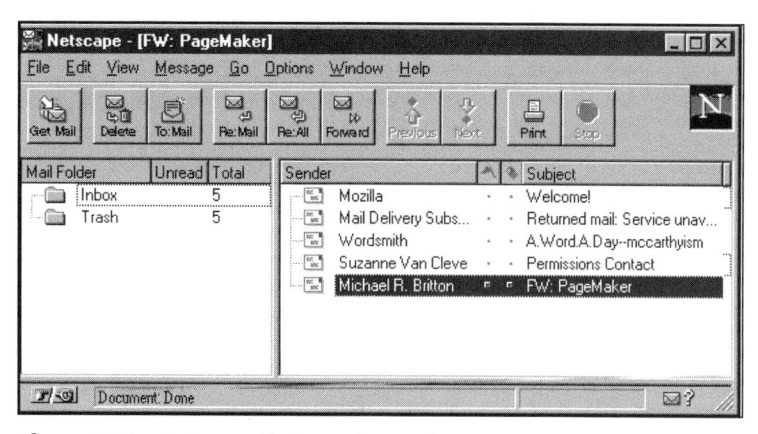

Figure 7-6 Netscape Navigator's e-mail

The Explorer e-mail, shown in Figure 7-7, is a cleaner interface, although users can easily get confused about the pop-up menu between inbox, outbox, and trash. The Address Book, shown in Figure 7-8, is a handy way to cross reference all of your contact information about an individual, including multiple e-mail addresses.

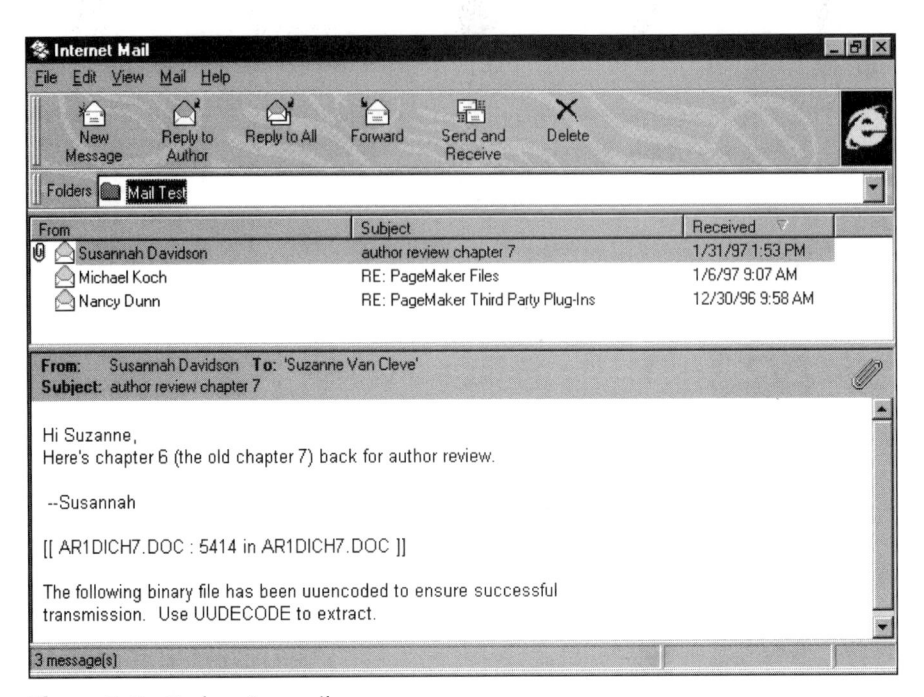

Figure 7-7 Explorer's e-mail

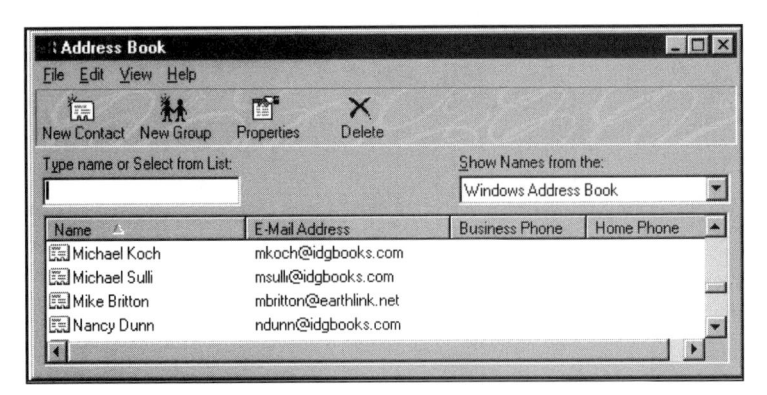

Figure 7-8 Explorer's Address Book

You can embed hyperlinks in both the Navigator and Internet Explorer e-mail programs, which is helpful for pointing your colleagues to specific locations in your intranet. They'll simply double-click the link in your e-mail to get to the specific page with most e-mail software. File attachments themselves are pretty simple, just choose the Attach button or menu option and navigate to the file you want. You can add multiple files to one e-mail. The complex part of e-mail is actually viewing the files at their destination, depending on what hardware and software the recipient is using. Mac-to-PC file transfers add another layer of difficulty. Standardization will pay off with e-mail attachments.

CAUTION: The Navigator mail interface can be confusing, especially for Macintosh users accustomed to a double-click opening a new window. Some of them won't see the message that appears below the Inbox window.

X-REF: For details on integrating e-mail with your intranet, see Chapter 13.

Working with Plug-ins

Plug-ins abound to add functionality to both browsers, although support varies depending on the plug-in and the browser your choose. Visit the Microsoft and Netscape Web sites regularly for the most updated list of compatibility.

Plug-ins are added easily to a folder within your Browser (most download automatically to the right folder), but it's important that all your users have the same plug-in set and that the plug-ins are updated regularly. Remember, innovation on the Web is constant, and the tools keep getting better. The downside is that add-ons, like plug-ins, can be outdated and not functional quickly. Keep your plug-in set limited for best results.

Plug-ins can add the following features to your browser:

- Multimedia players: Animation, sound, and video (including live video)
- High quality sound: Stereo sound
- Document viewers: For easy viewing of file attachments regardless of the source application
- 3D animation viewers
- Virtual reality viewers
- Image format viewers
- Presentation players: For viewing slides created in applications such as PowerPoint, Persuasion and Astound
- Chat features: For interactive discussions among members of your organization
- Image compression
- Video conferencing tools

WEB PATH: For the latest on streaming audio sound, visit the Real Audio site at:
http://www.realaudio.com

For the latest on plug-ins, including user critiques, new developments, usage tips, and more, visit:

http://www.cnet.com/Content/Reviews/Compare/Plugin/

BONUS

How to Customize Browsers

Your users can customize how they look at things in both browsers. Figure 7-9 shows Explorer's Options under the View menu to modify how your users see colors, links, and the toolbar. Be careful if they change some of these settings; you'll be directing them to click the blue underline elements (the default for hyperlinks) and they might have changed their default to purple. Other users will be tempted to add flashy background colors or patterns to the point of obscuring the content of the page. Users can also limit the items showing on their toolbar to maximize page viewing on their screen. Although you won't be able to control how users view pages, you can certainly educate them on the options and let them decide. Generally speaking, the appeal of a pink-spotted leopard background pattern will wear thin after a few days of eyestrain!

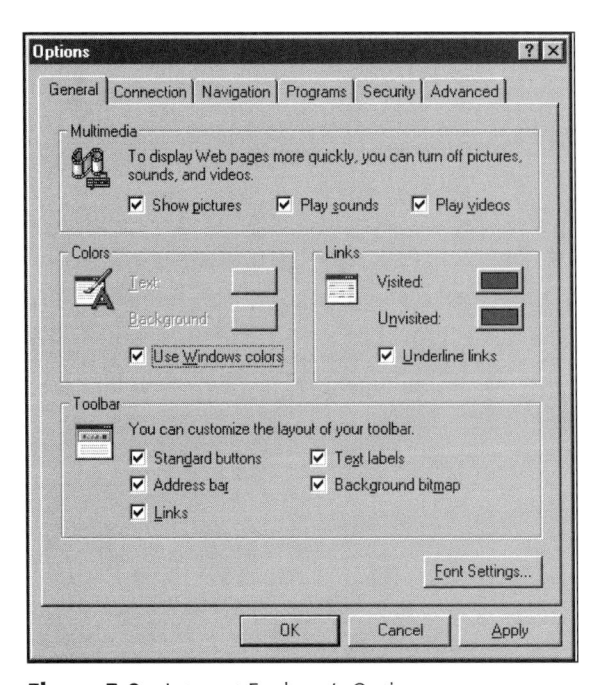

Figure 7-9 Internet Explorer's Options

Users can also determine whether they see video, sound, and pictures. For those with little patience, getting to just the text might be their ideal way to work. For others, all the flash adds to the fun and interest in your intranet and potentially boosts productivity.

Users can also customize their start page, which can launch them at the point in your intranet that matters most to them. Human resources can start in their area, newcomers can start in the employee directory, and so on.

In Navigator, users can modify similar General Preferences under the Option menu as shown in Figure 7-10. Toolbars can be set to words or pictures (again if space is a consideration, it's a good idea to use words or eliminate the buttons altogether). Users can customize the fonts to choose what's easiest for them to read on the screen (one of the dangers of Web page design), link and page background colors, and image color features.

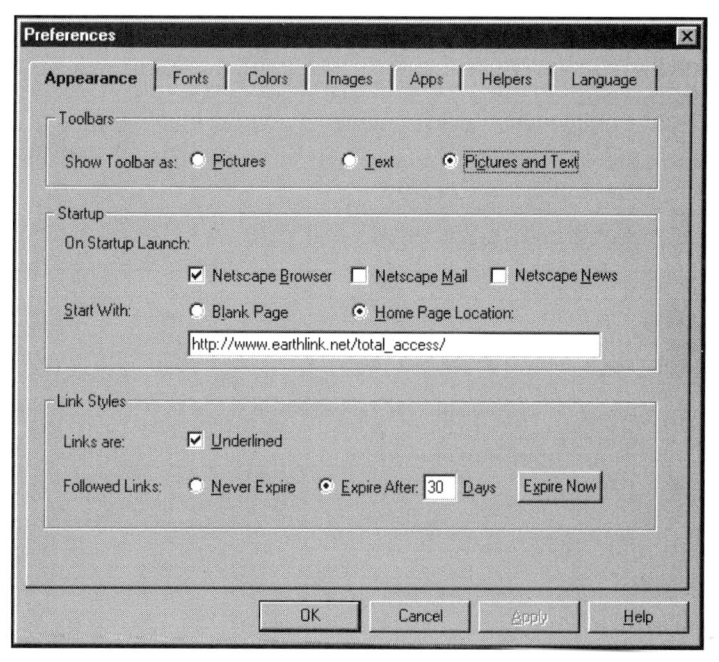

Figure 7-10 Netscape's Preferences

Users always want to add their personal touch to how they view things, and browsers offer a limited set of customizable features to enhance their viewing pleasure.

ALL ABOUT BROWSERS **123**

Summary

This chapter covered browsers used to view pages on your intranet, including:

The important features of browser navigation, bookmarks, plug-ins, and e-mail handling

The features of Microsoft Explorer and Netscape Navigator are very similar; pick one for your site to minimize complications

Plug-ins can expand the functionality of the browser, but support varies and the tools are being updated constantly

CHAPTER EIGHT
TOOLS FOR SITE MANAGEMENT

IN THIS CHAPTER YOU LEARN THESE KEY SKILLS:

HOW TO EFFECTIVELY MANAGE A SITE   PAGE 125

WHICH SITE-MANAGEMENT TOOLS TO USE
   PAGE 129

Once you've set up your intranet, you'll need a comprehensive, ongoing site management plan. The beauty of the digital format is that you (and your colleagues) can update information anytime, anywhere. The burden is never-ending version control to ensure that the right update is on the server for everyone to access. And as for all those nifty links — well, you'll be surprised how quickly they can become outdated.

The reputation of your intranet is at stake. Too many outdated documents or dead links will send your users back to paper documents in a flash. This chapter will cover the necessities of effective site management.

What Do You Need to Manage, Anyway?

An intranet is a dynamic medium, and people will respond to that by constantly changing the content. The very links between pages that make it a powerful web of information are easily broken if you do the following:

* Rename a page or an image file. Pages that are linked to the page or file will point to the name, and won't find the new one automatically.

* Move files, in and out of folders or between drives.
* Delete live files. Now that may sound obvious, but it's really hard to tell which files are still in use and which are outdated.

Managing these issues manually would be a time-consuming and tedious task, so it's great having a dozen site management tools available, with feature sets improving rapidly. But first, there are a few basic matters for effectively running your site.

File Management

Establish standards for file-naming conventions and how materials will be submitted for updating on your intranet. Your guidelines should include the following:

* Use the 8.3 file-naming convention for URLs (that's eight characters, a period, and a three-character file extension — a remnant of the DOS world), because you'll probably be using Macs and PCs on your intranet. Even though Windows 95 supports up to 32 characters in filenames, a Macintosh will not. You *can* use long filenames for the title of the HTML page, so choose something meaningful to your users.

  Also, avoid "funny" characters, such as spaces, slashes, asterisks, and so on. They can create problems when files are transferred to other platforms.

  Filename extensions (two characters to four characters) are also important because they are the most direct way for the browser to determine the file type.

* Keep the file extension (the last three characters) to identify the file format. For example: *.doc* = Microsoft Word; *.xls* = Microsoft Excel; *.mdb* = Microsoft Access, and so on.

* Establish a method for tracking revisions. Keeping the same filename reduces the chance of broken links, but it will be harder to track what's what on your hard drive in the revision stages. You can use the document header information to track dates of modification, creation, and comments. Document header information is available with all Microsoft and Adobe products, to name a few. Figure 8-1 shows a Microsoft Properties profile, which can be searched on the intranet.

X-REF See Chapter 2 for tips on tracking the project and the multiple documents involved in an intranet.

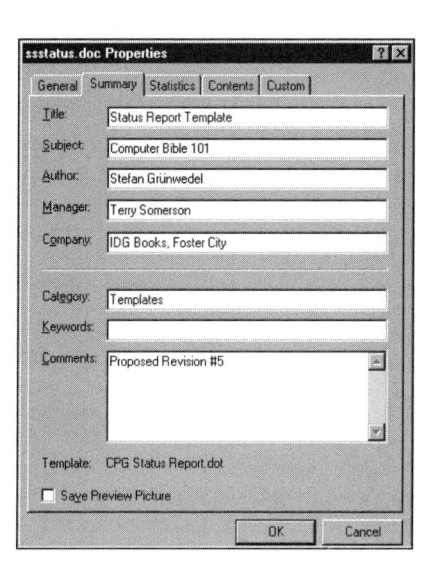

Figure 8-1 The Properties profiles provide detailed information about a file and can be used for managing numerous versions of files.

- Require the person submitting to provide the file header information, including:

    Author

    Date

    Subject

    Keywords

- Decide who will be responsible for reviewing updated material, and establish approval procedures if necessary. For example, if it's a update to the company calendar, you'll want to have someone in human resources approve it. If it's a change to an individual's classified ad, you may allow each individual to change his or her information.

- Put the approved files on your intranet and delete old files immediately. (Of course, you'll back them up somewhere off the intranet in case you find that you really do need them.)

X-REF For details on using Microsoft FrontPage to publish your pages on the intranet, see the section "Microsoft FrontPage Explorer" later in this chapter.

Maintaining Links

The easiest way to maintain your links is to pay attention to how you name files and where you put them. You can use a site management tool to survey all the links in your intranet, and report errors that you can correct by navigating to the right location or using a drag-and-drop feature directly from the page.

Updating Material

What's the best way to update the content? It all depends on your organization. Sometimes you'll need people to see the changes to the document (such as changes to rules for using the company logo); other times you'll just need to distribute the new file (such as a new medical claim form). You maybe want to designate someone in each functional area to be responsible for intranet content relative to his or her group, and that person can dictate update schedules and requirements.

Create schedules for submissions, and use e-mail to nudge users who owe you material. Automate the process as much as possible by using a To Do List, like the one in FrontPage, or a separate project management application.

Multiple Locations for Your Business

Site management is more complex if you have multiple sites and/or remote users, because you'll need to get those updates to various servers. But with the right site management tool, you can cut down dramatically on the amount of information you'll need to ship to other locations, whether in digital or paper form.

SIDE TRIP

LARGE-SCALE VERSION CONTROL

For large-scale version control — say for a site of 1,000 or more people or thousands of documents — consider a high-end intranet document management tool, such as RightSite from Documentum. This tool enables authors to export their work directly from the original application, such as Microsoft Word, and is designed to work in sync with your workflow; that is, all the steps you do to capture, edit, and reuse information.

RightSite also assists with filtering documents to the appropriate users — whether they want to receive it, or their manager thinks they should read it, and so on. RightSite is for large intranet applications, and includes a Library Services feature that enables users to check out documents for modification, Integrated Workflow for managing the flow of documents, and Dynamic Page Assembly for controlling page construction based on the user's rights, profiles, and preferences.

WEB PATH For more on RightSite, visit the Documentum site at:
http://www.documentum.com/

Site Management 101: The Tools

There are a dozen site management tools available, almost all of which are integrated closely with a Web page authoring module. It's easiest to use these "sister" applications so you'll be able to toggle between the site management functions and page editing functions.

Key Features of Site Management Tools

Most site management applications include the following features. Decide which are the most important to your intranet, and look at the user interface. Is it intuitive to you and your users based on applications you've used in the past? How much training do you think will be necessary to use it effectively? Don't forget, the workflow and information management aspects are as important as knowledge of the technical tool, so integrate that in your training program, formally or informally, depending on your organization.

X-REF For details on user training, see Chapter 12.

Features of site management tools include:

* A site view that shows all resources (pages, images, directories, scripts, and other files), page titles, and folders
* Warnings for missing links
* Automatic fixes for missing links wherever possible (for example, if the file is still on your intranet but in another location)
* Easy link creation by either browsing for a page or dropping a resource from the Site View onto a page
* Links to external Web addresses

Most site management applications contains several views:

* **Site View:** This view shows all site resources at a glance. You can usually double-click a page here to launch the editing application to modify that page. You can name, delete, and move resources between folders, and links are updated automatically. Figure 8-2 shows SiteMill's Site View.
* **Error View:** This view will enable you to repair broken links manually and will be used most often when you're first setting up your intranet. You simply click the broken link and browse to the new location for the linked item. Figure 8-3 shows SiteMill's Error View.
* **Page View:** This view includes WYSIWYG page editing so you can make changes on your page while seeing the type sizes and images in place. Figure 8-4 shows SiteMill's Page View. However, to see how the

page will look on your intranet, you'll need to preview the page in your browser.

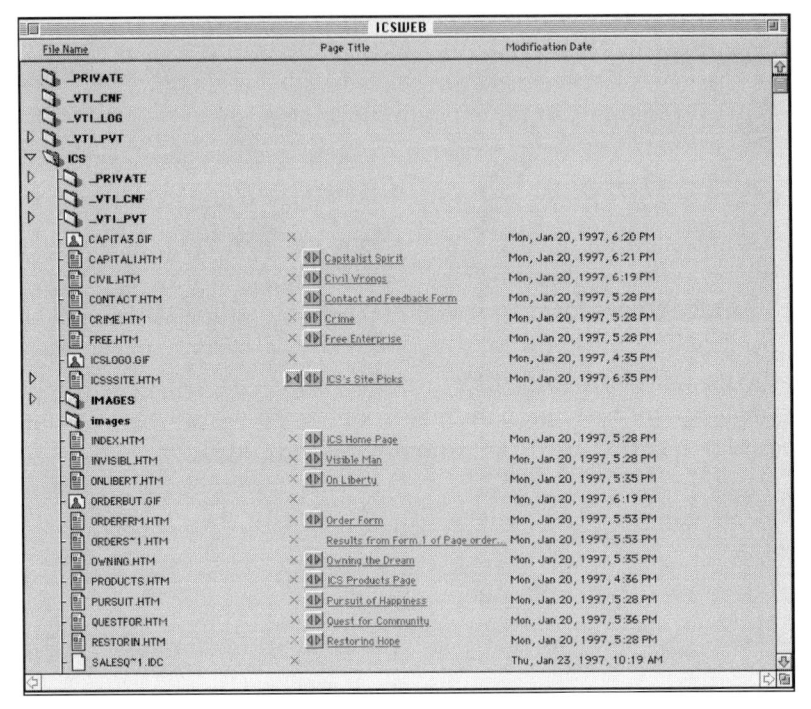

Figure 8-2 SiteMill's Site View

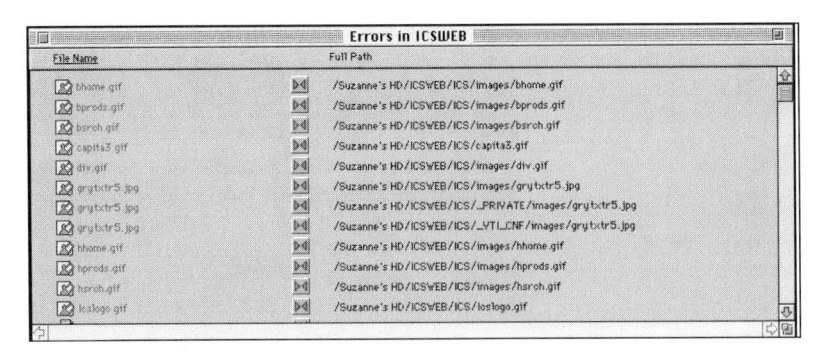

Figure 8-3 SiteMill's Error View

The site management tools offer similar functionality, but execute tasks rather differently because site management is an emerging genre of software. In the next section, we'll walk through basic site management tasks using FrontPage Explorer to demonstrate the process.

X-REF For details on indexing your site, another site management task deserving a chapter of its own, see Chapter 9.

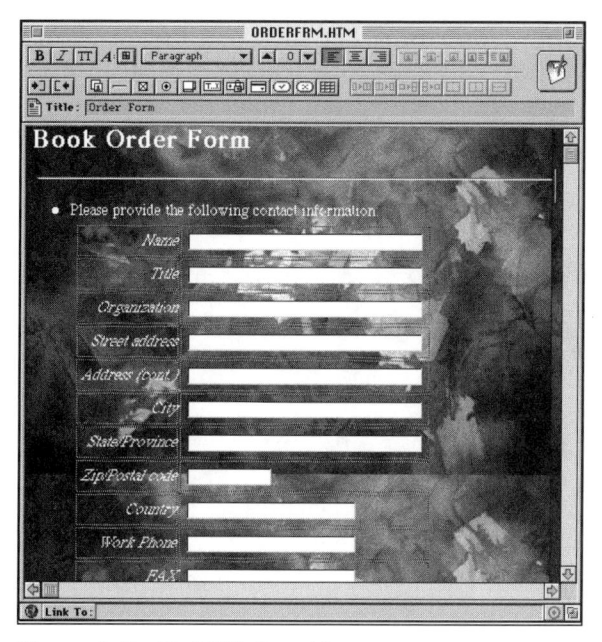

Figure 8-4 SiteMill's Page View

Microsoft FrontPage Explorer

FrontPage Explorer is the site management part of FrontPage, and it enables you to visually track all links. You can view the links between pages (together or separately), and the links between images and pages (useful if you're going to start changing some images around). From the Site View, you can visually see the layout of your intranet. By choosing Verify Hyperlinks, you'll get a full list of broken links, as shown in Figure 8-5. If you prefer the folder hierarchy as a way of managing things, choose the Folder View and see nested folders and files, as you would in old versions of Windows (3.1 and earlier) File Manager, or Windows 95 Explorer.

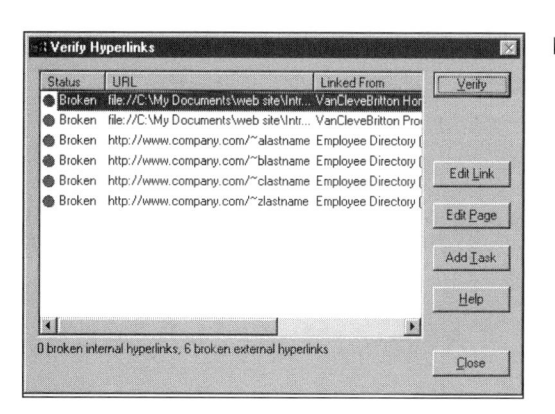

Figure 8-5 The FrontPage dialog box that summarizes broken links

TOOLS FOR SITE MANAGEMENT **131**

To fix broken links, you can either click Edit Page or Edit Link, which will launch FrontPage Editor. Edit Page takes you to the destination page; Edit Link takes you to the source page where the hyperlink is located. If you're editing page names, FrontPage conveniently alerts you to potentially broken links with the dialog box shown in Figure 8-6; save yourself time and choose Yes for FrontPage to update all links to that page automatically.

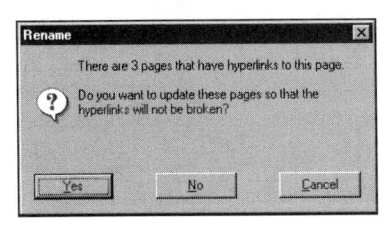

Figure 8-6 FrontPage's warning for breaking links

Or, you can use FrontPage's To Do List if you want to address all the broken links at a later date or delegate the chore to someone else. The To Do List, shown in Figure 8-7, is useful for effective site maintenance; you can get details on the outstanding items, as shown in Figure 8-8. You can launch immediately into the task because FrontPage will take you to the location for addressing it.

FrontPage Explorer includes a search tool to find occurrences of words throughout your intranet — quite helpful if your boss has just changed the department's name. The search, shown in Figure 8-9, works just like the Search and Replace tools in your word processor, and you can click Edit Page again to go to the source or Add Task to put the matter on your To Do List. You can spell check across your site, too — useful for those never-ending rushed updates.

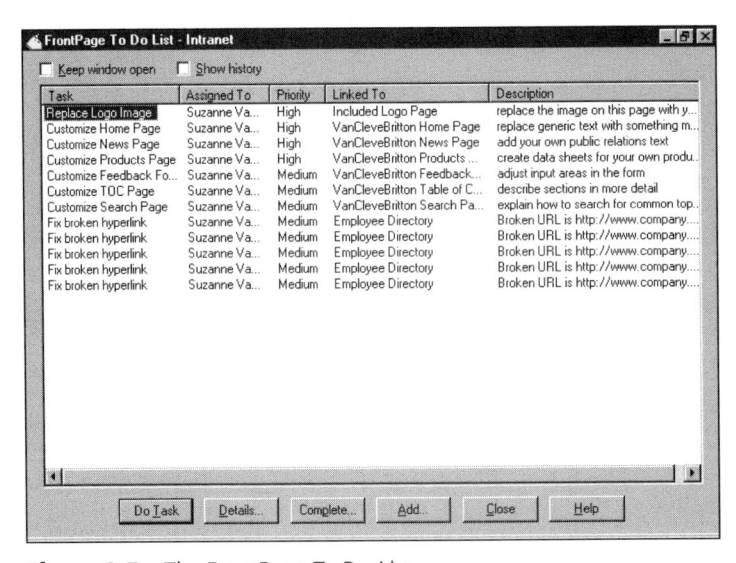

Figure 8-7 The FrontPage To Do List

132   HOW TO CREATE AND MAINTAIN AN INTRANET

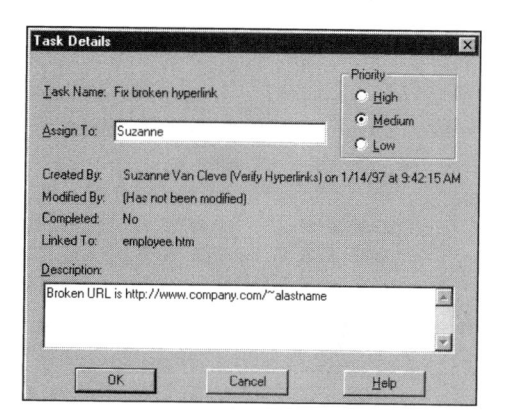

Figure 8-8 Details on tasks in the FrontPage To Do List

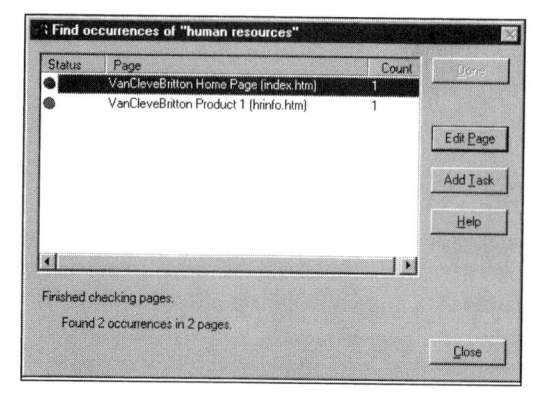

Figure 8-9 The FrontPage Search feature

FrontPage, like most of the site management tools, includes default settings to apply consistent contact information across your site. In one location you can enter and update your address, phone, e-mail, company name, department, and so on.

After all your links are connected, all your tasks are completed, and all your global changes are made, you *publish* your Web site, as shown in Figure 8-10. Publishing means to make your site accessible to your users. You'll choose the destination for your intranet. If you're modifying pages, you'll specify to Copy changed pages only. If you're adding a new segment, say another department has completed its material, you can choose Add to an existing FrontPage Web. Remember, you'll need to preview your pages in a Web browser to see how they'll look to your users.

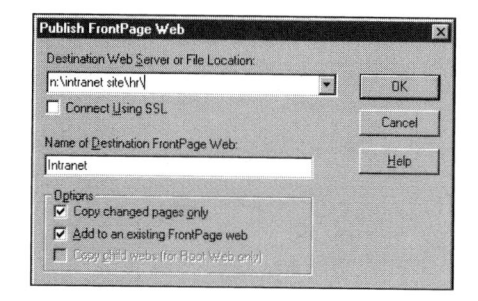

Figure 8-10 Publishing your intranet site from FrontPage

TOOLS FOR SITE MANAGEMENT **133**

DeltaPoint QuickSite

QuickSite is a project- and database-oriented approach to managing your intranet site. You can quickly see an overview of your intranet in a list format, as shown in Figure 8-11, but you'll sacrifice the visual aspect when editing your pages, as shown in Figure 8-12.

Figure 8-11 QuickSite's Site View

With QuickSite, all links are established automatically, and it adds elements to each page, such as e-mail icons and page dates. You can alter the feel of your site using predefined templates, which means you can change the look of your intranet in one dialog box — but the number of "looks" you have is limited. For example, you can choose a simple look, a contemporary look, a formal look, and so on.

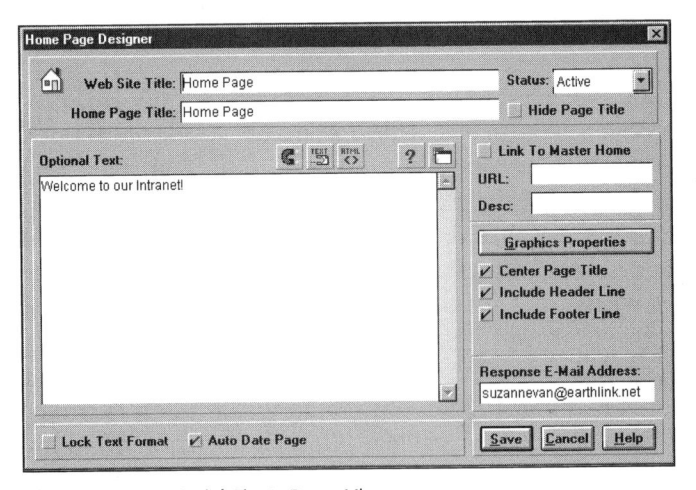

Figure 8-12 QuickSite's Page View

NetObjects Fusion

Fusion provides a graphical Site View that makes it easy to see the hierarchy and manipulate the position of pages and links, as shown in Figure 8-13. The Fusion Page View, shown in Figure 8-14, is fully editable by clicking and dragging on elements for quick updates right in the site management tool.

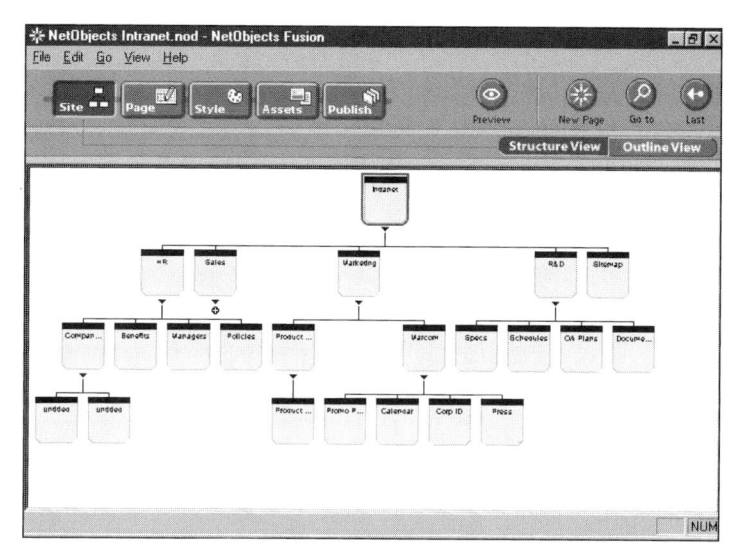

Figure 8-13 Fusion's Site View

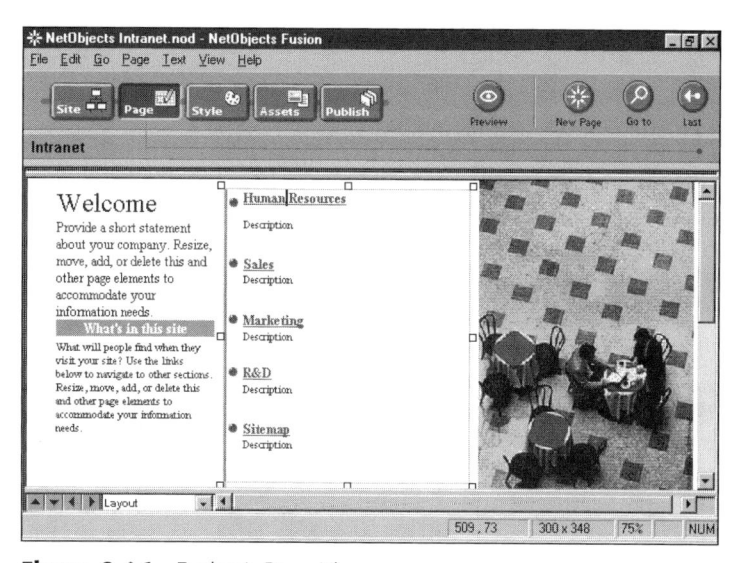

Figure 8-14 Fusion's Page View

Fusion includes MasterBorders and SiteStyles, which combine the strength of style sheets for text formatting and appearance with templates for consistent object positioning on your Web pages. For example, you can use MasterBorders to position buttons in the same location on every page on your intranet, and SiteStyle to set consistent type formatting, such as relative size and alignment. The MasterBorders can also be used to create reusable frames across your entire site, instead of having to manually create them for each page.

TOOLS FOR SITE MANAGEMENT **135**

Other site-management features from NetObjects include:

- **SiteMapper:** An advanced Java-based application that creates an instant map of the site for users to view and navigate through the site, especially useful if your intranet is undergoing rapid growth and frequent change.
- **NetObjects BBS:** A threaded discussion board to let your users interact on your site.
- **FormHandler:** A prebuilt CGI script that enables users to send instant feedback on the site.

Adobe SiteMill

SiteMill provides limited features for site management, but if your needs are limited to maintaining links between images and pages and pages to pages, SiteMill may suffice. It's easy to repair links by using the Error View: Simply click the broken link and navigate to the new location. You can also drag and drop elements between pages. SiteMill is being upgraded; look for more extensive site management features soon.

SIDE TRIP

LOTUS DOMINO: A BRIDGE TO AN INTRANET FOR NOTES USERS

What if you're in an organization that uses Lotus Notes? Is there any way you can share that information on your intranet? Yes, with a new tool called Lotus Domino that enables any Notes server to be accessed by any Web browser. You have all the access control and version control associated with Notes, the pioneer of groupware applications.

With its roots in groupware, Domino makes it easy to create threaded discussions on your intranet. This means a lot of people can share ideas with little maintenance on your part. You can also use the Notes full-text indexing feature for easy searching. If you need a lot of customization for features on your intranet, Lotus's rapid application development approach might be a good solution. Working in conjunction with someone who knows the nuances of Notes, you can quickly develop a complex application that would have taken months only a few years ago.

Lotus is also known for tight security controls, with multilevel access privileges for viewing, writing, editing, saving, and deleting files. It's a worthwhile consideration for a large, complex, and confidential intranet — if you've already got a Notes server in place.

WEB PATH → For details on Lotus Domino and to download a demo of the application, visit Lotus at:
http://www.lotus.com/

BONUS

Tips for Managing Intranet Sites

If you're the designated site manager, the following tips will help you dazzle your colleagues and earn you the esteemed title of Webmaster:

* Map the flow of documents and get concurrence from your users that work really does flow in that way.
* Manage the update schedule until you're satisfied that your intranet can handle the volume of regular revisions. Evaluate the need for updates with the respective department or divisional manager.
* Preview the work of new Web authors to ensure that their pages link properly and won't cause chaos on your intranet. Designate access and authoring privileges in sync with training programs or demonstrated ability.
* Provide templates for as many types of pages as possible. If you set the technical standards and encourage your users to get involved in the content creation, you'll have one happy combination.
* Check links regularly, everyday if possible, if you're updating your content frequently. Dead links are the biggest reason for your users to abandon the intranet.
* Limit the number of links to external Web pages unless you're certain the sites are established and stable. Check them regularly.
* Listen to feedback about your site from your users. Integrate features that can improve productivity within your technical and financial limits.

Summary

In this chapter you learned:

What features you need to effectively manage a site

The importance of version control

How to utilize the Site View for managing your intranet

Using the Page View for making modifications to your page

How to use To Do Lists to track needed repairs and upgrades to your intranet

CHAPTER NINE

TOOLS FOR SEARCHING YOUR INTRANET

IN THIS CHAPTER YOU LEARN THESE KEY SKILLS

NAVIGATING THE INTRANET   PAGE 139

USING BASIC SEARCH PRINCIPLES   PAGE 143

SEARCHING WITH ADVANCED TECHNIQUES   PAGE 146

USING INTERNET SEARCH ENGINES   PAGE 152

An intranet is a wonderful thing, if you can get instantaneous access to the information you want. If you've done the footwork outlined in previous chapters, you now have a solid directory structure that will aid users in finding what they want by navigating through menus. You can also add other tools, such as bookmarks, to help users find information. But what about those times when your topic isn't listed? Or you've become just plain tired of clicking through three levels of menus just to get to your weekly status report? Enter *search tools,* customizable search assistants that can streamline your ability to find things, once a day or only once a month, according to your needs.

Getting Around: Navigating Your Intranet

Before diving into search tools, think about the structure of your intranet and the navigation tools you can incorporate. By using tables of contents, bookmarks, frames, keywords, and indexes, you can improve the accessibility of your information.

Using a Table of Contents

Having a solid table of contents for your intranet home page will get users off to a running start. Mention the major subject areas in your intranet, which may include an employee directory, sales information, production guidelines, a product price list, calendars, special events, news, and various departments. Create links from the TOC to the main page for each area, and then do another TOC for each subsection. For example, you might want to provide a list of all the materials in your human resources area in one handy listing, so users know what is available from one location.

> **TIP** Try not to have more than three levels of clicking between entering your intranet and getting to the document to use.

Bookmarks

Users can easily "dog ear" the pages that they visit the most by using Microsoft Explorer's browser feature, Add to Favorites, and Netscape Navigator's Add Bookmark. The two browsers handle bookmarks a little differently, but both provide quick access to frequently visited pages.

To create bookmarks in Explorer, follow these steps:

1. Open the page to which you want to attach a bookmark.
2. Choose Add to Favorites from the Favorites menu, as shown in Figure 9-1.

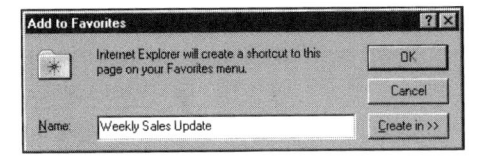

Figure 9-1 Explorer's Add to Favorites dialog box

3. Modify the name of the page so it's logical to you. The Name will default to the name of the page on your intranet.
4. Choose the appropriate folder in which to put the bookmark, or create a New Folder using the button. You can have as many folders as you need to easily access your bookmarks. File them in the same pattern that you'd set up a conventional paper-based file system.
5. From the Favorites menu or button, simply select the bookmark of the page to which you want to go. If you use the same browser for your Internet and intranet searching, you can access all of your bookmarks from one location and use the folder hierarchy to keep them sorted, as shown in Figure 9-2.

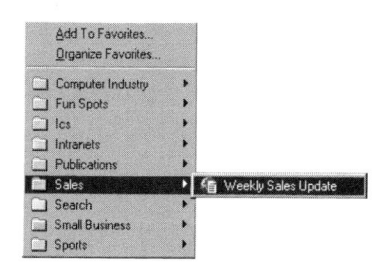

Figure 9-2 Accessing a bookmark from the Favorites button

Bookmarks are an easy way for every user of your intranet to customize his or her accessibility to information.

TIP Bookmarks are links to page locations, and if you move pages or rename them, the bookmarks will become invalid and cause an error message. If you must move pages around, leave a "forwarding address" by keeping the old page location active with a pointer to the new location for a certain period of time.

The biggest difference with Navigator is how bookmarks are managed; Figure 9-3 shows the separate Bookmarks window in Navigator. To move, edit, or delete bookmarks, open Bookmarks from the Window menu, click the bookmark you want to alter, and choose the appropriate menu action.

Figure 9-3 Navigator's bookmarks are easy to sort and modify.

Frames

Frames are a good way to use the structure of your page to enhance accessibility to information, but they're still quirky depending on the browser you use. Although frames can be used in a variety of configurations, the most common is a banner at the top with your logo, a narrow window down the left containing a list of contents, and the main window for viewing individual pages. Figure 9-4 shows a template for this standard configuration. Creating links from the contents frame to the appropriate pages helps users find information quickly. Keep in mind that frame technology is still developing and is something you should watch and consider for future use.

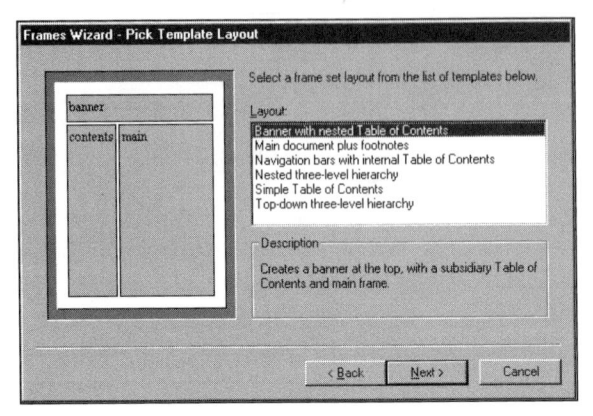

Figure 9-4 One basic configuration for using frames to help users find information

Keywords

Keywords are words or phrases that define the information users will seek.

The tricky part about keywords is, the English language is vast, and we have many different words that mean the same thing. For example, you might call a document "Production Guidelines" but your boss might be searching for "Book Submission Guides." Later in this chapter we get into details about expanding search terms, but for now let's just consider keywords.

Keywords should be simple — three or four words per phrase at most. Whenever possible, stick to what we call the stem of the word. A word stem is the root: *account* instead of *accounting* or *accounts; budget* instead of *budgets, budgeting,* or *overbudget;* and so on. Sample keywords for documents you're likely to have in your intranet are included in Table 9-1.

The easiest way to attach a keyword to a document is to use the Document Properties or Document Info menu found in many applications. Make a habit of creating those terms when you create the document, while the content is fresh in your mind. Trying to keyword 500 documents at once when producing your intranet will definitely lead to burnout, not to mention lousy keywords.

Keywording is a good investment because it gives faster access to the information in the long run. When using keywords, your search tool looks in the Properties header of your documents before scanning through all the text of all your documents. Your searches are therefore much faster.

TABLE 9-1 Sample Keywords

Intranet Document	Sample Keywords
PRESIDENT'S MESSAGE	1997 report, annual address, president's message
EMPLOYEE HANDBOOK	Policies, procedures, rules, handbook
JOB POSTINGS	Jobs, employment opportunities, job openings, positions available
E-MAIL POLICIES	Rules, spam, privacy, e-mail, e-mail, mail
GLOSSARY	Terms, glossary, definitions

> **TIP** Don't hesitate to create more than one descriptive keyword to a page because everyone thinks of things differently. Keywords are small, access is critical.

Indexes

You can also index all of the text in all of the documents on your intranet. This will ensure that the search tool, regardless of which one you use, checks everything. The search component of your intranet is usually a specific page dedicated to searching techniques and fields to enter keywords, phrases, or terms. For ease of access, you can provide links to this page from many other areas of your intranet. Searching all of the text can also turn up a lot of files that you don't really want. Be selective about what directories to include in your indexing, and monitor the speed of an index search.

Sifting for Gold: Basic Search Principles

If you've ever surfed the World Wide Web and done a search query to find some specific piece of information, you know how much garbage you can get. The same principles of searching large volumes of information apply to your intranet, but at least you have more control over keywording and index creation.

Your range of information to search isn't limited to materials created for your intranet. Your search may cover all of your corporate documents, internal discussion groups, news feeds compiled from various digital sources, and servers on the Web, all filtered through one search tool as shown in Figure 9-5.

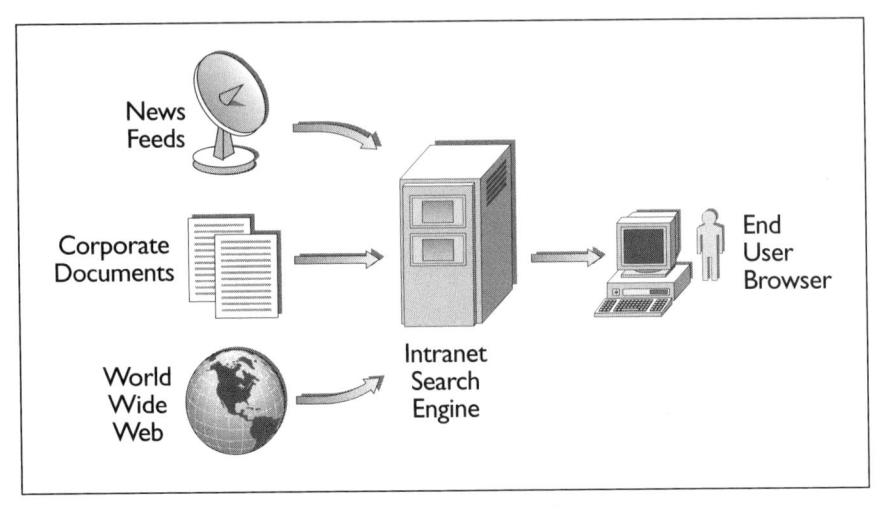

Figure 9-5 Your searchable information can come from many sources.

Using Search Tools

When creating your intranet, select one search tool, such as Verity's SEARCH '97. Search queries range from simple to complex, depending on the scope of your intranet. You can limit your query to a specific subset of your intranet to get faster results and fewer files to search through, if you're sure the information you want would be within that subset. For example, if you're searching for the December 1996 sales report from the Widgets division, you could rather safely target your query to search the Sales Reports and Widgets sections of your intranet.

You can also set the search tool to index keywords first. That way, users can focus their search queries to just those words indexed as keywords, and you avoid a lot of extraneous hits that result from indexing every word in every page on your intranet. For example, if you wanted to keyword a new job posting, you'd search using the terms jobs, employment opportunities, job openings, positions available. But there might be a large pile of proposals to expand job openings, reports on jobs in progress, employment statistics, and so on that would be found if you were searching all the text of the intranet. Keywords and searches on keyword fields allow you to focus information more effectively.

Finally, make sure you index all the text in all the pages on your intranet; you can search on the filenames of images as well (useful for maps of sales territories, graphics of financial reports, and so on). Be aware the full text indexing can create huge index files (often as big as half of the files in your entire intranet) and the first time will take hours to complete. Periodic updates will be faster and add incremental size to the index, but it's a must for the ever-changing content of your intranet.

To summarize: Keywords will enable quick access to documents and intranet pages if you consistently use the same terms, and take the time to add keywords when you're creating your intranet. Full text searches will find a term anywhere: any page or any document, which means you'll be able to find that morsel of information, but you also have to do some manual sifting through more hits to find precisely what you want.

Simple Queries

A simple query on keywords on an intranet can give you quick access to information from external sources as well. For example, let's say you're eager to track the sales and some other information on two products made by your department. For easy reuse, you can create a query with a summary topic and several query terms. Figure 9-6 shows a sample query for your sales information, including product sales, product competition, and marketing plans. Each time you run this query, you receive all the files on your intranet that contain all of these query terms, including news feeds (if your intranet contains that information).

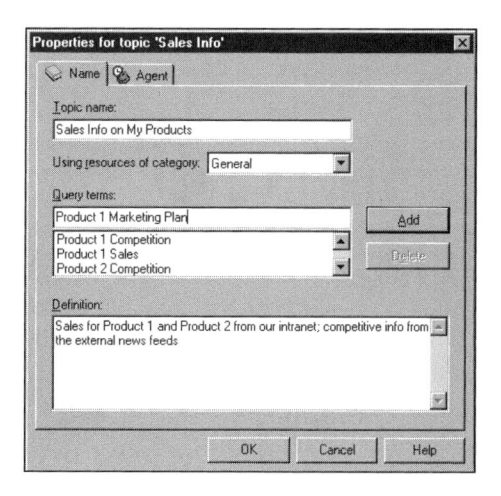

Figure 9-6 A simple search query

TIP Do include search tips for your users via a Search button on every page. Specify what type of operators your search tool recognizes, whether case matters, and include suggestions for narrowing queries. Also include a Boolean primer with examples of terms and searches that can be used on your intranet.

SIDE TRIP

SEARCHING AND USING NEWS FEEDS

Think how effectively you could keep tabs on your competition if every morning on your desktop was a folder of articles, clips, Web links, and other information covering a predefined list of topics or companies. Better yet, imagine you could rank the importance of those terms, and change the search criteria on a regular basis. And what if the tool you used was intuitive, and could "learn" from the way you sort out the delivered information?

Tools like NewsMagnet from CompassWare do just that. You preselect the news sources, create your keywords for searching, and set up the frequency of updates (hourly, daily, weekly). You need to tweak your searches to refine the information you get, but it's a lot easier than manually searching the multitude of sources.

WEB PATH For more information on NewsMagnet and CompassWare's intranet search tool, InfoMagnet, visit Web site at:

http://www.compassware.com

Get Out Your Magnifying Glass: Advanced Searching Techniques

More sophisticated searching techniques will enable you and your users to get to information faster and more accurately. The early days of electronic searching required the use of a lot of really obtuse terms, called *syntax operators,* to determine the relationships between words and designate the importance of each in the query. Today's search tools are increasingly better at recognizing both natural language queries, and "learning" what your preferences are, based on how you refine a search.

TIP Practice is the best way to learn search queries and optimize your time finding information. Start by entering the word or phrase as you think of it, and evaluating the number and quality of results. If you get too many hits, think about how to narrow down your scope, and try again. If you don't find anything, you might also need to broaden your terms to a more general category and try again.

To get the most out of a full text search, it's useful to learn a few terms of what's called Boolean logic. Essentially, the basics are four words: AND, OR, NOT, and NEAR. In the following example, let's say you're using an intranet to follow the development and production of this book, and you're going to use some query terms to find the information you need. (Yes, you could use the table of contents to navigate to the information, but maybe you just want to get there fast!)

AND: The AND operator means that all of the terms you enter into the search field are found. For example, let's say you want to find the schedule for a book project. If you enter **schedule AND "Discover Intranets"**, you get the schedule just for the book *Discover Intranets*, instead of hits on all of the schedules and all of the books.

The quotes mean that you want to find the title *Discover Intranets* as exactly those two words in that order, and not the hits on the individual words *discover* or *intranets*. Most search tools also ignore case unless you put in it quotes.

OR: Using the OR operator means that pages on your intranet with *any* of the terms you enter will be found. For example, if you enter **schedule AND "Discover Intranets" OR "Discover Desktop Conferencing with NetMeeting"**, you get schedules for *both* books.

NOT: You can use NOT to eliminate specifically certain words from your query. For example, if you enter **"Discover Intranets" NOT schedule**, you'll find all the information about the book except the schedule; that might be budgets, author information, contracts, marketing information, and so on.

NEAR: This operator will find words within a certain number of characters or words of each other. Depending on the search tool you use, you may be able to specify how close the words are. For example, if you enter **intranets NEAR Van Cleve**, you could find information on this book, without knowing the specific title of it.

> **CAUTION:** Every search tool uses a slightly different query syntax; that is, the way the search operators and punctuation are used to refine a search. Be sure to follow the specific tips for your search tool to get the best results.

Then there's the use of punctuation, for which the specifics vary by search tool, but the theories apply across the board.

Parentheses: This is back to basic algebra. For example, if you enter **schedule AND ("Discover Intranets" OR "Discover NetMeeting")** you find the schedules for both books.

Asterisks: Used as a wildcard to find any character, asterisks will let you find plurals or alternative spellings. For example, if you enter **discover***, you'll find *discover, discovered, discovering*.

Periods: Some search tools automatically stem words; that is, find all iterations of a term. To force the exact word, put a period at the end of the word. For example, if you enter **discover.** you'll exclude all other versions of the word.

Plus and minus signs: Plus signs require the word be included in the search, minus means the term is excluded. It's like the NOT operator. For example, if you enter **+discover -intranets**, you'd find all the books with *discover* in the title, but not intranets.

Intranet Search Tools

There are many intranet search tools available. Some are modified Web searchers, others are targeted specifically for intranet use.

Verity SEARCH '97 Intranet Spider

Verity's SEARCH '97 works through your browser to organize and index not only the intranet, but also your e-mail and attachments, and everything on your hard drive. Verity includes a built-in viewer for viewing documents in their native format (word processor, spreadsheet, database, HTML, PDF) with the search terms highlighted. This means you don't have to do a second search through each document to find the term you were looking for — it's a real time-saver.

SEARCH '97 will save your search queries, too. This is especially useful if you're doing regular searches through a lot of information, whether it's looking for your product name in news feeds, tracking information about one product among many in a large company, or getting really specific using Boolean queries that you'd rather not rethink each time.

WEB PATH For information on Verity's SEARCH '97 Intranet Spider, visit Web site at:

http://www.verity.com

Adobe Acrobat Search for PDF Collections

If you've moved a lot of material from the paper world to the electronic using Acrobat Capture or converted electronic files into Adobe Acrobat's PDF format, you can use the built-in Verity search tool to index and search on your files. Remember that Acrobat files can be viewed directly in your browser; you can also hyperlink PDF files to your intranet pages. Acrobat files can be indexed using Adobe Catalog, and accessed using search tools like Verity SEARCH '97. Results will be displayed on a newly generated intranet page.

Acrobat searches use a basic query structure as shown in Figure 9-7. You enter your query terms using Boolean search operators if you want, specify whether or not to use word *stemming* (that is, finding *discovering* even if you only entered *discover*), and other features. When creating PDF files, you can add keywords through the document information dialog box, shown in Figure 9-8, to expedite the search.

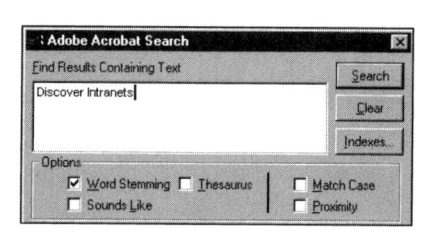

Figure 9-7 A basic search query in Acrobat

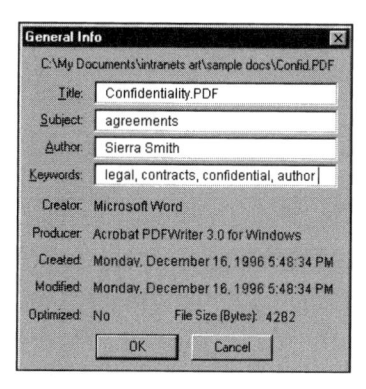

Figure 9-8 Acrobat document information fields for entering keywords

Creating indexes for your Acrobat files requires enough computer horsepower to generate and update the indexes, while the end user can search for the data on an average computer. Your users can choose which indexes to load and search, so it makes sense to name your indexes logically. Consider, for example, a huge library containing all the pages from all of the textbooks produced at a publishing company. If you create several indexes, say one each for Economics, Political Science, Literature, and so on, your users can narrow their search at the start by loading just the indexes in the discipline they want to search.

You can create and update multiple indexes using Acrobat Catalog, shown in Figure 9-9. You can select which directories to include and exclude, and you can eliminate certain words altogether from the indexing. This is useful for eliminating something called *stop words,* such as *a, the, an, or,* and *if,* and commonly used terms not useful for searching, like the publisher's name.

Overall, the Acrobat index is a quick way to catalog and access all files in PDF format in your intranet.

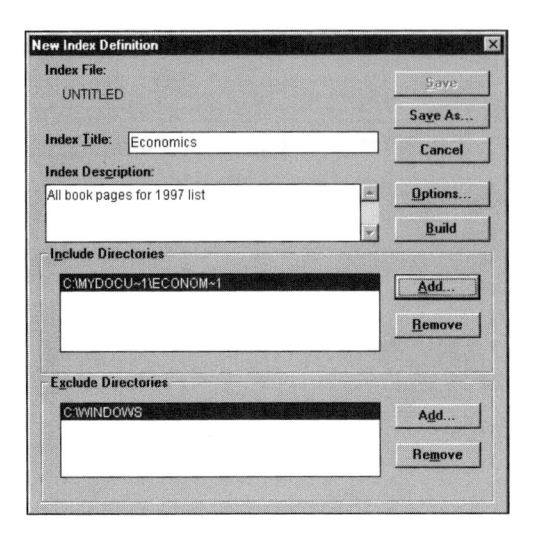

Figure 9-9 Creating an Acrobat index for PDF files on your intranet

CompassWare InfoMagnet

InfoMagnet uses its Magnet technology to *learn* what meaning or priority users attach to words, based on how they create queries and modify them. It combines natural language queries, dynamic query expansion, relevance feedback, and profiling. What do all those terms mean? Here's a summary:

Natural language queries: These are queries written in plain English.

Dynamic query expansion: This is an automatically generated thesaurus based on statistical relationships between terms that appear in the content. Queries are then expanded to include conceptually related terms.

Relevance feedback: Users can refine a query by giving feedback on retrieved results, and relevant terms are added to the revised query (this is the learning part!).

Profiling: This refers to saving user profiles, including what the user has designated as pertinent documents, for future use.

As illustrated in Figure 9-10, InfoMagnet lets you establish filters to sort out what is being searched. Returned hits for your queries can include summaries, as shown in Figure 9-11, of those pages or areas of your intranet provided someone has created them. This is similar to the use of keywords in the document summary of any file.

WEB PATH For more information about InfoMagnet, and for details about how the Magnet technology works, visit CompassWare's site at:

    http:/www.compassware.com

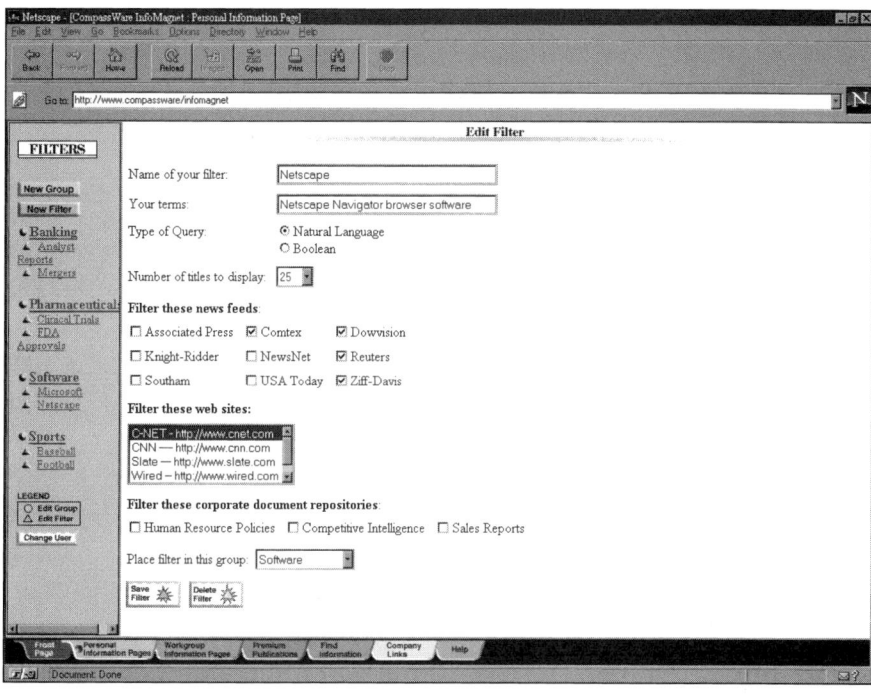

Figure 9-10 InfoMagnet provides filters for narrowing the area searched on your intranet

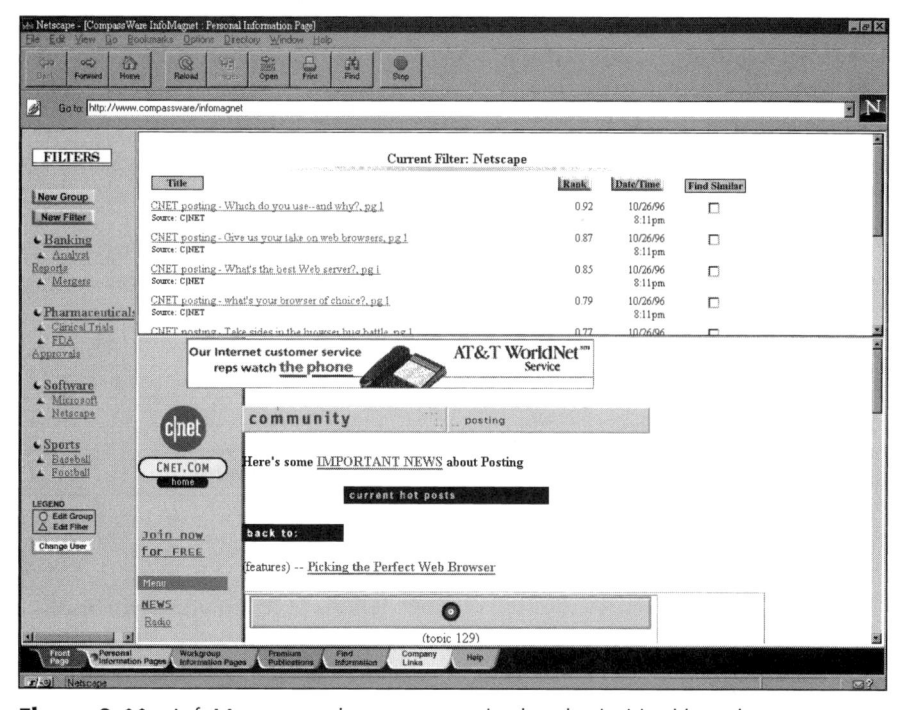

Figure 9-11 InfoMagnet results are summarized and prioritized based on your search criteria

TOOLS FOR SEARCHING YOUR INTRANET **151**

Quarterdeck WebCompass

WebCompass is a comprehensive search tool useful for surveying large sites and multiple types of information sources. If you do a lot of research or require constant updates on information that's posting in various locations on your intranet, WebCompass may be the tool for you. You can establish reusable topics and query terms, send out for updates at regularly scheduled times, and get summaries of the hits from the search. A Query Wizard walks you through the setup, but you need to spend time fine-tuning your terms for optimal results.

WEB PATH Try your skill at creating search topics and terms with WebCompass by downloading a 30-day trial version of its software at:

http://www.quarterdeck.com

The bottom line for searching is that you can quickly access the information you need if you spend a bit of time contemplating your needs. With a combination of TOCs and bookmarks, keywords, and full text searching, you and your users will be able to locate digital information significantly faster than the paper-based world.

BONUS

Test-Driving the Internet Search Engines

To experience searching on a fully developed resource, try visiting some of the leading search tools on the Internet as outlined in Table 9-2.

TABLE 9-2 Test-Driving Search Engines

Search Engine	Web Address	Comment
INFOSEEK GUIDE	http://www.infoseek.com	Will search the Web (like searching your intranet's pages), newsgroups (like your intranet's discussion groups), e-mail addresses (like your employee directory).

Search Engine	Web Address	Comment
EXCITE	http://www.excite.com	Does conceptual searching to find related items.
WEBCRAWLER	http://www.webcrawler.com	More manageable than some others.
HOTBOT	http://www.hotbot.com	Approaches searches with more restrictions; be sure to read the search tips.
ALTAVISTA	http:www.altavista.digital.com	A vast collection of full-text indexing, which will show you how tough it can be to narrow your searches to find anything useful.

Be sure to read the search tips on each site before beginning your queries. The tips will provide detailed instructions on using the Boolean terms discussed earlier in this chapter, and will define what punctuation is supported for narrowing your search. Try the same query on each of the sites and compare your results. You'll get a good idea of what search techniques and indexing schemes (keyword, full text, directory) will work best for your intranet.

Summary

This chapter introduced the principles of performing searches on your intranet. You learned:

Searching can be aided by using bookmarks, frames, and setting up logical tables of contents.

Creating keywords can expedite the search process by narrowing the range of searchable information.

Search queries can be simple or complex, using Boolean search operators to refine the scope of the information retrieved.

Search query technique takes a bit of practice, but is well rewarded by providing quick access to the information on your intranet.

CHAPTER TEN

HARDWARE NEEDS AND NETWORK STRATEGIES

IN THIS CHAPTER YOU LEARN THESE KEY SKILLS

THE HARDWARE AND EQUIPMENT YOU NEED PAGE 157

THE ROLE OF SERVERS PAGE 158

HOW TO CHOOSE THE NETWORK OPERATING SYSTEM FOR YOUR INTRANET PAGE 160

SELECTING YOUR DESKTOP COMPUTERS PAGE 161

THE IMPORTANCE OF SPEED PAGE 163

SOFTWARE THAT DETERMINES HOW YOUR DATA IS SENT OVER YOUR INTRANET PAGE 165

HOW TO KEEP ALL YOUR INFORMATION CURRENT WITH MULTIPLE USERS PAGE 166

We've been regaling you with tales of how great an intranet is; how it will improve your business processes, lower production costs, and freshen your breath without causing cavities.

But before you can reap the benefits of an intranet, you've got to build one. And that involves more than deciding what information to make available to your users and designing the right Web pages so they can access it. You also need an extensive conglomeration of computer equipment. Even though the activity of your system is ideally transparent to most users, there's a lot going on behind the scenes.

In this chapter, we'll take a look at the hardware and networking technology you'll need to successfully install and use an intranet in your organization. We'll also examine some of the technology you'll need to make full use of an intranet, both on-site and on the road.

First we'll look at the larger computers on your network, meaning the servers you need to handle your Web pages and pass them around to your users. How big a computer do you need to handle the intranet on a LAN (Local Area Network) or WAN (Wide Area Network)? A *LAN* is a local network, such as the network in your building; a *WAN* could be your company's entire network across numerous geographical locations. We'll examine the criteria for your server decision, along with the trickier question of which server platform you should use.

You're in for a pleasant surprise when it comes to client requirements: You may not have to spend very much on desktop systems if you've already got reasonably up-to-date systems online.

However, the intranet is generally a challenge for installed networking technology. You can probably manage to start your intranet using your installed LAN equipment (assuming you've loaded the right protocols), but you'll probably have to speed up your WAN connections. Figure 10-1 shows the difference between a LAN and the larger WAN.

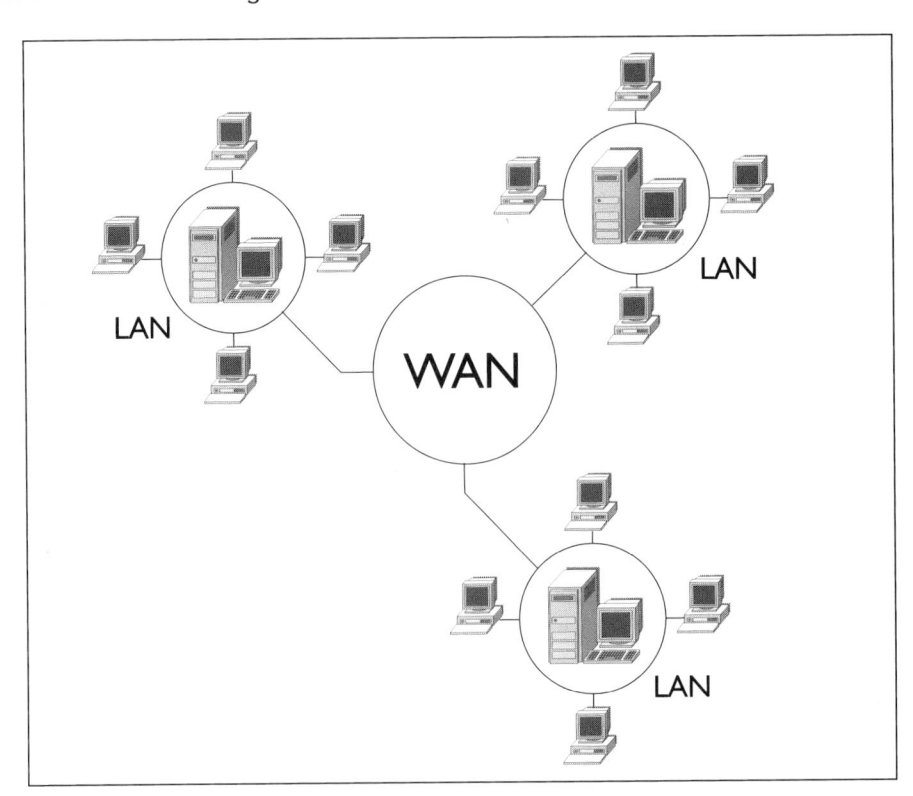

Figure 10-1 Several LANs are linked together to form a WAN that can transcend geographical boundaries. The LANs can be on different floors of the same building, in different cities, or across the world.

Making sure that everyone on those WANs has access to the same data is sometimes challenging, but it is possible with the proper data replication schemes. In this chapter, we'll take a look at how those out-of-the-loop users at remote locations can take advantage of the corporate intranet . . . after a fashion. We'll also discuss how to pass internal messages in your organization.

Gizmos, Gadgets, Hardware, and More

As you may have gathered by now, an intranet is a combination of the Internet and client/server (both existing technologies) computing over an internal computer network. The pages of information you'll supply will be in the standard Internet format of HTML, but you'll pass that data around based on the standard client/server architecture (in which a so-called *client* computer on a desktop asks a server system to perform various computing functions rather than do the computing itself).

Actually, that's good news, because you probably already have LANs and WANs in place in your organization. And if you have intercompany e-mail or collaborative computing capabilities, you've got an extra server or two in there as well. An intranet server actually has less work to do than most, because it only has to interpret browser code.

We sincerely hope you don't have to design your whole networking and client/server environments from scratch. If you do, you're going to have a *major* tax write-off next year. When building even a small LAN, you have to spend tens of thousands of dollars on hardware and networking equipment, as well as software and network design — not to mention the pain and suffering in your IS department. Putting up an intranet that connects numerous remote locations throughout the world is a million-dollar matter.

> **SIDE TRIP**
>
> ### WHAT WEB SERVERS REALLY DO
>
> For the sake of simplicity, we use the term *intranet server* to mean an internal Web server. However, a fully functioning intranet requires many servers; a Web server is only a small part of the solution. For example, Netscape offers SuiteSpot for intranets, which includes (software) servers for Web, e-mail, news, and proxy. So intranet servers do more than serve browser code, although one machine can easily handle the complete load. The Web server doesn't interpret any HTML code; it only handles HTTP requests from clients and sends back documents. The client handles the interpretation of HTML.

However, you're a forward-thinking, technologically savvy individual (you're reading this book, aren't you?) so of course you've already got some kind of LAN established in your facility. Assuming that you've already got PCs out there among your users, the hardware and networking costs of implementing an intranet could be relatively small — on the order of a few thousand dollars.

Service with a Smile

First, let's take a look at the server side of the equation. After all, the server does most of the work. In an intranet, the server fields all requests for information from users, finds the proper files from storage, and doles them out to its clients. (Picture a cook at a diner getting orders from a very limited menu, filling them in the kitchen, and whirling them out a little slot in the wall.)

Your intranet server will need to run server software and act as a repository for the intranet pages that you'll want available to your users. Typically, these servers are fairly high-end desktop computers running one of the standard operating systems (OS) such as Digital Equipment's Unix, Novell NetWare, Microsoft Windows, IBM OS/2, or the Apple Macintosh OS.

Server Needs

How many servers your intranet will need is tough to determine, especially because existing solutions are all over the map. One drug company has a dozen servers for 15,000 employees; a computer hardware company has nearly 2,000 machines to serve almost the same number. As a very rough rule of thumb, we recommend one server for every hundred or so active users.

But the raw number of users should be only one factor in determining your server needs. There are many other considerations, such as the number of people who will be using your intranet at the same time. In some ways, LAN speed is greatly affected by the number of people trying to access things simultaneously. Even a high-end server would show some degradation if asked to handle more than a couple of thousand tasks, such as finding or copying a file, especially if they were all demanding large files.

You also need to figure out how far away your users are from your servers. Data may travel quickly along dedicated lines, but it still takes awhile to get halfway around the world. At minimum, you'll want a server on every continent, and if you can swing it, a server in each office or business region.

Not every server has to contain the same information; one server can always ask information of another server on your intranet. Nevertheless, you'll need a certain number of *mirror sites* (sites that feature identical data). That's where trouble begins, and that's why you may want to keep your server numbers on the low side. Keeping mirrored sites updated can be a major pain in the tail.

The more servers you have, the harder time your IS people will have. That's generally a good thing to keep in mind when planning the makeup of your intranet. Some people believe that every desktop will eventually have intranet publishing capacity — that every desktop computer will be both client and server in turn. That may be true, but right now, that's a support nightmare we don't even want to think about!

Choosing the Speed of Your Server

Here's something that will seem a little backward. When shopping for a stand-alone PC, the first thing you look at is raw speed: What's the processing power of that baby? Well, clock speed isn't very important when picking a server. There's just not that much processing that needs to be done to run an intranet. The toughest task facing an intranet server may have nothing to do with the intranet; the tough job can be running one of today's mammoth network operating systems without choking.

You can't run an intranet with an Apple IIe, but you probably don't need the high-end of the Intel P Series either. We suggest shopping for last season's high-end — you know, the hardware that was pushed off the front page by last week's announcement. You'll get the advantage of that first big price reduction without having to worry about the hardware becoming immediately obsolete. You should be able to buy a better-than-adequate server from virtually any vendor for between $3,000 and $5,000.

Server Memory Requirements

Here's another issue you don't have to worry about. The memory requirements of most Web-server software is nothing compared to the requirements of today's operating systems. You can limp along with 16MB for almost any platform, but like most vendors, we recommend 32MB for most systems. In fact, why not live big and go up to 48MB, or even 64MB? At today's prices you can afford to get a little extra RAM; it almost always improves performance.

How much disk space you'll need is a little more difficult to evaluate. Network and Web-server software can take up the best part of a gigabyte of storage, but it's hard to tell how much storage you'll need for your corporate data. If you'll be mostly pulling out text, such as old legal briefs, your storage requirements will be pretty small. (A page of text is a few kilobytes of data.) On the other hand, if you've got lots of product photos online, which could be several hundred kilobytes, you're talking about a pretty massive library. Fortunately, disk storage isn't that expensive. You'll always find use for the storage space, even if it means doing more diligent backups in that extra space, so buy more than you think you'll need.

Picking Your NOS

Up to now, we've talked in generic terms about server capabilities. But eventually you're going to have to choose a specific server, and that means a specific operating system. With several flavors of Windows and even more versions of Unix, NetWare, Mac OS, and more out there, picking your NOS (network operating system) is a tough decision.

TIP Much of the success of a tool such as an intranet depends on your IS department's comfort level and continued use of the tool. In a client/server setup, especially with the various types of intranet servers, it doesn't really matter to the end user or department manager what types of hardware platforms are used. As long as they can communicate with each other (with protocols such as TCP/IP), any system can be used for the server or the clients.

When evaluating the various operating systems, consider the track record of the operating system, how easy it is to set up and configure a system, whether it's got all the functionality you need, and the amount of commitment third parties have shown to the platform. Table 10-1 compares your choices.

TABLE 10-1 Operating System Choices

Operating System	Ease of Installation	Expansion
WINDOWS NT	Intermediate	Cheapest
UNIX	Hardest	More expensive and complicated
NETWARE	Hard	Complicated; needs to be expanded by a Novell technician
MACINTOSH	Easiest	Easy to expand

Windows NT: Of all the various flavors of Windows, NT is best suited for a networked environment — that's what it was designed for. As an intranet server, NT conforms to the Windows reputation for ease of installation and use. Third parties are interested in anything Microsoft offers, so there are plenty of tools available. Intel and compatible platforms are plentiful and relatively inexpensive; you can get a serviceable intranet server for less than $3,000.

Unix: Unix is the grande dame of the operating system world; it's literally been around as long as all the other major operating systems combined! And because it's an open system that enables other companies to develop tools for it, there is a vast library of third-party products out there. Of course, anything that old is bound to be a bit crotchety, and Unix is notoriously hard to install and configure. It could cost you more than $4,000 to get a decent Unix server from Sun Microsystems or one of its competitors.

Novell NetWare: Like NT, NetWare is an operating system designed specifically for a network environment that runs on Intel and Intel-compatible hardware. NetWare does an excellent job, but it isn't particularly easy to install or change. And, perhaps because Novell tends to play its cards close to its chest, there aren't a heck of a lot of third-party tools out there. Novell intranet servers can be configured for less than $3,000.

Mac OS: Apple has always prided itself on how easy the Macintosh is to use, and the Mac OS helps it keep its well-earned reputation when used as a server. It's probably the easiest intranet server to set up and configure. There aren't as many third-party tools for the Mac OS as there are for some other platforms, but there are enough to get the job done. It should cost around $3,000 to buy a Macintosh that can function as an intranet server.

After choosing your platform, you'll need to determine server software. Although it's generally the domain of your IS department to select and manage server software, it's useful to know the differentiating capabilities of each.

X-REF For details on tools to manage intranet sites, see Chapter 8.

WEB PATH For links to current information on all of the network operating systems, go to a central directory such as Yahoo! (see Figure 10-2):

http://www.yahoo.com/Computers_and_Internet/Operating_Systems/

Choosing Your Desktop Weapons

Now that you've decided on your server hardware, you'll have to make a similar evaluation of your client needs. What kind of PC will you need to run the browser software? How much disk space will be required? How much is it going to cost?

Unless you're running absolute antiques in your office environment, you've got it covered. Establishing functional clients for an intranet requires nothing major in the way of processing power or disk storage. (If your desktop engines aren't powerful enough to act as intranet clients, your personnel have probably been complaining about them for years. It's time to upgrade.)

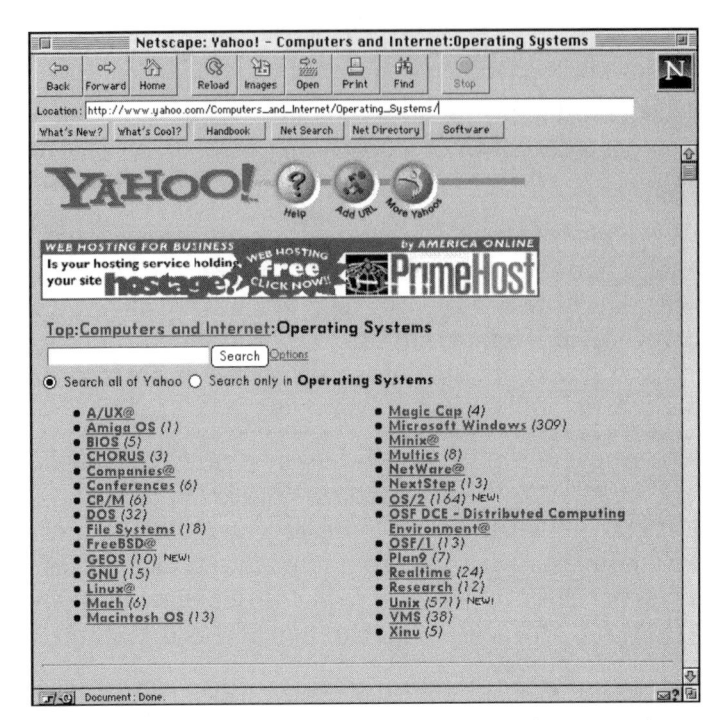

Figure 10-2 Yahoo!'s informative Computer and Internet Directory

An Intel 486 or Pentium processor with 8MB of memory is ample for running Netscape Navigator, Microsoft Explorer, or almost any other browser. You'll probably want 16MB of memory for a Windows 95 client, but that has more to do with the memory requirements of Windows 95 than with intranet functionality. You should be able buy that kind of machine (with a decent amount of disk storage) for less than $1,300.

In the Macintosh world, virtually all of the Macintosh II, Performa, or PowerMac lines come with enough processing power, memory, and storage to act as an intranet browser. For the record, Netscape recommends a 68030 processor or better with at least 5MB of memory known as *RAM* (Random Access Memory), although 8MB would be better. With some haggling, you should be able to buy a system for under $1,500.

As for a Unix client — if you've got a desktop system running Unix, you already have enough juice to run just about anything you want, so what are you worrying about? Or you could go with a low-end client system, such as a simple X-Terminal or an HP workstation available for a few hundred dollars.

TIP You are going to feel overcharged. Memory and storage prices are falling constantly. About three months after you buy your equipment, you'll look at the advertisements in the local paper and feel like you got ripped off. Well, you didn't. That's the nature of the peripherals business. Just keep telling yourself that if you had kept waiting, you'd have never launched this nifty intranet.

Okay, Speed Is of the Essence

Because an intranet is really nothing more than a specialized network implementation, you'll need a basic network architecture in place; a LAN for your local environment, and one or more WANs if you've got a number of regional facilities. Again, we're going to assume that you have *something* in place, because if you don't, you're in for months of planning and tens of thousands of dollars in expenses, and you have bigger things than intranets to worry about.

When it comes to communications, faster is better. That's why some people prefer Federal Express to the Postal Service, and why both are better for business than carrier pigeons. That holds true for network communications as well. The faster you can send data across your intranet, the better.

We are not contradicting what we said earlier. It really doesn't matter how fast your computers crunch numbers, because number crunching is a trivial part of the whole intranet environment. But naturally you want your data on your desktop as quickly as you can manage it. That's the speed of the network, not of the individual machines on it.

Of course, speed comes at a price. Federal Express may be faster, but it costs ten bucks or more to send a letter by overnight carrier and only 32 cents by first-class mail. (Carrier pigeons are extinct, so the parallel fails there. But you get the point.)

LAN Speed

Communications gurus measure data communications according to how many bits of information are transmitted per second. Until recently, the convention was to discuss Kbps (kilobits per second). A kilobit isn't actually 1,000 bits — it's 1,024 bits, for reasons nobody really wants to go into. Today's modems, for example, typically transmit and receive data at 28.8Kbps.

But people aren't talking about Kbps anymore — they're talking about Mbps (*mega*bits per second). Internal Ethernet connections are rated at 10Mbps, although they can only function at that speed for short bursts. Even so, you're talking about speeds easily 200 times faster than a top-of-the-line modem.

And if that weren't impressive enough, Fast Ethernet is becoming a standard throughout many installations. Fast Ethernet offers LANs 100Mbps connectivity, as do other emerging standards such as Fiber Channel. That's about 2,000 times faster than a modem, which means we owe carrier pigeons an apology. See Table 10-2 for a comparison of connection types.

TABLE 10-2 LAN Connection Types

Medium	Speed	Where Best Used
MODEM	Up to 33.36Kbps	Small office, home office
ETHERNET	10-20Mbps	Small to midsize office
FAST ETHERNET	100Mbps or more	Small to midsize office
FIBER OPTIC	400Mbps or more	Large or multisite office

If you're running a reasonably modern LAN system you shouldn't have much trouble setting up an intranet server. With normal Ethernet you can expect to grab a 1MB photograph in a second or so, unless there's a lot of traffic slowing down the transmission speed.

TIP Once your users get hooked on the intranet, they *really* get hooked. Your network traffic could easily double, triple, or more. Our advice is to plan on taking one more step up the bandwidth ladder.

WAN Speed

Propagating information throughout a WAN isn't nearly as quick as spreading the news around a LAN. There are a variety of solutions available for WANs, but they all require special cable and are only available in some areas. Expect to see improvements in this area: If you hear people talking about *bandwidth, the size of the pipe,* and *throughput,* they're referring to this subject. The high-speed options are shown in Table 10-3.

TABLE 10-3 WAN Connection Types

Connection	Speed	Where Best Used
ISDN CONNECTION	56Kbps	Small office
T1 CONNECTION	1.5Mbps	Small to large office
T3 CONNECTION	45Mbps	Large office with a lot of data to move

Chances are your WAN doesn't come near matching the speed of your LANs. Chances are your IS people wear a silly grin the moment you come into view.

With an intranet, you'll probably need more speed than you have today. In general, your network traffic is going to increase, and if you plan to keep your disk mirroring and replications up to snuff, you're going to end up with some terrific short duration, high-volume transmissions. As for video conferencing and other really high-volume transmissions, faster is better.

> **X-REF** Whether video conferencing is realistic based on transmission speeds and quality of video is a big topic of discussion. See Chapter 14 for details on audio and video conferencing.

Talk Is Cheap

By now, you're probably heartily sick of acronyms, but here's one more you will need for intranet technology: TCP/IP (it stands for Transmission Control Protocol/Internet Protocol, a fact known only to true data wonks, and can therefore be used to amaze your friends). After you've determined the speed at which your data will move within your LAN or WAN, TCP/IP tells the computer how to send data across a network.

Basically, TCP/IP is a software solution for computer connectivity. As far as intranets are concerned, TCP/IP is *the* communications solution. Intranet servers and browsers are all designed to work with TCP/IP. Rather like the American Express card, data can't leave home without it.

Unfortunately, if you've got a DOS or Windows-based facility, TCP/IP can be an added expense. Though an AppleTalk network is designed around IP and TCP/IP is native to the Unix world, you've got to coax Microsoft's products to accept TCP/IP. You'll need a hardware driver, as well as a software TCP/IP stack for each and every desktop computer that you want to attach to your intranet. It's not that expensive; there are numerous shareware and freeware products available to cover your needs for drivers, stacks, and Winsocks (don't ask). But it is troublesome and time-consuming; even an expert can have problems sweet-talking Windows 3.11 or NT into doing something for which it wasn't designed.

If you don't want to put TCP/IP on every desktop, you have a couple of choices. You can use something called a gateway in front of your server. A gateway is like your receptionist: The receptionist filters out the incoming matter (people, calls, mail), makes sure they're addressed properly or knows where they're going, and sends them on their way. Gateways translate TCP/IP into a protocol that Windows understands at the price of a bit of network speed. Or you can just limit the number of intranet terminals installed throughout your organization and make the employees share (at the price of some friction among colleagues).

> **TIP** TCP/IP is not too difficult to set up with Windows 95; the operating system itself can be configured for TCP/IP. For Windows 3.x (and also Windows 95), Winsock is a popular method of enabling TCP/IP.

Copy Cats

The problem of concurrent users on a WAN makes it a challenge to ensure that all the information is current all the time. If the whole idea of an intranet is to quickly propagate information, the entire setup is useless when the data isn't up to date. Fortunately, database vendors have been coping that problem for a long time. Their answer is called *data replication*.

Data replication copies information from one server to all the other servers in a WAN or LAN, so that the information they contain remains consistent. One server sends its contents to all the other servers on the network (either directly or routed through one or more central servers).

SIDE TRIP

TELECOMMUTERS CAN REACH THE INTRANET

Telecommuting means that almost anyone can be doing almost any job outside the office. What does that mean for the intranet user? Well, with due security considerations (more on that in Chapter 11), there's no reason why a remote user can't log on to the corporate intranet using a standard modem. There are plenty of Internet surfers who use their home computers.

Of course, there is one vital piece of equipment any remote user is going to need before logging on to the corporate intranet: a good book to help them pass the time.

If you're used to the 10Mbps–100Mbps speeds of an internal intranet, the speed of even a high-end 33.3 or 56Kbps modem can seem like a snail's pace. It's not uncommon for a Web page that appears instantaneously on your office machine to take minutes to appear on your remote terminal. There's not much Web designers can do about it (unless the page is intended for out-of-office use), except perhaps make sure that the photos on any Web page are relatively small — pictures take much longer to load than text. And the user can take comfort in the fact that most Web browsers have buffers of decent size, and once you've loaded a page, it won't take that long to return to it again during the same session.

Of course, it isn't a trivial matter to keep those servers in line. And the bigger your intranet, the bigger the issue is going to be. Say you have 22 servers, each with 2GB of data. It takes each server just under six minutes to send its contents to one other server, even on a T3 connection completely dedicated to the replication procedure. And if each server wants to communicate every time there's a change . . . well, it's obviously impossible.

The solution — or part of it — is to schedule data replication for times when the network isn't being used. Like sending 18-wheelers across a highway when there's no other cars to get in the way, the data can be transferred more quickly between, say, 3 a.m. and 5 a.m. than between 3 p.m. and 5 p.m. You can also schedule partial updates during regular hours, and (most important, perhaps) set an automatic backup every time something in a specified file is changed.

> **CAUTION**
> You could probably set up a WAN environment where every server mirrors every other one. But you should resist the temptation. Not everyone *needs* direct access to every Web page — who, outside of human resources, needs daily access to the corporate policy on maternity leave? Knowing how many resources must be dedicated to the task of data replication, and that you can always reach another server on the LAN in a matter of seconds, you might as well let each individual server grow in its own direction.

BONUS

What You'll Need for an Intranet

You can't just wave a magic wand and set up an intranet. (At least, we haven't seen it done yet.) As this chapter points out, there's lots of hardware and networking gear that has to be in place before you can launch your Web pages. A quick review of what you'll need is shown in the following checklist:

NETWORK RESOURCES
- ❏ Server (midrange desktop system or higher)
- ❏ Network-enabled operating system (Unix, Windows NT, Netware, Mac OS)
- ❏ TCP/IP driver or gateway
- ❏ LAN card for the server

❏ SMTP
❏ POP

CLIENT RESOURCES

❏ Desktop computer with at least 8M of RAM and 50M available hard drive space
❏ LAN card
❏ Internet browser software (Microsoft Internet Explorer, Netscape, or other)
❏ TCP/IP client software

Summary

In this chapter you learned the following about how to use hardware and network resources to set up your intranet:

Hardware and equipment needs

The role of servers

Network operating systems for your intranet

What type of desktop computers are best for your intranet

The importance of connection speed in setting up your intranet

CHAPTER ELEVEN

INTRANET SECURITY ISSUES

IN THIS CHAPTER YOU LEARN THESE KEY SKILLS

ADDING SECURITY YOUR INTRANET   PAGE 169

DECIDING WHETHER TO SECURE SEGMENTS OF YOUR INTRANET OR THE WHOLE SYSTEM   PAGE 170

THE IMPORTANCE OF BACKUPS FOR THE SAFETY OF YOUR DATA   PAGE 173

POTENTIAL SECURITY THREATS FROM THE INTERNET WITH A FIREWALL   PAGE 174

BATTLING COMPUTER VIRUSES   PAGE 178

Safe and Secure?

We've been discussing the benefits of disseminating data across your intranet. With all this talk about openness and free access to information, it sometimes sounds like the fall of the Soviet Union all over again.

Well, the corporate world isn't a democracy, and for a private intranet there can be such a thing as too much glasnost. There's a lot of internal material you don't want competitors — or even neutral third parties — getting ahold of. Heck, there's a great deal of material the rank-and-file employees shouldn't see.

You have to change your self-image as we work through this chapter. Get rid of the idea of the friendly trailblazer who clears the path, and acts as a tour guide for your more timid associates. You have to start thinking of yourself as a cop or security guard who keeps unwanted visitors out, and keeps valuables in.

Clearly, there are two competing impulses with which an intranet administrator has to deal. One is the desire to make sure that everyone in the organization has easy access to all the information they ever need, from the weather in the parking lot to the stock price at yesterday's closing. The other is the need to protect the company jewels by setting yourself up by the data bridge and warning in stentorian tones that "None Shall Pass!"

We trust you can find a happy medium. Settling the company policy of openness versus security should be a priority when designing your corporate intranet.

We can't make the evaluation for you, but we can recommend that this policy is a reflection of your overall corporate policy. For example: The manufacturer of Ben & Jerry's ice cream has a reputation for keeping its employees informed of business decisions as they're made. Its intranet would probably reflect this policy by making most of its Web pages accessible to employees. On the other hand, it's likely that Coca-Cola would want tighter security, if only to keep that formula for Coke a secret.

Blanket Security

Please don't take internal intranet security lightly. According to some estimates, 80 percent of all network security breaches come from inside a company (which makes sense, because insiders have much easier access to the network and its components). So it's wise to consider carefully who has access to what information, even on your internal intranet.

Elements of Intranet Security

Intranet security isn't all that different from standard network security. You've got to protect your data from encroachment, both intentional and accidental. (And far more damage is done to a computer network by innocent klutzes than by determined assailants.) You've got to make sure that you can restore your network quickly in case of catastrophe.

TIP It's important that you not only establish who can use what data, but who has the authority to change that configuration. In other words, if you're going to keep most of the doors locked, who's going to have the key? We recommend limiting the number of people with the ability to change access configurations to one or two per site. And more important, you should implement a strict procedure for opening various sites. Leave a clear paper trail so you know who left that door ajar, and when.

Restricting — or allowing — access to your intranet isn't too difficult. Most Web server software enables you to configure access by individual user or work group. In fact, some servers enable the Systems Administrator to limit access to unique Web pages — so that only the CFO has access to the real accounts receivable, for example. Frankly, we're not sure that's such a great idea: If the documents are *that* sensitive, why post them at all, even on a nominally secure intranet? Why do you think they make briefcases with secret compartments?

The Secret Word Is SwOrDfIsH

The first line of defense in your internal intranet security scheme should be, obviously, passwords. On the intranet, a password is typically a combination of letters, numbers, and punctuation marks — usually eight characters or more. All http servers, those computers that store and manage Web pages, can restrict access to both documents and databases based on such passwords. If you don't know the password, you can't get in the door.

Passwords are tricky. If they're obvious to the user, any hacker will be able to dope it out in short order. If they're complicated enough to fool an intruder, users may forget them. To make matters worse, you really have to change passwords frequently (every month or so is not amiss).

SIDE TRIP

FORGETTING YOUR PASSWORD IS NOT FUNNY

The trouble with passwords is that the really good ones are not only **hard to guess**, they're hard to remember. And, because writing down a password is a **cardinal no-no**, a good password can be as confusing for the user as it is for the hacker.

It reminds us of a speakeasy scene between Groucho and Chico Marx. Groucho, the user, wants to get in but doesn't know the password. Chico, the gatekeeper, wants to let Groucho in, but he can't because Groucho doesn't know the password (which is *swordfish*).

Groucho's predicament is familiar to many computer users with bad memories. He *knows* the password is the name of a fish and offers a number of guesses — all of which are wrong. Eventually, Groucho comes up with *swordfish*, but it does him no good: Chico has already changed the password.

We always knew the Marx Brothers were ahead of their time.

INTRANET SECURITY ISSUES

The Internet is full of documents offering advice on passwords. Unfortunately, some of that advice is contradictory. Here are some password don'ts from the experts:

- Don't use your first or last name, the names of any relatives, or the names of your pets. Anyone serious about hacking a system can do enough research about a user to find out that basic information.
- Don't use social security numbers, tax numbers, or telephone numbers. The preceding reasons apply.
- Don't use the user ID as the password, because that's *stupid!* A hacker already knows the user ID.
- Don't use any obscene words or phrases. This isn't prudishness; it's just obvious. There aren't that many, and experienced hackers apparently try them early in the search.
- Don't use any obvious keyboard patterns, such as *qwerty* or *asdfg*. If they're obvious to you, they're obvious to a hacker.
- Don't use any common English words. This one startled us, but determined hackers will apparently hook up a spell-checker dictionary, and try each and every word in the English language to find the password. In fact, some advise not to use two words put together for the same reason.

Well! With all those don'ts, how do you come up with a decent password? Some people believe that spelling a common word backward, such as *drawkcab*, makes a decent password. Others say that even that is too obvious, and recommend a word that is spelled *incorrektly*. Inserting capital letters into a password *raNdoMly* is favored by some, though the more cautious types say that every password should include at least two *nu3b2rs* or *pun!ua%ion* marks to complicate things further.

We have our own favorite way of generating a password that uses none of those techniques. Take a well-known phrase, or line of poetry:

"To be, or not to be: That is the question."

And take the first letter of each word: *TBONTBTITQ*.

Now you have a password that's easy to remember but has no apparent pattern. You can pretty it up, by taking the second letter of each word: *OEROOEHSHU*, or typing it backward: *QTITBTNOBT*, or substituting punctuation marks for one or more of the letters. There are many possible permutations, all of which can be easy to remember but difficult to decipher.

TIP We've given you a bunch of good ideas for passwords. Feel free to use any of the techniques we've outlined, but *please* don't use any of the specific examples. You're not the only one reading this book, you know — at least we hope not!

Back to Backups

Security on your intranet is more than making sure no one trespasses in your data preserves. It's also the knowledge that if something goes wrong, you can recover the data in a timely fashion. Backing up network data, like data replication, is a challenge that network engineers have been addressing for some time.

How to Back Up Your Intranet

Backing up your intranet means taking existing data and storing it on some kind of removable medium. Backing up also implies restoration, of course, and the software that copies the data will usually automate the recovery process as well.

There are several reasons for backing up your data, but mainly it is life insurance. There's really no going back — once your company depends on the intranet to do business, it may be impossible to go along without it.

Disaster can strike your intranet for a number of reasons. A hacker might break in, despite your best defensive efforts, and corrupt or erase files. Or, the elements might conspire against you in the form of fire or flood. Or, and this the most likely scenario, one of your users may screw up. (Before you dismiss the notion, how many times have you clicked Yes mistakenly when asked if you want to delete a file?)

There is a lot of software designed specifically for backing up network environments, especially for the NetWare arena. Some have even been tailored to the Internet. Generally running on a separate server, backup solutions such as Cheyenne's ARCserver and Legato's NetWorker copy the contents of such disks automatically as the systems administrator designates.

As with data replication, the backups have to be scheduled and are typically done overnight, although incremental backups of critical data are often done more frequently. And also similar to data replication, the larger the network, the more difficult it is to find time to do that backup.

The real headache is in the restoration if your server fails for any reason. It could be a hardware failure, a power problem, or a software problem. File-by-file restoration is a fairly slow process, but the good news is you will be back in business eventually. New products, such as JETserve and SnapBack take "images" of large chunks of a storage disk and copy it exactly. Restoring an individual file is more difficult, but restoring a network completely is sometimes improved by an order of magnitude.

CAUTION: It's possible to become too concerned about hackers. For someone really interested in finding corporate secrets, there are easier routes than the intranet. For example, where do you keep your tape backups? What's keeping them from walking out the door under someone's shirt? We're not suggesting that backups aren't necessary — far from it! But it's possible to get so wrapped up in the esoterica of network computing that we forget the obvious.

When hunting for a backup solution, as with most intranet solutions, keep in mind ease of use. Is the system difficult to install? And is it difficult to configure once you've installed it? Simplicity is a pleasant convenience when things are going well. But when the system's down and an administrator is breaking out in a cold sweat, an easy-to-use system is a necessity. (Network administrators are even harder to replace than network data.)

Backup Storage Media Compared

It's amazing how reactionary network designers can be sometimes. Even though magnetic disks and optical media have been around for a decade or more, most network archive and backup data are stored on some form of tape. And that's a bit surprising, because tape storage is slower than magnetic disk to write and restore, and isn't as stable as an optical disk. (Not to mention the fact that it's a two-dimensional medium, and can't be easily searched for individual files.)

Nevertheless, tape storage seems to be the medium of choice. It's cheap and high capacity (with automated tape libraries, you can store terabytes of data). Besides, after all these years, designers are used to tape's idiosyncrasies.

According to a survey from Strategic Research Corp., PC and Unix-base LAN servers are most frequently backed up by 4mm Digital Audio Tape (DAT) systems or by 8mm tape storage devices. The quarter-inch tape (QCI) tape drive, in vogue several years ago, is falling out of favor in today's network. The upstart Digital Linear Tape (DLT), with its high speed and capacity, is gaining in popularity — although not too many installations are presently using them.

The survey didn't mention them, but there are any number of the old reel-to-reel tape storage devices still out there. A lot of irreplaceable data is archived on those tapes, and most companies don't have the time or budget to transfer it to other formats. Besides, we think administrators get a secret kick out of watching the reels go 'round and 'round.

Enter the Internet

With restricted access, passwords, and possibly data encryption (which we'll discuss later), you'll have a decent handle on your internal intranet security problems. But eventually your users will want to push outward to the Internet. And that opens up a whole new set of security problems.

As Sun says on its WWW site, "The Internet is known as a haven of hackers and misfits." (Its user community might well take umbrage if they read that.) There are millions of Internet users in the U.S. alone, any one of whom — armed with the right equipment and the proper will — could infiltrate your intranet.

An intruder on your intranet could steal files and sell your vital corporate data, insert viruses to foul up your computers, erase sensitive files, or even crash your whole system. Tossing a real monkey wrench in the works would cause less damage.

So if it's so dangerous, why maintain an Internet presence at all? There are several good reasons. For one thing, it may well be to your advantage to let customers or just the general public have access to some areas of your business — a parts catalog, for example. Another reason is there's a lot of business information out there that can benefit you, from census data to competitors' prices and everything in between.

The Internet also offers a communications gateway to the world through e-mail, enabling you to reach any other Internet user around the world with great savings of time and energy (not to mention money). And while you can keep your intranet, Internet access, and e-mail separate, having one integrated solution simplifies matters.

SIDE TRIP

HACKERS LOVE A CHALLENGE

You've probably gotten the image by now of Internet hackers as fiendish monsters bent on destroying humanity, or as black-hatted spies intent on stealing your vital corporate secrets. And, well, some hackers are like that — and worse.

But on balance, most hackers are relatively benign. They're computer enthusiasts who are interested mostly in the challenge of working with computers and playing around in networks. This doesn't mean they aren't dangerous — blundering around in a network can be just as damaging in the long run as a determined sabotage effort. And hackers are noted for a . . . ahem . . . juvenile sense of humor that can lead to damage for the "fun" of it.

What this means is you may be visited by hackers precisely *because* you have a particularly efficient security system. There's a large underground of hackers sharing tips and information across the Internet. If your company gets a reputation as a tough nut to crack, not only will you be besieged by hackers eager to take on the challenge, but once they've cracked your system they may post some of your secrets on the Net!

There's really not much you can do about this, except keep vigilant. Oh, and try not to boast about how secure your intranet is. That's just like saying "I dare you" to the hacker community.

And, perhaps more important, it's cheaper and more convenient to extend the corporate intranet over the Internet than to invest in a WAN solution (if you don't already have one in place, that is.)

No, the Internet is too big an asset to leave untapped. (If you don't believe us, check out the huge rack of Internet books in the bookstore near where you found this one.) It just means more security procedures — yes, more headaches.

Fighting Fire with Firewalls

Protecting your innocent intranet from incursion by invaders can be a tiring, frustrating job. You may have to institute a fortress mentality, and adopt a defensive posture not unlike that of a feudal lord protecting his castle. Small wonder that one of the key intranet security devices has been dubbed a firewall, as shown in Figure 11-1.

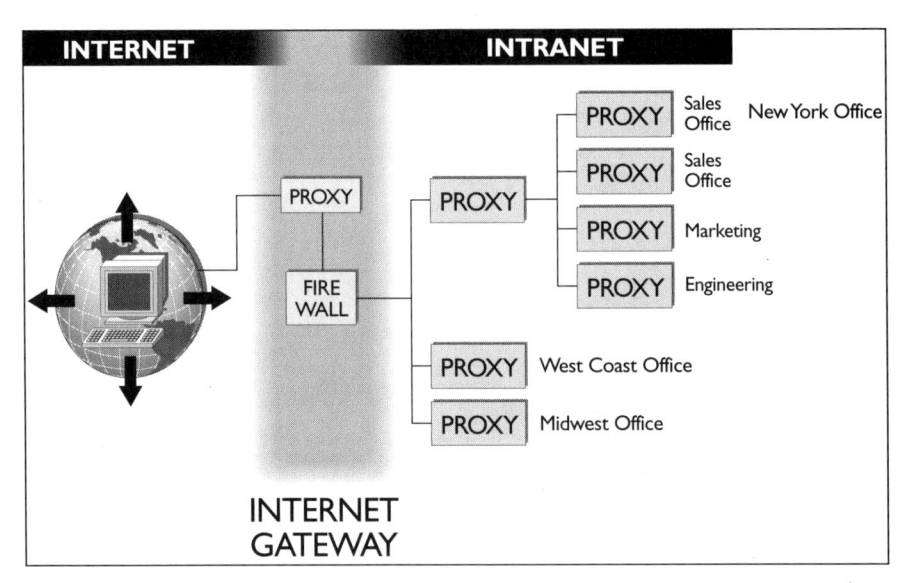

Figure 11-1 A combination of proxy servers and a firewall will provide security for your intranet.

A *firewall* is a computer system that sits between your intranet and the Internet beyond. The firewall has two functions: blocking traffic that you don't want on your intranet, and mediating and tracking the traffic that you do want. The idea is that the more you can keep your intranet insulated from outsiders, the less chance there is of trouble.

You can build your firewall from freeware, or buy the latest and greatest software from specialists. You could put one together in a week at no expense (other than skull sweat), or you could take more than a month and spend more than

$100,000. The new, hot (you should pardon the expression) firewalls are increasingly user friendly, with graphical interfaces and fine-grain controls for determining what data is and isn't allowed through.

Though firewalls tend to slow down that traffic, they don't have to be obtrusive. A good firewall is rather like a polite Swiss customs agent who asks gently if you happen to have anything that you might wish to declare. A poor firewall, on the other hand, is more like brutish border guard who delights in strip searching innocent tourists.

Checkpoint Charlie

Firewalls really do function as customs agents. They stop each data packet and piece of information traveling into your intranet from the wider Internet. Firewalls provide a checkpoint where visitors have their credentials examined and are then granted or denied admittance. A firewall will examine names, application types, Internet addresses, and other characteristics and compare them to criteria established by you. Packets that pass the comparison test are allowed through. The rest are bounced.

Firewalls go about their jobs in a couple of ways. Under the packet-filtering scheme, a router (acting like a traffic cop) examines each incoming packet and checks its source, destination, or address. Under packet filtering, specific data types are barred. In other words, you have to specify what packets are *not* allowed through. This makes them easy to control, but also relatively easy to crack.

Application gateways work the opposite way. Data from specific types of applications only (such as e-mail or FTP) can pass through this type of firewall. Application gateways are considered more secure, but they're higher maintenance — each time you want to add a new application, your network manager has a sizeable task on his or her hands.

Proxy servers are probably the most complicated firewalls, but they certainly are the most secure. A proxy server does just as its name implies; it acts as a proxy for internal clients, listening to data requests and forwarding them to Internet servers outside the firewall. Think of a proxy server as one of those bright office kids you send out for coffee so you don't have to go yourself. Because no incoming traffic ever goes onto the intranet directly, proxy servers provide some of the best network security available. They also make it easy to log all transactions, and trace any trouble back to its source. Unfortunately, proxy servers frequently cause noticeable performance delays. But combined with a dedicated firewall, you'll have a more comprehensive security system.

TIP   It's the same old problem: When you install a firewall, you're trading performance for security. Is it worth it? Well, think how much faster you could drive if you didn't obey those pesky traffic lights. . . .

Listen, firewalls aren't the perfect solution. They're generally difficult to set up and maintain, because someone has to design and implement access policy. Also, a good firewall is going to create *more* work for your support staff, because it will keep a detailed record of all the Internet traffic flowing in either direction.

Firewalls don't offer complete security because they don't affect internal usage. If someone inside the company is bent on espionage or sabotage, they're already past the firewall and the system can't offer you any protection.

Data Encryption

If you really enjoy playing spy, the security measure for you is data encryption. Just like in the classic espionage stories, data encryption lets you pass coded messages back and forth across a network.

There are a couple of reasons for seeking data-encryption capabilities. The first is to prevent a third party from snitching information (e-mail, spreadsheet files, and so on) as they're passed along your intranet. If encryption keys are unique and kept confidential, then only the receiving party can decode your message successfully.

Second, a coded message can serve as authentication, a kind of caller ID for the Internet. A confidential message is guaranteed to be authentic if it comes in properly encrypted.

Today, you can equip all Internet servers and browsers with encryption technology so that every packet sent over the corporate intranet is encoded and readable by the intended recipient only. You can even lease encrypted lines from telephone providers, which is good news for remote users.

Don't Bug Me!

You've doubtless read about computer viruses, those nasty little programs that somehow sneak into your computer system and cause untold havoc. It should come as no surprise that the more your company uses the Internet, the more likely you are to come down with a case of the electronic flu. If you want to learn more about the latest viruses, you might start out at Yahoo!'s directory on computer security, shown in Figure 11-2. If you know the name of a specific virus, enter it in the search field and Yahoo! will find you information on it.

Very simply, computer viruses are programs that reproduce themselves and attach themselves to other codes without permission. They are almost always damaging to the computer system that contracts them. Simple viruses may copy themselves over and over until they devour all their disk space. Others, when triggered, may delete all *.exe* files, including the virus itself. According to one survey, more than 70 percent of businesses suffer some kind of financial loss due to computer viruses.

The good news is, catching a computer virus is kind of like catching a real virus — you have to come in contact with someone who already infected. Viruses have traditionally been contracted through the medium of removable storage; infected floppy disks or tapes were passed from user to user, and when the files they contained were copied to a PC's hard drive, the virus was passed along as well. In fact, this is still probably the most common way of contracting a computer virus. (It was and is possible to introduce a computer virus directly into a computer by entering it on a keyboard. But it's a lengthy and difficult process — almost the equivalent of designing a true virus by genetic engineering.)

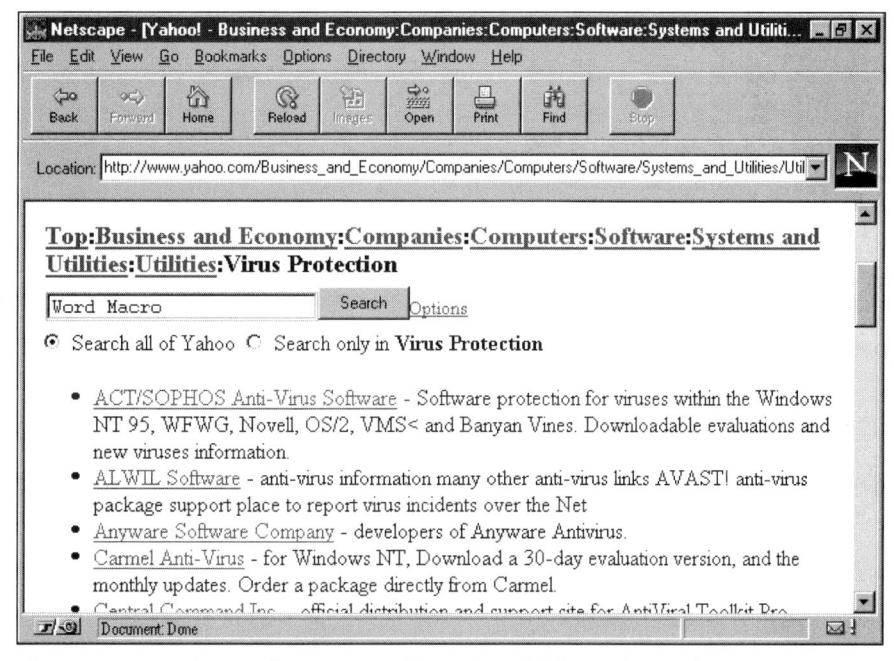

Figure 11-2 Yahoo!'s directory provides updated information on known viruses, with links to specific resources. Text and artwork are copyright 1997 by YAHOO!, INC. All rights reserved. YAHOO! and the YAHOO! logos are trademarks of YAHOO!, Inc.

Unfortunately, the Internet has made it much easier for your systems to "catch cold." There are hundreds of thousands of files out there available for download, from White Papers (presumably unbiased studies on a particular product or technology) to the latest in shareware games. And each of these files could contain a computer virus.

There's hope, though. There are antivirus packages out there; software that will sort through the files on a disk, detect viruses or other questionable programs, and "scrub" the disk clean. The difficulty is making sure the packages are used regularly by every user. Every client computer should be loaded with antivirus software, and it should be part of the computer's boot-up routine. Figure 11-3 shows Norton Anti-Virus options for scanning files.

In the past, firewalls weren't much help with viruses, because while they were tops at detecting known patterns, there were just too many ways a virus could be designed to stop them. But some of today's firewall providers are catching on, and licensing antivirus software to be run as part of the firewall routine. The big drawback is, as you might imagine, it takes time to read and scrub all those messages as they arrive.

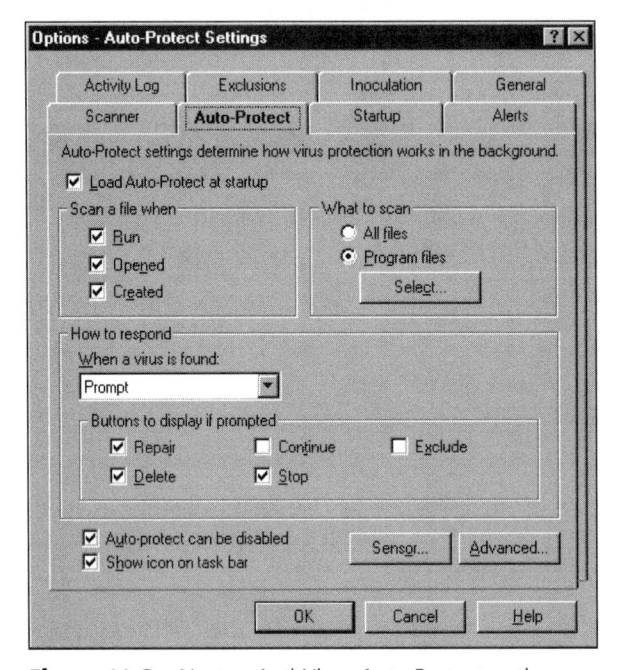

Figure 11-3 Norton Anti-Virus Auto-Protect options

TIP You know how you used to be afraid of catching something from a toilet seat? Well, your fear of catching something from e-mail is about as logical. The best word we've gotten to date is that there's no way to catch a virus by just reading an e-mail itself. Viruses propagated in this manner are passed through the attachments found frequently with e-mail. So go ahead and read your junk mail! Just don't open any attachments.

On the Road Again

You have spent a lot of time and effort securing your intranet. You've set up firewalls, encryption, and passwords so secure that a flea couldn't climb in without your noticing. But we forgot to mention remote users.

According to some estimates, more than 10 million people telecommute to the office at least part of the time. Those folks want access to the corporate intranet, even though you've just done your best to make sure that no outsider can. (Stop banging your head against the wall. You'll chip the paint.)

> **More than 10 million people telecommute to the office, and will want access to the corporate intranet.**

Most often, remote users use their modems to call a network server. Their mobile device pretends it's a local network client. With the proper log-in and password, the telecommuter can work just as he or she does from the office (except for the ponderously slow modem hookup, of course).

That's great for the user, but it's a headache for the network administrator. The network server doesn't know anything about this "new" client device, and none of the onsite security measures are in effect. Not only that, you don't even know if the line is secure!

There are a couple of things you can do to improve this condition. First, the firewall you put in place to protect you from outsiders can be used to screen remote users, too. You just have to configure your firewall correctly. You might, however, have to limit the remote user's access to some sensitive information.

We mentioned earlier that data encryption can be used for user authentication. With an advanced encryption algorithm or chip, you should be able to "tag" every remote user — the same way they do endangered species on *Wild Kingdom*.

Or, you could instigate dial-back techniques. When the user wants to telecommute, he or she calls the network from the remote location. But instead of logging in, he asks the network to call him back. The server does so — at a prearranged telephone number. The fact that a computer answers that number is validation of the user's identity.

BONUS

Keep up with Hackers, Viruses, and Other Foes

Nothing's harder than trying to keep up with the changes in the network security area. But we've found a number of sources that will keep you in the loop. Here are a few of them:

Publications

- *Network World*: One of the past masters, *Network World* has been covering networks forever. It's not dedicated to intranets, but it's sure to cover any breaking stories in fine detail.
- *LAN Times*: A biweekly publication dedicated to Local Area Networks, it frequently carries intranet and security-related stories.
- *Web Week*: A newer, sassier trade publication that, like *Network World*, covers a lot more than just intranets. But the paper likes to be the first to break stories.
- *Intranet Journal*: An online publication dedicated to all things intranet. We especially recommend Soundings, a moderated newsgroup. It's full of helpful folks who can answer most of your questions — and, because it's moderated, there is almost no advertising! Check it out at:
  http://www.intranetjournal.com

Web Sites

There are dozens of Web sites on intranet security issues. These are a few that struck our fancy, for one reason or another. Be careful; many Web sites (including some of the following examples) are trying to sell you something, and they may not be completely objective.

- **Computer Virus Alert Page**
  http://www.antivirus.com/alert.html

  This site has a fairly comprehensive list of specific computer viruses and their symptoms.

- **System and Network Security Links**
  http://www.mc2-csr.com/~lglaze/security.html

This site offers an excellent selection of links to other sources, including several from the seamy underbelly of computing.

- **Virus Bulletin Home Page**
  http://www.virusbtn.com

This is the Home page of a monthly technical journal on developments. It's an excellent academic resource.

- **Firewall Product Overview**
  http://www.access.digex.net/~bdboyle/firewall.vendor.html

A roundup of existing firewall products, it features links to many of the vendors, as well as some product comparison.

- **National Computer Security Association**
  http://www.ncsa.com

A good resource for general network security information, NCSA is designing computer security certification strategies.

Usenet Groups

In today's digital age, Usenet groups may be your best source for up-to-the-minute information. The following list isn't exhaustive, but it will give you a place to start.

CAUTION Most of these sites aren't moderated, meaning that there's no one screening the messages. Generally, we approve of this free flow of ideas, but it does mean that newsgroups are full of rumor, innuendo, and junk mail.

Never gone Usenet surfing? It's a rather free-form digital bulletin board that literally spans the world. Ardent Usenet fans consider it an network unto itself, separate from the Internet.

You can probably dive into a directory of Usenets from the home page of your Internet Service Provider.

WEB PATH For a good description of Usenet and how to use it, visit the Big Dummy's Guide to the Internet at:
http://wwwpc.hrz.th-darmstadt.de/bdgtti/bdg_7.htm

- alt.security.pgp: A newsgroup dedicated to encryption issues
- cern.security.unix: From CERN, the home of the World Wide Web, this group discusses security issues relating to the Unix operating system (don't forget, Unix is the backbone of an intranet).

- comp.virus : This newsgroup dedicated to computer viruses is full of infighting, but has important news and rumor faster than almost any other source.
- comp.security.misc: Friendly folk here, but there's a relatively high noise-to-news ratio.
- comp.lang.java.security: A quite specific newsgroup dedicated to the challenges Java brings to the Internet table. Quite hardheaded, the posters here are capable of head-banging, too.
- comp.risks: A newsgroup with information about risks to the public in computers and related systems

Summary

This chapter covered security issues for your intranet, including:

Ways to secure your intranet

Safeguarding your data by backing up all of your files

How Internet access can be a security threat, and what you can do about it

How a firewall can protect your intranet

Methods for battling computer viruses

PART THREE

ADVANCED INTRANET FEATURES

THIS PART CONTAINS THE FOLLOWING CHAPTERS

CHAPTER **12** TRAINING AND SUPPORT

CHAPTER **13** INTEGRATING ADDITIONAL SERVICES

CHAPTER **14** AUDIO AND VIDEO CONFERENCING

CHAPTER **15** EXPANDING YOUR INTRANET TOOLBOX

CHAPTER **16** MAKING YOUR INTRANET ORGANIC

When you're ready to expand your intranet, there are several additional features you can add — and the list keeps growing. You can also use your intranet to provide various types of training and support.

This part covers adding services such as collaboration, discussion groups, calendars, access to legacy data, news servers, and extranets; audio and video conferencing; and expanding your toolbox with tools such as Java, ActiveX, and Shockwave. Finally, we'll look at how to get feedback from your users so you can continually meet their information needs.

BOOK SALES INFO FLIES OVER AN INTRANET

A book publisher with 300 sales reps nationwide was distributing a weekly sales report of 200 pages, shipped by UPS. Reps complained, because information was usually a week old by the time it arrived in Peoria. In addition, reps estimated that they each spent three hours per week sorting through the one standard report to get the information they needed. Textbook, trade, children's, and reference book sales were mixed together, while each rep was responsible for only one category based on selling channels.

Last year, the field reps were liberated with the debut of an e-mail system and laptop computers, getting electronic files of the same report. The company chose Adobe Acrobat as the standard file format, converting pages from the proprietary sales management system. This made information current to the day — and somewhat searchable — but it still required rep time to repackage the information into a useful format.

One Web-surfing rep approached the VP of sales about an intranet, citing the flexibility of information retrieval and postings, and the sharing of information among reps as benefits not available under the current system. Reps could interact with the system instead of just being recipients. They could share new information on competing products so their colleagues could access and act on that new data quickly. In addition, the production department could post early proofs of the books, so that sales reps could access the material and show it to customers with an online demo or local printing. The new process could save shipping costs and time getting new products out into the customers' hands.

This year, the company has implemented a companywide intranet containing all these features, and it's still growing with input from the field sales team. New modules, including desktop video conferencing, are being considered for implementation this year. As for the Web-surfing rep . . . well, she's now Webmaster of the intranet.

CHAPTER TWELVE
TRAINING AND SUPPORT

IN THIS CHAPTER YOU LEARN THESE KEY SKILLS

USING YOUR INTRANET AS A TRAINING TOOL
PAGE 188

QUIZZING YOUR STAFF TO IDENTIFY WHAT THEY
KNOW — AND DON'T KNOW   PAGE 191

FINDING TOOLS TO CREATE YOUR TRAINING
PROGRAMS   PAGE 192

TEACHING PEOPLE TO USE UNIQUE ELEMENTS OF
YOUR INTRANET   PAGE 195

SETTING UP A SUPPORT SYSTEM   PAGE 197

Training for Your Intranet

You've probably heard that intranets are "no brainers" when it comes to training users. After all, it's all within a Web browser, and your ten-year-old has been doing that for months. But wait: Investing in a training program will return substantial dividends, both immediately and long term.

Because the complexity of intranets ranges dramatically, from simple information-sharing sources to complex systems interlaced with database queries to outside systems, your training needs will vary. If you create a flexible and modular system, your training program will grow comfortably alongside your intranet.

Computers as Teachers

Your intranet can be a vital educational tool within your organization, both for teaching your people how to use the intranet and for other areas of the company as well. Think of it as a new medium enabling ongoing instruction, anytime, anywhere.

There are online training resources that offer instruction over the Web, including DigitalThink and Street Technologies. Both companies will also develop custom training modules for use on your intranet, on virtually any topic you need.

WEB PATH

Visit DigitalThink at:
http://www.digitalthink.com

Visit Street Technologies at:
http://www.streetinc.com

DigitalThink uses the school metaphor consistently. This includes a Locker page that contains all of your enrolled courses and necessary materials, as shown in Figure 12-1. Students can participate in Chats, as shown in Figure 12-2, to share information with or pose questions to people simultaneously online. It's a virtual classroom in which all participants can share and collaborate, either as a group or individually. To add to the sensation of instructor-led courses, DigitalThink has audio clips of teachers throughout the site.

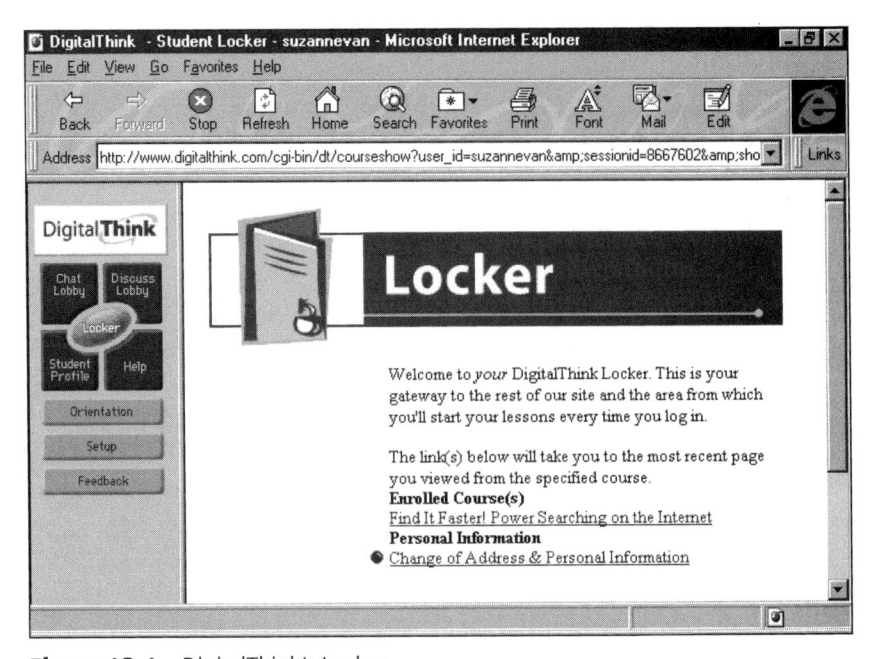

Figure 12-1 DigitalThink's Locker

Copyright 1997 DigitalThink, Inc.

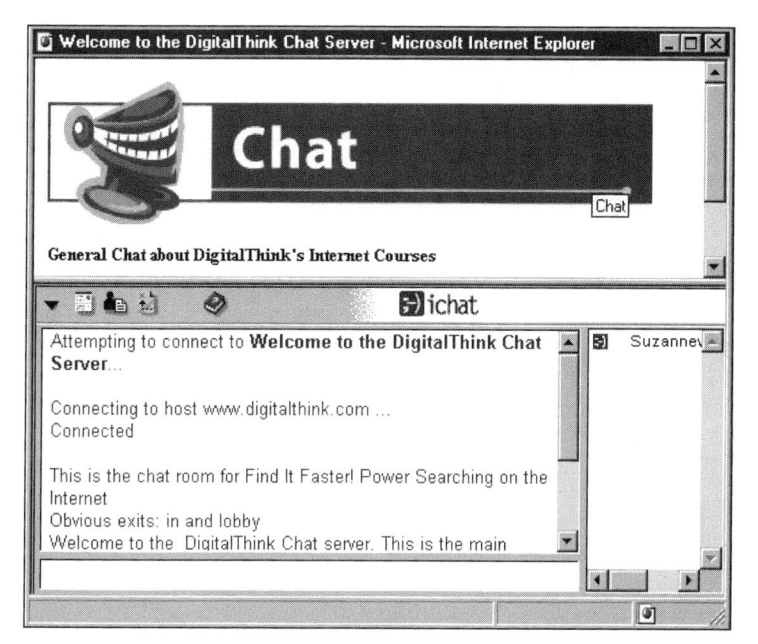

Figure 12-2 DigitalThink's Chat

Copyright 1997 DigitalThink, Inc.

DigitalThink courses are modular, so students learn at their own pace. Also, the progress is tracked, so students can return to their last location easily. Courses include links to additional resources online, search engines to get to information directly, side trips to further explain details, exercises to tap into the interactive capabilities of the digital medium, quizzes to monitor understanding, and so on. Figure 12-3 shows a quiz for a free demo course on "Power Searching on the Internet." Figure 12-4 shows an exercise from the same course.

Think about the uses of this new learning technology for your organization: how to use the intranet training, other computer software training, sales training, new hire orientation, distributing details on new products, budget preparation techniques, and so on.

Training for Use of the Intranet

Use the intranet to teach the intranet. With a combination of organized lessons, online tutorials, and classroom instruction, this tool is a learning mechanism for itself. Consider, for example, the popular Tip of the Day feature that's found in Windows 95, most Microsoft products, and others. You're spoon-fed a little bit of information each day. Even die-hard technologists can learn something new that saves time or makes working in the digital world a bit more rewarding. If you build in tidbits, people will nibble constantly.

Depending on the technological savvy of your people, you might want to launch general use of your intranet with some classroom instruction, but also spread that out over time.

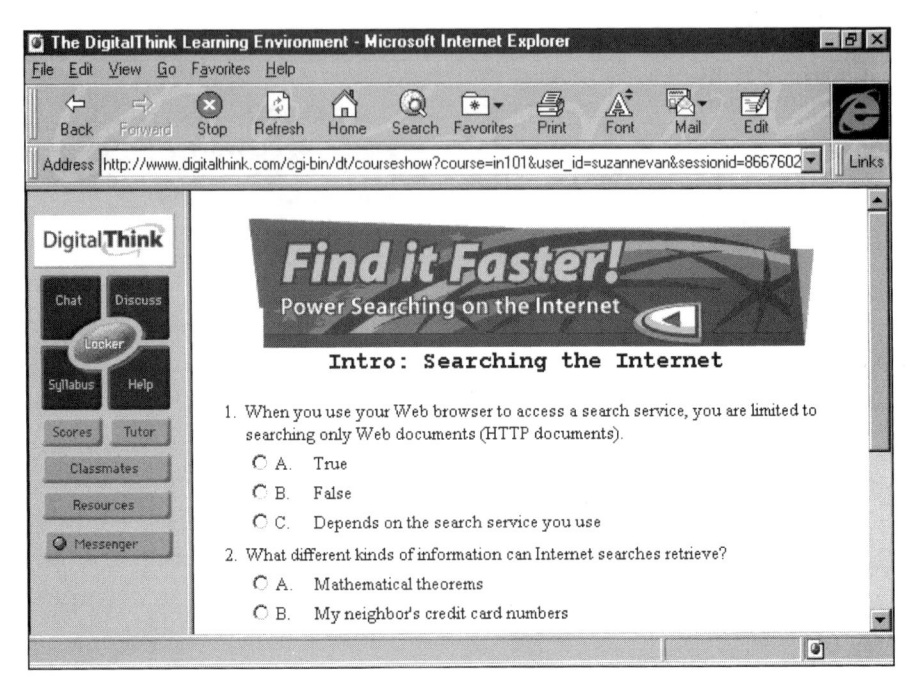

Figure 12-3 A sample quiz from DigitalThink's "Power Searching on the Internet"

Copyright 1997 DigitalThink, Inc.

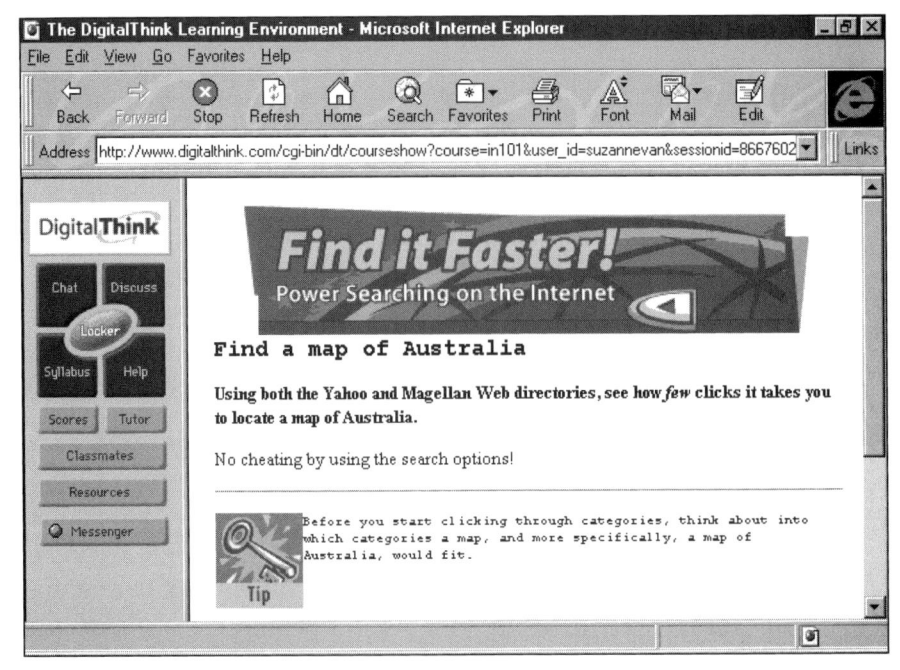

Figure 12-4 A sample exercise from DigitalThink's "Power Searching on the Internet"

Copyright 1997 DigitalThink, Inc.

TIP Back to the limited attention span concept: People can absorb new information in a training environment for about two hours a day. After that, they're fried and more likely to be worrying about the work piled up on their desks. Spread out training over several days; better yet, several weeks. Your users will be able to implement what they've learned between sessions, they'll probably have constructive questions, and they'll retain more from your efforts.

Training for Other Aspects of Your Operation

You can use your intranet for training needs in your organization well beyond using computers. Human resources training materials have been available on CD-ROM for several years, and these tools are now migrating to the intranet. Consulting firms have used CD-ROMs to help employees keep pace with changes in audit, tax, and other consulting issues. But with an intranet, training materials can be updated faster and at a lower cost, and are available immediately to employees worldwide.

TIP Tools such as Macromedia's Shockwave enable integration of audio into training materials for your intranet. Combined with its Authorware application, you can integrate video, interactive quizzes, flexible navigation, and more. But, Authorware isn't easy to learn or use — unless you plan a large and ongoing training program, you're probably better off hiring out the task.

WEB PATH For a great online resource of training ideas and solutions, events, and a national directory of training centers, visit:
http://www.trainingnet.com/

It's Quiz Time

How can you determine who knows what? And in the case of senior management, how can you determine this and still keep your job? The effectiveness of your training program will depend greatly on the openness of your potential trainees.

You have several options:

* Create a formal, paper-based survey. It's paper, it's comfortable, and you'll probably get results.

- Create and distribute an online survey. It's digital, easily calculated, and scheduled, because all the data is already entered.
- Conduct personal surveys. It's a time-consuming but often much-appreciated approach, especially with upper management. When constructing a survey, create separate sections for job functions or types. That will enable you to schedule training for groups with similar jobs, and then into subgroups of similar skill levels. Ask users to rate themselves as novice, intermediate, or proficient in the following areas:
    - Basic Windows skills, including file management, and the taskbar
    - Basic e-mail skills, including file attachments
    - Browser use, including navigation techniques, storing and printing documents
    - Custom features of your intranet (for instance, sales tracking reports)
    - Preparing electronic documents for the intranet from basic office applications like word processing, spreadsheet, database, and presentation software
    - Audio and video conferencing techniques

TIP You might use the survey for intranet skills as an opportunity to study overall computer skills in the company. Add another section or two to assess basic computer skills, e-mail skills, word processing, or other tasks.

Intranets 101

There are many alternatives for training, from the full-service, company training center to computer-based training (known as CBT) over your intranet. IBT (*Internet-* and *intranet-based training*) has just begun and promises substantial improvements in how we teach and learn.

Your intranet will really be just the distribution medium, and your current training programs can be transferred. The degree of complexity depends on the current format of your materials — are they on paper, electronic, some combination? How current are they?

The benefit of distribution on the intranet is that the HTML-based standard can be viewed by anyone with a Web browser. CBT creators have locked companies into their proprietary formats for many years. Now you can access, modify, and distribute materials easily.

A chunk of your training can be bought ready made: how to use the PC, network, e-mail, and other basic functions. These materials are available as books, videos, and online tools.

CAUTION Look out for copyright issues! You may only have one-time rights to use training materials from an outside source, and you may be prohibited from updating the materials, or even copying them — regardless of whether it's on paper or in a digital file. Know your rights before you duplicate or modify any material from outside your organization. Even better, know what rights you're getting before you buy training materials.

X-REF Entire training program on paper? Don't panic. See Chapter 5 for details on converting paper-based documents into electronic formats.

Books, Video, CD-ROMs

The number of books, videos, and CD-ROMs for computer training can be daunting. Your choice will depend largely on presentation of material, style, and preferred medium. Again, there are numerous sources to review materials and determine what works best for you.

Some people prefer books — something tangible to sit on their desk for reference. Some of your eager staff members may actually read the entire book; put these people in an important role for your intranet. Other people prefer to watch a video, either in the office or at home, although sometimes it's harder to apply what they've seen if there's a time gap between the viewing and actually doing. Then there are CD-ROMs, which have the advantage of taking up very little space and often include sound and video to propel the learning process. A lot of people like the glitz of the multimedia world; just be sure they're learning what they need to function successfully on the intranet.

Online Instruction

Online instruction tools are available from many sources on the Web. Some are actually purchased via 800 numbers (and then the product is shipped to you), and others are downloadable right off the Web with proper payment.

You should experiment with the online tutorials before buying large scale. Many training material companies will provide free samples for testing, which you can loan out physically with a library-style checkout system, or post them on your intranet with a set number of simultaneous users. Remember, you need to buy the applications before rolling out your program.

SIDE TRIP

COMPUTER BOOKS ABOUND

It's rather ironic that the business of computers, the world in a digital format, have created a huge book publishing market. From simple beginner titles to introduce new users to the basics, to complex bibles that include every technical detail, there's a book to fill your thirst for knowledge.

You can either peruse the local bookstore for offerings, or jump on the Internet and do online searches for subjects, authors, or titles that interest you. Amazon.com and BookZone are the largest online booksellers. A simple search for books on the subject of Netscape will reveal over 70 titles, and you can click through to see book summaries and helpful review comments posted by other readers, the author, or the publisher.

If Amazon doesn't have any titles on your topic, say Training for Intranets, you can try its Personal Notification Service to receive an e-mail when a book on that subject becomes available.

For a comprehensive list of the computer training books available, visit Amazon or BookZone at:

```
http://www.amazon.com/
http://www.bookzone.com
```

Classroom Instruction

Classroom instruction is the most complex and expensive proposition, but if you're working with a large organization and a hearty intranet, it may be the best solution. Keep in mind you need fully loaded workstations, a segment of the network to minimize disruptions to a live system, video projection equipment, and a room or two to house it all. You'll need instructors and someone to manage the facility and scheduling.

On the upside, your people can interact, ask questions, and refocus the class as needed to get the most information quickly. If they collaborate, they'll come up with new ideas and ways of using the intranet just because they're exploring it together.

Alternatively, you can outsource the classroom training to one of the many national services that provide the same curriculum in multiple cities, using their own equipment and space. It's a viable option if you foresee a large-scale but one-time training program.

SIDE TRIP

AUDIO AND VIDEO STREAMING

First there was text, then images, then sound, and finally video — all coming into our computers. But downloading and launching these files quickly became a drag, and we wanted everything in real time. Now we have it, in the form of *streaming* audio and video, which means we can see and hear in real time through our browsers.

You can run a demonstration in one window, with a voice-over in another; you can show a slide presentation in one window, while listening to the speaker; or you can broadcast your next annual meeting live to all your associates via the intranet — if your computer is powerful enough to display these memory-intensive multimedia formats.

Audio and video streaming is something you need to experience online to sense how much both can heighten the training experience. Visit Vxtreme at:

http://www.vxtreme.com/

Intranets 201

The second part of your training program will be to teach people to use the elements unique to your intranet, whether it's your company phone directory, queries to the sales database, the multisite video conferencing system, or other features. There are a number of tools available to expedite the learning process.

You can use a basic word processor, and of course export the text to HTML for publication on the intranet as shown in Figure 12-5. If your staff uses Microsoft Word, the add-on Internet Assistant is an easy way to create nice-looking documents that are ready to publish on the intranet.

You can use a more sophisticated page makeup program like PageMaker to create prettier pages with indexes, tables of contents, and bookmarks. You could then export the PageMaker files into Adobe Acrobat for publication on your intranet. Or you can use more customized multimedia tools like Macromedia Authorware or Director to create animations and interactive sequences.

WEB PATH For a demonstration of Macromedia's Authorware and Director, visit its Web site at:

http://www.macromedia.com/

TRAINING AND SUPPORT

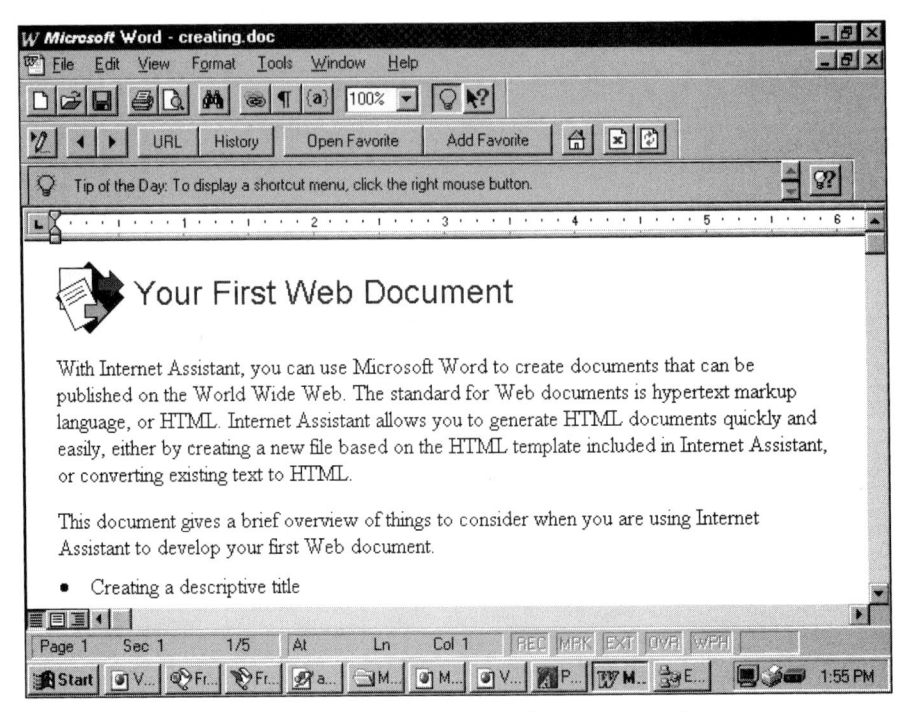

Figure 12-5 Microsoft Word's Internet Assistant is an easy way for your users to create documents for an intranet.

SIDE TRIP

TEST PREP TOOL

Stanford Testing Systems, a company that emphasizes SAT prep materials, is the publisher of IBTauthor, a tool for creating Internet and intranet-based training courses. IBTauthor can create lessons, multiple-choice questions, fill-in field answers, or clickable image questions.

IBTauthor is fully customizable, so your users will see only your material, not the shell provided by IBT. Modules can be fun, interactive, and easy to use.

To experience this yourself, test yourself with a sample course, or download a free trial version of the software at:

    http://ibt.testprep.com/

Creating Your Rescue Squad

You need to support your users as they embark on a new style of working. There will be those crisis moments when a report must be in the hands of a manager in two minutes, an e-mail must get to the Vice President before his 9 a.m. meeting, or the company phone directory becomes corrupted again. For this, you need two types of support: the technical emergency pros from a help desk or a similar centralized source, and the local experts who can see, sort, and manipulate the content quickly.

The help desk is best situated in a core IS area, in order to troubleshoot any technical emergency. It should handle software configuration and support the server, all hardware, and the network (including connecting individual workstations to the network).

After that, cultivate the local experts. They're closest to the operations of the department or segment of the company, they know the information that resides on your intranet, and can quickly become sharp enough to sort through the intranet to find the critical information. Give the local experts the tools they need: time for training and learning new software, and recognition for their contribution.

BONUS

Top Five Skills Your Staff Needs

Your users need the following skills to effectively use an intranet:

* File management: Save, retrieve, and most importantly find documents, as shown in Figure 12-6.
* Use e-mail: Open messages, respond, create Address Books, attach files.
* Make bookmarks or shortcuts to return to the places most useful to them, as shown in Figure 12-7.
* Construct effective search queries, like using a search page in Figure 12-8.
* Create material that is easily posted on the intranet, to ensure contributions from all areas of your organization.

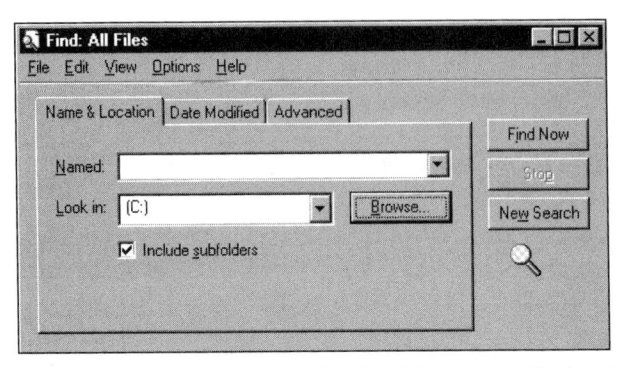

Figure 12-6 Your users need to be able to use a Find tool, like this Windows 95 Find dialog box.

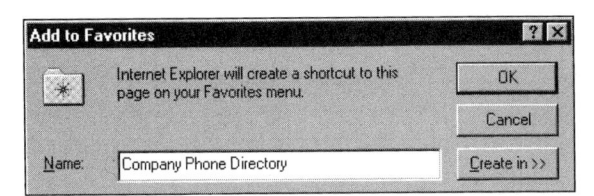

Figure 12-7 Adding URLs or local pages is easy with Microsoft's Add to Favorites in Internet Explorer.

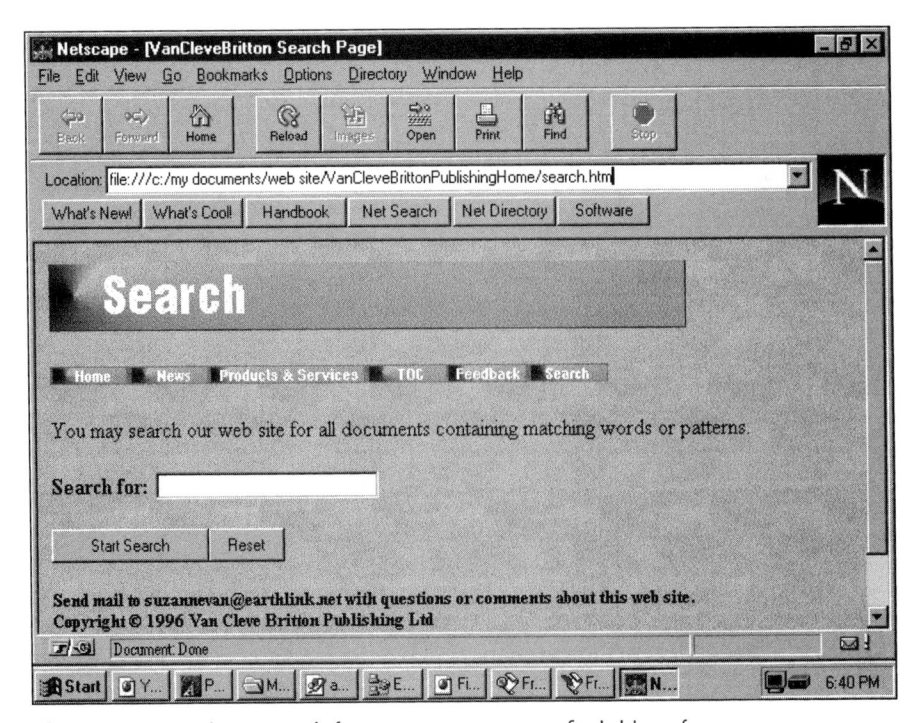

Figure 12-8 Using a search feature, your users can find things fast.

198   ADVANCED INTRANET FEATURES

Summary

In this chapter, you learned the following:

Training is important, even though an intranet may seem very simple at face value. Use your intranet to train people how to use it.

Your intranet can be used to train people both on technology and other learning needs for your organization.

By surveying your staff's computer knowledge, you can create training programs that better fit their skills and needs.

There are a number of tools to expedite the creation of training materials, both for simple print distribution and more complex interactive tools.

Setting up a support system is critical, for both technical and information needs.

CHAPTER THIRTEEN

INTEGRATING ADDITIONAL SERVICES

IN THIS CHAPTER YOU LEARN THESE KEY SKILLS:

INTEGRATING GROUPWARE INTO YOUR INTRANET
PAGE 202

INCORPORATING E-MAIL INTO YOUR INTRANET
PAGE 212

ACCESSING LEGACY DATA FROM OTHER COMPUTER SYSTEMS   PAGE 214

EXPANDING TO AN EXTRANET   PAGE 216

AUTOMATICALLY DISTRIBUTING INFORMATION
PAGE 216

After you decide on the basic framework of your intranet, you'll want to consider the additional services your users could access from this one consistent source. Technology tools are heading toward across-the-board compatibility, regardless of type of computer, operating system, or software. Your intranet can bridge that gap for many services now, including integrating groupware functions previously reserved for dedicated systems such as Lotus Notes.

You can integrate critical communications tools such as e-mail, both in-house and via the Internet. You can collaborate with others using online discussion groups or chat rooms.

There's the matter of all your critical information locked in a proprietary system managed by IS. You can access a lot of legacy system information (*legacy* being a term for data in a large-scale and often proprietary system managed by your IS department) with hooks from your intranet.

Finally, once you have a terrific intranet up and running, you're going to want to share your success with others: vendors, partner companies, customers, and so on. This leads us to the concept of extranets, which we will discuss later in this chapter.

Groupware Everywhere

Groupware can include any application that seeks to enhance collaboration among people. It can be a digital library of corporate documents with indexing, discussion groups that enable people to share ideas on specific topics, e-mail with more structure than your average e-mail software, extensive modules of customizable applets to meet the demands of your business, and more. One groupware application, Open Text's Livelink Intranet, is accessible through a Web browser. Figure 13-1 shows Open Text's Livelink Intranet demo available on the Internet.

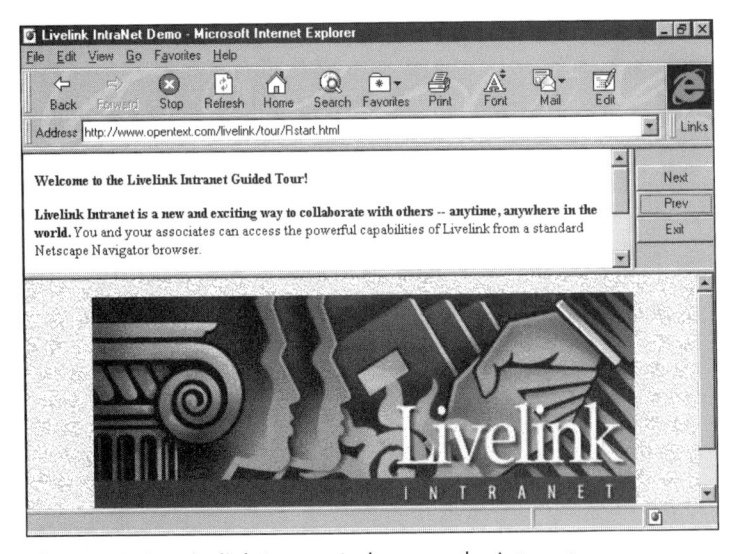

Figure 13-1 Livelink Intranet's demo on the Internet

WEB PATH Experience Livelink firsthand at the Open Text site:
http://www.opentext.com/

TIP The three buzzwords sometimes attached to groupware are *communication, collaboration,* and *coordination.* These are "the three Cs" representing messaging systems, team-based applications, and project management-type applications, respectively. Admittedly, the line between each of these is fuzzy, but effective groupware applications include elements of all three.

How's groupware different from your intranet? It's not very different at all, it's just committing your organization to one developer's suite of tools instead of the more open standards of Web-compatible solutions. Figure 13-2 shows e-mail from Livelink's Intranet, which may look different than your current e-mail software, but it does function in the same way and fulfill the same tasks. Figure 13-3 shows a document workflow map from Livelink, a feature that's found more often in groupware than an intranet.

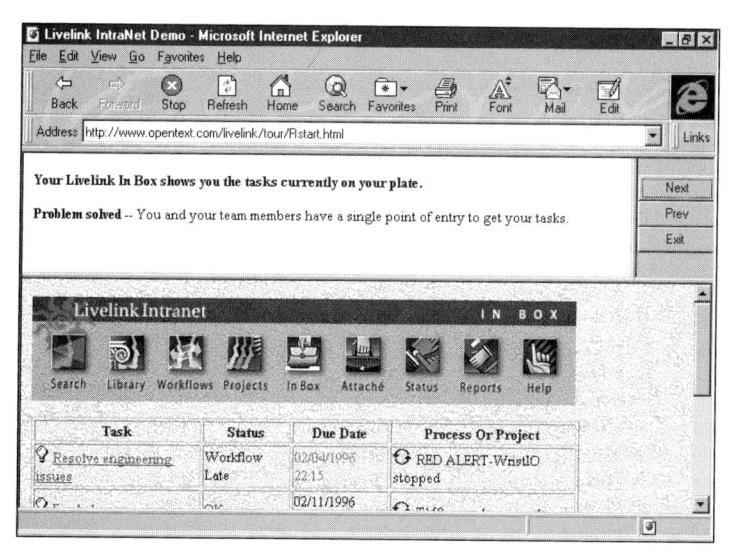

Figure 13-2 Livelink Intranet's Inbox

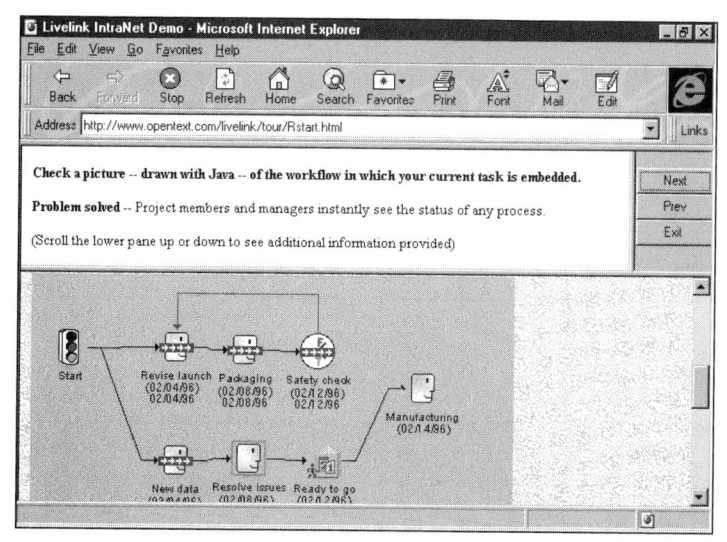

Figure 13-3 Livelink Intranet's document workflow

INTEGRATING ADDITIONAL SERVICES   **203**

Groupware is something of a religion; those who got on the wagon at the beginning with Lotus Notes, the first of the breed, are strong advocates of a dedicated groupware application. Lotus Notes is now Web enabled with Lotus Domino, which means companies that have dedicated substantial resources to Notes can migrate their information onto an intranet.

Companies just starting to use groupware often prefer tools that are Web savvy (and by extension intranet savvy), because they're designed for compatibility and extensibility. The major players in the groupware market are shown in Table 13-1. Visit their Web sites for additional information, and in some cases, free downloadable demos.

TABLE 13-1 Groupware Solutions

Application	Key Features/Comments	Web Site
LOTUS NOTES/DOMINO	Notes now contends with other Web-savvy products, now that Domino is available	www.lotus.com
MICROSOFT NETMEETING	Fits snugly with other Microsoft applications, like Office 97 and Exchange, the new e-mail server	www.microsoft.com
NETSCAPE SUITESPOT	Big on threaded discussions and conferencing	www.netscape.com
NOVELL GROUPWISE	Uses messaging strength to support discussions, document sharing	www.novell.com
OPEN TEXT LIVELINK	A documents and project-management application that is now Web savvy, good for large organizations, and includes several collaborative applications	www.opentext.com

Choosing a groupware application can mean faster setup time for your intranet, but you sacrifice some customization when you have to use built-in templates. The best approach is to make a list of features that you need the most in your intranet from the following list, and find the products that support your needs:

* Integrated e-mail with attachments and integrated page links
* Collaboration, including discussion and/or chat groups

- A detailed document management system
- A digital library of corporate documents with indexing capabilities
- Access to legacy data
- Access to existing groupware documents
- Access to outside nonemployee users, such as vendors and customers
- Ease of setup
- Ease of administration
- Internet connectivity, for grabbing news feeds, e-mail, and other information
- Applications development, for features you need that aren't integrated in the package

> **SIDE TRIP**
>
> ### INTRANETS IN A BOX
>
> When Lotus Notes, the granddaddy of groupware applications, decided to leave the proprietary world and join in Web browser accessibility, Lotus added a toolbox of modules for expediting intranet development. The Domino Action development system includes features such as:
>
> - Page templates, which can include corporate trademarks all linked together for easy updating (read mergers and acquisitions!)
> - Human resources modules: job postings, corporate policies, company profile
> - Customer/partner relationships (great for extranets): communication, registrations
> - Discussion databases
> - Document library
> - Products and services
> - Feedback and frequently asked questions (FAQs)
>
> Two additional features for Domino include Domino.Merchant, which handles sales transactions, and Domino.Service, an Electronic Data Interchange (EDI) type of capability to do things like handle help desk inquiries.

Netscape Communicator: A Web-based Groupware Solution

The race for Web-based groupware solutions has just begun, with new versions coming soon from most of the major software companies. To give you an idea of what groupware can do for your intranet, this section will explore Netscape Communicator, a multipart application to be available from Netscape in summer 1997. The product includes the components that are key in any groupware solution:

* **Netscape Navigator:** The core browser application, with new and improved interface, as shown in Figure 13-4.

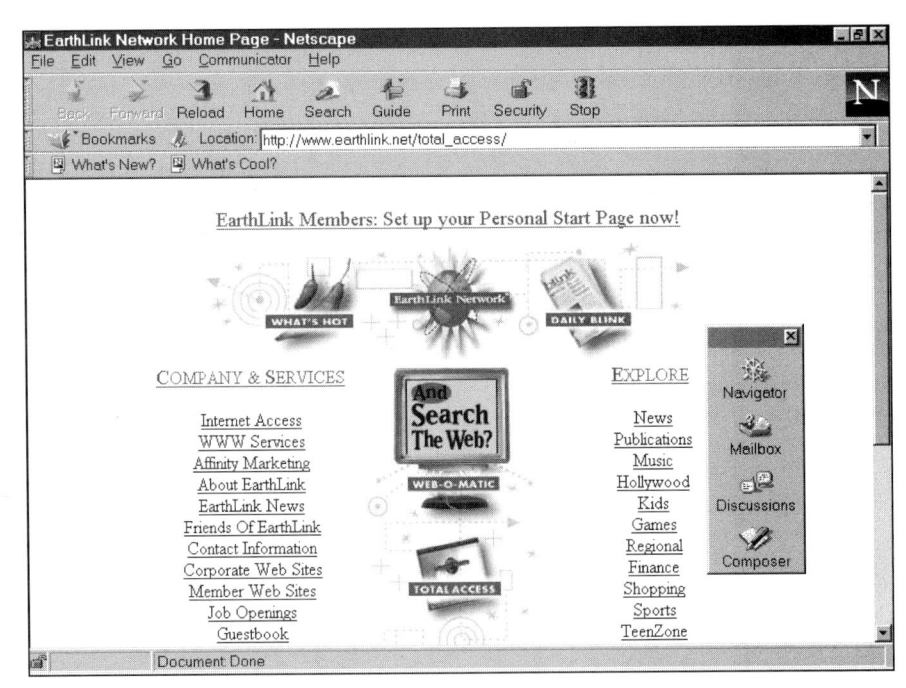

Figure 13-4 Netscape Navigator's new interface

* **Netscape Conference:** For creating conferences with multiple participants, primarily text-based for now, but with audio capabilities coming soon.

X-REF For details on Microsoft's Net Meeting, including robust audio and video conferencing features, see Chapter 14.

* **Netscape Composer:** A basic word processor that integrates seamlessly with the rest of the package. Think about it: No more waiting for

Microsoft Word to load, or tell you it's out of memory for unknown reasons. Composer, shown in Figure 13-5, provides the necessities of written communication.

* **Netscape Messenger:** E-mail with plenty of filing features for sorting, routing, and storing the ton of e-mail you receive daily. Figure 13-6 shows the new Netscape mail interface.

* **Netscape Collabra:** Managing discussion groups is important if you're going to benefit from them. Otherwise, you'll end up with piles of electronic information that is useless because of its sheer volume. Figure 13-7 shows the easy method for subscribing to a newsgroup. Figure 13-8 shows Netscape Communicator's navigation bar, which helps you navigate among the different elements of Communicator.

* **Netscape Netcaster:** Netcaster is a "push" distribution tool, so you can automatically distribute news and other important messages to your employees. The difference with push technology is that the employees do not have to actively seek out the information, and you can track what you've sent to whom as evidence of your communication.

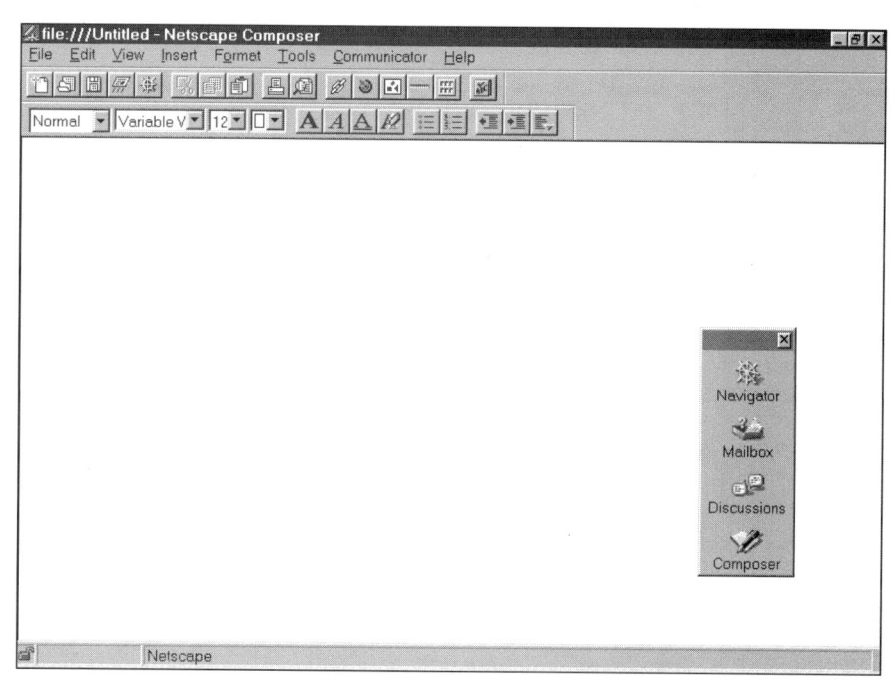

Figure 13-5 Netscape's Composer

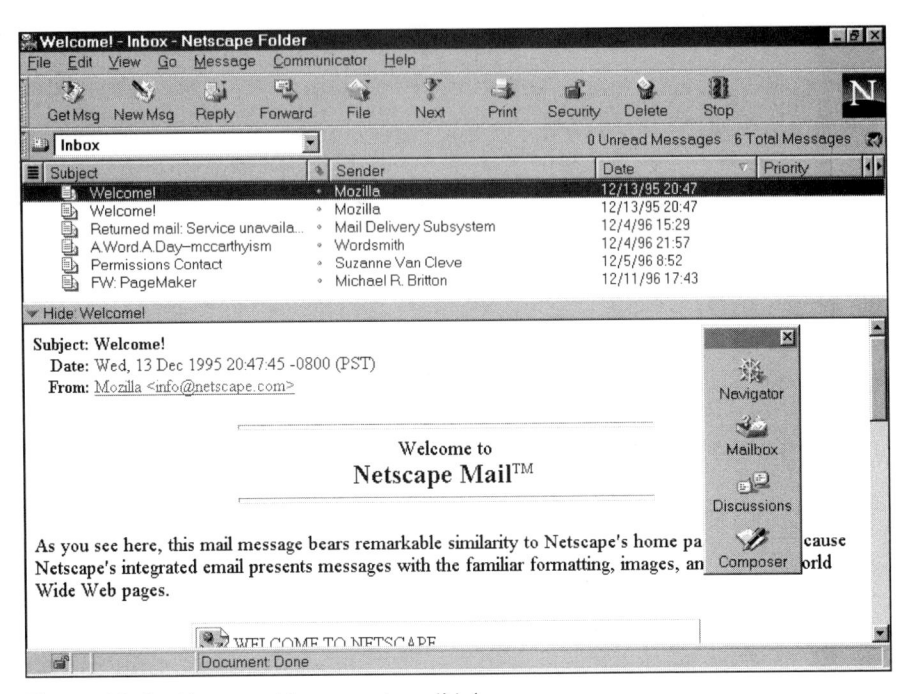

Figure 13-6 Netscape Messenger's mail inbox

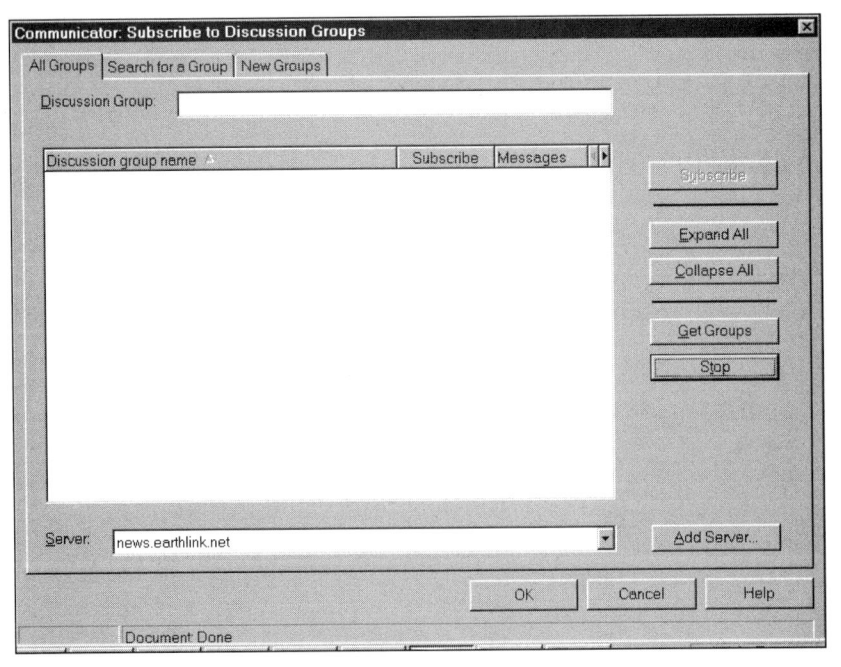

Figure 13-7 Subscribing to a newsgroup in Communicator

Figure 13-8 Netscape Communicator's navigation bar

In addition, Netscape is producing a "professional edition" that will include the following:

* **Netscape Calendar:** Finally, some standards are coming to calendaring applications so you can schedule meetings by checking your schedule, checking the schedules of your colleagues, and checking availability of room and equipment.
* **Netscape IBM Host On-Demand:** For integration with legacy systems, and access to information through a browser.
* **Netscape AutoAdmin:** Access privileges and other administration tasks for managing your groupware package.

Communicator includes a handy navigator bar so you can quickly move between the components of the groupware suite. You can essentially conduct all your necessary communication — e-mail, conferencing, discussion groups, an Internet phone call, Web surfing — all from the same interface. This lowers the learning curve for your users and means you can get an electronic information system implemented and in use much faster than proprietary systems. Properly managed, an integrated groupware suite can also cost you less in terms of system implementation, and ongoing maintenance.

Communicator also uses hierarchical folders for managing bookmarks, which your users will likely use to mark the pages of your intranet to which they will return often.

DYNAMIC HTML: THE NEXT GENERATION

Netscape Communicator features something called Dynamic HTML, which takes HTML-based content from a static page to a more interactive format. Dynamic HTML includes the new specifications for style sheets and JavaScript. The best part of Dynamic HTML is that all the activity takes place on your users' computers, which means a faster response and less network traffic.

Dynamic HTML includes definitions for positioning and layering elements, text, graphics, and applets by specifying x and y coordinates for that section of HTML. You can overlap images and text, and specify which element goes on which layer, adding more page make-up capabilities to HTML. Using JavaScript, you can animate and manipulate elements, and since it is HTML-based, anyone with a current Web browser can view the elements. (Remember the days when you had to distribute a copy of PowerPoint viewer so that everyone could read your presentation? Remember the hassle when the VP couldn't open the file? Well, this next generation of HTML provides a common denominator that anyone can use.)

DYNAMIC STYLE SHEETS: DEFINE IT ONCE, USE IT REPEATEDLY

Netscape Communicator includes dynamic style sheets, which means you can define colors and text sizes once, save those specs as a style sheet, and use it over and over. For example, you can create templates for employees to use for posting reports, memos, schedules, and the like, and keep a consistent look and user interface. There are two types of style sheets currently being evaluated by the World Wide Web Consortium (known as WC3), which is a "governing body" of sorts of key corporations who develop technology products. The style sheets being considered are Cascading Style Sheets (CSS1) and JavaScript-accessible Style Sheets. Dynamic style sheets are a subset of CSS1, and can be programmed using JavaScript. Say, for example, you want to know the user's browser window size before a page is downloaded to their computer. Using dynamic style sheets, you could set up an automatic query in JavaScript to evaluate the viewer's window size, and then display margins and fonts on the page by an automatic calculation for proportions.

Communicator also supports dynamic fonts, so users can view the exact font, not a default font specified in the browser. This eliminates the limitation of the Font Face tag, which can use fonts that your users have installed on their computers. However, the Font Face tag is still useful because it doesn't require an additional font to be downloaded.

DISCUSSION GROUPS: ANYTIME, ANYWHERE FORUMS TO SHARE IDEAS

With the Collabra tool of Communicator, you and/or your users can create discussion forums. You can reduce your responsibility, as well as the potentially large burden of managing discussion groups, by delegating moderation tasks to your users. And now, you can use meaningful discussion groups names, without having to link all the words together with dots in between. So if your employees want to gather in the digital way to gripe about status meetings, you can name the group Mindless Meetings R Us.

You can also quickly navigate through *threads*, that is, long streams of related ideas, comments, and thoughts from the various participants in the discussion. You and your users can set the rules for monitoring or ignoring threads, to more effectively manage the flow of information into your inbox.

MEETINGS AND MORE: FINALLY, COMPATIBLE CALENDARS

Digital calendars have been around for a few years, including programs such as Now Up to Date, Lotus Agenda, Microsoft Schedule, and Meeting Maker.

Individuals could plan their schedules, keep track of contacts, created To Do Lists, and so on, but sharing all this information across an organization was difficult. None of the calendaring, or personal information manager, programs were compatible — thus, the advent of HTML-based calendar applications such as Netscape's Calendar segment of Communicator.

What's Next in Groupware?

Groupware promises to evolve dramatically over the next year or two. Look for the following developments:

A merger between OS and browser. The next stage of HTML-based groupware will be a "merger" between the operating system (Windows, Macintosh, Unix) and the browser (Netscape Navigator, Microsoft Internet Explorer, and others). Browsers may soon be driving computers, creating a system that will enable a "push" application to take control of the computer and turn it into a front end for legacy system tasks.

Workflow management tools. Workflow diagramming is just the beginning; you'll be able to set up templates to forward and track documents within your organization. Combined with document management tools, you and your users can "check out" files, work on them, approve them, return them, and always know where things are. (Sure beats hunting through your entire organization looking for that one ad that needs multiple approvals.)

Applications development tools. With expansions on JavaScript, Java, CGI, and other automation tools, you and your users will be able to create custom "modules" to plug into your intranet at any time. Relying on prebuilt segments of code, you can plug them together to streamline a variety of tasks.

Industry leaders are saying that the groupware choices come down to Lotus, Microsoft, and Netscape, but it's too early to pick a winner in the race. The good news is standards are much more open than any genre of computer software in the past, and the real winner then becomes the users and those responsible for managing information.

Audio and video conferencing capabilities. Audio conferencing is becoming more mainstream, with the addition of sound cards, microphones, and speakers being affordable and functional. Bandwidth requirements for audio are acceptable, especially on an intranet with direct network connectivity. Audio conferencing software is simple to set up and use. Video conferencing is still in its infant stages, with expensive hardware requirements and serious bandwidth limitations, even on one local area network. However, the savings in cost and time associated with audio and video conferencing make it worth keeping and eye on in the next few years.

X-REF For more details on audio and video conferencing with Microsoft NetMeeting, see Chapter 14.

The tools will become more tightly integrated, more powerful, and easier to maintain with common standards in place. Groupware, and the whole idea of collaborative computing, will simply become the way we all work, and will be as much of a core business tool as the fax machine and voice mail are already today.

E-Mail: It's Worse Than Snail Mail

Electronic mail is becoming increasingly important in the modern office environment. Between e-mail, fax machines, and voice mail systems, it's possible to work for months with people without ever actually speaking to them. Implementing e-mail on an intranet isn't exactly trivial, but Internet technology can certainly handle the challenge . . . it's been designed to do it.

But on the downside, e-mail can pile up worse than the old-fashioned U.S. Post Office variety. Consider how easy it is for anyone to create a message, and then instantly zap it to one, ten, or hundreds of people with no additional effort on their part. No envelope addressing or stamp licking required!

TIP Teach e-mail etiquette to your intranet users. It's important for them to understand and appreciate the difference in impact between face-to-face communication and the written word. Something said in jest verbally is usually accompanied by a grin or a shrug that lets the receiver know it wasn't serious. People miss those cues in an e-mail message.

If you've got a network running now, you probably have e-mail of some sort like Lotus cc:Mail, one of the Microsoft mail applications, or other software. It may not work effectively (it seems most don't yet, due to overloads or poor connections), but you've got something in place. Linking your e-mail system to your intranet will bring you closer to having one consistent, compatible system: attachments and intranet page addresses can be easily integrated into your e-mail.

Linking your e-mail system to your intranet will bring you closer to having one consistent, compatible system.

To properly establish e-mail across an intranet, you may well need a dedicated server. Many recommend a PC clone, but that's sheer chauvinism, as an Apple or Unix engine would work just as well. In fact, for a larger network, you may need the power of a RISC workstation. The machine has to run the Simple Mail Transfer Protocol (SMTP) that communicates with other mail servers and — as its name strongly implies — simply transfers mail between them.

In putting together the mail system, you also need a Post Office Protocol (POP) server, though there's no reason it can't run on the same server running your SMTP software. That server communicates with the clients in your LAN, enabling them to read and send mail. Each desktop machine also needs a package that enables it to read and send mail. Most of the major browsers come with such a package, though.

SIDE TRIP

SCHEDULING

Until recently, anything that looked like a calendar on an intranet page required a lot of time and effort dabbling in HTML. The best you could do was get something that resembled a printed calendar, without any interactive features for querying other people for dates, or finding available conference rooms.

With new calendar tools targeted for the Internet and intranet, you can easily share your schedule with others. The details of your meetings and appointments can be accessed like any other hyperlink; double-clicking will take you to another page that can include a list of participants, proposed alternative dates and times for the meeting, location (city, building, conference room), media required (for audio and video conferencing), agendas, and any other pertinent documents attached.

Now Software's Up-to-Date Web Publisher lets you generate HTML-based calendars and contact lists automatically, complete with frame-based navigation. Other people can review your calendar or contact list using any Web browser, as shown below.

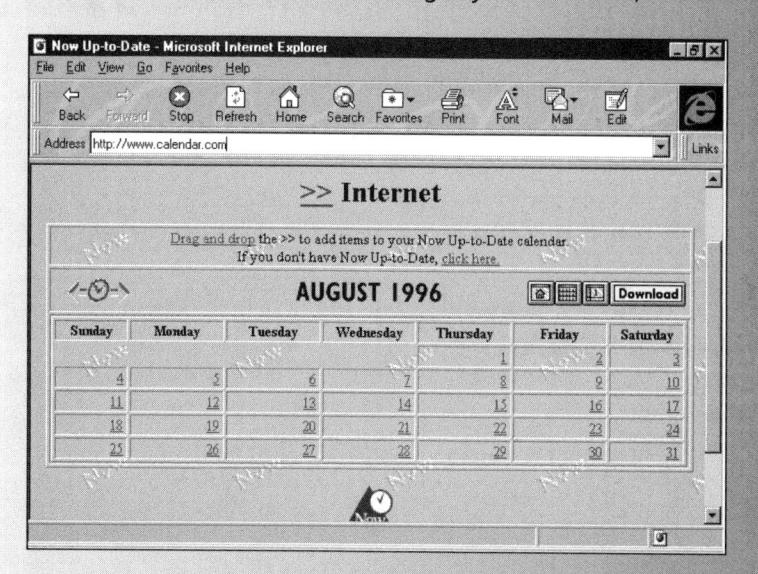

WEB PATH For a free downloadable demo of the Now Up-to-Date tool, visit:
http://www.nowsoft.com

INTEGRATING ADDITIONAL SERVICES **213**

There are any number of commercial e-mail packages available — and groupware applications usually have a built-in e-mail application. The commercial e-mail packages are usually more user-friendly when it comes to installation, configuration, and control; but in terms of capabilities, the only real difference we can think of is that the intranet mail system doesn't have a built-in user directory. That particular problem is easily addressed, though, by the simple expedient of putting a list of addresses up on a Web page.

Digging Up Your Data

Linking to legacy data, that vast pool of information residing on a complex computer system that's managed by your IS department, is possible via your intranet. Legacy data can be your sales information, financial and accounting information, and other types of mostly quantitative data. Your organization may also refer to it as client/server applications, where your PC is the client and the host computer storing all the information is the server.

You need an experienced programmer to make the links between your intranet and the other data. Be prepared ahead of time by considering the following issues:

- Specify the information you and your colleagues need to see. This is your opportunity to customize information in ways not possible before. Remember the days spent trying make a minor modification to your sales database so that your sales people could actually use it? Seize this opportunity to get the data you want.

- In what format do you want to receive the information? Consider including some default reports that you can publish for others to read. For example, as sales manager, you might create a report and post it on your intranet as an Adobe Acrobat file. Everyone can read it, but no one can change it.

- What about customizable reports? Do you and your colleagues need to be able to generate "what if" scenarios or view different slices of the data? For example, your regional reps might want to see how product sales are doing in specific geographic areas.

- How frequently do you want information updated? (Depending on the location of your legacy system, there might be a bandwidth problem.) Does your sales information change daily? Would a weekly report be more meaningful and get more attention?

Here's one scenario of how you can access the data: Working with a programmer, you set up a query form on your intranet in which users enter the information they want. For the user, it functions just like the search queries in a browser, as discussed in Chapter 9. You set up a hyperlink to a *common gateway interface script* (CGI script), which will pass through your intranet Web server to query the legacy data system, get the information you need, and return it to the user on the intranet. Alternatively, you can use an application programming interface (API), developed by vendors like Microsoft and Netscape, to access the information and return it to your browser.

CGI is the tool for connecting your static intranet page to programs or scripts that create a new intranet page automatically. CGI programs can receive input from the user, as well as assess the user's profile (type of computer, browser, etc.), and then automatically construct a Web page with the requested information. Like other Web content, CGI input and output are platform independent, which means you can exchange data among PCs, Macintoshes, Unix computers, and others, all via your intranet. CGI works in several basic steps, as outlined below and shown in Figure 13-9.

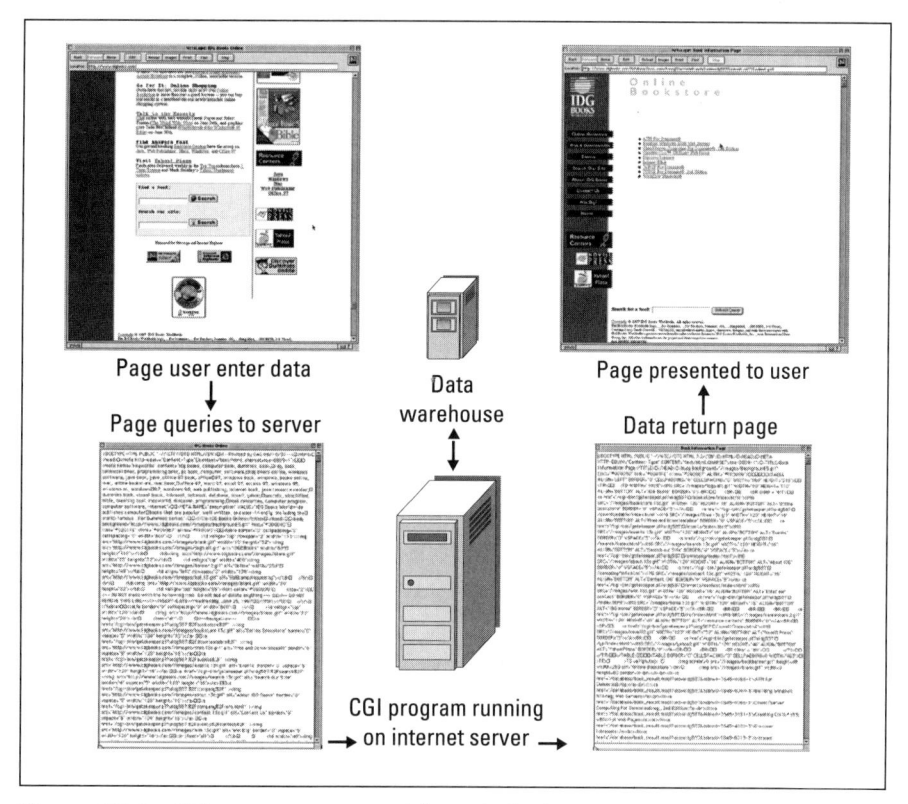

Figure 13-9 CGI requests are routed through the intranet.

The following steps show how CGI requests are processed:

1. Your browser makes a CGI request through a special Uniform Resource Locator (URL), which is the address of the page or program that contains any raw data. You can enter your request though a form on your intranet. (You need a CGI-capable Web server to receive the request, launch the CGI program, and interpret the information entered by the user.)

2. The CGI program sorts though various data resources, including local and external databases, files, and other programs.

3. The CGI program takes the information and *translates* it into an HTML-based page that can be viewed on your intranet.

4. The user receives a customized page containing the information requested.

That's CGI simplified, but now you start to see the potential for connecting to the vast pool of information your organization already has in digital format.

Extranets: Turning Your Intranet Inside Out

After you have your department and organization running with an intranet, you may want to consider expanding the range of access to people outside your organization. For example, through your intranet you may now distribute weekly status reports on products, updates to product specifications, and templates for products. You may use the e-mail feature to nudge colleagues on due dates or ask for clarifications. You may publish your employee directory, press releases, and other corporate information.

Depending on your business, your customers, vendors, and partner companies could benefit immensely from access to this current information. Imagine not having to send those ever-changing product specs to the vendors working on your products, or not having to e-mail press releases to your partner companies. Say you're a distributor and you spend most of your time creating and delivering reports to your customers about sales and delivery schedules.

You can push the burden of getting current information to those outside, by giving them password-protected access to a specific segment of your intranet, an idea that has been labeled *extranets*. Again, the compatibility and ease of access of the Internet and intranets makes it easier than ever before for different computers to communicate in one common language.

News Distribution

If your staff is the kind that will try to duck you by saying, "I couldn't find it on the intranet," consider the new tools known as *personal broadcast networks*. That means if your users don't access information themselves (like new due dates, meeting notices, competitor information, and so on), you can set up a system that automatically routes specific documents to users you designate. The same tool can be applied to customers on your extranet who need regular updates from you.

You can create group profiles to receive regular updates, urgent notices, and such, knowing your customers will receive them right on their desktop, instead of having to wade through the intranet to find it. For example, you can create a group for your department, and specify that they passively receive your weekly status report in their e-mail inboxes, rather than assuming they'll actively look for it on the intranet. Or you can create individual profiles. Say you gather competitive product information from the Internet and post it on your intranet, but you want to ensure that your internal product managers are all reading the information pertinent to their line of goods. Simply set individual profiles linked to keywords on the incoming news feeds, and the information will be automatically routed to the individuals' inboxes.

PointCast and IntraExpress

Two leaders in this field include PointCast and IntraExpress.

PointCast's I-Server is like TV programming, letting you control the corporate channel. Information can be delivered as a screen saver, and you designate timing on delivery of information. This is particularly useful if you need to get a companywide notice out to everyone at the same time. (It sure beats the mailroom chaos of paper memos, for both time and accuracy of delivery.)

PointCast's interface is lively and well organized for accessibility. Its Internet application, called the PointCast Network, gives you a feel for the I-Server interface that would include your corporate information.

WEB PATH → PointCast's Internet software will give you an idea of how push-pull technology works. For a free copy, visit:

http://www.pointcast.com

Diffusion's IntraExpress includes Wizards to set up your delivery system, including New Distribution, New Release, Manage Distribution, and Manage Recipients, as shown in Figure 13-10. It's targeted toward effective collection, analysis, distribution, and action on sales information, but can be applied to other vital information as well. If it's critical data that needs to get to specific individuals quickly, IntraExpress may be a good solution.

With IntraExpress, you set a distribution profile once: What type of information is important, who needs to see it, and delivery schedules (hourly, daily, weekly). Your colleagues set their recipient profiles to determine: the information they want to receive (listen, you can't force them to open interoffice mail either!); the preferred delivery medium (e-mail, fax, pager, or printer); and file format. IntraExpress matches the two profiles to quickly and accurately distribute the right information.

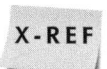

X-REF Verity's SEARCH 97 can also be configured to help users filter for information. For details, see Chapter 9.

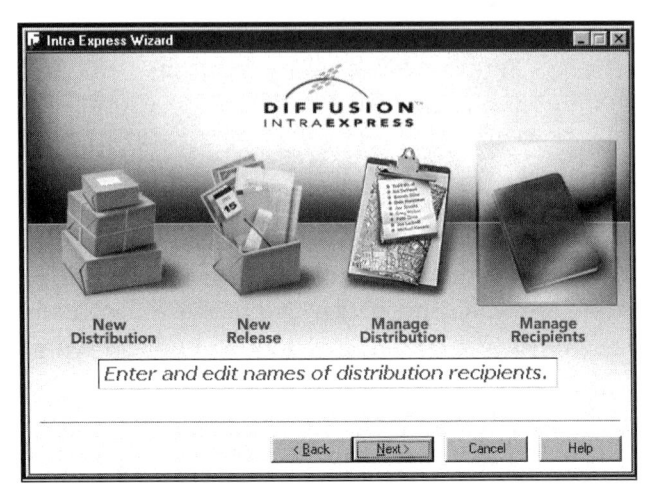

Figure 13-10 IntraExpress' Diffusion

"Push" It out There

One growing area on the Web and particularly on intranets is "push" technology, which includes news distribution and more. The present "pull" approach means that your users must manually browse and search for information, tag frequently visited pages with bookmarks, and remember to visit in the future for updated information.

Push technology delivers information proactively to users, or Web surfers, without them having to specify a URL to actively search for information. On the upside, you'll have a mechanism for keeping your employees informed; on the downside, you're shoving even more information their way.

> **CAUTION** Think "TV advertising" and you'll get a feel for the potential intrusiveness of this medium. The real debate is whether push technology will help your organization better manage the clutter of electronic information. Do you really need all the material that's coming your way, and can you intelligently set rules that limit the inflow of data and sort it in some meaningful way?

Push tools are evolving, and the range of services and potential uses on your intranet varies. Table 13-2 shows current push tools.

TABLE 13-2 Push Technology Tools

Product	Company	Description	Web Site
Arrive Network	Ifusion Com Corp.	Delivers graphic-oriented and sophisticated media that resembles television. You can personalize the items that will be pushed to specific users.	www.ifusion.com
BackWeb Inc.	BackWeb	Designed to deliver InfoPaks, which can contain InfoFlashes as floating banners or other multimedia elements. BackWeb can also be used to deliver software updates.	www.backweb.com
IntraExpress	Diffusion Inc.	Created specifically for intranet information delivery, the application includes templates for storing and delivering your content.	www.diffusion.com
Marimba Castanet	Marimba Inc.	Marimba projects the bulk of its business will come from intranets, with software upgrades and maintenance being key for large companies. Information is conveyed through a Transmitter (the server) and the Tuner (the client). Download the free Marimba Tuner, and test-drive the application from a variety of Channels at the Marimba site. You can also get a free evaluation copy of Marimba Transmitter for a limited time.	www.marimba.com

(continued)

TABLE 13-2 Push Technology Tools *(continued)*

Product	Company	Description	Web Site
NETdelivery	NETdelivery Corp.	NETdelivery is more of a commercial e-mail system, but it can facilitate the distribution of up-to-date corporate information through an intranet.	www.netdelivery.com
PointCast	PointCast Inc.	The first of its kind, PointCast defined the early push market on the Internet. The new I-Server is specifically for intranet applications. Updates are fast and easy, and the interface is consistent and friendly. Download the free PointCast viewer and test drive the Internet version.	www.pointcast.com
Wayfarer	Wayfarer Communications Inc.	Wayfarer targets business content, and has a simple interface for your users to broadcast messages to colleagues.	www.wayfarer.com

Marimba Inc.'s: Castanet Dancing on the Intranet

Some call it Webcasting, the ability to distribute information to your users just like television. You can send a file, an image, a Java applet, or even a software update to a thousand users in one click. It's powerful, and potentially an ideal corporate solution, especially for large and multisite businesses.

Castanet is a complete package that uses the TV analogy to educate about the technology. Essentially, you as the intranet manager control the transmitter that sends out a signal over a channel on the intranet. While these channels can handle more complicate code, the application is targeted toward HTML(*). Your users will receive the channel using the Castanet tuner. Tuner is available free on the internet if you're developing an extranet and want your customers to be able to receive the channels, too. Castanet Tuner will also be included in the Netscape Communicator. Castanet channels are being created in a flurry; Figure 13-11 shows a few Channel choices from the Tuner.

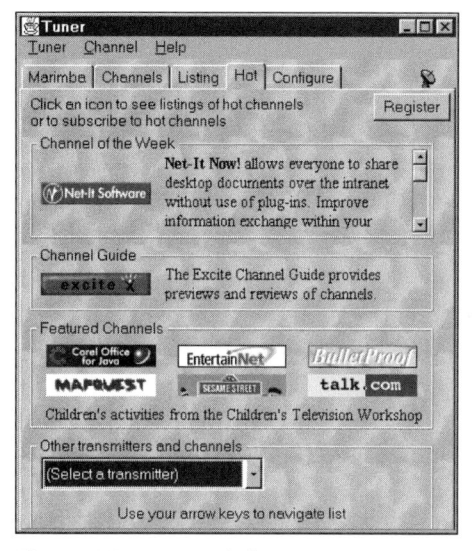

Figure 13-11 Marimba's Castanet Tuner

On the other hand, the real benefit of Marimba's technologies isn't in the HTML-type applications, but rather full-fledged applications (such as Corel Office for Java). Castanet content is converted to a Java application and then transported, which is an inefficient way of sending HTML across a network. So depending on your goals, Castanet can either be the right solution or just more overhead.

You might be wondering why you need this, when you could just distribute Java applets throughout your company. Castanet is designed to handle more robust Java applications. Java applets are small elements, such as an animation, which are part of the intranet page and download quickly. In contrast, Java applications are usually much larger and thus slower and longer to download, require more flexible security (for retrieving and writing data), and need more memory and processing power. With Castanet, you only download the channel once, which puts the Java application on your computer. Updates and fixes to the application are retrieved automatically.

Instead of a Web server, the Castanet Transmitter distributes channels, and their patent-pending technology to merge HTTP information on a single TCP circuit eliminates much of the overhead of transmission. Once your users subscribe to a channel, the bulk of the information is downloaded to their computer, and future updates are fast and almost unnoticeable. Figure 13-12 shows some Transmitter hosts available on the Internet.

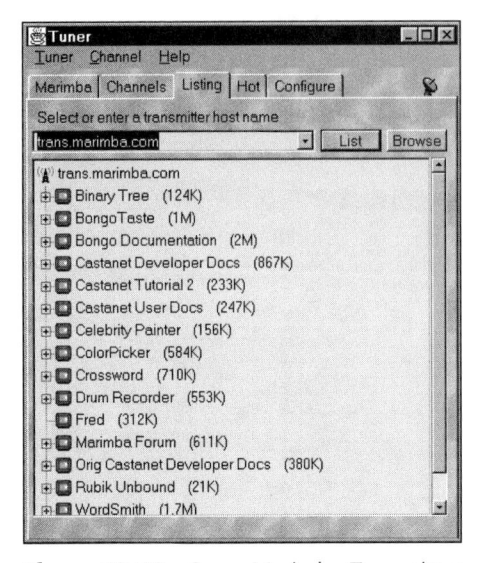

Figure 13-12 Some Marimba Transmitters

So how difficult is it to create channels? Not very, using Castanet wizard-like publishing tools to convert items like existing Java applications or HTML pages. To create channels from scratch, you can use Marimba's Bongo to import and create text and graphic elements.

BONUS

Windows NT Peer Web Service: A Virtually Instant Intranet for a Small Workgroup

"Windows NT?!" you exclaim. Just when you've mastered Windows 95, along comes yet another innovation from Microsoft, but this time it promises not to change the interface you know, at least not very much. Windows NT Workstation is designed for high-powered workstations used by mere mortals. It adds 32-bit addressing, which means your applications will be more reliable, secure, and Internet/intranet accessible than Windows 95, which is a 16-bit power scheme.

It's bundled with TCP/IP and the Microsoft Internet Explorer Browser, and something called peer Web services for creating a small workgroup intranet quickly. Peer Web services are based on Microsoft's Internet Information Server, and offer the performance, management, and administration features you need to get a small intranet running. You can use WebPost Wizards to quickly publish to the server through a series of prompted steps. Of course, all of it works well with Microsoft Office products, especially when adding Internet Assistants available for a free download, or using the new Microsoft Office 97 suite.

WEB PATH → **For more information on peer Web services, visit Microsoft at:**
http://www.microsoft.com

Summary

This chapter looked at groupware applications as a tool for building an intranet, and additional features for your intranet, including:

Incorporating e-mail as an extension of your intranet to easily route information

Accessing legacy data from your corporate computer system via your intranet

Expanding to an extranet for customers, vendors, and others outside your organization

Automatic distribution of information via push-pull products like PointCast and IntraExpress

CHAPTER FOURTEEN
AUDIO AND VIDEO CONFERENCING

IN THIS CHAPTER YOU LEARN THESE KEY SKILLS

THE CONCEPT OF AUDIO AND VIDEO CONFERENCING PAGE 226

MICROSOFT NETMEETING, ONE EXAMPLE OF AUDIO AND VIDEO CONFERENCING PAGE 228

HOW TO USE NETMEETING PAGE 233

Audio and video conferencing is a revolutionary way to improve communication within your office using your intranet. As with any new process involving your computer, you need to learn new software. But in the case of audio and video conferencing, you also need to learn a new way of communication. This compounds the learning issue, but the rewards and benefits are great. This chapter is an overview of the new world of audio and video conferencing over your intranet.

You'll take a tour of Microsoft's conferencing product, NetMeeting, which you can download and test-drive for free. You will also discover the benefits of an audio and video conferencing solution that can be implemented using your Intranet. So bring on the microphone and the camera and dig into audio and video conferencing.

X-REF For a more detailed look at the world of audio and video conferencing, read *Discover Desktop Conferencing with NetMeeting 2.0*, by Suzanne Van Cleve and Mike Britton (IDG Books Worldwide, 1997).

Concept of Audio and Video Conferencing

Think of your intranet as an e-mail system. You can send a message to anyone on your Local Area Network (LAN) or your Wide Area Network (WAN). You launch your e-mail software, address your message, type a subject in the appropriate blank, key your text, and press the Send button. It's that simple to communicate with another associate in your office or a remote office location. The data you have keyed shoots across the network in search of the e-mail address you entered, and then appears on the recipient's computer.

Just as text zooms across the intranet, audio and video can also be digitized and sent across the intranet. The digital data sent between two or more computers results in a real-time conversation, and, if effective, results in an appropriate action. That's the concept of audio and video conferencing — achieving a response through digital communication.

Desktop audio telecommunication software was first introduced in 1995, so the technology is very young and still has a way to go before it becomes a common means of communication. For now comparing an e-mail message with a digital audio and video signal will help you understand how your voice and picture get from your desk to your associate's desk just by using your computer.

See It, Hear It

As mentioned earlier, NetMeeting software is free and there are minimal hardware costs needed to establish audio and video conferencing capabilities. For under $500 per user, your organization can possess the capability to have virtual meetings. This in turn will offer you some fantastic benefits.

Travel Savings

A trip to a remote location in your company can cost you thousands of dollars in airfare, meals, hotels, and entertainment. Multiply this by the number of people attending the conference and you have a significant investment for every meeting scheduled. By using audio and video conferencing capabilities, you virtually eliminate these costs. In the meeting you can transfer data, draw on a whiteboard, and take minutes electronically. All while viewing each other and verbally communicating. It's just like being there. Well, almost.

Time Savings

Beyond the "hard dollars" that you spend in T&E expense, you spend "soft dollars" in time and effort whenever you attend a remote meeting. For instance, you spend airplane time, transfer time to and from the airport, waiting time because the airline doesn't coordinate with your meeting schedule, hotel time, and let's face it, goofing-off time because you're on a business trip. All of these add up.

You still spend a great deal of time if the meeting is just down the hall. Coordinating schedules, waiting for people to arrive, and arranging for coffee all amount to time that could be spent in creating new revenue streams.

Audio and video conferencing gives you back the wasted meeting time. A simple click of the software and your meeting is in progress.

> **CAUTION**
> The business trip is an institution of the American businessperson. No matter how much your employees complain about travel, they look forward to these trips. Being mandated by your company to use audio and video conferencing instead of flying to beautiful San Diego will not be received well, especially if you're located in North Dakota and it's 20 below. Also, a friendly handshake and personal communication is a benefit to your employees. Go ahead and reduce your costs by using audio and video conferencing, but don't cut out all of the trips. Intersperse virtual meetings with actual face-to-face meetings.

Retrieving Lost Opportunities

Given the information described earlier, your travel and entertainment budget probably makes your head spin. However, you must realize that many needed meetings don't get scheduled because of the expense. This results in lost opportunities — a cost that can't be calculated.

Audio and video conferencing enables your employees to meet whenever the need arises. Ad hoc meetings will replace scheduled meetings, making everyone more productive. Let's face it, you attend way to many meetings. Corporate America is meeting-crazy. A simple click of the NetMeeting button will have two associates talking and sharing information in ways that were not possible before audio and video conferencing.

Telecommuting

Connecting to the company intranet from home is another benefit of audio and video conferencing. Associates have the ability to work at home, connect through their Internet service to the company intranet, and conference with audio, video, and data — just as if they were in the office. This, of course, can be a cost savings, a time savings, and a fringe benefit that you can offer.

The ability to connect to the company intranet from home is one benefit of audio and video conferencing.

CAUTION Working at home is a radical and unpleasant change for some. The office environment is a necessary part of social life for many office workers. If you can't manage time wisely, working outside the office is not for you. If you feel the need to be with others, telecommuting is not an option. Use telecommuting when ever it makes sense and go to the office when it doesn't. Remember, don't force the issue.

Overview of Microsoft NetMeeting

There are many software products that offer audio-conferencing solutions. Fewer products offer a video solution. Microsoft's NetMeeting offers both, and in addition it sports several other features that make it an all-around conferencing winner. Furthermore, the software is free — that's right, absolutely no cost. This makes NetMeeting a fantastic tool to add to your intranet. This section focuses on the basic features of NetMeeting so you can test-drive the concept of audio and video conferencing on your intranet.

NetMeeting Main Window

When you launch NetMeeting you see the Main Window, as shown in Figure 14-1. All features of NetMeeting are accessed from the Main Window. You need to understand the features in this window to use the software effectively.

The Main Window contains the following elements:

- Title Bar
- Menu Bar
- Main Toolbar
- Audio Toolbar
- ULS Pop-up Menu
- Directory Window
- Connection Window
- Status Bar

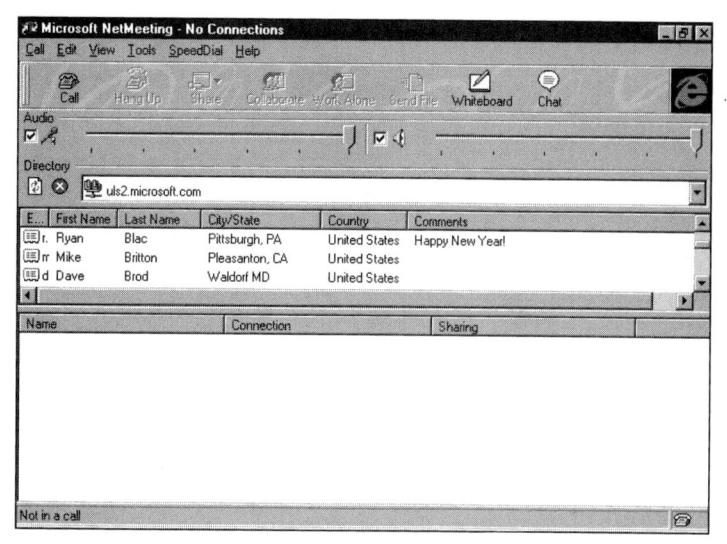

Figure 14-1 The NetMeeting main window

Title Bar: The title bar shows the program name and the name of your NetMeeting connection, if there is one. It also contains the Windows Minimize, Maximize, and Close buttons and menu.

Menu Bar: The menu bar lists the menu names for the application. From this area you can access all of the functionality of NetMeeting.

Main Toolbar: The toolbar is a graphical representation of frequently used commands from the menu, and is designed to save time. You can click the appropriate button to select a command instead of accessing the command from the menu bar.

Audio Toolbar: The audio toolbar enables you to adjust microphone and speaker settings.

ULS Pop-up Menu: The User Location Service (ULS) pop-up menu shows your current connection and enables you to specify the ULS server to which you want to connect. The ULS server is a dynamic phone book housing everyone in your organization who is currently running NetMeeting. This means they are available for an audio or video conference.

Directory Window: The directory window lists the NetMeeting users who are currently connected to the ULS server.

Connection Window: The connection window shows your current NetMeeting connections.

Status Bar: The status bar shows your current connection status.

AUDIO AND VIDEO CONFERENCING **229**

A Tour of NetMeeting's Features

The NetMeeting program is a combination of several communication methods. Voice, video, data, pictures, sounds, and text make up the NetMeeting product. In this section, you learn how NetMeeting uses these communication methods by discovering the following eight major features of the software:

- Internet phone
- Application sharing
- Shared clipboard
- File transfers
- The whiteboard
- Chat feature
- Video conference
- The User Location Service Directory (ULS)

THE INTERNET PHONE

You can place a voice call to an associate over your intranet without picking up the phone, or make a sales call to the far side of the globe over the Internet without paying any additional phone charges. The Internet phone uses a range of compression formats that optimize the audio signal for the speed of your network or modem connection. Your computer needs no additional software to accomplish the task; however, you do need a sound card, microphone, and speakers to take advantage of this feature. This can be obtained at a minimal expense, especially when compared to the cost benefits. Refer to the "See It, Hear It" section of this chapter.

APPLICATION SHARING

Application sharing enables you to share a program, such as Excel shown in Figure 14-2, with others in the conference. They will see the same information that you see on your computer. Taking this one step further, you can choose to collaborate with your conference attendees, giving them the opportunity to edit and control the application. The conference attendees do not need to have the software application in order to collaborate. They can see, edit, and control the program as if they had the software.

SHARED CLIPBOARD

The shared clipboard feature functions with the application sharing feature. You can share the contents of your clipboard with other participants in a conference. You can copy information from any document and paste it into a shared application using the copy/paste operation.

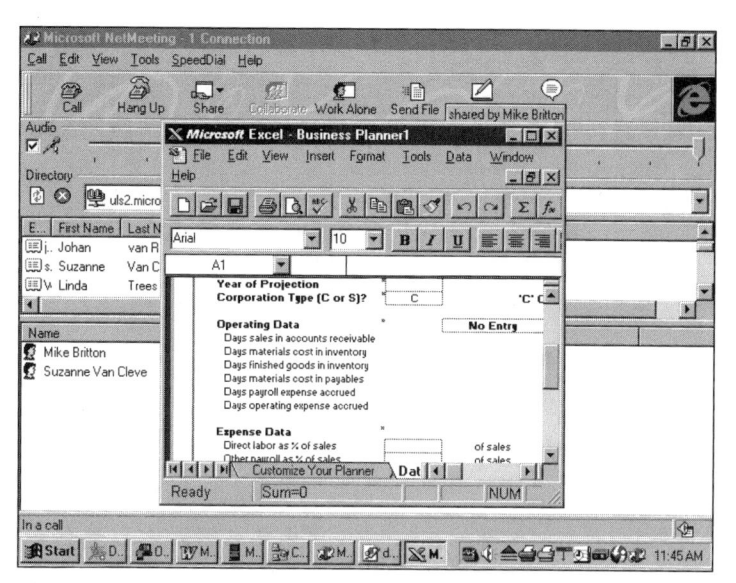

Figure 14-2 The application sharing feature sharing an Excel spreadsheet

FILE TRANSFER

The file transfer feature enables you to send a file to one person or to a group of people in a conference. You can send any file saved on your computer. The file transfer happens in the background so you can continue to participate in the conference while your file is being sent.

THE WHITEBOARD

The whiteboard is the most creative feature in NetMeeting. It is a multipage, multiuser drawing application that enables you to sketch diagrams and display graphic information. Figure 14-3 shows the whiteboard feature. There are many uses for the whiteboard, and it's fun to communicate using the tools provided in this feature. Whether you are Picasso or a person who has a hard time drawing a straight line, the whiteboard is the perfect compliment to the audio and video features of NetMeeting.

THE CHAT FEATURE

The chat feature provides a text-based method of communication. This is essential because not everyone in your organization will have the hardware to send and receive audio and video transmissions. The chat window, shown in Figure 14-4, functions like other chat applications and can be used in combination with all NetMeeting features.

Figure 14-3 The whiteboard

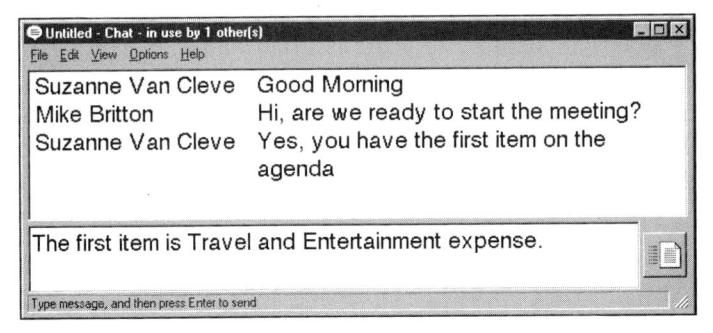

Figure 14-4 The Chat window

VIDEO CONFERENCE

The video conference feature is new to NetMeeting 2.0. Video conference enables you to send and receive live video communications. As with the audio feature, you do not need any additional software; however, you do need a video camera to send a video image. You can receive video messages even if you don't have a video camera connected to your computer. Figure 14-5 shows the Video conference window.

Figure 14-5 The Video conference window

THE USER LOCATION SERVICE DIRECTORY (ULS)

ULS is a dynamic phone book. Associates currently running NetMeeting are accessible directly from within NetMeeting or from a Web page on the intranet. Microsoft has established a network of ULS servers, but you can create your own within your company. This will segment you from the outside world and enable you to see only those on your LAN or WAN who are available currently for a conference. Microsoft has complete information on establishing your own ULS server on its Web site.

> **WEB PATH** For information on establishing your own ULS server, see the following Microsoft Web page:
> http://www.microsoft.com/netmeeting/
>
> To download a free copy of Microsoft NetMeeting, visit:
> http://www.microsoft.com

Making an Audio and Video Call in NetMeeting

NetMeeting is free and can be obtained in two ways. You can download the software itself from the Microsoft site, or you can download Microsoft Explorer, which contains NetMeeting, from the Microsoft site. However you get it, you will want to jump right in and see how it works.

AUDIO AND VIDEO CONFERENCING **233**

If your organization doesn't have its intranet implemented yet, you can still test NetMeeting by using a 28.8kpbs modem and your connection to the Internet. When your intranet becomes available, the software will function in exactly the same way. So it doesn't really matter which comes first. You can get a feel of audio and video conferencing anytime you wish.

In this section, you learn the basic steps to accomplish an audio and video connection using NetMeeting. For audio and video conferencing to be an effective tool, you need to learn how to configure the software, adjust the settings, and maximize the performance.

Follow these steps in NetMeeting to establish an audio and video connection:

1. Launch NetMeeting and address a call by typing a name in the Call dialog box.

2. An incoming dialog box will appear on the computer of the person you are trying to call. The dialog box gives the recipient the option of accepting or ignoring the call. The dialog box is shown in figure 14-6.

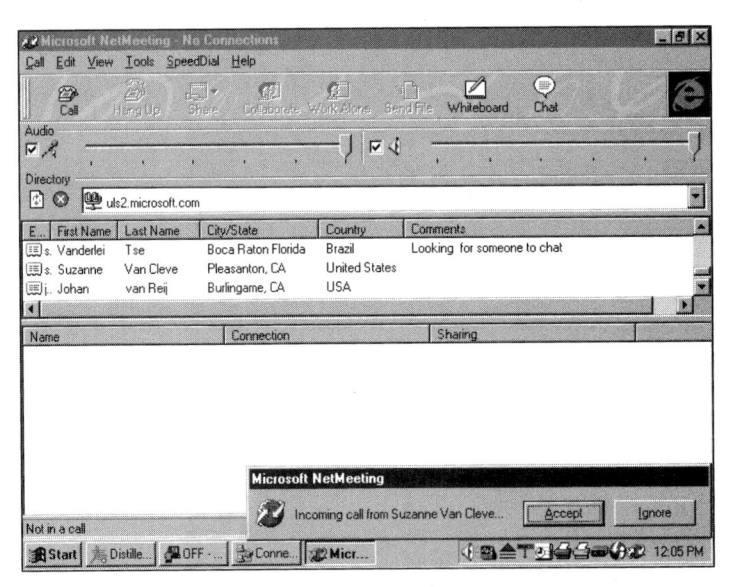

Figure 14-6 The Incoming call dialog box

3. Upon acceptance of the call, the Connection window will list you and the recipient. The status bar will show that the person you called has joined the conference.

4. If you have trouble hearing or your voice is distorted, you can use the Audio Toolbar to adjust the microphone and the speaker volume. You can use the mute boxes to turn off your microphone or speakers temporarily.

TIP NetMeeting provides an Audio-tuning Wizard to help you adjust the audio setting of the software. The Wizard can be summoned whenever you are not in a call.

5. Choose View → Video → Myself from the menu bar to access the video feature. After you have made all of the necessary adjustments, you are ready to conduct your conversation. Talk into the microphone, look into the camera, and listen through the speakers.

CAUTION NetMeeting supports meetings of up to 32 people. However, only the first two people connected can participate in an audio and video call. All other participants must use a text or graphic feature in order to communicate. That's why the other features of NetMeeting are so important to learn.

6. When it's time to conclude your call, notify the participants in the conference that you are hanging up and click Hang Up on the main toolbar.

7. You are now ready to make another call or exit the program. To make another call, just follow the previous instructions. To exit the program, choose Call → Exit from the menu bar.

BONUS

Getting a Camera

One of the video cameras available on the market is the QuickCam from Connectix. QuickCams attach directly to your computer, so they're very simple to configure and use. And because of the simplicity in design, they are also very affordable. The black-and-white version costs around $100, while the color version is close to $200. These are excellent prices for such a useful tool to use with this technology. You can find more details at the Connectix Web site, at:

http://www.connectix.com/

The quality of the image will vary significantly depending on your office environment, lighting specifically. You'll notice that most photos taken in your office make your complexion look pretty sickly, and unattractive shadows darken your eyes and other features. Adding additional lighting to your work or conference area will help.

Thus, you may find that springing the extra hundred dollars for the color camera to be a waste, and you might actually convey a clearer, brighter image with a black-and-white camera. Buy one and test it in your actual video conferencing space before buying one for every member of your team.

Summary

This chapter covered some of the basics of audio and video conferencing, including:

The concept of audio and video communication

The benefits of using audio and video conferencing in your business

The basic steps in making an audio and video connection in NetMeeting

CHAPTER FIFTEEN

EXPANDING YOUR INTRANET TOOLBOX

IN THIS CHAPTER YOU LEARN THESE KEY SKILLS:

ADDING NEW FUNCTIONALITY TO YOUR INTRANET WITH JAVA APPLETS   PAGE 238

EXPANDING THE INTERACTIVITY OF YOUR INTRANET WITH ACTIVEX   PAGE 240

ADDING MOTION AND SOUND TO YOUR INTRANET WITH SHOCKWAVE   PAGE 241

CREATING ANIMATIONS   PAGE 242

MAKING THE MOST OF NEW FEATURES IN PAGE-AUTHORING TOOLS   PAGE 252

New tools for building your intranet are emerging at a rapid pace. Sun's Java programming language and Microsoft's ActiveX both enable you to create self-running mini applications that can be used on any kind of computer: PC, Mac, Unix, or even the much-touted network computer. These two tools enable your users to pull applications right off the intranet server, rather than installing software on their local computer.

Shockwave is the Web and intranet tool for delivering multimedia content on your intranet, whether it's videos, audio, self-running tutorials, and so on.

The tools for making intranet pages continue to improve; more features are being added, others are being simplified. The competitive market for Web-authoring software drives the need for constant improvement — making your job of building and managing an intranet easier.

Perk Up Your Intranet with Some Java

Java began spreading like wildfire in 1996, with a lot of media hype. Because developers were creating products with more interactivity, the issue of software's capability to run on any type of computer was critical. Java solves this problem, because Java applications and applets can run on just about any computer platform. Java applets, a small application written with the Java programming language, also initiated the idea of something called a *thin client*, a tool that would let users pull applications off the intranet.

There's some confusion about what's what with Java. Java *itself* is a high-powered programming language. A Java *application* is a full-fledged piece of software that can run over the intranet, and a Java *applet* runs inside a Web browser. Both applications and applets are platform independent, meaning users of PCs, Macs, and Unix machines can all run the same software. Java applets abound on just about any topic you can think of: a 401K calculator, a self-running training tutorial, a form to collect feedback on a project, and so on.

WEB PATH For a terrific introduction to the concepts behind Java, including an interactive tutorial, visit the Sun site at:
http://www.javasoft.com/doc

There's also something called JavaScript, which is Netscape's HTML-based scripting language. Web authors use JavaScript to manage objects and actions. This scripting language can add interest and interactivity to your intranet, with a little work on your part. The full-powered Java programming language uses code compiled to create applications your users can run within their browsers, but can't modify. In contrast, JavaScript code is embedded in the HTML page and is viewed through the browser. JavaScript is also useful for manipulating the content and appearance of the Web page itself.

Examples of JavaScript you might use in an intranet include registering users who visit certain pages, greeting your users with personalized messages, and distributing a report from a custom database.

JavaScript can do the following:

* **Manage forms:** While CGI will pose your user's query to the server, JavaScript monitors the forms as users enter information. For example, if you want phone numbers as extensions only, and a user begins to enter the whole number, JavaScript can send up an alert button as soon as the user moves to the next field.

* **Customize information for your users:** You can set up a log-in screen to keep track of who's reading what material, and show users what's new since their last visit. JavaScripts can collect information about the user (who, when, what, and so on) and create a *cookie*, which contains and remembers this information for the user's next visit. The

cookie is a file that contains information about the user and the locations he or she visits in the intranet. For example, if a user visits a new product development area frequently, a cookie can record that information.

* **Manage the appearance of the intranet page:** Want to hide the toolbar on your users' browsers so you can use the full screen? Want to promote an upcoming meeting by flashing an alert box when they log into a section of the intranet? Want to add banners? JavaScripts can do it all.

* **Connect to plug-ins and applets:** The feature is called Netscape's LiveConnect, and joins other tools for multiple use. For example, if a user visits a new product development area frequently, a cookie can mark that and automatically send updates about those products to that user.

WEB PATH For more information on JavaScript and LiveConnect, visit Netscape's site at:
http://www.netscape.com

Also visit Gamelan, the official Java directory, at:
http://www.gamelan.com/

SIDE TRIP

COREL OFFICE FOR JAVA

Corel has seized the idea of Java with a new office product that is small, modular, platform independent, and distributable across an intranet. Imagine an office suite — including word processor, spreadsheet, charting, tool, scheduler, and e-mail — requiring less than 5MB of hard drive space(?!).

The software is updated on the central server, eliminating the frustration of users being on different versions on incompatible software. Also, Corel's centralized document management means users can share documents across the intranet.

Worried about your existing files in Microsoft Word and Lotus 1-2-3? Fear not, because Corel Office for Java includes filters to import and export to the leading mainstream applications.

Tiptoe into Programming with ActiveX

ActiveX, which only runs on Windows 95 and Windows NT, runs inside a Web page, like Java applets. ActiveX is based on the idea of a *control,* a piece of programming that you add to your intranet page. For your intranet, the easiest way to integrate ActiveX is to build on controls created by a developer, customizing them for your use. ActiveX controls enable you to add Checklist buttons, shown in Figure 15-1, and pop-up menus, shown in Figure 15-2.

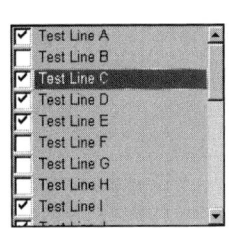

Figure 15-1 Checklist buttons created with ActiveX

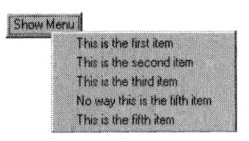

Figure 15-2 Pop-up menus created with ActiveX

With ActiveX controls, you can add the following:

* **Sound:** Add a clip of your CEO's latest presentation, a recent news conference, or other verbal reports.
* **Images:** Video and fixed images can be automatically delivered to your users.
* **Customizable page appearance:** Your viewers can choose options from fonts, background page colors, and so on.
* **Site mapping:** Users can automatically generate an overview of your site for their use.
* **Form elements and design:** Create forms and charts for quick visual interpretations of data.
* **Database access:** Create links to your other data resources.
* **Report writing:** Write accessible reports of data pulled from other resources.
* **3D/VRML (Virtual Reality Modeling Language):** Use this to develop training modules.
* **Conferencing:** Multiple users can communicate simultaneously.

One of the most popular ActiveX controls is the scrolling marquee included with FrontPage 97. You can enter a phrase, such as, "The CEO's State of the Company Speech Has Been Postponed," and set such elements as the timing, the scrolling pattern, alignment, size, and color, as shown in Figure 15-3. The result is a flashing notice that your users won't miss.

CAUTION When using Java or ActiveX, know what applets/controls you are downloading before allowing them to run on the system. As an extreme example, there is rumor of an ActiveX control that can search your hard drive for Microsoft Money and retrieve financial information. The cautionary advice Microsoft gives is never to allow an unfamiliar ActiveX control to access your system or network if there is sensitive information on it.

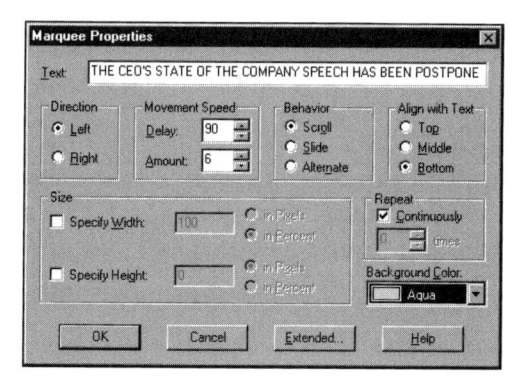

Figure 15-3 A sample marquee

ActiveX controls are directly supported by Microsoft Explorer, and there's a plug-in available for support by Netscape Navigator.

WEB PATH For a great resource center on ActiveX, visit Microsoft's component library at:
http://www.microsoft.com/activex/controls

Wake Them Up with Shockwave

Besides Java, another way to deliver multimedia on an intranet is with plug-in technology that acts as a player for a file. With plug-ins, the user doesn't need to purchase Macromedia's Director program to play a multimedia clip written with Director. The user can just download the Shockwave plug-in from Macromedia — for free — and play the file. The upside is that people used to creating training materials and presentations using existing tools like Director can continue to use those tools, and end users can view the results on their browsers using the free plug-in.

Astound's WebMotion is a presentation tool, great for creating slide shows and demos, and can be delivered to your users as a *streaming* animation. Streaming means that the file will download as users are viewing it, and it doesn't require any plug-ins to make it work. Astound presentations can also be delivered as animated GIF files.

WEB PATH For a sample of Shockwave, download the player from the Macromedia Web site and experience the samples at:
http://www.macromedia.com/shockwave/epicenter

Creating Animations for Your Intranet

Animations may not be critical to the content on your intranet, but they sure are fun. Animations can be GIF, Shockwave, or Java format; GIFs are the easiest and smallest and are the best way to get started with animations for your intranet.

CAUTION Even with an intranet, you should always consider the size and download time of your animation. Remember, for the most part the animations are entertainment and secondary to your content, and so should be available quickly to your users.

Used sparingly, animations can:

* Be used as metaphors to communicate your message
* Add humor or entertainment value to otherwise boring information
* Flag really important information (again, be selective about how and when you use it)
* Create a unique digital signature or provide a consistent look for your company

GIF Animations

GIFs are attractive because they're small, easy to deliver, and easy to view. They work just like the little cartoon animation books that you hold your thumb on and flip through the pages quickly to make it appear that the characters move. To create a GIF animation, you need an image to animate and a GIF-animating program. You then set frame options for timing and changes, and set loops.

Animated GIFs are attractive because they're small, easy to deliver, and easy to view.

WEB PATH ➡ For a demo version of GIF Construction Set for Windows, visit Alchemy Mindworks at:
http://www.mindworkshop.com/alchemy/gcsdemo.html

Microsoft's GIF animator, which is freeware, is available at:
http://www.microsoft.com/imagecomposer

GIFs are simple. They don't require any programming, plug-ins, or wait time. You can overlap GIFs for movement of multiple objects (say a character and a background) and they're transparent, which means you won't have a nasty white box outlining your image. GIFs are frequently used to animate corporate logos and department names.

Getting Animated with GIF Construction Set

GIF Construction set is a nifty piece of shareware, which means if you like the product and use it you should send the mere $20 to the creators. (Do it — shareware developers work hard on their products and deserve to be paid just like the software giants.) There are other tools, notably the shareware GIF Builder (but it's only on the Macintosh), and other programs you can purchase, but check out GIF Construction set first.

GIF Construction Set for Windows can do the following:

* Create looping animation GIF files for Netscape/Explorer-enhanced Web pages
* Create transparent GIF files
* Create interlaced GIF files
* Compress GIF files to for faster downloading
* Create animated LED signs
* Generate quick, animations with a wizard

WEB PATH ➡ For more details on GIF Construction Set, visit the Alchemy sites at:
http://www.mindworkshop.com/alchemy/gifcon.html

Creating animations with the GIF Construction Set is pretty straightforward if you go through the animation wizard as described below. You'll need to create GIF files, including the interim stages of the animation, in a separate application such as a paint program. Think of the cartoon flip books, the ones that you hold your finger on the corner and flip quickly through the pages to make a figure appear in motion. That's how animated GIFs work.

Follow these steps to build a GIF animation:

1. Select `Animation Wizard` from the `File` menu, as shown in Figure 15-4.

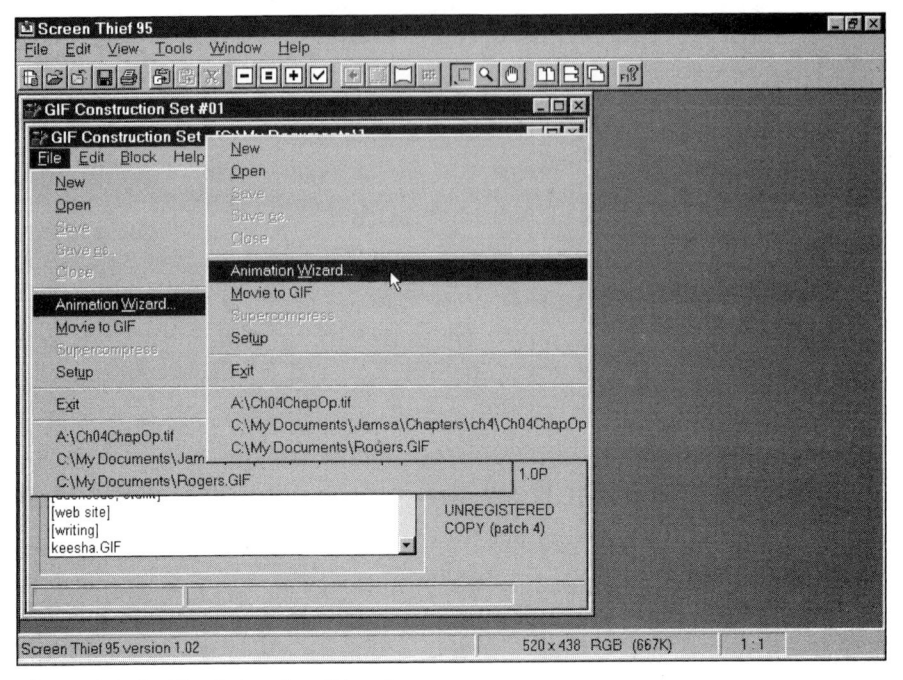

Figure 15-4 The Animation Wizard

2. Decide if you're going to use the animation on a Web page or elsewhere. Click OK.

3. Decide if you want your GIF to animate indefinitely, or play once and then stop. Click OK.

4. Choose whether you want the image to be Photorealitic, Drawn, Drawn in sixteen colors, or Matched to the first palette, as shown in Figure 15-5. Click OK.

5. Choose how much time you want between frames, as shown in Figure 15-6. Click OK.

6. Choose GIF files from your system. You can hold down the Ctrl key and click each filename in sequence. Click Open when you're done

NOTE **You must select at least two images to create a GIF animation. The more images you include between movements, the smoother your animation will appear.**

7. When you're done choosing GIFs, choose Cancel in the Open dialog box. You'll be back at the Animation Wizard window. Click Next.

8. Click Done. Animation Wizard will build your animation. The animation files will appear in the main window, as shown in Figure 15-7.

9. Preview your animation by selecting View. Save your animation to a new GIF file by selecting `File` → `Save As`. The animated GIF is shown in Figure 15-8.

TIP The visual appeal of your first frame is critical, because most browsers will display this as a fixed GIF until the animation begins.

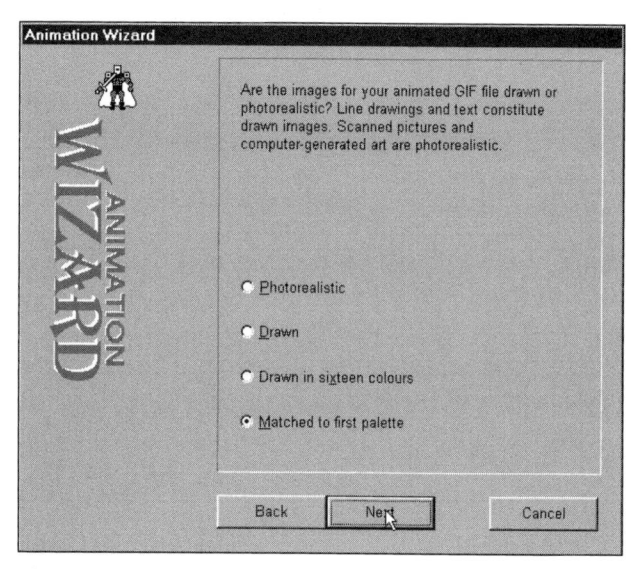

Figure 15-5 Select how you want your figure drawn.

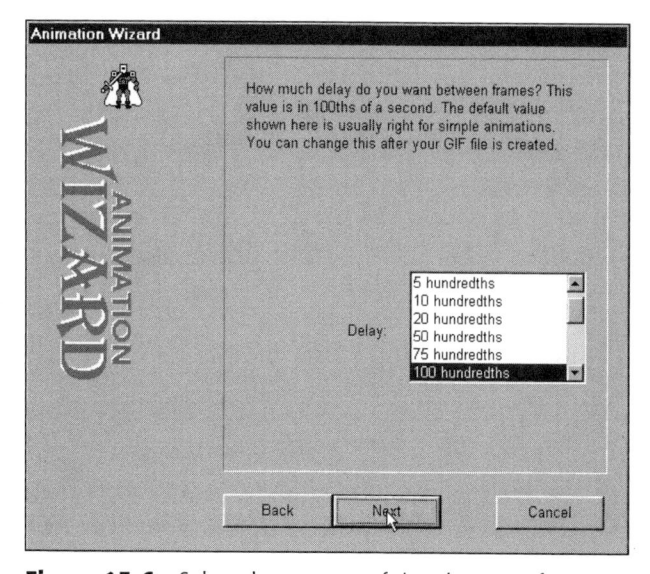

Figure 15-6 Select the amount of time between frames.

EXPANDING YOUR INTRANET TOOLBOX **245**

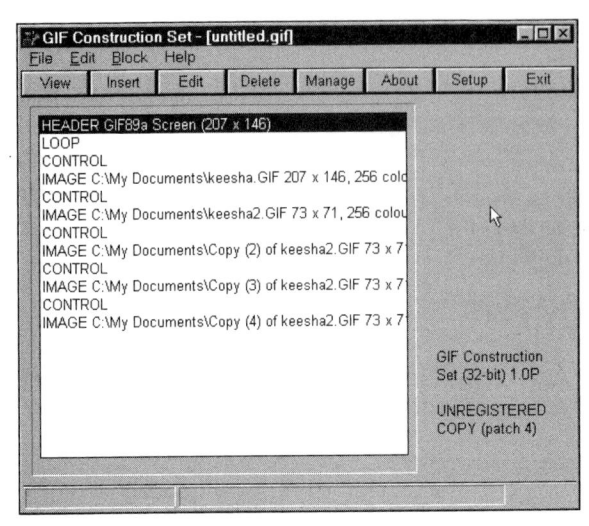

Figure 15-7 All of the individual GIF files in your animation appear in this window.

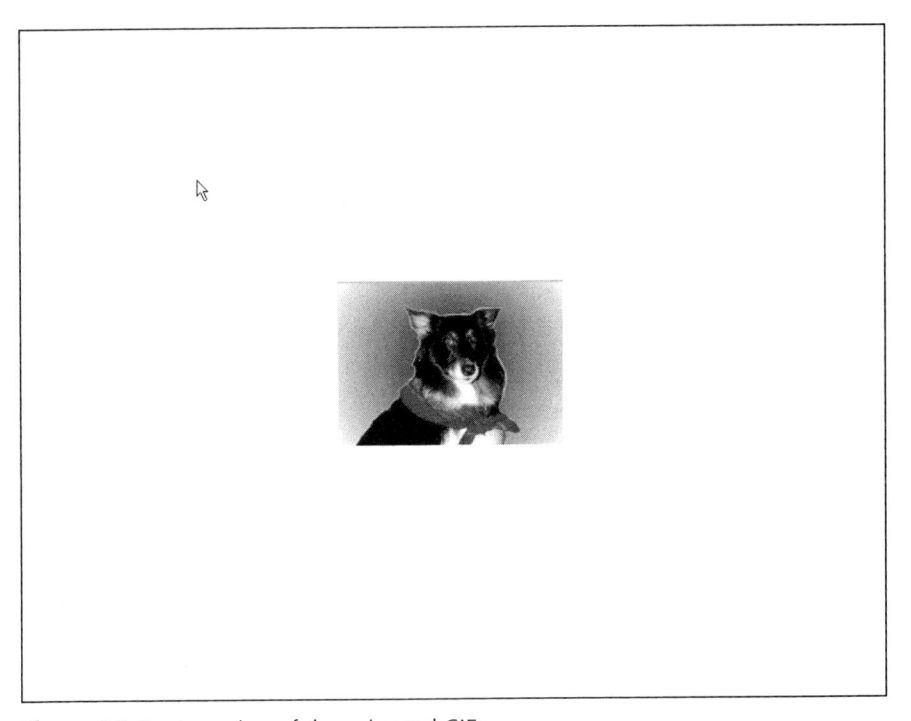

Figure 15-8 A preview of the animated GIF

So, now you've created your first animated GIF, but you decide that having a transparent background would be much more appealing that an ugly box behind your image.

Follow these steps to create an animated GIF file with transparency:

1. Open the animated GIF from the last section and go to the `Block` menu and select `Manage`.
2. Click the Select All button.
3. Select Set All Existing Controls.
4. Click Apply in the Control Block group.
5. From the Control Block editor, choose enable the Transparent Colour option, as shown in Figure 15-9.

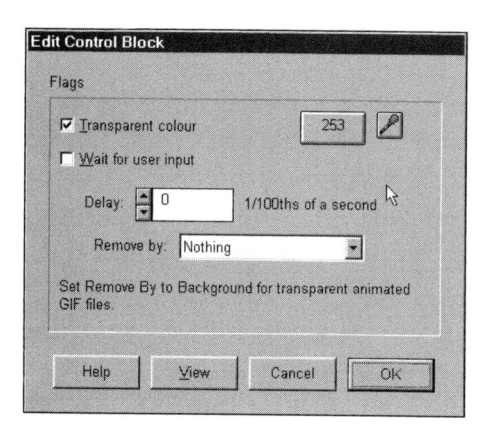

Figure 15-9 Setting the transparency color

NOTE This assumes that the area you want transparent is the same color. If it's not so, a solid background color will flash in your animating GIF file. You will have to set background colors by hand to edit each of the Control blocks.

6. Click the Eyedropper tool, and the first image in your GIF file will appear.
7. Click the area to make transparent. The image will close and the Control Block editor will reopen.
8. Open Remove By dialog box and select Background.
9. Click OK. Save your GIF file.

Interlaced GIF file displays in coarse pixels in a Web browser when it begins to download, and becomes more clearly defined as the download proceeds. It displays in single lines in GIF Construction Set, which are ordered to ultimately display the entire image. Interlaced GIF files offer no performance improvements — they're wholly cosmetic.

Interlaced GIF Files for a Quick Preview

What's an interlaced GIF file? It's an image that draws in passes, to give your users a fuzzy preview of the whole image that gets clearer in each pass as more image information is added. Should you interlace animated GIFs? No, because the way animation works, it won't help reduce download time. But interlacing your nonanimated GIFs is worthwhile because it gives your users something to preview while they're waiting for the page to download.

To create interlaced GIFs, follow these steps:

1. Select File → Open.

2. Choose the GIF file to make interlaced.

3. Double click the Image block to open the Edit Image dialog box, shown in the following figure.

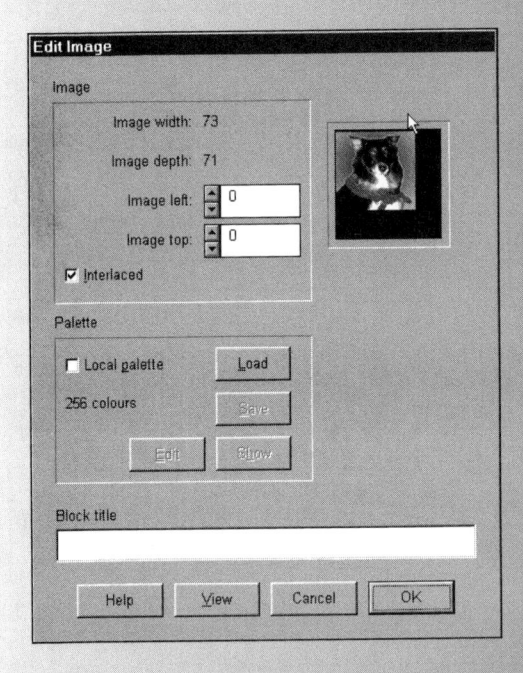

4. From the Edit Image dialog box, choose Interlaced.

5. If you want to select a special color palette, such as the 216 Web safe colors, click the Local Palette button and navigate to your color palette.

5. Click OK and save your file.

6. Choose View to see your interlaced GIF file.

248 ADVANCED INTRANET FEATURES

Note that while you can create interlaced animated GIF files with GIF Construction Set, Web browsers will not display them as such — they'll deinterlace the downloaded image frames before they're displayed. There's no worthwhile reason for creating such a GIF file.

LED SIGNS

LED signs are like those flashing or marquee signs you see in Times Square, public transportation terminals, or your local convenience store. With GIF Construction Set, you can create digital LED signs quickly and easily. Figure 15-10 shows the LED sign options, which include controlling the height of your text, the colors used, the scrolling rate, and whether your animation is continuous or one time only. Figure 15-11 shows a preview of an LED sign.

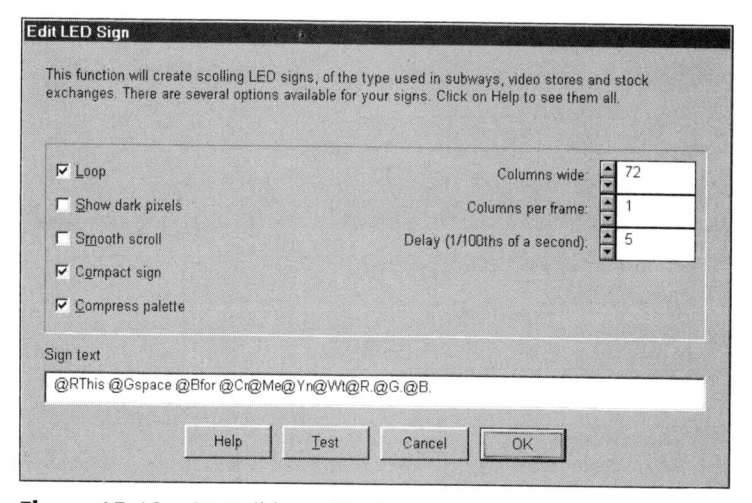

Figure 15-10 GIF Builder's LED signs options

With GIF Construction set, you can create LED signs that are:

* Of varying display speed and scrolling ability
* Large or small
* In seven LED colors
* Adjustable length for your message

BANNERS AND TRANSITIONS

It's easy to add banners and transitions with GIF Construction set by simply selecting the options you want from the appropriate dialog boxes. Banners are great for calling attention to recently added items on a page.

Figure 15-11 A preview of an LED sign

Figure 15-12 shows the Banner dialog box, which includes options for looping, rolling, setting transparent backgrounds, text color and background, size, and font. You'll also set the delay; remember that you want your message to be read, so don't make it move too fast. Enter your message in the Banner Text field, and keep your message short enough to be read quickly. Use contrasting colors for the text and the background.

Preview your banner by choosing the test button. Figure 15-13 shows a sample banner.

Transitions are another great option for easily adding pizzazz to your intranet pages. With GIF Construction Set you can make items appear, make them disappear, make them loop, make them pause, set their size, and choose from a variety of transition affects, as shown in Figure 15-14.

Figure 15-12 GIF Construction Set's Banner dialog box

Figure 15-13 A preview of a banner

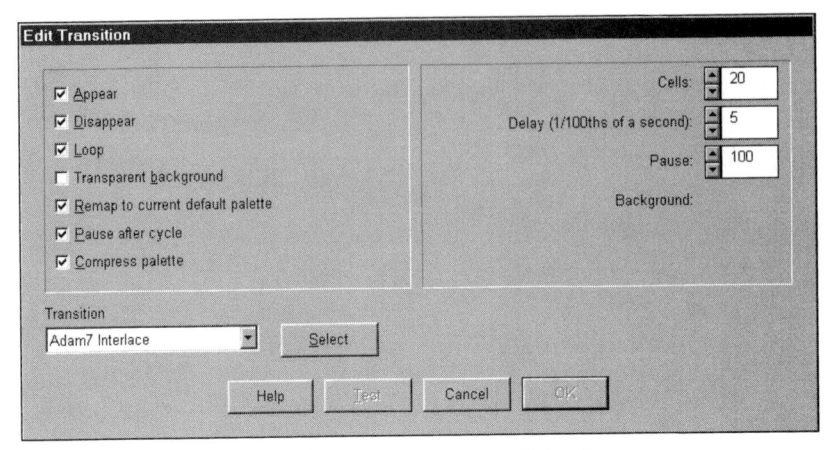

Figure 15-14 GIF Construction Set's Transition dialog box

It's Getting Better All the Time

In addition to the advanced tools discussed earlier in this chapter, the basic Web authoring tools themselves continue to improve with each revision.

Templates

You'll see more and more templates in the future, including intranet pages for specific business functions. Forms and target pages will be easy to modify from these templates, giving fast access to feedback in an organized manner. Other page templates will include those designed specifically for human resources functions, including all the dreaded insurance forms, employee directories, job postings, and the like. Additional templates will include pages designed to connect to databases and publish the results; public relations pages, including press release listings; product pages; table of contents pages; meetings, agendas, and minutes; search pages; and more. Plus, you can create your own reusable templates for pages that work for your intranet. By storing these in a central location on your intranet, you can make the templates easily accessible to everyone, and lend some consistency to your intranet site.

Style Sheets

Style sheets, the standard for which is still being determined, would enable you to set type styles for the heads and main body, and apply them consistently throughout your Web site. This saves enormous amounts of time, especially if you're converting documents from a word processor that are already styled.

The benefit is being able to globally change all the elements of the same type with one command, instead of having to laboriously go through every page and make the change.

Frames

Frames, which enable quick access to the contents of your intranet, are getting easier to use with object-oriented tools like PageMill, as shown in Figure 15-15. With the early page-authoring tools, frames were created blindly. You'd have to toggle back and forth from your tool to a preview in your browser, and back to your tool. The newer tools work with frames in a very visual way, so you can see how your page will look while you're building it.

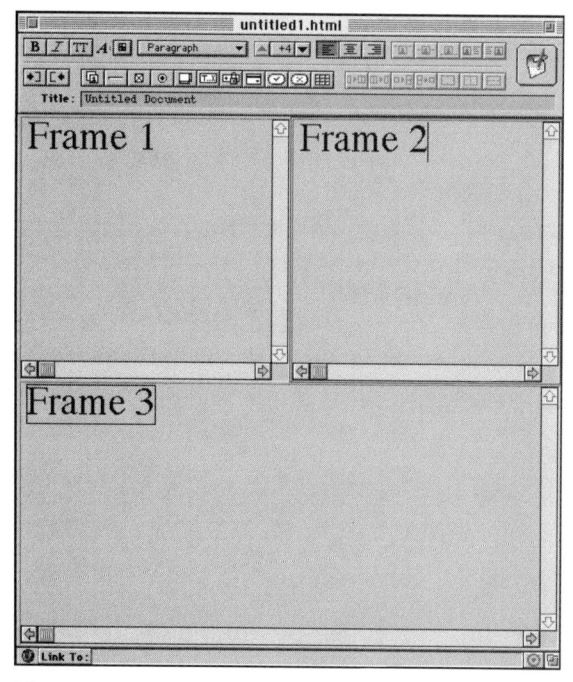

Figure 15-15 PageMill's graphical interface for creating frames

BONUS

3D: The Interface on the Horizon

Remember just a few years back, when the idea of windows and icons was radical? Today it's commonplace, so you're probably wondering what's next.

Enter 3D interfaces, where information is *vitally real.* The idea is to make the interface intuitive enough so users don't need training or help files to access information. For example, your human resources area might look just like your HR department's reception area: insurance forms on the rack on the wall, job postings on the bulletin board, a company directory on the counter, the receptionist behind the desk to answer questions, and so on. By simply clicking the appropriate element, the user would get to the information needed, or be prompted for additional input.

With a 3D interface, the user can see the structure of the information much faster and quickly navigate in and out of areas that are much more familiar than the flat world of two dimensions.

Summary

This chapter covered:

Java applets and ActiveX controls for adding functionality to your intranet

Shockwave and other multimedia tools to add motion and sound to your intranet

Using GIFs for animations

New features of page-authoring tools, including styles sheets, easier frames, and templates

CHAPTER SIXTEEN

MAKING YOUR INTRANET ORGANIC

IN THIS CHAPTER YOU LEARN THESE KEY SKILLS

SOLICITING FEEDBACK FROM YOUR USERS ON YOUR INTRANET   PAGE 256

KEEPING YOUR INTRANET ENERGIZED WITH NEW FEATURES AND INFORMATION   PAGE 259

A successful intranet is an organic creature. By that we mean it is changing constantly, growing with your organization, and changing structure and content as needed to fulfill your demands for information.

If you're open to suggestions, your users will provide adequate feedback for you to enhance and fine-tune your intranet — provided you're listening. Whether it's a formal survey or a walk down the hall (you can still actually talk face to face, you know!), you'll get ideas to keep your intranet lively.

The beauty of this medium is that you and your colleagues can make changes on the fly, relatively easily and with little cost. This chapter helps you evaluate the effectiveness of your intranet, and take steps to ensure that the beast illustrates the Japanese term *kaizen* — constant, never-ending improvement.

Ask Them What They Think . . . and Brace Yourself

Asking your users what they like and what they don't can be a very humbling experience. You've probably invested a lot of time and energy creating the monster, and you've battled the political wars to get the required approvals and financing. You've spent hours wrestling with your organizations workflow process, trying to make sense of it before putting the business onto an intranet. And now you're asking people to evaluate the project — it's not easy.

CAUTION Both the intranet and the Internet are highly interactive forums in which people will respond fast to anything. Remember, people are likely to be more forthcoming (and potentially harsh) when they can write the words instead of having to speak to you directly. If you do receive abusive feedback, don't take it personally. If you want to address it, call the person rather than zapping back a defensive message.

You can solicit feedback through the intranet itself with feedback forms, a sample of which is shown in Figure 16-1. You can set up a Web page on your intranet to collect and tabulate the results of these surveys, which is particularly useful if you have a large organization. You can create a discussion group for an ongoing dialogue about the intranet and appoint someone to moderate.

If you want people to give you feedback on a regular basis, respond to their comments as often as possible.

Or, you can do it the "old-fashioned" way and talk to people informally. The only drawback with face-to-face communication is that your responses may not be as candid, depending on the organizational status of you and the person with whom you're chatting.

If you want people to give you feedback on a regular basis, respond to their comments as often as possible. That can be done with a quick e-mail (cheat a little and create a generic letter that you can customize if you have time), posting on the intranet (such as in a What's New area), or other internal public relations measures. Your acknowledgment of people's ideas will go a long way.

You'll probably want to explore the following topics for feedback.

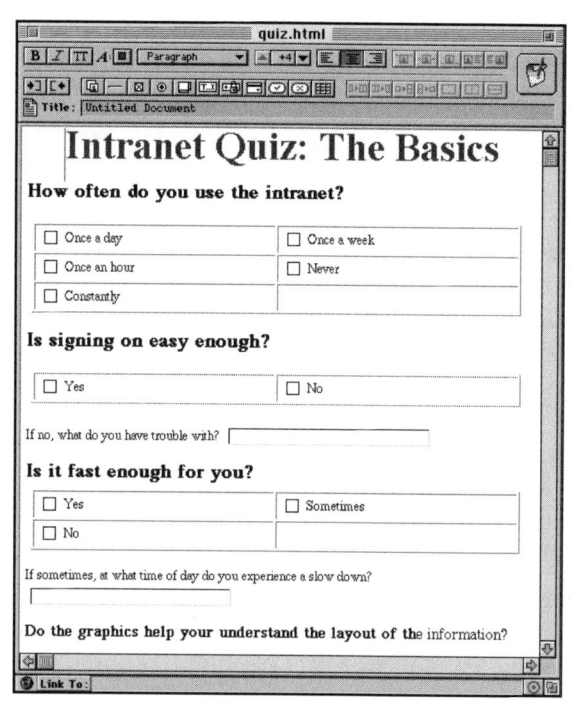

Figure 16-1 A form to collect feedback

Writing Style

Writing for the intranet is different than writing on paper. Remember that people are looking for morsels of information and don't want to scroll. If your users complain about the length or the complexity of copy, try the following:

Keep your pages short. Make more than one page rather than scrolling, if possible.

Use formatting logically. Even though HTML formatting is limited, you might be unnecessarily cluttering your pages with styling that doesn't improve the delivery of information.

Write summaries. Remember that people have very limited attention spans these days; everyone loves an "executive summary."

Consider developing a style manual. If you have a large number of contributors with mixed writing abilities, consider setting some standards. Readers/users can get confused if terms are used inconsistently.

Content

Find out if the content you're delivering is useful to people. Inquire if they understand the material, want other information, think the quality is good, want to contribute, and so on. If your users respond that the content isn't on the mark, consider doing the following:

Create a glossary. Very often people can get lost right away when they trip on terms they don't understand. Create a glossary with definitions, and hyperlinks to examples if possible. Make sure users know the glossary exists.

Consider timeliness. If your information is out of date, your users may start reverting to their old paper-based ways. Set up a process for regular updates of information, and appoint someone to monitor the content in areas where timing is critical. If it's regular reports from an external source, see if you can increase the frequency of updates.

Think about accuracy. If your users say that the content is incorrect, appoint someone to review the materials, similar to managing editor of a magazine. You may need multiple people if your content covers many topics.

Find a champion with an editorial background. It's easy to think that anyone can manage content in a digital format, but having someone who understands editorial content can improve the effectiveness of your intranet dramatically. Take a look around your organization and you'll probably find someone with an English degree or journalism background who'd be willing to lead the effort.

Structure

You'll want to know if your information is accessible. Can users find what they want within a reasonable number of clicks? Can they use the search engine effectively? Do the metaphors make sense or do they get in the way? If your users say the structure needs improvement, try the following:

Fine-tune your search tool. Is your search tool hitting on a lot of "stop words" such as *a, the, an,* the company name, and others? Make sure you're including instructions for creating good search queries. Help your users set up reusable queries for cumbersome and repeated searches.

Reevaluate your keywords. Do your keywords work? Are you creating keywords that aren't in the terminology your users would enter? Get someone from each department or functional area to contribute to establishing keywords for documents frequently accessed by their area. Revamp your keyword approach as soon as possible.

Limit the number of clicks to useful information. If your users say they're spending too much time hunting, consider adding frames or other navigation devices, such as buttons, to improve the speed of navigation.

Evaluate if your metaphors are working. Some metaphors are overdone and don't add much to the structure of an intranet. If your metaphor is for fun and doesn't impede information access, that's fine. But if your users are tripping on images, colors, or elements that don't make sense to them, cut them out or try labeling them for clarity.

Performance

Your users might be griping about slow access time for finding pages, moving between links, finding results on searches, and request processing. You'll probably forward the requests to your IS department, but check the following first:

Are images small and fast drawing? If not, downsample the images to the smallest possible memory size with a quality deterioration that's acceptable to you. Consider reducing the physical size of the images, too.

Are your links current? Use a site management tool to keep your links up-to-date for better retrieval times.

Other performance issues of speed are likely network structure and/or capacity issues.

Energize Your Intranet

If your users respond that your intranet isn't much better than paper, you might be lacking enough interactivity to set it apart from the paper world. It's the idea that anything digital should be dynamic: changing and intriguing, flexible and worth revisiting.

If your users are demanding more interactivity and liveliness on your intranet, consider the following solutions:

Create something fun and interactive that changes regularly. Whether it's company trivia (how long have you been in the business of making widgets?), an employee contest (name the new product and win a weekend trip to San Francisco), call for new business ideas (new products, new processes), or any other subjects that interest your users. Post the results; you'll be amazed how quickly people will participate.

Make sure your search tool is accessible. If your users find your site to be somewhat static, add more access to your search tool from different segments of your intranet.

Add a few bells and whistles. Although sound and video are more glitz than substance, users expect something extra when they're accessing information online. With a few easy additions, you can add a bit of dazzle to your intranet to keep your users entertained. Add slide presentations, audio of recent presentations, and so on.

Add CGI programs to access more data. Does your organization have something called a "data warehouse" that seems to contain all the vital information your colleagues need? Remember, you can link these other data resources to your intranet though CGI programs that can be constructed as easy-to-use forms. Your users enter the information they need, a request is sent to the data warehouse or any other location where raw data is stored, and an easy-to-access intranet page is returned to your user.

> **X-REF** For details on CGI, see Chapter 15.

BONUS

A Online Quiz for Your Users

Create an easy-to-use form that your users can complete in five minutes or less. If you expect a large number of responses, focus on answers using check boxes or radio buttons to select from a list, or a pop-up menu. If you want more narrative results that you will read through, use text fields in which the user can fill in details. Figure 16-2 shows both check boxes and text fields.

If you're the type who wants to know a lot from your audience, change the questions on your response form on a regular basis. Ask about content one week, structure the next, and then design, performance, and so on. Rotate back to the beginning if you're making substantial upgrades to your intranet.

Consider posting your results so that your users can see what people are thinking. Best of all, you'll now have working templates that you can use to collect information about many issues that matter to your organization.

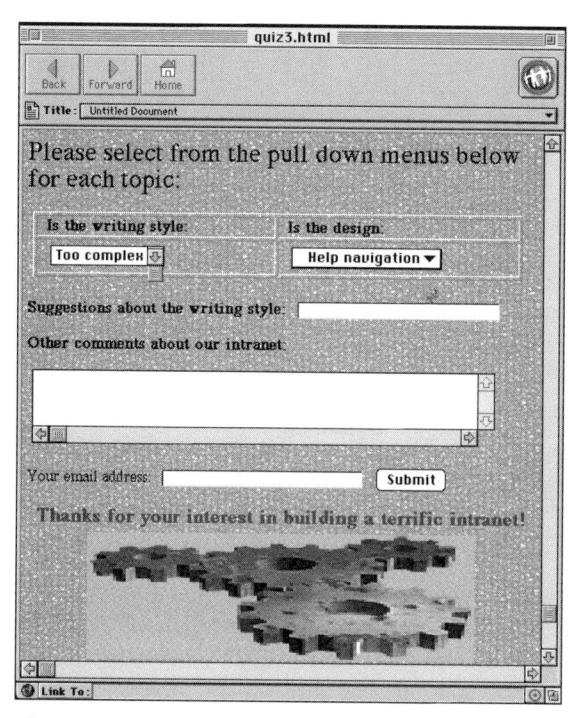

Figure 16-2 Check boxes and text fields in a feedback form

Intranet Quiz: The Basics

How often do you use the intranet?

- ❏ Constantly
- ❏ Once an hour
- ❏ Once a day
- ❏ Once a week
- ❏ Never

Is signing on easy enough?

- ❏ Yes
- ❏ No

If no, what do you have trouble with?

Is it the intranet fast enough for you?

- ❏ Yes
- ❏ No
- ❏ Sometimes

If sometimes, at what time of day do you experience a slow down?

Do the graphics help you understand the layout of the information?

- ❏ Yes
- ❏ No

Suggestions to improve graphics:
Is the content:

- ❏ Timely?
- ❏ Accurate?
- ❏ Interesting?

What else would you like to see included?

What isn't useful information via the intranet?

Does the structure:

- ❏ Enable easy navigation to information you need?
- ❏ Have too many layers requiring too much clicking?

Is the writing style:

- ❏ Too complex for online reading?
- ❏ Too fragmented across various pages?
- ❏ Just right?

Suggestions about the writing style:

_____
_____
_____

Summary

This chapter explored how to keep your intranet lively and a place where your colleagues will visit on a regular basis. You learned:

How to solicit feedback from your users on the core functions of your intranet, including writing style, content, structure, and system performance.

How to keep your intranet energized with new features and information.

DISCOVERY CENTER

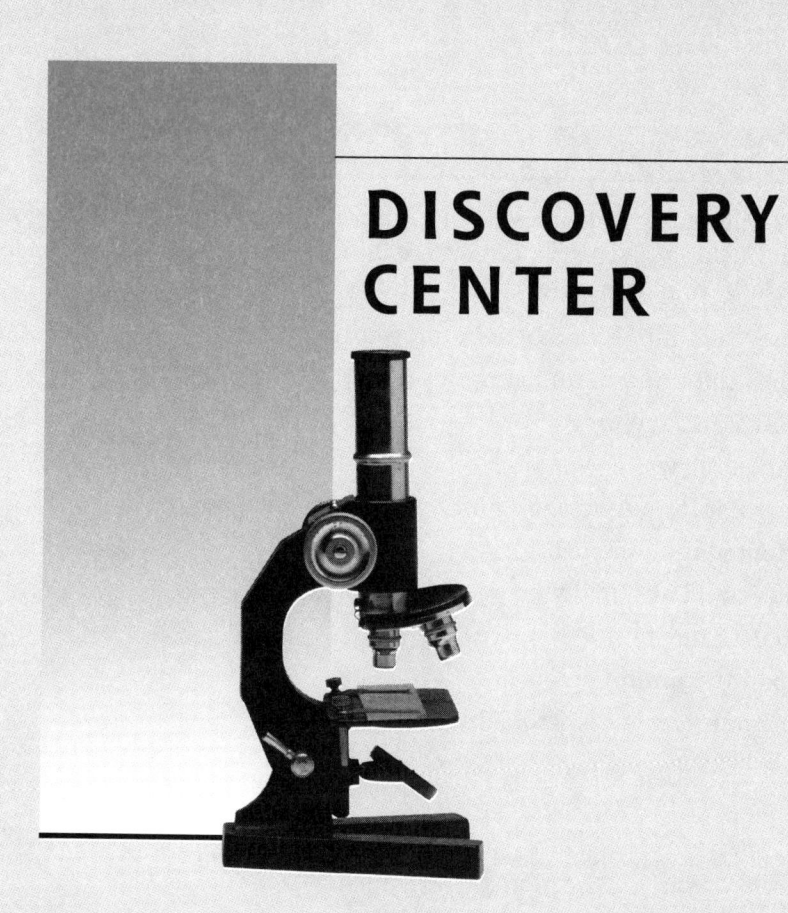

In this section, you'll discover many of the important steps for creating an effective intranet. The Discovery Center is a handy reference to the most important tasks in the chapters. The quick summaries include page references referring you to the chapters if you need more information.

CHAPTER 1

What You Can Do with Your Intranet (page 9)

An intranet is literally a network within a corporation; it can be used to manage information, including creation of content, routing and approval, publishing, document usage, and archiving. Use your intranet for:

- Employee manuals and benefit information
- Product information and current pricing
- Project status reports
- Company news
- Personal information (announcements, classified ads, and so on)
- Document management
- Routing and approvals
- Help desk functions
- Corporate training programs
- Reusing information across divisions

CHAPTER 2

How to Assess Your Content (page 26)

The intranet becomes the living example of your organization's structure and process, which is why a time-out to assess your operation is in order. The degree of content and process assessment is up to you; we've found that the law of diminishing returns applies to this task. We'll also look at some of the organizational and political barriers you may encounter along the way.

1. Start by gathering paper-based materials that you use on a regular basis, in the form they presently exist, whether it's 8 ½"-×-11" paper, multipart forms, odd-size slips, or whatever. Take paper files and sort them using the tools you know: paper folders, hanging folders, file cabinets, and so on. This is a visual and tangible method that will be familiar to everyone.

2. Gather your historical paper documents (contracts, old reports and letters, completed projects). Categorize and file them.

3. Gather your electronic files into one location, regardless of the application used. Use the folder hierarchies of Windows as shown in Figure 2-1 to create a structure, using the same theory of folders and file cabinets as noted above. Think carefully about the labels you use for hierarchies, and you'll have the beginnings of your process, discussed later in this chapter.

4. Gather your historical electronic documents and evaluate what can be archived offline and what needs to be accessible live on your intranet.

5. Clean house while you're at it. Look for duplicate forms and functions, and outdated materials. Decide on a time frame that you consider the useful life of a document for your business, and discard anything older than that.

6. Decide which documents can be combined and improved. Decide whom in your organization is best equipped to do so.

7. Create a wish list of materials that you don't currently have but would like to add in an intranet. Again, think about who's best situated to create the new materials.

8. Actively solicit input from the future users of the intranet for potential content and ways they want to use information. You will be surprised what you'll hear that you haven't thought of yet.

CHAPTER 3

How to Write an Intranet Plan (page 36)

1. Create a one-page executive summary.
2. Propose your intranet team.
3. Plan an implementation schedule.

How to Nurture the Intranet into the Office Culture (page 38)

1. Get as many people on the intranet as you can.
2. Market your intranet as you would your products.
3. Get support from top management.

Who You Need on Your Intranet Team (page 39)

You need to find people to cover these functional areas:

- Writing/editing
- Project coordination
- Design
- Technical development
- Testing
- Production
- Site administration

How to Figure Out Cost and Savings (page 44)

When estimating costs for your intranet, use spreadsheet software to determine hardware, software, and application-development needs.

This Excel worksheet shows projected intranet costs:

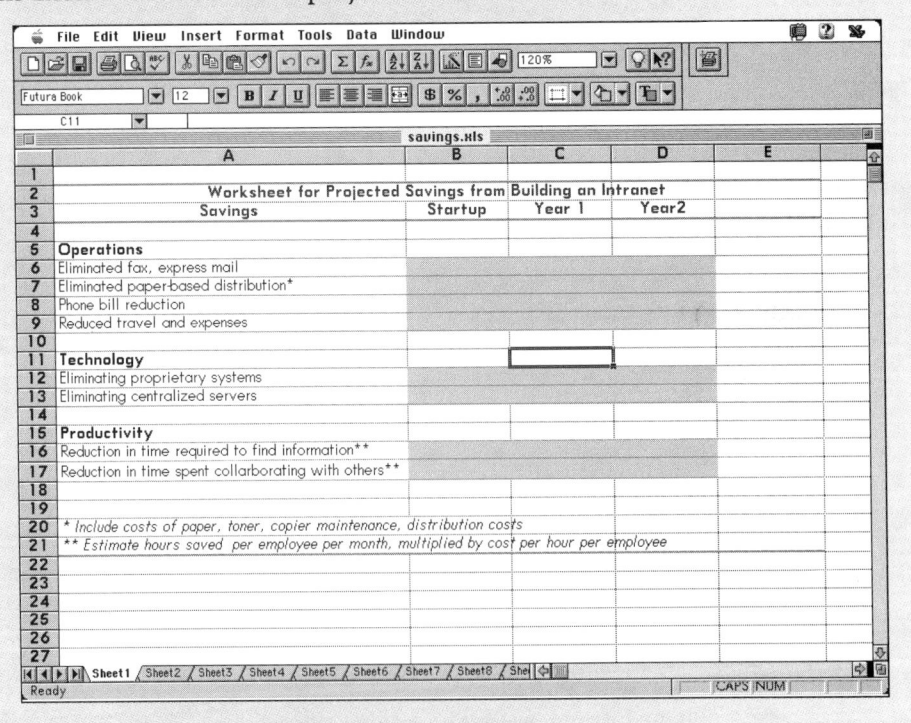

Intranet savings can translate into 100 percent a year or more. Use a worksheet like the following to estimate savings:

268 DISCOVERY CENTER

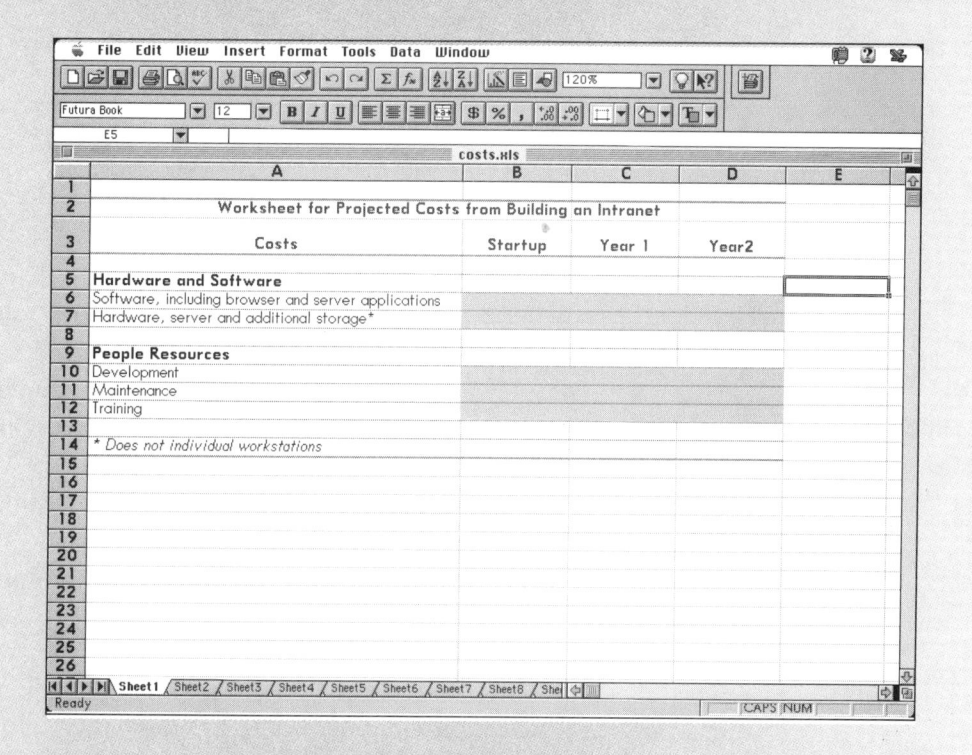

How to Create an Intranet Prototype (page 48)

Use Adobe PageMill or Microsoft FrontPage to create a prototype of your intranet. You should follow these steps:

1. Start with a paper-based prototype
2. Set up dummy pages
3. Add links
4. Add additional functions if necessary, using plug-ins
5. Make sure the prototype is ready when you present your plan

Building an intranet is tough work, but if you dedicate yourself to developing a comprehensive plan, you'll have a solid road map to follow. Most aspects of building an intranet can be facilitated with electronic tools. The more you work in the digital world, the more natural and preferable it will become. You'll eliminate redundant tasks by entering or gathering information once. You can evaluate, process, route, and archive all in the digital format, improving your speed and accuracy in the competitive business environment.

DISCOVERY CENTER

CHAPTER 4

Questions to Ask Your Users (page 52)

Designing your intranet is a critical step in determining how accessible and inviting your intranet will be. Consider the following questions before developing your design:

- How do users categorize the information they use? Do they think of information by project, by department, or something else?
- For what fields of information would they search? For example, would they search by product number or name, due dates, projects that they're responsible for, subject, or other fields?
- How often does this information change? Would it help to have more frequent updates?
- How do they manage information now? Find out what manual tools they use, what electronic tools they have, and what they'd like to have at their fingertips.
- How do they think an intranet makes them more productive? Can they project how much time and money can be saved by having information more accessible?

Design Issues to Address (page 52)

1. **Interactive or published pages.** Will your users need to enter information, or sort the information presented? Or, will your users be more recipients of published information?
2. **Complex or simple.** Do you users want just the facts, and how much data are you going to be handling? Will you need a lot of tables for posting details?
3. **Searchable or directory-oriented.** Should your home page include clickable elements to get users to subsections quickly, or are they going to enter keywords to search your site?
4. **Cross-referencing or hierarchy.** Do your users need a lot of pointers within your intranet to get around? You'll always want to point them back to your home page, but you might want links between pages, too.
5. **Digital and paper formats.** Will your users print out some segments of your intranet onto paper? Whether it's reports for group meetings, or forms to be taken off-site, you'll need to plan your page dimension to either fit the screen or be scrollable.

How to Effectively Use Icons and Backgrounds (page 58)

* How your intranet looks is as important as what it says — like it or not, it's got to be pretty to be read.
* Metaphors quicken the learning curve, and they don't necessarily need to be glamorous to succeed. The most successful intranets have a distinguished look without being overpowering.
* Try to create enough variety to keep your site intriguing and fun, but don't tease your visitors with "under construction" signs, demands for user feedback, or dead link as seen in the figure below.

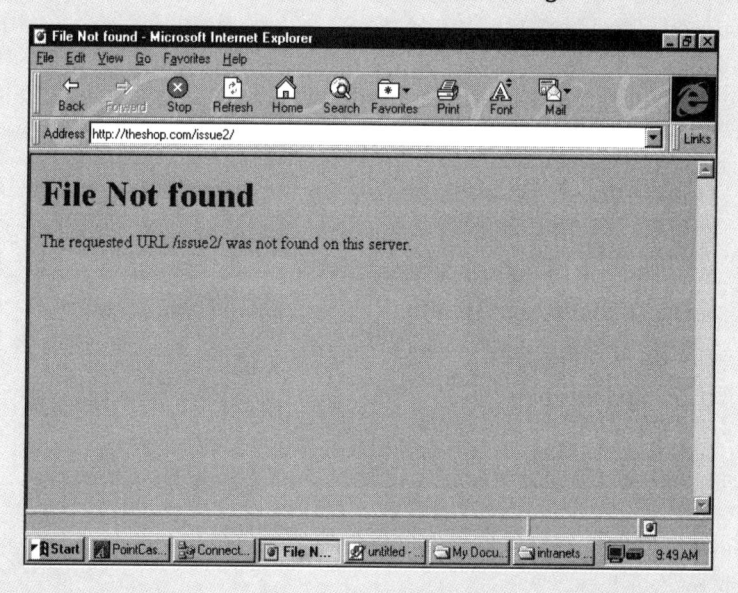

CHAPTER 5

Scanner Categories (page 73)

Scanners come in three categories:

* Personal scanners
* Desktop scanners
* High-end, high-volume scanners

What You Can Do with Scanners (page 75)

From business cards to receipts, invoices to articles, any document can be included in your intranet once it's in a digital format. Using a variety of scanners, you can take paper-based information and easily distribute it over your intranet.

Scanning software can do the following:

* Create simple images of your files
* Do complete conversions into editable text
* Capture images

Ultimately, you'll have digital documents to integrate into your intranet. These screen captures show typical office documents scanned with Visioneer's Paperport, an easy-to-use personal scanner that costs less than $300.

The following figures show a receipt, invoice, and a newspaper clipping scanned using the Paperport scanner.

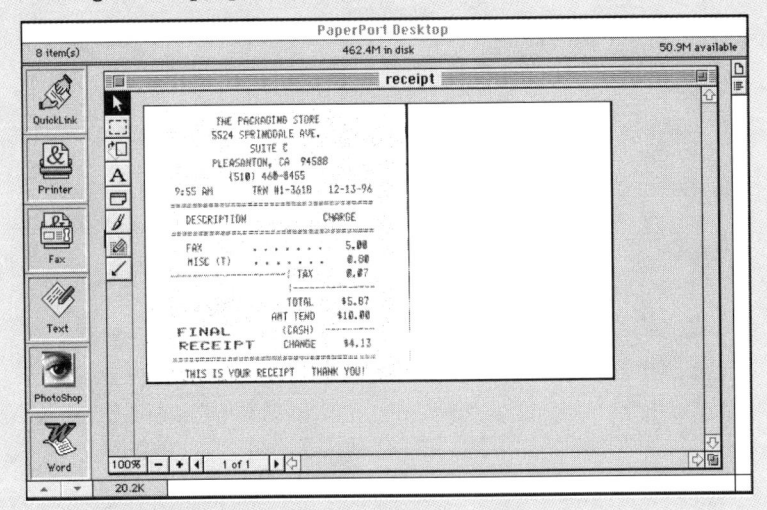

DISCOVERY CENTER

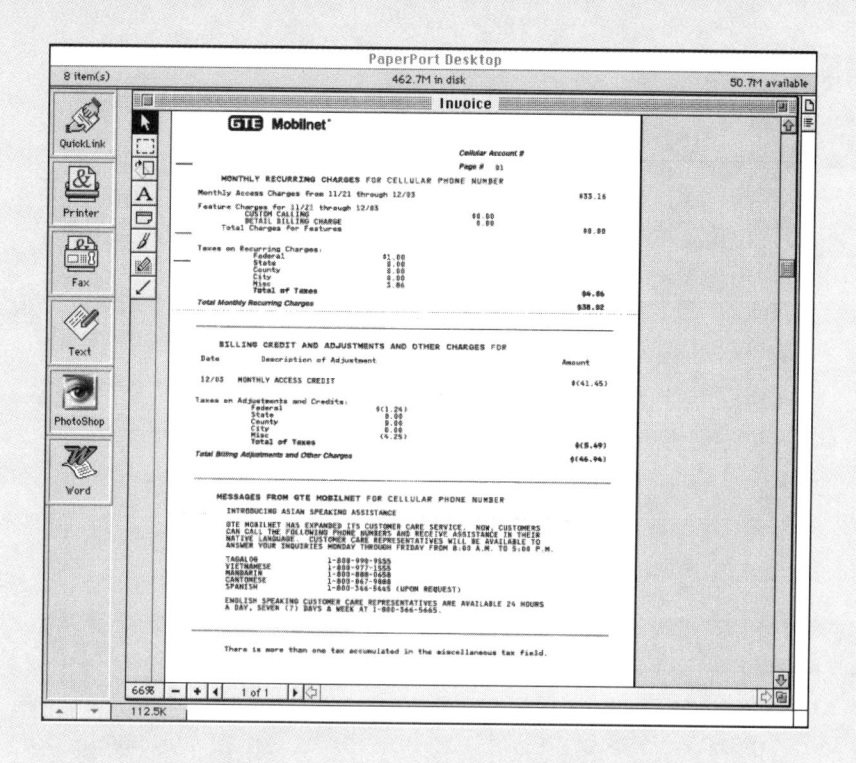

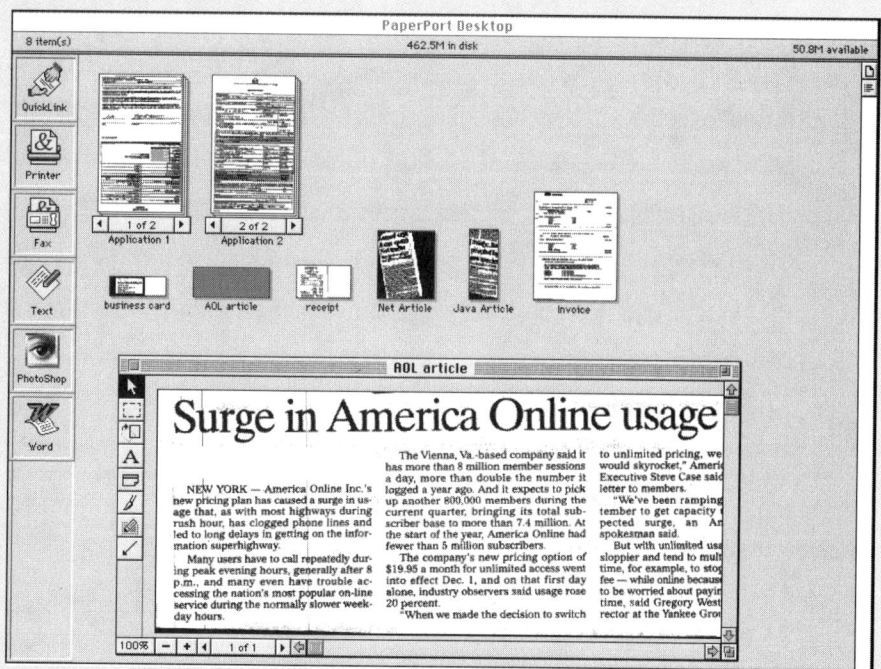

CHAPTER 6

Intranet and Web-Authoring Tools (page 95)

There are many technology tools to choose from when building the pages for your intranet. Building a Web page is really two phases: building the pages, and then testing them in a browser such as Explorer or Navigator.

The most prominent Web page authoring tools are the following:

- Microsoft FrontPage
- Adobe PageMill
- DeltaPoint QuickSite
- Netscape Navigator Gold
- NetObjects Fusion
- Macromedia Backstage Designer

How to Create Intranet Pages Using Wizards (page 99)

Most of the tools have step-by-step wizards to walk you through the creation of basic pages and your site, as shown in the DeltaPoint QuickSite screens here.

1. First, create text for your home page.

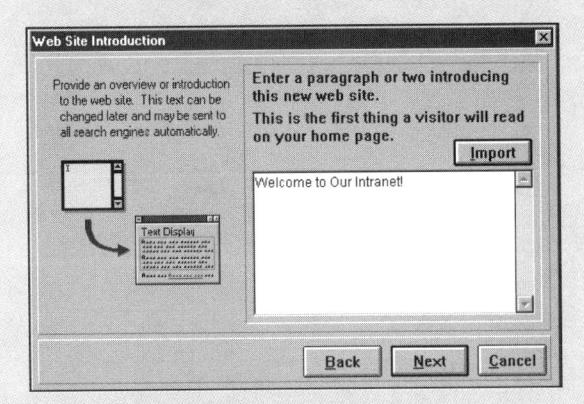

2. QuickSite prompts you to form a Web site structure.

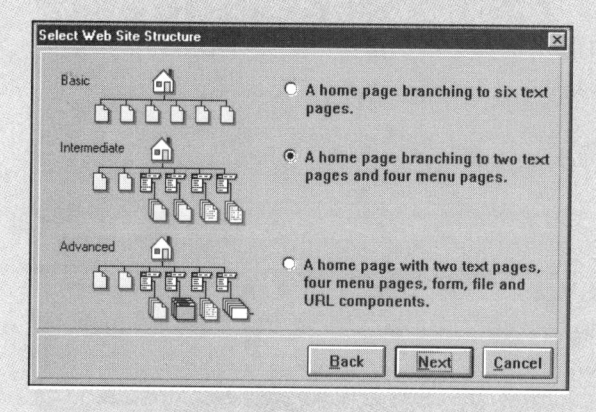

3. Next, style your pages.

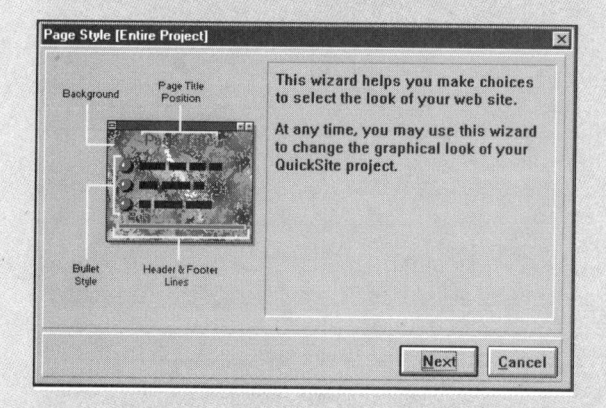

4. Review your site structure.

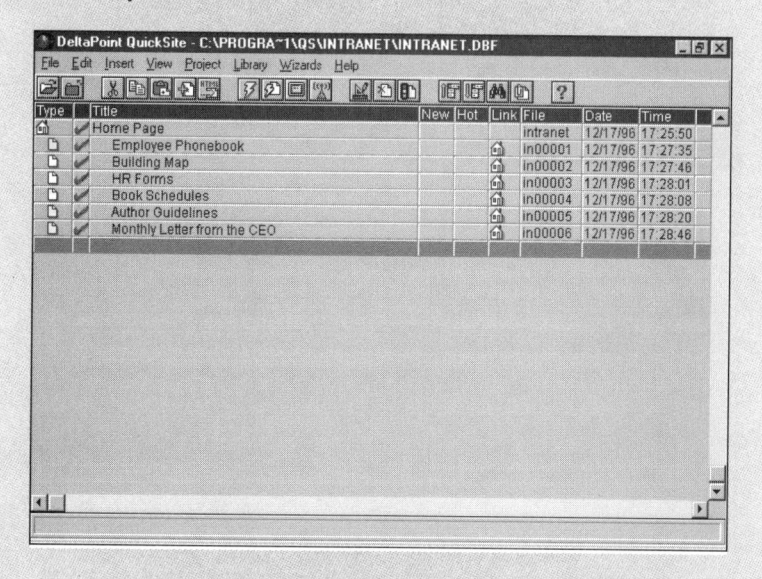

5. Finally, you can view your completed home page.

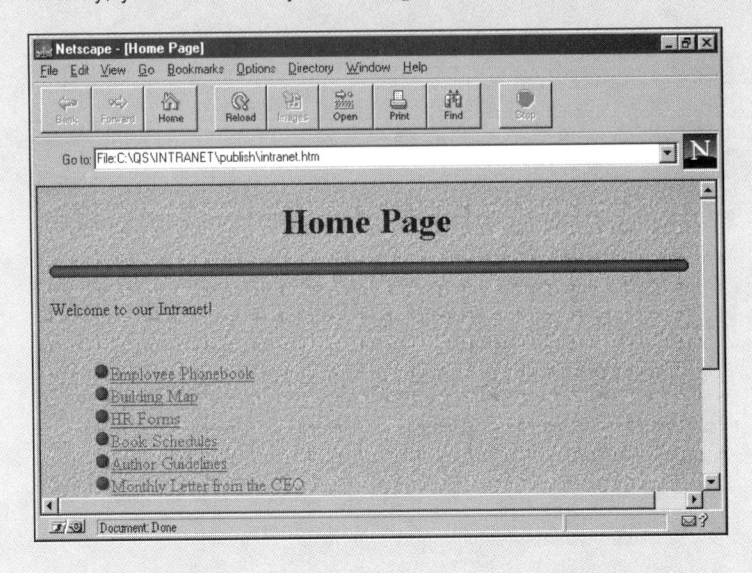

CHAPTER 7

Browser Similarities (page 116)

The browser is the looking glass for your intranet. For general viewing of text and images, your pages will look the same regardless of the browser. The Employee Directory page shown here looks the same whether it's viewed with Microsoft Internet Explorer or Netscape Navigator.

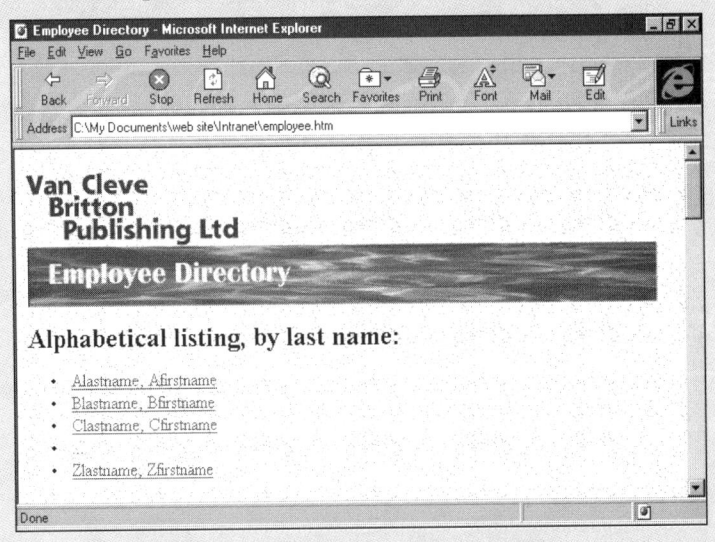

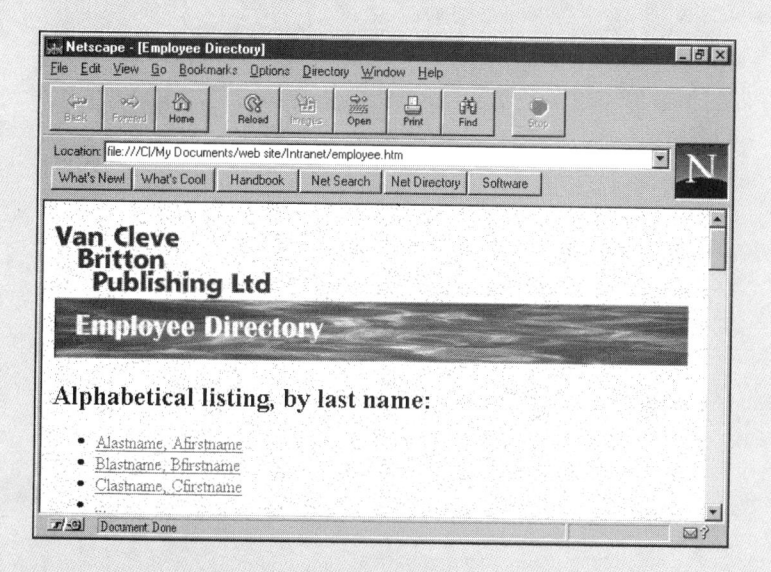

Browser Differences (page 117)

For browser features such as frames, interactive components, ActiveX elements, and marquees, you may see significantly different results when viewed with the different browsers. The intranet News page shown here looks different in Explorer, which shows the marquee successfully highlighting the promotion. Notice that the frames appear different in Navigator and Explorer, even though they're set to the same percentage in the Web page authoring tool.

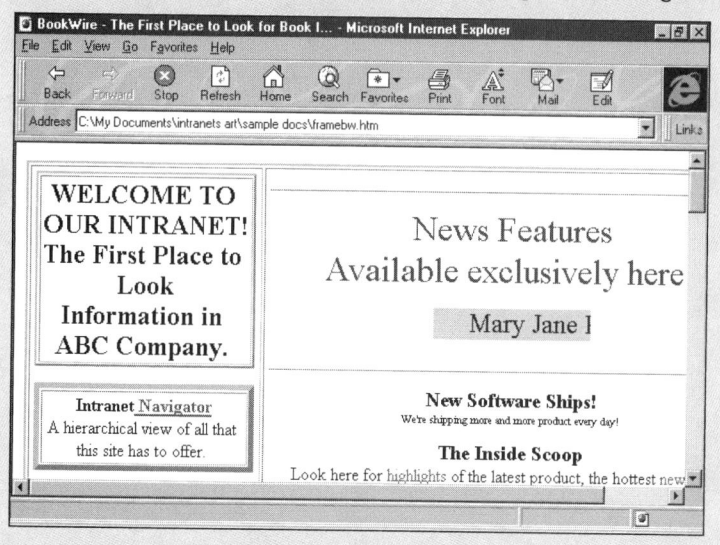

DISCOVERY CENTER **277**

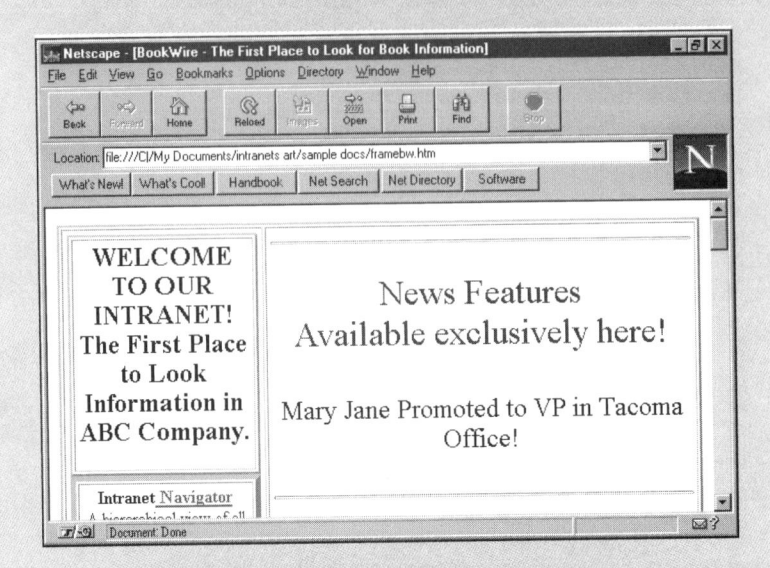

The bottom line: Pick one browser and stick to it for all the users of your intranet. You're in a closed environment and can dictate these things, so take advantage of it! You'll save yourself a lot of time in testing and modifying pages.

CHAPTER 8

Rules for Site Management (page 126)

Managing the files in your intranet is an important foundation when it comes to running and maintaining a site. You'll want to:

- Make sure everyone uses the 8.3 filenaming convention of that DOS world for URLs of your Web pages; you can use up to 32 characters for the Title of your page.
- Keep the file extension (the last three characters) to identify the file format.
- Establish a method for tracking revisions.
- Keep the filenames the same.
- Use the document header information to track dates of modification and creation, and comments.
- Require the submitter to provide the file header information, including:
  - Author
  - Date
  - Subject
  - Keywords

* Decide who will be responsible for reviewing updated material, and establish approval procedures if necessary.
* Put the approved files on your intranet and delete outdated files.

Features of Site Management Tools (page 129)

* A site view that shows all resources

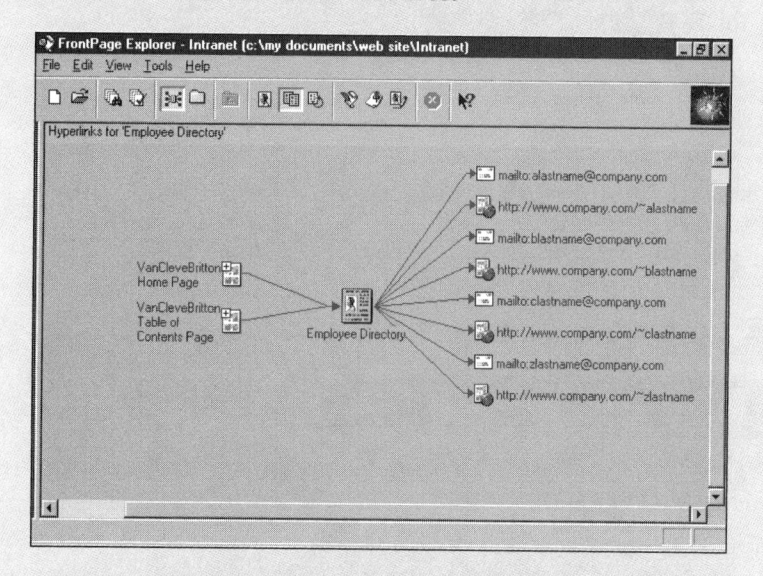

* Warnings for missing links

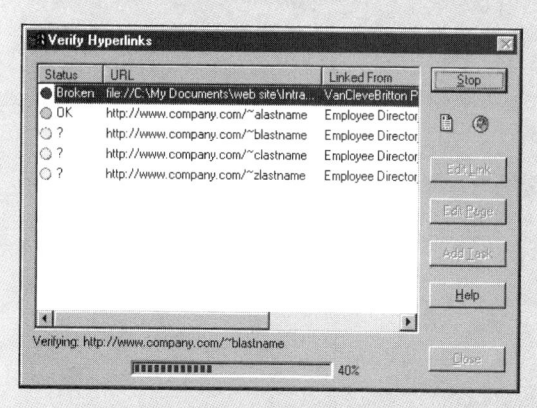

* Automatic fixes for missing links
* Easy link creation
* Links to external Web addresses
* A To Do List to track tasks

CHAPTER 9

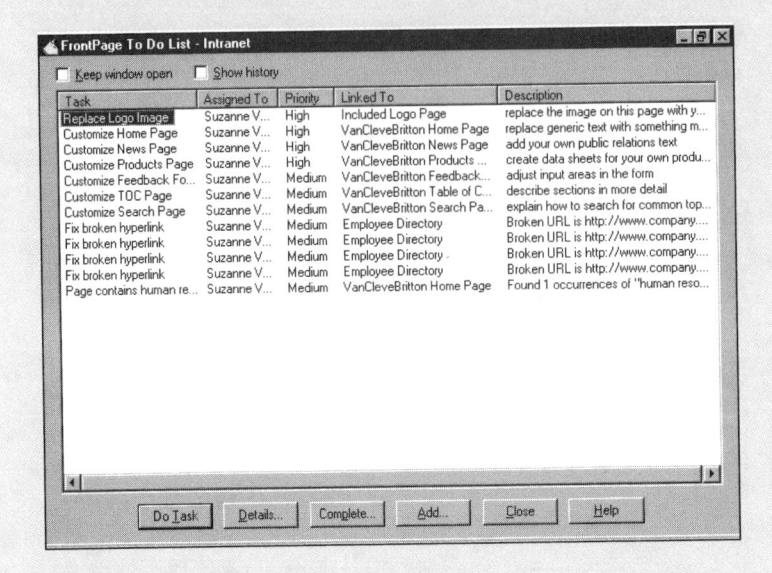

How to Use Keywords (page 142)

Keywords are vital to creating quick access to your intranet. The easiest way to attach a keyword to a document is to use the Document Properties or Document Info found in many applications. Add those terms when you create the document; that way the content will be freshest in your mind. Keywords should be simple — three or four words at most per phrase.

For example, if you wanted to keyword a new human resources medical coverage policy, you'd likely use the terms: insurance, medical plan, HMOs, PPOs, healthcare, and so on. Your users may think about medical coverage under any of those phrases, and you'd want them to be able to find the document easily.

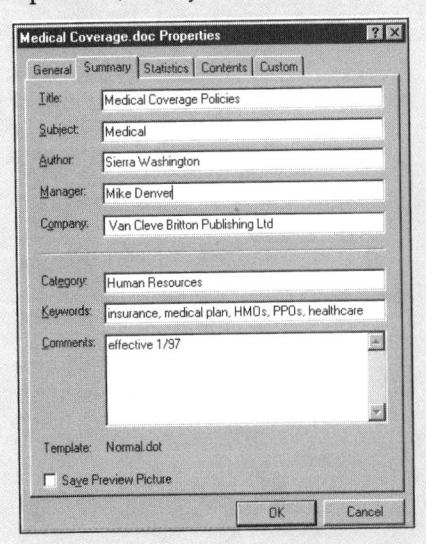

How to Use Boolean Queries (page 145)

If you're looking at a full text search instead of just keywords, you'll need a few terms of what's called Boolean logic. Essentially the basics are four words: and, or, not, near. *And* means the search must include all the words, *or* means either will do, *not* excludes a word, and *near* means it must be close in proximity.

For example, if you wanted to find the update on your company's medical coverage, but you wanted to exclude PPOs, you could enter *Medical Coverage NOT PPOs* to get your results.

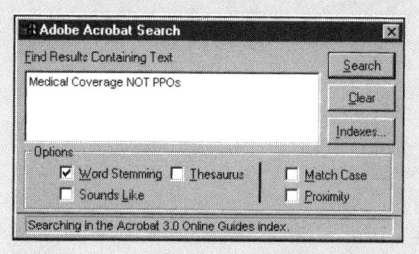

CHAPTER 10

Intranet Servers to Consider (page 158)

You'll need an intranet server to run server software, and act as storage for the intranet pages that you'll want available to your users. These servers are typically high-end desktop computers running one of the standard operating systems such as:

- Digital Equipment's Unix
- Novell NetWare
- Microsoft Windows
- IBM OS/2
- Apple Mac OS

You'll probably have your Information Systems people implement and manage your intranet server, while you focus your time and energy on the content. But it will help the overall planning picture if you work with IS to determine your needs because you know the user community and the information it will be managing.

Server Information to Consider (page 158)

When planning to buy a server, consider the following:

- How many people you'll have accessing the intranet at the same time
- How far apart your users are — it does take data longer to travel farther

* Speed and memory requirements
* Storage needs

CHAPTER 11

Importance of Intranet Security (page 169)

It took the business world a long time to realize that computer data is a resource. In fact, it's one of the most valuable resources available to an organization. That's why an intranet is so important: It lets your personnel use that valuable resource more effectively.

But you're also going to have to make sure that nobody else gets to use that valuable resource. That's why security on the corporate intranet is so important.

Security Rules (page 170)

* Develop a good, healthy paranoia. In the world of computing, consider yourself surrounded by enemies within and without.
* Floods, fire, static electricity, and other acts of God can wreak havoc with your computer equipment.
* Never, ever underestimate the power of human error.
* Secure your intranet even before your people start using it.
* Decide who gets access to what information, and making sure that *only* those people can get it, is an early way of keeping your valuable information resources from the clutches of those who don't deserve them.
* Passwords are an absolutely indispensable way of making sure that only those who are approved for access actually *get* access to sensitive material.
* If you should lose some of those valuable resources (either to accident or vandalism) the successful functioning of your organization will require that you get that data back on the intranet as quickly and as accurately as possible. Storage media is vital.
* Firewalls — systems that act as buffers between the intra- and Internet — can help improve your system's security from the outside world.
* Data encryption, a method of codes that — hopefully — keeps anyone but the intended recipient from reading a given file.

CHAPTER 12

Training Needs (page 189)

Your users will need to know how to use the basic browser you install, whether it's Microsoft Explorer or Netscape Navigator. Yes, there are a few others still alive, but these two players already own most the market and are certainly your best bet.

Both applications offer Web tutorials and help files. You can use these online if you have access to the Internet; you can also download the tutorials and post them on your intranet for local access. The functionality of using a Web browser on your intranet and on the larger Internet are the same; the differences will be your custom design and structure, and links to other applications unique to your organization.

These tools will get you started, but to fully utilize all the capabilities of your intranet, some organized training will go a long way.

For an engaging and fun introduction to browsers, visit the Netscape handbook at:

```
http://www.netscape.com/eng/mozilla/2.0/handbook/docs/intro.html#C1
```

Beyond training on how to use the intranet itself, or other computer applications, consider online training for: new hire orientation, new product information training, budget preparation guidelines, production instructions, and more.

CHAPTER 13

File and Document Management with Livelink (page 202)

The screen shots here show the guided tour of Livelink intranets, with a descriptive window up top detailing the features of the tool in the window below. These examples show you how one groupware application handles file management in your inbox, and document management with workflow diagrams.

Take one for a test-drive, and consider the applications for your organization. Whether you choose a groupware solution for building your intranet, or a more modular approach with a variety of tools, the theory and features are very similar.

* Livelink's opening screen starts your journey into the demo.

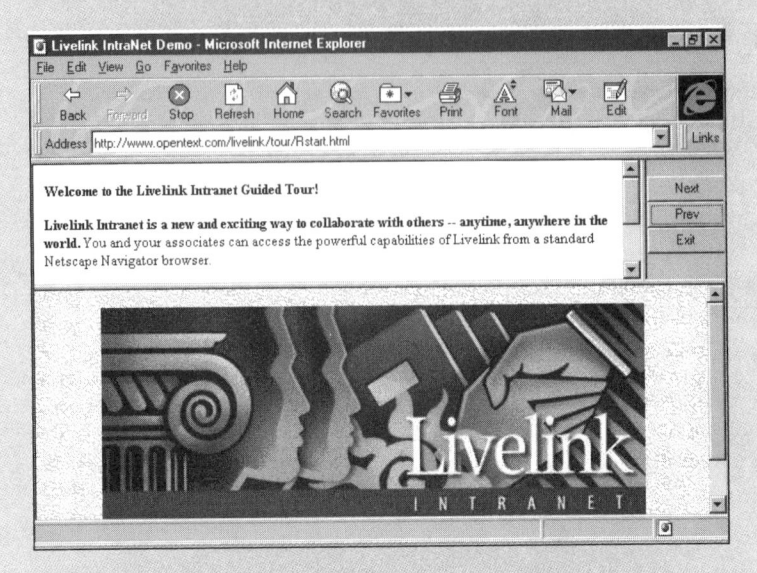

✹ The Livelink Inbox shows how you can review and manage your e-mail.

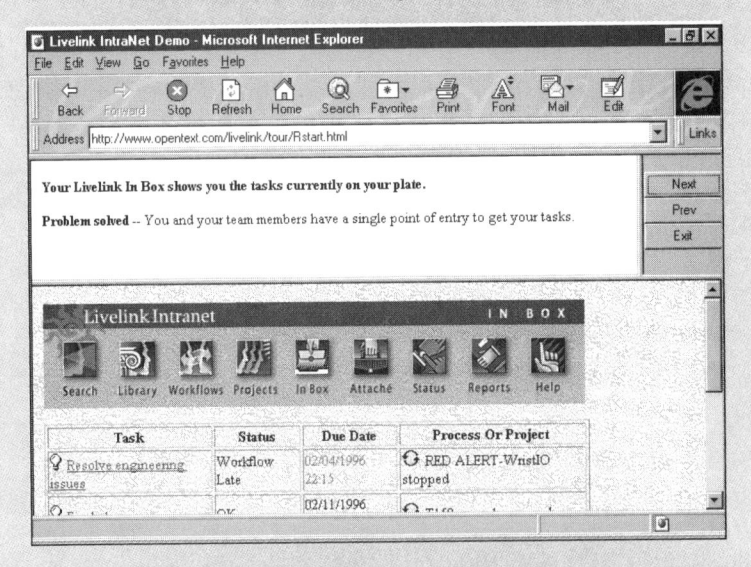

✹ Workflow diagrams streamline document management

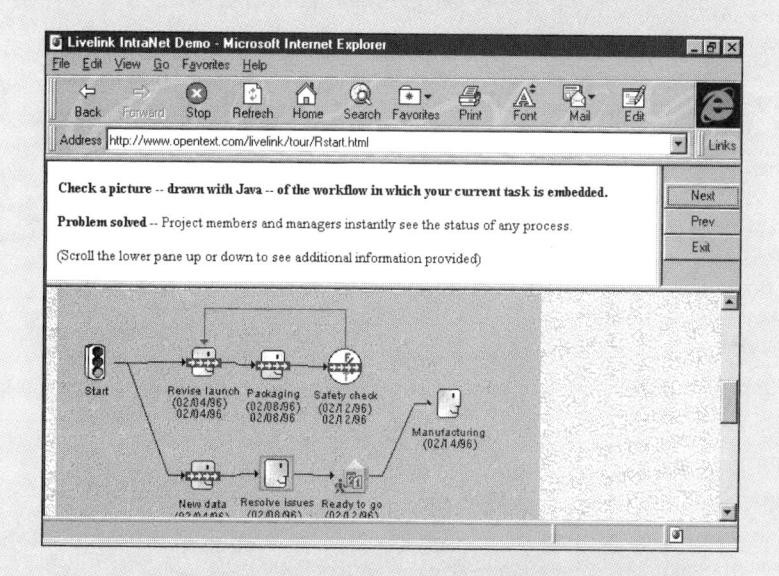

Groupware Applications You Can Use (page 204)

There are many different features you can add to expand the capabilities of your intranet, much of them following applications that are labeled groupware. Most groupware applications are now Web compatible, meaning you can use the best of both on your intranet.

Many of the groupware applications offer free demos or tours on their Web sites:

Application	Web Site
LOTUS NOTES/DOMINO	www.lotus.com
MICROSOFT NETMEETING/EXCHANGE	www.microsoft.com
NETSCAPE SUITESPOT	www.netscape.com
NOVELL GROUPWISE	www.novell.com
OPEN TEXT LIVELINK	www.opentext.com

DISCOVERY CENTER

CHAPTER 14

Touring NetMeeting's Main Features (page 230)

Feature	Definition
THE INTERNET PHONE	Talk over the Internet.
APPLICATION SHARING	Share a program with a group of people.
SHARED CLIPBOARD	Copy and paste information across the country.
FILE TRANSFERS	Send files to one or a group of people.
THE WHITEBOARD	Use graphics to communicate your message.
CHATTING	A text-based method of speaking in NetMeeting.
VIDEO CONFERENCE	Send and receive live video communications.
USER LOCATION SERVICE DIRECTORY	The worldwide dynamic phone book.

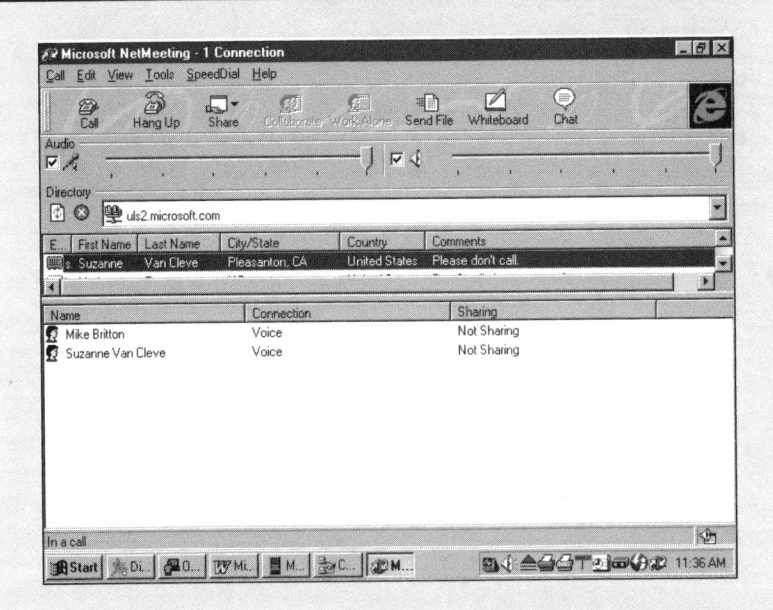

Making an Audio and Video Call (page 234)

1. Launch NetMeeting and address a call by typing a name in the Call dialog box.

2. An incoming dialog box will appear on the computer of the person you are trying to call.

3. Upon acceptance of the call the Connection window will list you and the person you called.

4. Choose View → Video → Myself from the Menu Bar to access the video feature.

5. Conduct your audio and video conference.

6. When it's time to conclude your call notify the participants in the conference that you are hanging up and click Hang Up from the Main Toolbar.

7. You are now ready to make another call or exit the program.

DISCOVERY CENTER **287**

CHAPTER 15

You can expand your intranet toolbox with Java and ActiveX, both of which can enhance the interactivity of your intranet.

What JavaScripts Can Do (page 238)

- Manage forms
- Customize information for your users
- Manage the appearance of the intranet page
- Connect to plug-ins and applets

What ActiveX Controls Can Add (page 240)

- Sound
- Images
- Page appearance
- Site mapping
- Form elements and design
- Database access
- Report writers
- 3D/VRML
- Conferencing
- Calendars (see the following figure)

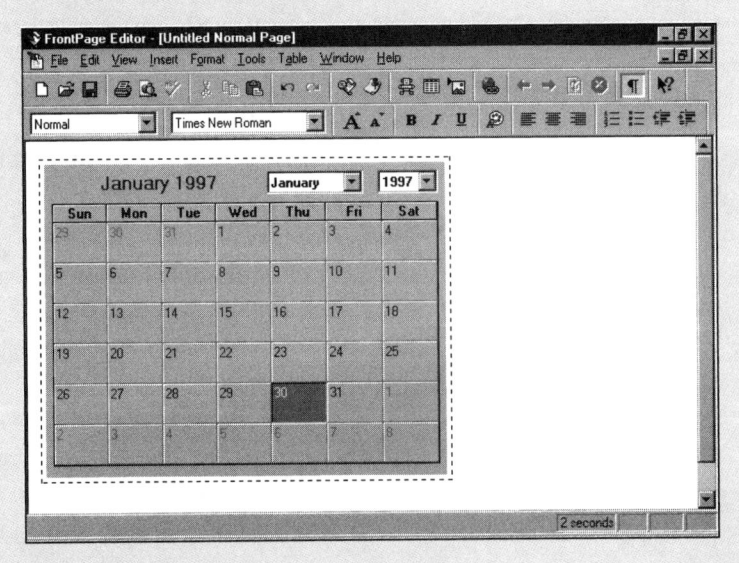

288   DISCOVERY CENTER

CHAPTER 16

User Feedback Elements (page 256)

After launching your intranet, you're not finished! In fact, the task of maintaining the digital creature has just begun.

You'll want to get feedback from your users in the following areas:

Writing Style: Writing for the intranet is different than paper-based documents. Remember that people are getting pieces of information, and don't like to scroll through multiple screens of information.

Content: Find out if the content you're delivering is useful to most of the people. Inquire if they understand the material, want other information, think the quality is good or not, want to contribute, and so on.

Structure: You'll want to know if your information can be accessed easily. Can users find what they want within a few mouse clicks? Can they use the search tool to effectively find information? Do the metaphors make sense or get in the way?

Performance: Your users might be complaining about access time being slow for accessing pages, moving between links, finding on searches, and request processing.

Ask them what they think, and listen. You'll get a bounty of ideas for keeping your intranet fresh and worth visiting often.

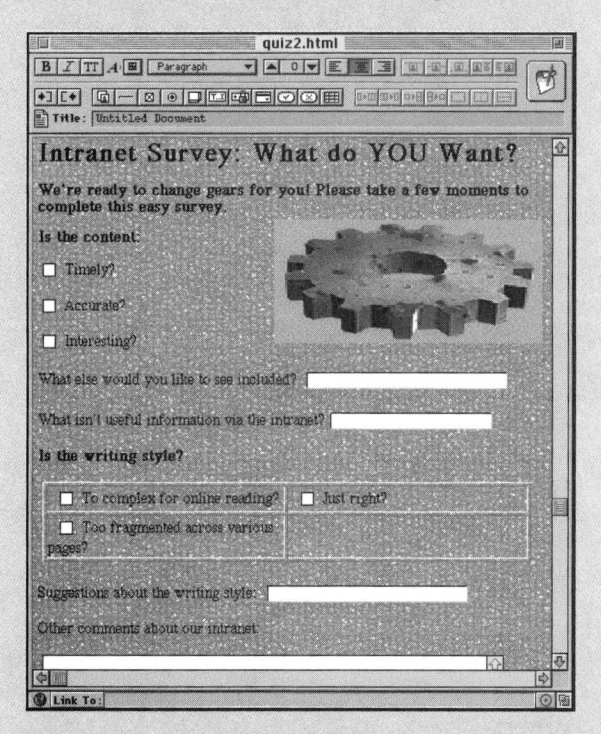

DISCOVERY CENTER

Interactive Solutions (page 259)

- Create something fun and interactive that changes regularly
- Make sure your search tool is accessible
- Add a few bells and whistles
- Add CGI programs to access more data

VISUAL INDEX

An HTML File

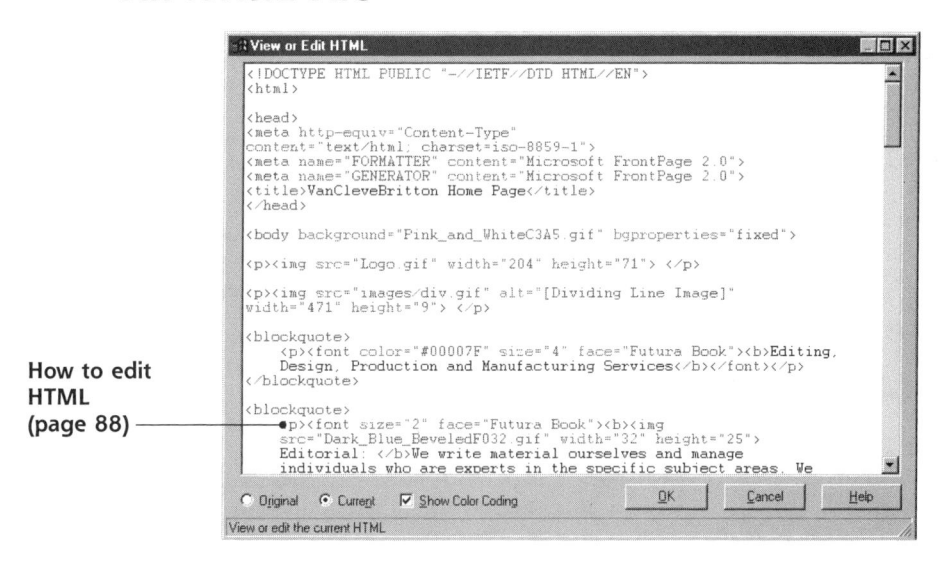

How to edit HTML (page 88)

Basic Home Page

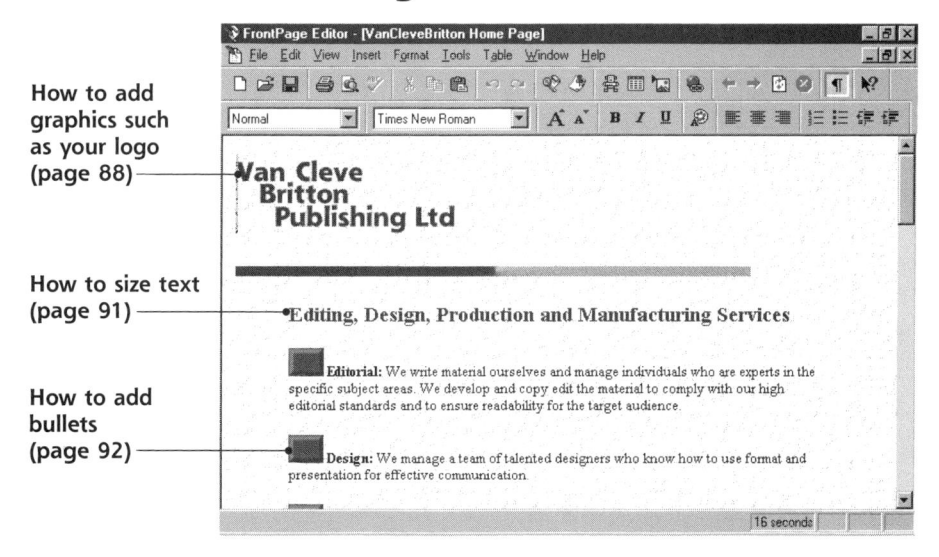

How to add graphics such as your logo (page 88)

How to size text (page 91)

How to add bullets (page 92)

291

Home Page with Frames

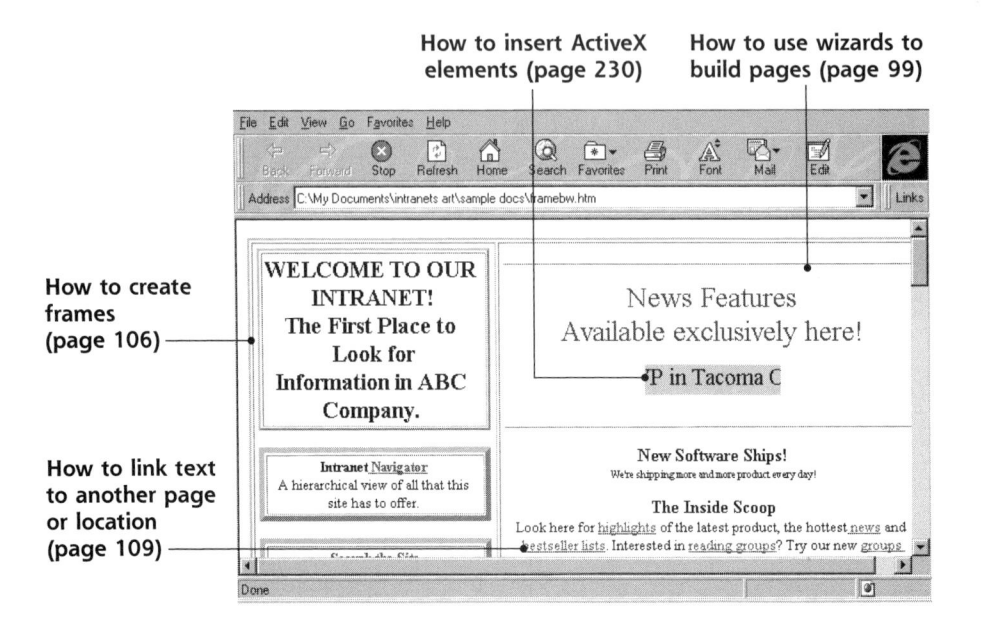

- How to create frames (page 106)
- How to link text to another page or location (page 109)
- How to insert ActiveX elements (page 230)
- How to use wizards to build pages (page 99)

Site Management

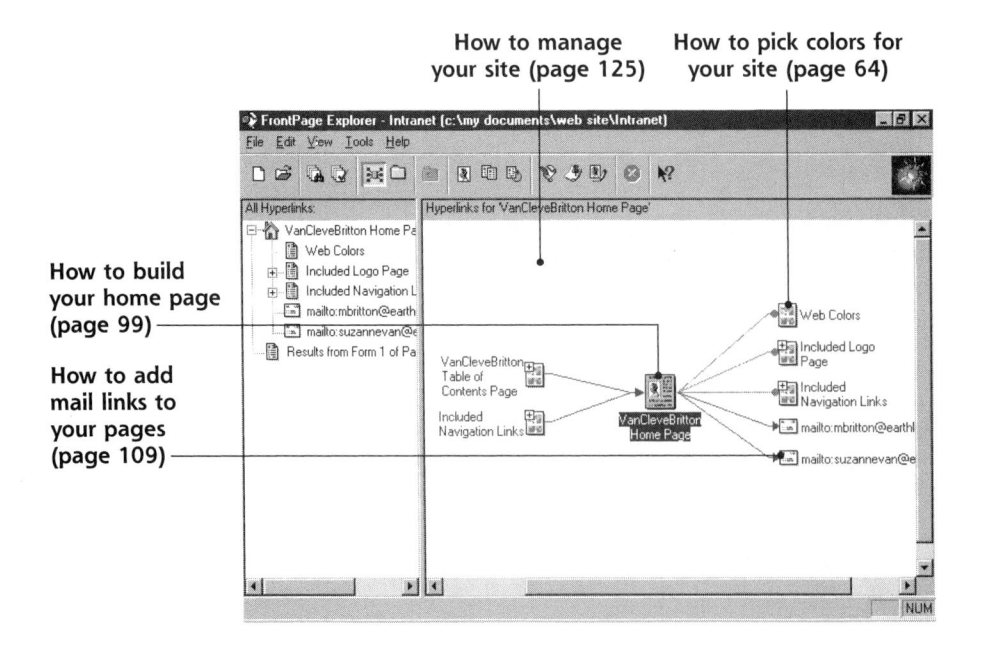

- How to build your home page (page 99)
- How to add mail links to your pages (page 109)
- How to manage your site (page 125)
- How to pick colors for your site (page 64)

Linking Your Intranet Together

How to add text over graphics (page 104)

How to create tables (page 104)

How to add a link to email the Webmaster (page 109)

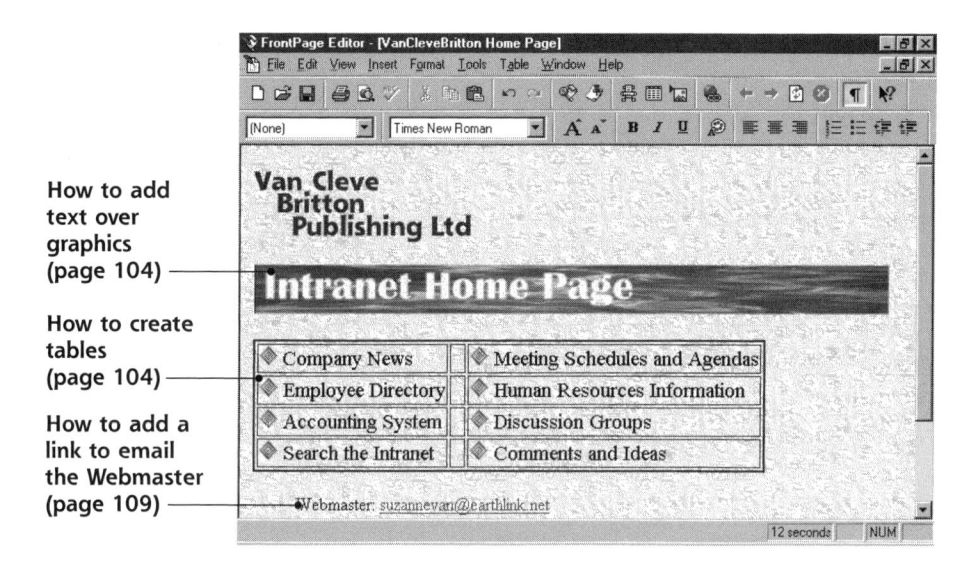

Forms

How to create forms (page 106)

How to create field labels (page 106)

How to add data fields (page 106)

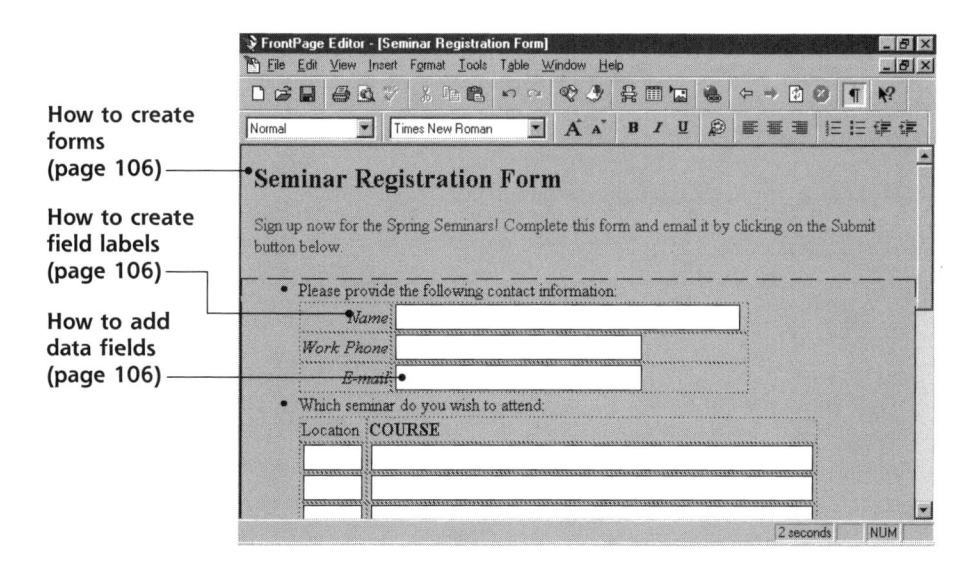

VISUAL INDEX **293**

Publishing Your Intranet

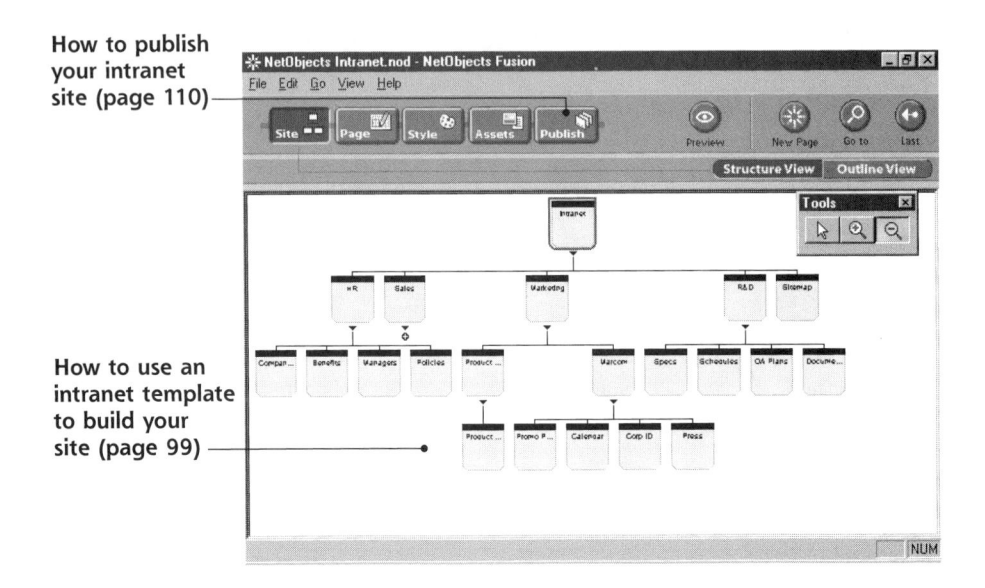

How to publish your intranet site (page 110)

How to use an intranet template to build your site (page 99)

Bookmarks

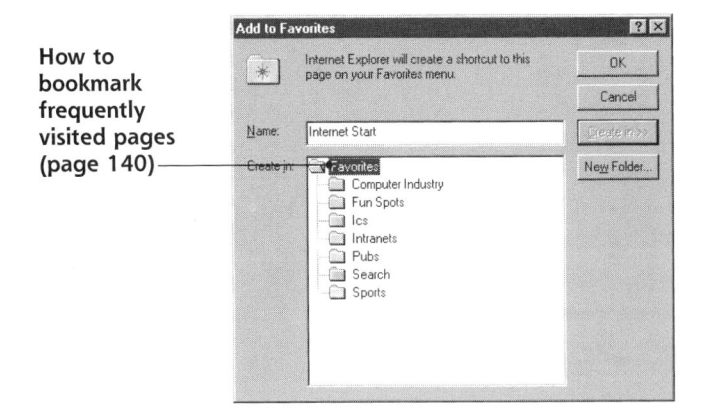

How to bookmark frequently visited pages (page 140)

294   VISUAL INDEX

Customizing Your Browser

How to change what toolbars show in your browser (page 122)

How to change the color of visited links (page 122)

How to change colors that you view with your browser (page 122)

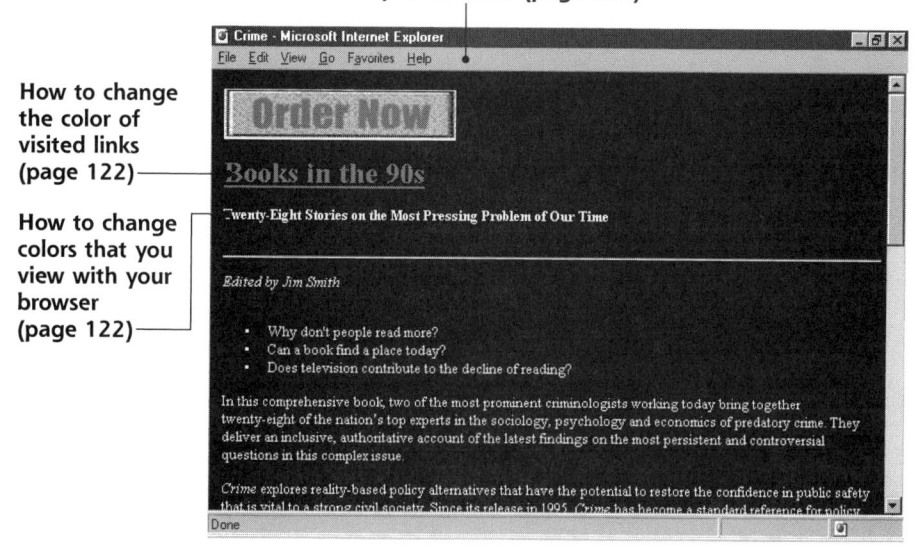

Searching Your Intranet

How to set up automatic searches of your intranet (page 144)

How to set up query terms for a search (page 142)

How to define query terms for a search (page 145)

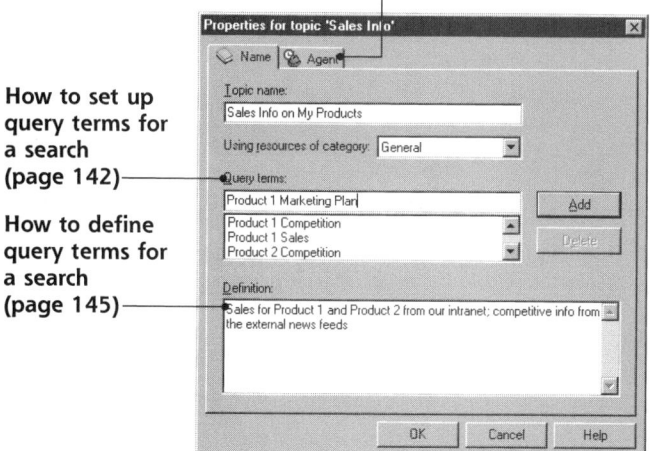

VISUAL INDEX **295**

APPENDIX A

AN INTRODUCTION TO HTML BASICS

Throughout this book we've focused on the content and process of your intranet, because if the content is irrelevant to your audience, all the coding and aesthetics in the world won't make your intranet useful.

However, at some point you may need to mess around with HTML. Keep in mind that HTML is an evolving language, so visit the Web sites listed in this appendix for up-to-date information. You can write and edit HTML in stand-alone HTML editors, such as the shareware or freeware shown in Table A-1.

You can use just about any text editor, such as the NotePad in Windows, or any word processing program, such as Microsoft Word, WordPerfect, and so on. Microsoft Office, WordPerfect Suite, and Lotus SmartSuite all have features that enable you to automatically convert (or publish) the word processor document into an HTML document.

You can also edit HTML within a Web authoring program such as Microsoft FrontPage, DeltaPoint QuickSite, or Adobe PageMill. Usually, you'll have a menu option for View → Source, which will open the raw HTML document for easy editing. It's useful to know some HTML codes to supplement the many automated HTML-generating features in these applications.

TABLE A-1 Freeware or Shareware HTML Editors

Product	Description	Web Site
Easy HTML	An interactive editor for HTML files that prompts you through the process of creating and editing an HTML document via a Web browser.	http://ox.ncsa.uiuc.edu/easyhtml/easy.html
AOLPress (Formerly GNNPress)	A WYSIWYG tool so you can create and view your document in the same window. It supports tables, forms, and various body attributes.	http://www.aolpress.com/press/index.html

(continued)

TABLE A-1 Freeware or Shareware HTML Editors *(continued)*

Product	Description	Web Site
Home Page	Free from Claris, Home Page includes both a WYSIWYG and text-only mode. Supports custom tables, frames, page templates. Get it now before it becomes commercial and costs money!	http://www.claris.com/products/clarispage/enquirer/Docs/download.html
HotDog	The shareware sibling of the commercial and recognized Hot Dog Professional, this shareware application gets rave reviews.	http://www.sausage.com/
HoTMetaL	This free sibling of HoTMetaL Pro supports page templates.	http://www.sq.com/products/hotmetal/hm-ftp.htm

> **WEB PATH** For general information about HTML including plans for new versions, see:
>
> http://www.w3.org/hypertext/WWW/MarkUp/MarkUp.html

Before we dive into doing HTML, a bit of background on the state of HTML as a language is helpful. There are several versions of HTML in use today, primarily HTML 2.0 and HTML 3.2. HTML 3.2 is a specification for HTML, developed in 1996 by the World Wide Web Consortium (know as the W3C) and big computer companies such as IBM, Microsoft, Netscape, Novell, and Sun Microsystems.

HTML 2.0 and earlier versions were grossly simplistic versions of the much more sophisticated SGML (Standardized General Markup Language) used for years by technical and mathematical publishers. Early HTML was limited to about 20 different styles for an entire Web site — extremely limiting when you think about the variety of information that you want to present on your intranet. HTML 3.2 adds important new features for intranet creators, including tables (which enable Web pages to more closely resemble book or magazine pages), applets (which can add interactivity and functionality to intranets), and more styles than ever before. Future versions of HTML promise style sheets such as page make-up applications, which means you can apply styles to specific elements and globally change the *definition*, or appearance and format, of that element at any time.

So, consider HTML a language in early development — it's now ready to use and will improve in subsequent editions, making your job as an intranet manager easier with each revision.

So What Are HTML Tags?

HTML tags are nothing more than codes that define how elements, such as text or graphics, should be displayed on your intranet page. Each code is surrounded by angle brackets like <this>.

If you've already started building your intranet, or you've just inherited the management of your intranet from someone else, be brave and choose Show Source, probably from the Edit menu of your browser. All that code you see is HTML, and if you don't panic, and dissect it into a piece at a time, you *can* do HTML.

The bare bones framework of an intranet page is something like this:

```
<HTML><HEAD><TITLE> Your Intranet Page's Title
</TITLE></HEAD><BODY>
The Body of Your Intranet Page
</BODY>
</HTML>
```

* The <HTML> </HTML> tags tell the browser (remember, Netscape Navigator, Microsoft Explorer, and so on) that the page is indeed HTML code. Every HTML code has a start tag, and many have an end tag being signified by the slash </> in the end code. When in doubt, use the end tag.
* The <HEAD> </HEAD> tags are the heading of your page, and the title of the page is placed inside the heading.
* The <BODY> </BODY> tags identify the core part of your page that will be displayed.

Basic HTML Tags

So what's the least you need to know about HTML? There are a set of fundamental tags that will help you in designing your intranet pages.

Text Tags

If you're just beginning to venture into HTML tags, keep it simple by focusing on the basic text tags necessary to create intranet pages. Text and the whole idea of font usage (and the accompanying copyright implications) is still under development. The only way to truly guarantee that any font other than Times or Helvetica will appear correctly is to create the text element as a GIF or JPEG image and link that image onto your intranet page. That approach becomes a hassle if someone (probably your boss!) decides to make last minute text changes to your pages, which will send you back to your photo manipulation program for a long night of work.

If you also consider that your users can change their default type font at whim, even if you tell them not to, you will never really be sure how the type font will look on a page.

However, you can control the size and the alignment of type with HTML tags; the basic tags for managing your text are shown in Table A-2.

TIP If you preview you page and get unexpected results (translation: a mess!), check for your end tags which are probably missing. More sophisticated HTML editing programs will alert you to this error early on, and prompt you to insert an end tag. Some HTML tags are "single" tags, without an ending </> tag. Some of these are <BR>, <DIV>, <DT>, <META>, <FRAME>, **and** <HR>.

TABLE A-2 HTML Body and Text Tags

Tag	Description
<B></B>	Bold text.
<BLINK></BLINK>	Blinking text.
 </BR>	Hard return to start a new line.
<CENTER></CENTER>	Centers elements, such as text or graphics.
<FONT COLOR=*FFFFFF*></FONT>	To make your text a specific color, where "FFFFFF" is a number that represents the color you want to display.
<FONT = *Font Name*></FONT>	Defines a specific font to be imaged on the page, where "Font Name" is the name of the font you want to use.
<FONT SIZE=+1></FONT>	Indicates the font size you want to use, ranging from +1 to +7. The size that it actually displays depends mostly on the browser being used.
<I></I>	Italic text.
<P></P>	New paragraph, with a optional end tag.

CAUTION: You must use the exact PostScript or TrueType font name in the `<FONT>` tag. If you don't, the text within the tag will image in the default type font.

The `<FONT FACE>` tag is new, and will raise some flags about copyright, although Microsoft positions its use of the tag creating read-only fonts. This means your users can't copy the fonts onto their hard drives and use them for any purpose other than viewing the page with the tag. Watch for future announcements on font handling.

There are a few other important items to note regarding HTML tags and text, particularly spacing. HTML does not recognize more than one space, so multiple spaces (more than one carriage return) will appear as a single space on your Web page. Because HTML interprets returns as spaces, special tags must be used for returns at the end of a line (carriage returns). The `<BR>` tag creates one return, and `<P>` makes two returns.

There is also a No Break tag. It tells the browser that the enclosed text should not be broken up unless absolutely necessary, which is really helpful if you're concerned about how proper names or URLs will break on the page. The No Break tag looks like this: `<NOBR>` text not to be broken `</NOBR>`.

Color Your World: Tags to Add Color

Now on to color, the first step of dazzle on your intranet page. HTML colors are coded as a rather obtuse 6-digit hexadecimal number that represent the values of Red, Green, and Blue in the color that will display on your page. Why Red, Green, and Blue, and not maybe the CMYK colors of the print world, representing Cyan, Magenta, Yellow, and Black? Because HTML defines the colors available in the digital world, the computer monitor, which is RGB.

Netscape (v2.0 and higher) and Internet Explorer (v3.0 and higher) will also recognize colors when they are specified by name. For example, Netscape accepts the following font colors: Black, Olive, Teal, Red, Blue, Maroon, Navy, Gray, Lime, Fuchsia, White, Green, Purple, Silver, Yellow, and Aqua.

The amount of Red, Green, and Blue that will be present in a color on your intranet page ranges from 0 to 255, which is 00 to ff in the lingo of hexadecimal. Because every color is a mix of the three primary colors, each taking 2 digits to represent in hex (which for you math types is base 16), one whole color takes 6 digits. The following hexadecimal numbers can be used to color your text:

Red = FF0000
White = FFFFFF
Blue = 0000FF
Lt. Blue = 00FFFF
Lt. Blue = 00CCFF
Black = 000000
Gray = CC9999

Green = 00FF00
Yellow = FFFF66
Purple = CC33FF

TIP Colors can be used in several ways to liven up your site, such as background, text, or links (unvisited, visited, and active).

So now you know how it's done! But honestly, using the color picker of your Web authoring tool might be a bit simpler, don't you think? At the very least, begin to explore the HTML source code of Web pages or intranet pages (although they are admittedly harder to get a hold of!) that you like, and look up the color references they use.

Tags to Make Lists

Lists are an important element for providing structure to a series of information on your intranet site, whether it's random points in a bulleted list or sequential points in a numbered list. List tags include a start tag, end tag (prefaced by a slash / like other HTML tags), and "in-between" tags that denote each item in the list. List tags are shown in Table A-3.

CAUTION All HTML tags can be nested; that is, tags can appear within tags, such as a bulleted list within body text, or a color within a font size tag. Again, be sure to include end tags where needed, no matter how many other tags appear in between.

TABLE A-3 HTML Tags for Lists

Tag	Description
`<DL><DT><DD></DL>`	Definition List `<DT>`=term, `<DD>`=definition
`<DIR><LI></DIR>`	Directory List, with `<LI>` before each list item
`<MENU><LI></MENU>`	Menu List, with `<LI>` before each list item
`<OL><LI></OL>`	Ordered List, `<LI>` before each list item
`<UL><LI></UL>`	Unordered List, `<LI>` before each list item

CAUTION List tags can also be nested, such as the `<LI>` tag for List Item. You can also nest different types of lists, such as starting with a bullet list, and then have a numbered list within that bulleted list.

APPENDIX A

Intermediate Tags: Tables, Frames, Links, and Meta

If you're comfortable with the basic tags, venture into what we consider the intermediate league: tags for creating tables, frames, and links. With tables, you can add more visual structure to your pages instead of being limited to one vertical element appearing at a time. Frames add multiple viewing windows within the browser to your intranet, enhancing the accessibility of information. While most of the Web authoring tools now provide some frame features, look for these features to improve dramatically in the near future. Finally, link tags create the Web-like hypertext effect which differentiates the world of digital information from piles of unconnected paper files.

Making Tables: Tags to Add Structure

First, tables are several elements: a caption, heads for columns, and the actual rows of data. Within the cells of a table, you can have text, multiple paragraphs, lists, and headers. For more page make-up flexibility, you can merge cells (to create a headline over multiple cells) and change the size of cells.

NOTE Table tags have evolved significantly with HTML 3 as described in this section, and the proposed specification for HTML 3.2 will be even easier to use. Make sure your users have the current versions of the browsers for best viewing results.

Information in a table is specified in HTML line by line. Each row is coded with a <TR> and </TR> tag. The information in each row of the table (think *cells* if you're accustomed to a spreadsheet such as Microsoft Excel), is defined using the <TH> and </TH> tags for heading text, and <TD> </TD> tags for data text.

For example, a table could contain the following information:

TABLE HEAD

Col Head 1	Col Head 2	Col Head 3
Data Item 1	100	200
Data Item 2	300	400

The HTML code for this table would be:

```
<table>
<caption>Table Head</caption>
<tr>
<th>Col Head 1</th> <th>Col Head 2 </th> <th>Col Head 3 </th>
</tr>
<tr>
<td>Data Item 1</td><td>100 </td> <td>200 </td>
</tr>
<tr>
<td>Data Item 2 </td> <td>300 </td> <td>400 </td>
</tr>
</table>
```

Table A-4 shows the basic table tags.

TABLE A-4 HTML Tags for Tables

Tag	Description
`<CAPTION> </CAPTION>`	Caption, or head to a table
`<TABLE> </TABLE>`	Begins and ends a table
`<TD> </TD>`	Table cell text (often data), in plain text
`<TH> </TH>`	Table column headers, in bold text
`<TR> </TR>`	Separates table rows

NOTE ALIGN is used for positioning text or graphics within the cell, and is used within the `<TR>` and `<TD>` tags: for example, `<TR ALIGN=LEFT>` or `<TD ALIGN=CENTER>`. Also, `VALIGN` is the attribute used for vertical alignment of the table contents. `BORDER` is also an attribute tag used within the `<TABLE>` **tag to specify the border thickness. For example:** `<TABLE BORDER=2> . . . </TABLE>`.

TIP You could start the whole table code with `<TABLE BORDER>`, **which tells the browser to draw lines around each cell. You can use the tag** `<BORDER=#>` **where the number sign represents the size of the table border edge in pixels, which are roughly one dot on the computer monitor.**

Tables can be of any size — as many rows and columns as you need and will fit on the screen. The browser will automatically format the rows, and will vertically center cell contents.

CAUTION Tables are complicated, and one missing tag can wreak havoc with your intranet page. Web authoring tools, such as Microsoft FrontPage, Claris HomePage, and Netscape Navigator Gold all include tools for simplifying the process and ensuring you have start and end tags properly positioned.

Multiple Windows: Tags to Make Frames

With frames, you can display more than one HTML page at a time by dividing one page into any number of pages, although three is probably the effective limit for frames on a page. Frames don't have the <BODY> </BODY> tags of an ordinary Web page. Instead, you would use <FRAMESET> </FRAMESET> to indicate the start and end of the group of frames, similar to the way <TABLE> </TABLE> tags wrap a table element. Like the tags inside the TABLE tag, the <FRAME> tag is used to specify the contents of the frame. Your users will also need to be using Netscape Navigator 2.0 or higher, or Internet Explorer 2.0 or higher, or another browser that supports frames.

NOTE Some browsers don't fully support frame tags yet, but they most likely will soon.

Frames can be sized in either fixed sizes or percentages of the viewer's browser window. This gets a bit tricky because your users might be using everything from a standard 12" office monitor to a gigantic 21" graphic arts workstation.

TIP Look at Web sites that use frames effectively to get an idea of how to use them on your intranet. While you're there, take a peek at the source code for technical insights.

Frame Tags are shown in Table A-5.

TABLE A-5 HTML Tags for Frames

Tag	Description
<FRAME SCROLLING="YES|NO|AUTO">	Scrollbar on (yes) or off (no)
<FRAME SRC="*URL*">	Definition of frame and source of document
<FRAMESET BORDER=*n*>	Border Width

(continued)

TABLE A-5 HTML Tags for Frames *(continued)*

Tag	Description
`<FRAMESET BORDERCOLOR="#nnnnnn">`	Border Color
`<FRAMESET COLS=*></FRAMESET>`	Column Widths, where * is the relative size
`<FRAMESET COLS ></FRAMESET>`	Column Widths, in pixels or %
`<FRAMESET FRAMEBORDER="yes|no">`	Borders on (yes) or off (no)
`<FRAMESET ROWS=*></FRAMESET>`	Row Heights, where * is the relative size
`<FRAMESET ROWS=,,,></FRAMESET>`	Row height in pixels or %
`<FRAMESET></FRAMESET>`	Start and end of a set of frames

> **CAUTION** Frames are also complicated, and one missing tag can destroy your Frameset. Web authoring tools, such as Microsoft FrontPage, Claris HomePage, and Netscape Navigator Gold include tools for simplifying the process.

Tags to Make Links

Links are what make your HTML-based intranet page a living and interlinked entity; it's the whole idea that the Internet is a Web superimposed on your internal intranet.

> **NOTE** While you may look at it as three types of links (to another spot on the same page, another page in your intranet, or another Web site), the only real type of link is that to another URL. A URL can be another page, an image, a link to an FTP site, and so on. To link to a specific location within the page (instead of the top of the page), anchor the location itself using: `<A NAME="insert name"></A>`. Then create a link to that section of the page in the form: `<A HREF="#insert name"> . . . </A>`.

Link Tags are shown in Table A-6.

TABLE A-6 HTML Tags for Links

Tag	Description
`<A NAME>`*Text*`</A NAME>`	Link to other text
`<IMG SRC=`*filename of image*`>`	Link to an image
`<A HREF=`*URL*`></A>`	Link to a URL

For example, you can use the text link to link to another location on the same page, or a line of text on another page on your intranet. You can use the image link to view GIF or JPEG images on your intranet page, and the HREF tag to link to other pages, other intranets in your company if you have more than one, or out onto other pages on the World Wide Web.

Meta Tags for Easier Accesss

The `<META>` tag is used to describe the contents of any page in your intranet. The `<META>` tag can contain key words that can be indexed by a search engine and make it easier for your users to immediately get to specific pages on your intranet. This enables you, the manager of the intranet, to have more control over what's considered prominent on a page, rather than having the search engine simply index the first 200 words on a page. With the `<META>` tag, you can assign keywords to pages that are image-oriented and might not be found during a text search.

META tags are shown in table A-7.

TABLE A-7 HTML Tags for META data

Tag	Description
`<META NAME = `*description*`>`	Usually a sentence description of the page
`<META NAME = `*keywords*`>`	Individual keywords describing the contents of a page

HTML in Action: Tags to Pages

To illustrate the power of HTML code when display visuallyed, here is a look at our Web page (Figure A-1) and its corresponding code. While it may look overwhelming at first glance, it's really pretty logical, and with practice, can be mastered to expand the features on your intranet. The Van Cleve Britton home page integrates images and tables.

WEB PATH → **To view the source code live, visit our site at:**
http://www.vcbweb.com

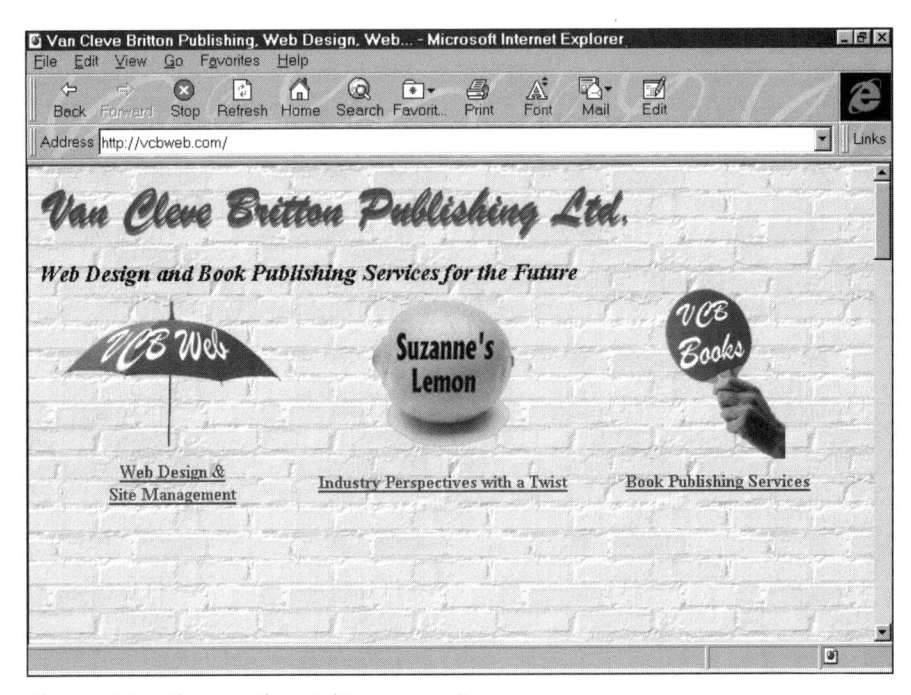

Figure A-1 The Van Cleve Britton Home Page

```
<!DOCTYPE HTML PUBLIC "-//IETF//DTD HTML//EN">
<html>
<head>
<meta http-equiv="Content-Type"
content="text/html; charset=iso-8859-1">
<meta name="description"
content="Customized web design for business, personal, and
education! Van Cleve Britton makes your Internet presence easy,
fun and affordable. San Francisco based. Your personal, affordable
Webmaster! Worldwide Web hosting. Offers all types of publishing
services including authoring.">
<meta name="keywords"
content="web design, web hosting, ISP, Webmaster, San Francisco,
Van Cleve, Britton, publishing, Internet, publishing services,
book publishing, business web design, personal web design,
education, school, author, publisher, designer, web marketing,
book sales, book marketing">
```

```html
<meta name="GENERATOR" content="Microsoft FrontPage 2.0">
<title>Van Cleve Britton Publishing, Web Design, Web Hosting, Site Management, Publishing Services, Author, Editorial </title>
</head>

<body background="Light_Grey_Brick8212.gif">

<h1><img src="VCBlogoDS.gif" width="547" height="54"></h1>

<table border="0" cellpadding="0" cellspacing="0" width="100%">
<tr>
<td colspan="3"><font size="5"><em><strong>Web Design and Book Publishing Services for the Future</strong></em></font></td>
</tr>
<tr>
<td width="33%"><p align="center"><a href="#VCB Web"><img src="VCBumb.gif" border="0" width="208" height="133"></a></p>
</td>
<td width="33%"><p align="center"><img src="SVCLemmon.gif" width="142" height="133"></p>
</td>
<td width="34%"><p align="center"><a href="#VCB Books"><img src="VCBBooks.gif" border="0" width="123" height="155"></a></p>
</td>
</tr>
<tr>
<td width="33%"><h3 align="center"><a href="#VCB Web">Web Design &amp;<br>
Site Management</a></h3>
</td>
<td width="33%"><h3 align="center"><a href="#Suzanne's Lemmon">Industry Perspectives with a Twist</a></h3>
</td>
<td width="34%"><h3 align="center"><a href="#VCB Books">Book Publishing Services</a></h3>
</td>
</tr>
</table>

<p> </p>

<p> </p>
</body>
</html>
```

INDEX

Note: Page numbers in *italics* refer to illustrations or charts.

SPECIAL CHARACTERS

3D interfaces, 254

A

ABC FlowCharter, flowchart tools, 33
accessing content, ease of, 15–16, 17, 22
ActiveX controls, 240–241
    scrolling marquees, 241
ad hoc meetings, audio and video conferencing, 227
Add to Favorites dialog box, Internet Explorer, *140, 198*
Adobe Acrobat Exchange. *See* PDF documents
Adobe PageMill, 96–97
Adobe SiteMill, 136
    views, 129–130, *131*
advanced searching techniques, 146–148
    Boolean logic, 146–147
    punctuation, 147–148
    syntax operators, 146
Agfa scanning guide, 75
Alta Vista, Internet search engines, *153*
Amazon.com, online book sales, 194
AND operator, advanced searching techniques, 147
Animation Wizard, GIF Construction Set, 243–245
animations, 242–252
    GIF Construction Set, 243–252
    uses of, 242
antialiasing, graphics formats, 62
AOLPress, shareware HTML editors, *291*

applets, Java, 238
application sharing, Microsoft NetMeeting, 230, *231*
applications, Java, 238
applications development tools, future of groupware, 211
archives, process mapping, 32
Arrive Network, "push" technology, *219*
assessing content, 26–27
    Quick Tour, 1–2
attachments, e-mail, 120
audio streaming, training and support, 195
audio and video conferencing, 225–236
    ad hoc meetings, 227
    concept of, 226
    Connectix QuickCam video camera, 235–236
    future of groupware, 211
    Microsoft NetMeeting, 228–235
    telecommuting, 227–228
    time savings, 227
    travel savings, 226
Audio-tuning Wizard, Microsoft NetMeeting, 235
authoring tools, 87–99
    See also graphic-oriented tools
    flow charts, 33–34
    graphic-oriented, 89–99
    HTML and, 53–55
    HTML editors vs. graphic-oriented, 88–89
AutoAdmin, Netscape Communicator, 209

B

backgrounds
   intranet design, 59, *60*, 104
   Quick Tour, 3
backups, 173–174
   storage media, 174
BackWeb Inc., "push" technology, *219*
bandwidth. *See* speed
banners, GIF Construction Set, 249–250, *251*
BBEdit HTML editor, Macintosh computers, 90
benchmarking, process mapping, 30
benefits of intranets, 15–20
   distributed information, 19–20
   easy access, 15–16, 17, 22
   needs-based publishing, 19
   productivity gains, 19
   rapid development, 19
body tags, HTML, *294*
bookmarks
   See also Favorites
   navigating intranets with, 140–141
   Netscape Navigator, 118, 140, 141
   Quick Tour, 5
books, training and support, 193, 194
BookZone, online book sales, 194
Boolean logic, advanced searching techniques, 146–147
borders, NetObjects Fusion MasterBorders, 135
bridges to proprietary systems, 13–14, 84
broadcast networks. *See* personal broadcast networks
Broderbund, OrgPlus flowchart tool, 33
browsers, 115–124
   See also Internet Explorer; Netscape Navigator
   customizing, 122–123
   e-mail and attachments, 119–121
   frame tags and, 299–300
   HTML and, 54
   Lotus Notes and, 136
   merging with operating systems, 211
   navigation buttons, 116–118
   performance comparison, 116
   plug-ins, 121
   searching with, 119
budget variations, financial issues, 46–47
building intranet pages. *See* creating intranet pages
bullets, intranet page creation, *103*

C

Caere Corporation's OmniPage Pro, OCR (Optical Character Recognition), 75
calendars
   HTML, 213
   Netscape Communicator, 209, 210–211
cameras
   digital, 63
   QuickCam video, 235–236
Castanet. *See* Marimba Castanet
CD-ROMs, training and support, 193
CGI (Common Gateway Interface)
   scripts and legacy systems, 214–216
   usability testing, 260
champions, human resources, 32
character recognition. *See* OCR (Optical Character Recognition)
chat feature, Microsoft NetMeeting, 231, *232*
classroom instruction, training and support, 194
clients, 161–162
   memory requirements, 162
   resources, 168
   thin, 238
clipboard sharing, Microsoft NetMeeting, 230
Collabra, Netscape Communicator, 207
color
   background, 59
   intranet page, 104
   loading Web site into Photoshop, 64
   typeface, 61
color management, intranet design, 64
color range, scanners, 73

color tags, HTML, 295–296
Common Gateway Interface. *See* CGI
Communicator. *See* Netscape Communicator
CompassWare InfoMagnet, search tools, 150, *151*
Composer, Netscape Communicator, 206, *207*
conferencing
   See also audio and video conferencing; video conferencing
   interactive tasks, 15
   Netscape Communicator, 206
connection types
   LAN (Local Area Network), *164*
   WAN (Wide Area Network), *164*
Connectix QuickCam video camera, 235–236
content, 25–29
   assessing, 1–2, 26–27
   information as power, 25
   managing, 27–29
   updating, 128
   usability testing, 258
controls, ActiveX, 240–241
converting documents. *See* document conversions
cookies, JavaScript, 238–239
coordinating efforts, organizational issues, 40
Corel Office, Java, 239
cost and savings projections. *See* financial issues
creating intranet pages, 99–111
   See also designing intranets
   adding pages for specific tasks, 107–109
   backgrounds, 104
   bullets, *103*
   color, 104
   editing HTML source code, 109, *110*
   employee directories, *108*, 109
   forms, 106, *107*
   frames, 106
   hyperlinks, 109
   importing and formatting text, 104
   importing graphics, 103
   publishing pages, 110
   sound, 104
   tables, 104, *105*
   video, 104
   wizards, 99–101, *102*
cultural change, organizational issues, 38–39
customizing browsers, 122–123

D

data
   See also content
   encryption, 178
   replication, 166–167
databases, interactive tasks, 15
DeltaPoint QuickSite, 98
   site management tools, 134
designing intranets, 51–67
   See also creating intranet pages
   backgrounds, 59, *60*
   color management, 64
   elements of, 65
   graphics, 61–63
   HTML and, 53–55
   icons, 58, *59*
   issues, 40–41
   metaphors as road maps, 55–59
   overview, 51–52
   Quick Tour, 3
   rules for effective design, 66
   structure and, 52–53
   tables, 61
   typefaces, 60–61
desktop clients. *See* clients
desktop video conferencing. *See* video conferencing
Diffusion, IntraExpress (personal broadcast networks), 217, *218*
digital cameras, graphics and, 63
digital integration, 14–15
DigitalThink, training and support resources, 188–189, *190*

INDEX **313**

discussion groups
  See also newsgroups
  Netscape Communicator, 210
distributed information, benefits of intranets, 19–20
document conversions, 71–85
  bridges to proprietary systems, 84
  electronic documents, 78–84
  HTML and, 82–84
  scanning paper, 72–78
Document Information dialog box, PDF documents, *80*
documents
  See also content; creating intranet pages; home pages; Web sites
  converting. *See* document conversions
  electronic, 78–84
  recognition applications (OCR), 75, 76
  scanning, 72–78
Documentum, RightSite large-scale version control, 128
Domino Action development system, Lotus Notes, 136, 204, 205
Dynamic HTML, Netscape Communicator, 209–210
dynamic style sheets, Netscape Communicator, 210

E

e-mail, 119–121, 212–214
  attachments, 120
  disadvantages of, 212
  embedding hyperlinks in, 120
  etiquette, 212
  interactive tasks, 14
  POP (Post Office Protocol) servers, 213
  servers, 212–213
  SMTP (Simple Mail Transfer Protocol), 212
ease of use, graphic-oriented tools, 92
easy access, benefits of intranets, 15–16, 17, 22
Easy HTML, shareware HTML editors, *291*

editing
  with graphic-oriented tools, 91, 94
  HTML source code, 90, 94, 109, *110*, *291–292*
  organizational issues, 39
electronic documents, 78–84
  Adobe Acrobat PDF, 79–82
embedding hyperlinks in e-mail, 120
employee directories, intranet page creation, *108*, 109
encryption, data, 178
Error View, Adobe SiteMill, 129, *130*
etiquette, e-mail, 212
Excite, Internet search engines, *153*
Explorer. *See* Internet Explorer; Microsoft FrontPage Explorer
Extended Attributes dialog box, Microsoft FrontPage97, *110*
extranets, 216

F

Favorites
  See also bookmarks
  Add to Favorites dialog box, *140*, *198*
  Internet Explorer, 118
feature creep, prototypes and, 48
file formats, graphics, 62
file management, site management tools, 126–127
file transfers, Microsoft NetMeeting, 231
files. *See* content; documents
financial issues, 43–47
  budget variations, 46–47
  cost and savings projections, 44–45
  hardware and software costs, 46
  human resources, 46
  Payback Periods, 50
  Return on Investment (ROI), 49–50
  savings potentials, 44
finding data. *See* search tools
firewalls, 176–178
  defined, 176
  gateways and, 177
  packet filtering, 177

proxy servers, 177
viruses and, 180
flow charts
    process mapping, 30, *31*
    tools, 33–34
FlowCharting PDQ, flowchart tools, 34
fonts, HTML text tags and, 295
Form Page Wizard, Microsoft FrontPage97, *107*
formats, graphics file, 62
formatting text on Web pages, 104
FormHandler, NetObjects Fusion, 136
forms, 106, *107*
    graphic-oriented tools, 94
    managing with JavaScript, 238
    scanning, 77, *78*
frame tags, HTML, 299–300
frames
    adding to Web pages, 106
    graphic-oriented tools, 93
    navigating intranets via, 141, *142*
    as tools, 253
Frames Wizard, Microsoft FrontPage97, 106
freeware, HTML editors, *291–292*
FrontPage. *See* Microsoft FrontPage97; Microsoft FrontPage Explorer
FTP (File Transfer Protocol), defined, 10
Fusion. *See also* NetObjects Fusion

G

gateways and firewalls, 177
GIF Construction Set (animations), 243–252
    Animation Wizard, 243–245
    banners and transitions, 249–250, *251*
    building animations, 243–245
    functions of, 243
    interlaced GIF files, 248
    LED signs, 249, *250*
    transparencies and, 247
GIF graphics format, 62
Giles, Rick, HTML Editor, 90
Gophers, defined, 10

graphic-oriented tools, 89–99
    See also authoring tools
    Adobe PageMill, 96–97
    CGI (Common Gateway Interface), 94–95
    DeltaPoint QuickSite, 98
    ease of use, 92
    editing with, 91
    forms, 94
    frames, 93
    HTML source code editing, 94
    HTML tools comparison, 88–89
    importing graphics, 92, 103
    Microsoft FrontPage 97, 95–96
    multimedia, 93–94
    NetObjects Fusion, 98–99
    Netscape Navigator Gold, 98
    overview, 90
    ScreenTips, 91, *92*
graphics, 61–63
    digital cameras and, 63
    file formats, 62
    image maps, 63
    importing, 92, 103
groupware, 202–212
    applications development tools, 211
    audio conferencing, 211
    future of, 211–212
    interactive tasks, 15
    intranet comparison, 203
    Lotus Notes, 136, 204, 205
    merging browsers and operating systems, 211
    Netscape Communicator, 206–211
    Open Text's Livelink Intranet, 202, *203, 204*
    video conferencing, 211
    workflow management tools, 211

H

hackers, Internet connections and, 175
hardware, 155–160, 161–165
    clients, 161–162

(continued)

hardware *(continued)*
   cost of, 46
   LAN speed, 163–164
   servers, 158–159
   WAN speed, 164–165
help desks, training and support, 197
Hewlett-Packard ScanJets, personal scanners, 74
Home Page, freeware HTML editors, *292*
home pages, RedTraktor site, *13*
HotBot, Internet search engines, *153*
HotDog, shareware HTML editors, *292*
HoTMetaL, freeware HTML editors, *292*
hotspots, image maps, 63
HTML editors, 90, *291–292*
   graphic-oriented tools comparison, 88–89
HTML (HyperText Markup Language), 53–55, 291–303
   authoring tools, 53
   browsers and, 54
   calendars, 213
   document conversions, 82–84
   Dynamic (Netscape Communicator), 209–210
   editing source code, 94, 109, *110*
   graphic-oriented tools vs. HTML editors, 88–89
   history of, 292–293
   line breaks, 60
   resources, 55
   source code, *88*, 94, 109, *110*
   tags, 53–55, 293–303
   versions of, *292*
   View Source command, 55
human resources, 32–33
   champions, 32
   financial issues, 46
   NetObjects Fusion site, *112*
   RedTraktor site, *16*
   shepherds, 33
   Webmasters, 33
Hyperlink command, HTML document conversions, *82*

hyperlinks
   defined, 10
   embedding in e-mail, 120
   image maps, 63
   Insert Hyperlink command, *82*
   intranet page creation, 109
   site management tools, 127
   Verify Hyperlinks dialog box, *131*

I

I-Server, PointCast (personal broadcast networks), 217
IBM Host On-Demand, Netscape Communicator, 209
IBTauthor, training and support tool, 196
icons
   intranet design, 58, *59*
   Quick Tour, 3
Image Composer, Microsoft FrontPage97, *95*, *96*
image maps, graphics with hyperlinks, 63
images. *See* graphics
importing graphics
   graphic-oriented tools, 92
   intranet page creation, 103
importing text, intranet page creation, 104
Incoming Call dialog box, Microsoft NetMeeting, *234*
indexes
   navigating intranets and, 143
   PDF documents (Adobe Acrobat Exchange), 149
   search tools, 144
InfoMagnet search tool, 150, *151*
information. *See* content
information systems page, RedTraktor site, *14*
InfoSeek Guide, Internet search engines, *152*
infrastructures, technical issues, 43
input/output, process mapping, 31
Insert Hyperlink command, HTML document conversions, *82*

316   INDEX

Insert Table dialog box, Microsoft FrontPage97, *105*
integrating services, 201–223
    e-mail, 212–214
    extranets, 216
    groupware, 202–212
    legacy data, 214–216
    news distribution, 216–222
    Windows NT peer Web service, 222–223
interactive tasks, 14–15
    conferencing, 15
    databases, 15
    e-mail, 14
    groupware, 15
    usability testing, 259–260
interfaces
    3D, 254
    Common Gateway. *See* CGI
interlaced GIF files, GIF Construction Set (animations), 248
interlaced graphics formats, 62
Internet
    defined, 10
    intranet simulations, 16–17
    ISPs (Internet Service Providers), 17
    search engines, *152–153*
Internet Assistant (Microsoft Word)
    HTML document conversions, 82–84
    training and support, *196*
Internet connections, 174–178
    firewalls, 176–178
    hackers and, 175
Internet Explorer
    See also browsers; Netscape Navigator
    Add to Favorites dialog box, *140, 198*
    customizing, 122–123
    e-mail, 119–121
    Favorites, 118
    toolbar buttons, 117
Internet phone, Microsoft NetMeeting, 230
IntraExpress
    personal broadcast networks, 217, *218*
    "push" technology, *219*
Intranet AutoSite, NetObjects Fusion, *112*

Intranet Journal, 182
Intranet Module, NetObjects Fusion, 111, *112*
intranet servers, workings of, 157
intranets, 9–24
    assessing content, 1–2, 26–27
    audio and video conferencing, 225–236
    backgrounds, 3
    backups, 173–174
    benefits of, 15–20
    bridges to proprietary systems, 13–14, 84
    browsers and, 115–124
    costs of. *See* financial issues
    defined, 10
    designing, 3, 40–41, 51–67
    digital integration, 14–15
    e-mail and, 119–121, 212–214
    extranets, 216
    firewalls, 176–178
    functions of, 11
    groupware comparison, 203
    growth of, 12–15
    hardware, 155–160
    integrating services, 201–223
    interactive tasks, 14–15
    Internet connections, 174–178
    Internet simulations, 16–17
    justifying, 35–50
    management and, 21–22
    management tips, 5–6
    navigating, 139–143
    network resources, 167–168
    organic nature of, 255–263
    organizational issues, 38–43
    overview, 10–11
    page creation, 99–111
    publishing on, 78
    questions to ask users, 2–3
    quiz, 23–24
    requirements for, 167–168
    ROI (Return on Investment), 49–50
    sacrifices of, 20–21

(continued)

intranets *(continued)*
    search tools, 139–153
    security, 169–184
    TCP/IP, 165–166
    technical issues, 43
    telecommuters and, 166
    tools, 87–99, 237–254
    training and support, 187–199
    usability testing, 256–262
    video conferencing, 6, 15, 232
    wizards. *See* wizards
ISPs (Internet Service Providers), 17

J

Java, 238–239
    See also Marimba Castanet
JavaScript, 238–239
JPEG graphics format, 62
juggling metaphor, intranet design, 56
justifying intranets, 35–50
    financial issues, 43–47
    organizational issues, 38–43
    plans for, 35–38
    technical issues, 43

K

keywords
    navigating intranets via, 142, *143*
    PDF documents (Adobe Acrobat Exchange), 149
    search tools and, 144, 145

L

LANs (Local Area Networks)
    connection types, *164*
    defined, 156
    LAN Times, 182
    speed of, 163–164
large-scale version control, site management tools, 128
LED signs, GIF Construction Set (animations), 249, *250*
legacy systems, CGI scripts and, 214–216

line breaks, HTML, 60
link tags, HTML, 300–301
links. *See* hyperlinks
list tags, HTML, 296
Livelink Intranet, groupware, 202, *203*, *204*
Lotus Notes, Domino Action development system, 136, 204, 205

M

Mac OS, operating systems, 161
Macintosh, BBEdit HTML editor, 90
Macromedia Shockwave, multimedia players, 241–242
Magnet technology, InfoMagnet, 150, *151*
mail. *See* e-mail
management, intranet, 21–22
management tips, Quick Tour, 5–6
managing content, 27–29
maps, graphic image, 63
Marimba Castanet ("push" technology), *219*, 220–222
    See also Java
    Transmitters, 221, *222*
    Tuner, 220–221
    TV analogy, 220–221
marketing, planning intranets, 36
marquees, ActiveX controls, 241
MasterBorders, NetObjects Fusion, 135
meetings. *See* audio and video conferencing; video conferencing
memory requirements
    clients, 162
    servers, 159
Messenger, Netscape Communicator, 207, *208*
META tags, HTML, 301
metaphors as road maps, 55–59
    backgrounds, 59, *60*
    card catalog, *58*
    common, 57
    icons, 58, *59*
    juggling, 56
Micrografx, ABC FlowCharter tool, 33

Microsoft FrontPage97, 95–96
    Extended Attributes dialog box, *110*
    Form Page Wizard, *107*
    Frames Wizard, *106*
    Insert Table dialog box, *105*
    Microsoft Image Composer, 95, *96*
    WebBots, 95
    wizards, 95, 100–101, *102*
Microsoft FrontPage Explorer, 131–133
    fixing broken links, 132
    publishing Web sites, 133
    Search feature, 132, *133*
    To Do Lists, 132, *133*
    Verify Hyperlinks dialog box, *131*
Microsoft Image Composer, 95, *96*
Microsoft Internet Explorer. *See* Internet Explorer
Microsoft NetMeeting, 228–235
    application sharing, 230, *231*
    Audio-tuning Wizard, 235
    chat feature, 231, *232*
    clipboard sharing, 230
    conferencing guidelines, 233–235
    file transfers, 231
    groupware, *204*
    Incoming Call dialog box, *234*
    Internet phone, 230
    main window, 228–229
    ULS (User Location Service) directory, 233
    video conference feature, 232
    video conferencing, *233*
    whiteboard, 231, *232*
Microsoft Project, schedules, 47
Microsoft Word
    HTML document conversions, 82–84
    Internet Assistant, *196*
    Print dialog box (PDF documents), *79*
    Web Browse feature, *83*
mirror sites, server, 158
multimedia players
    graphic-oriented tools, 93–94
    Macromedia Shockwave, 241–242

N

naming files, site management tools, 126
navigating intranets, 139–143
    See also search tools
    bookmarks, 140–141
    frames, 141, *142*
    indexes, 143
    keywords, 142, *143*
    tables of contents, 140
navigation buttons, browser, 116–118
NEAR operator, advanced searching techniques, 147
needs-based publishing, 19
Netcaster, Netscape Communicator, 207
NETdelivery, "push" technology, *220*
NetMeeting. *See* Microsoft NetMeeting
NetObjects Fusion, 98–99, 134–136
    BBS, 136
    cost of, 99
    FormHandler, 136
    Human Resources core page, *112*
    Intranet AutoSite, *112*
    Intranet Module, 111, *112*
    MasterBorders, 135
    Page View, 134, *135*
    Site View, 134, *135*
    SiteMapper, 136
    SiteStyles, 135
    technical development, 41
Netscape Communicator, 206–211
    AutoAdmin, 209
    Calendar, 209, 210–211
    Collabra, 207
    components of, 206–209
    Composer, 206, *207*
    Conference, 206
    discussion groups, 210
    Dynamic HTML, 209–210
    dynamic style sheets, 210
    IBM Host On-Demand, 209
    interface, *206*
    Messenger, 207, *208*
    navigation bar, *209*

(continued)

Netscape Communicator *(continued)*
  Netcaster, 207
  newsgroups, *208*
  professional edition, 209
Netscape Navigator
  See also browsers; Internet Explorer
  Bookmarks, 118, 140, 141
  customizing, 123
  e-mail, 119–121
  toolbar buttons, 117
Netscape Navigator Gold, 98
Netscape Suitespot, groupware, *204*
network dependence, sacrifices of intranets, 20
networks
  local area. *See* LANs
  Network World, 182
  operating systems (NOS). *See* operating systems
  resources, 167–168
  wide area. *See* WANs
news distribution. *See* personal broadcast networks
news sources, search tools and, 146
newsgroups, 183
  See also discussion groups
  Netscape Communicator, *208*
NOT operator, advanced searching techniques, 147
Notes. *See* Lotus Notes
Novell Groupwise, groupware, *204*
Novell NetWare, operating systems, 161

O

OCR (Optical Character Recognition), 75–77
  Adobe Acrobat Exchange, 75, 77
  character recognition applications, 75
  defined, 76
  document recognition applications, 75, 76
  OmniPage Pro, 75
online quiz for users, usability testing, 260–262
online resources, training and support, 188–191, 193
online services, 17
Open Text's Livelink Intranet, groupware, 202, *203*, *204*
operating systems, 160–161
  Mac OS, 161
  merging with browsers, 211
  Novell NetWare, 161
  Unix, 160–161
  Window NT, 160
OR operator, advanced searching techniques, 147
organic nature of intranets, 255–263
organizational issues, 38–43
  coordinating efforts, 40
  cultural change, 38–39
  design, 40–41
  feature creep, 48
  planning, 36
  production, 42
  prototypes, 48–49
  Return on Investment (ROI), 49–50
  schedules, 47
  site administration, 42
  team meetings, 43
  team-building, 39
  technical development, 41
  testing, 42
  writing/editing, 39
OrgPlus, flowchart tools, 33
outsourcing
  scanning of documents, 73
  technical issues, 43

P

packet filtering, firewalls, 177
Page Views
  Adobe SiteMill, 129–130, *131*
  DeltaPoint QuickSite, *134*
  NetObjects Fusion, 134, *135*
PageMaker Acrobat PDF dialog box, PDF documents, *81*
PageMill. *See* Adobe PageMill

pages
   creating intranet. *See* creating intranet pages
   viewing. *See* browsers
Paperport, personal scanners, 74
passwords, 171–172
Patton & Patton, FlowCharting PDQ tool, 34
Payback Periods, financial issues, 50
PDF documents (Adobe Acrobat Exchange), 79–82
   Document Information dialog box, *80*
   electronic documents, 79–82
   forms, 77, *78*
   indexes, 149
   keywords, 149
   Microsoft Word Print dialog box, *79*
   OCR (Optical Character Recognition), 75
   PageMaker Acrobat PDF dialog box, *81*
   search tools, 148–149, *150*
peer Web services, Windows NT, 222–223
performance
   browser, 116
   usability testing, 259
personal broadcast networks, 216–222
   PointCast and IntraExpress, 217
   "push" technology, 218–222
personal scanners, 74
phones (Internet), Microsoft NetMeeting, 230
Photoshop, loading Web site color into, 64
physical locations, multiple, 128
pictures. *See* graphics
plans for intranets, 35–38
   elements of, 36–38
   purposes of, 36
   style sheets, 37
plug-in connections, JavaScript, 239
plug-ins
   browser, 121
   defined, 13
PointCast
   personal broadcast networks, 217

"push" technology, *220*
POP (Post Office Protocol) servers, e-mail, 213
process issues, sacrifices of intranets, 21
process mapping, 29–32
   archives, 32
   benchmarking, 30
   flow charts, 30, *31*
   input/output, 31
   publishing, 32
   revisions, 32
   routing and approval, 32
production, organizational issues, 42
productivity gains, benefits of intranets, 19
proprietary systems, bridges to, 13–14, 84
prototypes, organizational issues, 48–49
proxy servers, firewalls, 177
publications, intranet-related, 182
publishing, 78
   intranet page creation, 110
   needs-based, 19
   process mapping, 32
   Web sites with Microsoft FrontPage Explorer, 133
punctuation, advanced searching techniques, 147–148
"push" technology, 218–222
   See also personal broadcast networks
   defined, 218
   Netscape Netcaster, 207
   tools, *219–220*

Q

Quarterdeck WebCompass, search tools, 152
queries, search tool, 145
questions to ask users
   See also quizzes; testing
   Quick Tour, 2–3
Quick Tour, 1–6
   assessing content, 1–2
   backgrounds, 3
   bookmarks, 5

(continued)

Quick Tour *(continued)*
    design issues, 3
    icons, 3
    management tips, 5–6
    questions to ask users, 2–3
    video conferencing, 6
    wizards, 4
QuickCam video camera, 235–236
QuickSite. *See* DeltaPoint QuickSite
quizzes
    See also questions to ask users; testing
    "Are you ready for an intranet?," 23–24

R

RAM. *See* memory requirements
RedTraktor site, 12–13
    home page, *13*
    human resources page, *16*
    information systems page, *14*
    search page, *18*
    site map, *18*
    visiting, 16–17
reengineering, sacrifices of intranets, 21
replication, data, 166–167
resolution, scanner, 73
resource requirements, sacrifices of intranets, 21
resources
    client, 168
    HTML (HyperText Markup Language), 55
    human, 32–33
    network, 167–168
    online training and support, 188–191, 193
revisions, process mapping, 32
RightSite, large-scale version control, 128
ROI (Return on Investment), 49–50
routing and approval, process mapping, 32

S

sacrifices of intranets, 20–21
    network dependence, 20
    process issues, 21
    reengineering, 21
    resource requirements, 21
saving data, backups, 173–174
savings projections, financial issues, 44–45
ScanJets, personal scanners, 74
scanners, 72–75
    color range, 73
    comparison of, *73*
    criteria for selecting, 72–73
    personal, 74
    resolution, 73
scanning documents, 72–78
    Agfa scanning guide, 75
    forms, 77, *78*
    OCR (Optical Character Recognition), 75–77
    outsourcing, 73
    physical aspects, 72
    scanners, 72–75
    software, 75–78
scheduling, organizational issues, 47
ScreenTips, graphic-oriented tools, 91, *92*
scripts, CGI (Common Gateway Interface), 214–216
scrolling marquees, ActiveX controls, 241
search page, RedTraktor site, *18*
search tools, 139–153
    See also navigating intranets
    Adobe Acrobat PDF documents, 148–149, *150*
    advanced searching techniques, 146–148
    browser, 119
    CompassWare InfoMagnet, 150, *151*
    indexes, 144
    Internet search engines, *152–153*
    keywords, 144, 145
    Microsoft FrontPage Explorer, 132, *133*
    news sources, 146
    overview, 143–145
    Quarterdeck WebCompass, 152
    queries, 145

security, 169–184
   administrators, 170
   backups, 173–174
   data encryption, 178
   elements of, 170–171
   firewalls, 176–178
   Internet connections, 174–178
   overview, 169–170
   passwords, 171–172
   publications, 182
   telecommuters and, 181
   Usenet newsgroups, 183–184
   viruses and, 178–180
   Web sites, 182–183
servers, 157, 158–159
   data replication, 166–167
   determining needs for, 158–159
   e-mail, 212–213
   memory requirements, 159
   mirror sites, 158
   proxy, 177
   speed of, 159
shared applications, Microsoft NetMeeting, 230, *231*
shared clipboards, Microsoft NetMeeting, 230
shareware
   Giles HTML Editor, 90
   HTML editors, *291–292*
shepherds, human resources, 33
Shockwave, multimedia players, 241–242
simple queries, search tools, 145
site administration, organizational issues, 42
site management tools, 125–137
   DeltaPoint QuickSite, 134
   features of, 129–130
   file management, 126–127
   hyperlinks, 127
   large-scale version control, 128
   Microsoft FrontPage Explorer, 131–133
   multiple physical locations, 128
   NetObjects Fusion, 134–136
   overview, 125–126
   tips, 137
   updating content, 128
   views, 129, *130*
site map, RedTraktor site, *18*
Site Views
   Adobe SiteMill, 129, *130*
   DeltaPoint QuickSite, *134*
   NetObjects Fusion, 134, *135*
SiteMapper, NetObjects Fusion, 136
SiteMill. *See* Adobe SiteMill
SiteStyles, NetObjects Fusion, 135
skill requirements, training and support, 197, *198*
SMTP (Simple Mail Transfer Protocol), e-mail, 212
software
   See also tools
   cost of, 46
   operating systems, 160–161
   scanning, 75–78
sound
   intranet page creation, 104
   multimedia formats, 94
source code
   editing HTML, 94, 109, *110*
   HTML, *88*
speed
   hardware, 163–165
   server, 159
staff. *See* human resources
Stanford Testing Systems' IBTauthor, training and support, 196
storage media, backup, 174
structure
   intranet design, 52–53
   usability testing, 258–259
style sheets
   dynamic (Netscape Communicator), 210
   plans for intranets, 37
   as tools, 252–253
styles, NetObjects Fusion SiteStyles, 135
support. *See* training and support
syntax operators, advanced searching techniques, 146

INDEX **323**

T

table tags, HTML, 297–299
tables
    Insert Table dialog box, *105*
    intranet design, 61
    intranet page creation, 104, *105*
tables of contents, navigating intranets, 140
tags (HTML), 53–55, 293–303
    body, *294*
    color, 295–296
    fonts and, *295*
    frame, 299–300
    link, 300–301
    list, 296
    META, 301
    overview, 293
    table, 297–299
    text, 293–295
    Van Cleve Britton home page, 302–303
TCP/IP, 165–166
team meetings, organizational issues, 43
team-building, organizational issues, 39
technical development, organizational issues, 41
technical issues, 43
technology tools, 22
telecommuters
    audio and video conferencing, 227–228
    intranets and, 166
    security and, 181
telephones (Internet), Microsoft NetMeeting, 230
television analogy, Marimba Castanet ("push" technology), 220–221
templates, as tools, 252
testing
    See also questions to ask users; quizzes
    organizational issues, 42
    training and support, 191–192
    usability, 256–262
text, importing and formatting, 104
text tags, HTML, 293–295
thin clients, defined, 238
threads, discussion group, 210
3D interfaces, 254
throughput. *See* speed
To Do Lists, Microsoft FrontPage Explorer, 132, *133*
toolbar buttons
    Internet Explorer, 117
    Netscape Navigator, 117
tools, 237–254
    See also software
    ActiveX controls, 240–241
    animations, 242–252
    authoring, 87–99
    frames, 253
    GIF Construction Set (animations), 243–252
    graphic-oriented, 89–99
    Java, 238–239
    search, 139–153
    Shockwave multimedia player, 241–242
    site management, 125–137
    style sheets, 252–253
    templates, 252
    WYSIWYG. *See* graphic-oriented tools
tracking sheets, managing content, 27–28
training and support, 187–199
    audio and video streaming, 195
    books, 193, 194
    CD-ROMs, 193
    classroom instruction, 194
    DigitalThink, 188–189, *190*
    forms of, 192–194
    help desks, 197
    Internet Assistant, *196*
    online resources, 188–191, 193
    skill requirements, 197, *198*
    Stanford Testing Systems' IBTauthor, 196
    testing, 191–192
    video, 193
transitions, GIF Construction Set, 249–250
Transmitters, Marimba Castanet ("push" technology), 221, *222*
transparencies, GIF Construction Set and, 247

travel savings, audio and video conferencing, 226
Tuner, Marimba Castanet ("push" technology), 220–221
tutorial. *See* Quick Tour
TV analogy, Marimba Castanet ("push" technology), 220–221
typefaces, intranet design, 60–61

U

ULS (User Location Service) directory, Microsoft NetMeeting, 233
Unix, operating systems, 160–161
updating content, site management tools, 128
usability testing, 256–262
    See also questions to ask users; testing
    CGI programs, 260
    content, 258
    interactive features, 259–260
    online quiz for users, 260–262
    performance, 259
    structure, 258–259
    writing style, 257
Usenet newsgroups, security issues, 183–184
User Location Service (ULS) directory, Microsoft NetMeeting, 233

V

Van Cleve Britton home page, HTML tag samples, 302–303
version control, large-scale, 128
video
    intranet page creation, 104
    training and support, 193
video cameras, QuickCam, 235–236
video conferencing
    See also audio and video conferencing
    future of groupware, 211
    interactive tasks, 15
    Microsoft NetMeeting, 232, *233*
    Quick Tour, 6

video streaming, training and support, 195
View Source command, HTML, 55
viewing Web pages. *See* browsers
views
    Adobe SiteMill, 129–130, *131*
    DeltaPoint QuickSite, *134*
    NetObjects Fusion, 134, *135*
    site management tools, 129
viruses, 178–180
    firewalls and, 180
    YAHOO! directory, *179*
Visioneer Paperport, personal scanners, 74

W

WANs (Wide Area Networks)
    connection types, *164*
    data replication, 166–167
    defined, 156
    speed of, 164–165
Wayfarer, "push" technology, *220*
Web Browse feature, Microsoft Word, *83*
Web browsers. *See* browsers
Web pages
    creating. *See* creating intranet pages
    viewing. *See* browsers
Web sites
    See also site administration; site management tools
    large-scale version control, 128
    publishing with Microsoft FrontPage Explorer, 133
    security-related, 182–183
Web Week, 182
Web-authoring tools. *See* authoring tools
WebBots, Microsoft FrontPage97, 95
WebCompass, search tools, 152
WebCrawler, Internet search engines, *153*
Webmasters, human resources, 33
whiteboard, Microsoft NetMeeting, 231, *232*
Windows NT
    operating systems, 160
    peer Web services, 222–223

wizards
    creating intranet pages with, 99–101, *102*
    Microsoft FrontPage97, 95, 100–101, *102*
    Quick Tour, 4
workflow management tools, future of groupware, 211
writing, organizational issues, 39
writing styles, usability testing, 257
WYSIWYG tools. *See* graphic-oriented tools

Y

Yahoo! directory, virus resources, *179*

DUMMIES PRESS

The Fun & Easy Way™ to learn about computers and more!

10/31/95

Windows® 3.11 For Dummies, 3rd Edition
by Andy Rathbone
ISBN: 1-56884-370-4
$16.95 USA/
$22.95 Canada

Mutual Funds For Dummies™
by Eric Tyson
ISBN: 1-56884-226-0
$16.99 USA/
$22.99 Canada

DOS For Dummies, 2nd Edition
by Dan Gookin
ISBN: 1-878058-75-4
$16.95 USA/
$22.95 Canada

The Internet For Dummies, 2nd Edition
by John Levine & Carol Baroudi
ISBN: 1-56884-222-8
$19.99 USA/
$26.99 Canada

Personal Finance For Dummies™
by Eric Tyson
ISBN: 1-56884-150-7
$16.95 USA/
$22.95 Canada

PCs For Dummies, 3rd Edition
by Dan Gookin & Andy Rathbone
ISBN: 1-56884-904-4
$16.95 USA/
$22.99 Canada

Macs® For Dummies, 3rd Edition
by David Pogue
ISBN: 1-56884-239-2
$19.99 USA/
$26.99 Canada

The SAT® I For Dummies™
by Suzee Vlk
ISBN: 1-56884-213-9
$14.99 USA/
$20.99 Canada

Here's a complete listing of IDG Books' ...For Dummies® titles

Title	Author	ISBN	Price
DATABASE			
Access 2 For Dummies®	by Scott Palmer	ISBN: 1-56884-090-X	$19.95 USA/$26.95 Canada
Access Programming For Dummies®	by Rob Krumm	ISBN: 1-56884-091-8	$19.95 USA/$26.95 Canada
Approach 3 For Windows® For Dummies®	by Doug Lowe	ISBN: 1-56884-233-3	$19.99 USA/$26.99 Canada
dBASE For DOS For Dummies®	by Scott Palmer & Michael Stabler	ISBN: 1-56884-188-4	$19.95 USA/$26.95 Canada
dBASE For Windows® For Dummies®	by Scott Palmer	ISBN: 1-56884-179-5	$19.95 USA/$26.95 Canada
dBASE 5 For Windows® Programming For Dummies®	by Ted Coombs & Jason Coombs	ISBN: 1-56884-215-5	$19.99 USA/$26.99 Canada
FoxPro 2.6 For Windows® For Dummies®	by John Kaufeld	ISBN: 1-56884-187-6	$19.95 USA/$26.95 Canada
Paradox 5 For Windows® For Dummies®	by John Kaufeld	ISBN: 1-56884-185-X	$19.95 USA/$26.95 Canada
DESKTOP PUBLISHING/ILLUSTRATION/GRAPHICS			
CorelDRAW! 5 For Dummies®	by Deke McClelland	ISBN: 1-56884-157-4	$19.95 USA/$26.95 Canada
CorelDRAW! For Dummies®	by Deke McClelland	ISBN: 1-56884-042-X	$19.95 USA/$26.95 Canada
Desktop Publishing & Design For Dummies®	by Roger C. Parker	ISBN: 1-56884-234-1	$19.99 USA/$26.99 Canada
Harvard Graphics 2 For Windows® For Dummies®	by Roger C. Parker	ISBN: 1-56884-092-6	$19.95 USA/$26.95 Canada
PageMaker 5 For Macs® For Dummies®	by Galen Gruman & Deke McClelland	ISBN: 1-56884-178-7	$19.95 USA/$26.95 Canada
PageMaker 5 For Windows® For Dummies®	by Deke McClelland & Galen Gruman	ISBN: 1-56884-160-4	$19.95 USA/$26.95 Canada
Photoshop 3 For Macs® For Dummies®	by Deke McClelland	ISBN: 1-56884-208-2	$19.99 USA/$26.99 Canada
QuarkXPress 3.3 For Dummies®	by Galen Gruman & Barbara Assadi	ISBN: 1-56884-217-1	$19.99 USA/$26.99 Canada
FINANCE/PERSONAL FINANCE/TEST TAKING REFERENCE			
Everyday Math For Dummies™	by Charles Seiter	ISBN: 1-56884-248-1	$14.99 USA/$22.99 Canada
Personal Finance For Dummies™ For Canadians	by Eric Tyson & Tony Martin	ISBN: 1-56884-378-X	$18.99 USA/$24.99 Canada
QuickBooks 3 For Dummies®	by Stephen L. Nelson	ISBN: 1-56884-227-9	$19.99 USA/$26.99 Canada
Quicken 8 For DOS For Dummies, 2nd Edition	by Stephen L. Nelson	ISBN: 1-56884-210-4	$19.95 USA/$26.95 Canada
Quicken 5 For Macs® For Dummies®	by Stephen L. Nelson	ISBN: 1-56884-211-2	$19.95 USA/$26.95 Canada
Quicken 4 For Windows® For Dummies, 2nd Edition	by Stephen L. Nelson	ISBN: 1-56884-209-0	$19.95 USA/$26.95 Canada
Taxes For Dummies,™ 1995 Edition	by Eric Tyson & David J. Silverman	ISBN: 1-56884-220-1	$14.99 USA/$20.99 Canada
The GMAT® For Dummies™	by Suzee Vlk, Series Editor	ISBN: 1-56884-376-3	$14.99 USA/$20.99 Canada
The GRE® For Dummies™	by Suzee Vlk, Series Editor	ISBN: 1-56884-375-5	$14.99 USA/$20.99 Canada
Time Management For Dummies™	by Jeffrey J. Mayer	ISBN: 1-56884-360-7	$16.99 USA/$22.99 Canada
TurboTax For Windows® For Dummies®	by Gail A. Helsel, CPA	ISBN: 1-56884-228-7	$19.99 USA/$26.99 Canada
GROUPWARE/INTEGRATED			
ClarisWorks For Macs® For Dummies®	by Frank Higgins	ISBN: 1-56884-363-1	$19.99 USA/$26.99 Canada
Lotus Notes For Dummies®	by Pat Freeland & Stephen Londergan	ISBN: 1-56884-212-0	$19.95 USA/$26.95 Canada
Microsoft® Office 4 For Windows® For Dummies®	by Roger C. Parker	ISBN: 1-56884-183-3	$19.95 USA/$26.95 Canada
Microsoft® Works 3 For Windows® For Dummies®	by David C. Kay	ISBN: 1-56884-214-7	$19.99 USA/$26.99 Canada
SmartSuite 3 For Dummies®	by Jan Weingarten & John Weingarten	ISBN: 1-56884-367-4	$19.99 USA/$26.99 Canada
INTERNET/COMMUNICATIONS/NETWORKING			
America Online® For Dummies, 2nd Edition	by John Kaufeld	ISBN: 1-56884-933-8	$19.99 USA/$26.99 Canada
CompuServe For Dummies, 2nd Edition	by Wallace Wang	ISBN: 1-56884-937-0	$19.99 USA/$26.99 Canada
Modems For Dummies, 2nd Edition	by Tina Rathbone	ISBN: 1-56884-223-6	$19.99 USA/$26.99 Canada
MORE Internet For Dummies®	by John R. Levine & Margaret Levine Young	ISBN: 1-56884-164-7	$19.95 USA/$26.95 Canada
MORE Modems & On-line Services For Dummies®	by Tina Rathbone	ISBN: 1-56884-365-8	$19.99 USA/$26.99 Canada
Mosaic For Dummies, Windows Edition	by David Angell & Brent Heslop	ISBN: 1-56884-242-2	$19.99 USA/$26.99 Canada
NetWare For Dummies, 2nd Edition	by Ed Tittel, Deni Connor & Earl Follis	ISBN: 1-56884-369-0	$19.99 USA/$26.99 Canada
Networking For Dummies®	by Doug Lowe	ISBN: 1-56884-079-9	$19.95 USA/$26.95 Canada
PROCOMM PLUS 2 For Windows® For Dummies®	by Wallace Wang	ISBN: 1-56884-219-8	$19.99 USA/$26.99 Canada
TCP/IP For Dummies®	by Marshall Wilensky & Candace Leiden	ISBN: 1-56884-241-4	$19.99 USA/$26.99 Canada

Microsoft and Windows are registered trademarks of Microsoft Corporation. Mac is a registered trademark of Apple Computer. SAT is a registered trademark of the College Entrance Examination Board. GMAT is a registered trademark of the Graduate Management Admission Council. GRE is a registered trademark of the Educational Testing Service. America Online is a registered trademark of America Online, Inc. The "...For Dummies Book Series" logo, the IDG Books Worldwide logos, Dummies Press, and The Fun & Easy Way are trademarks, and ---- For Dummies and ... For Dummies are registered trademarks under exclusive license to IDG Books Worldwide, Inc., from International Data Group, Inc.

For scholastic requests & educational orders please call Educational Sales at 1. 800. 434. 2086

FOR MORE INFO OR TO ORDER, PLEASE CALL ▶ 800 762 2974

For volume discounts & special orders please call Tony Real, Special Sales, at 415. 655. 3048

DUMMIES PRESS™
IDG BOOKS

The Internet For Macs® For Dummies®, 2nd Edition	by Charles Seiter	ISBN: 1-56884-371-2	$19.99 USA/$26.99 Canada
The Internet For Macs® For Dummies® Starter Kit	by Charles Seiter	ISBN: 1-56884-244-9	$29.99 USA/$39.99 Canada
The Internet For Macs® For Dummies® Starter Kit Bestseller Edition	by Charles Seiter	ISBN: 1-56884-245-7	$39.99 USA/$54.99 Canada
The Internet For Windows® For Dummies® Starter Kit	by John R. Levine & Margaret Levine Young	ISBN: 1-56884-237-6	$34.99 USA/$44.99 Canada
The Internet For Windows® For Dummies® Starter Kit, Bestseller Edition	by John R. Levine & Margaret Levine Young	ISBN: 1-56884-246-5	$39.99 USA/$54.99 Canada

MACINTOSH

Mac® Programming For Dummies®	by Dan Parks Sydow	ISBN: 1-56884-173-6	$19.95 USA/$26.95 Canada
Macintosh® System 7.5 For Dummies®	by Bob LeVitus	ISBN: 1-56884-197-3	$19.95 USA/$26.95 Canada
MORE Macs® For Dummies®	by David Pogue	ISBN: 1-56884-087-X	$19.95 USA/$26.95 Canada
PageMaker 5 For Macs® For Dummies®	by Galen Gruman & Deke McClelland	ISBN: 1-56884-178-7	$19.95 USA/$26.95 Canada
QuarkXPress 3.3 For Dummies®	by Galen Gruman & Barbara Assadi	ISBN: 1-56884-217-1	$19.95 USA/$26.99 Canada
Upgrading and Fixing Macs® For Dummies®	by Kearney Rietmann & Frank Higgins	ISBN: 1-56884-189-2	$19.95 USA/$26.95 Canada

MULTIMEDIA

Multimedia & CD-ROMs For Dummies®, 2nd Edition	by Andy Rathbone	ISBN: 1-56884-907-9	$19.99 USA/$26.99 Canada
Multimedia & CD-ROMs For Dummies®, Interactive Multimedia Value Pack, 2nd Edition	by Andy Rathbone	ISBN: 1-56884-909-5	$29.99 USA/$39.99 Canada

OPERATING SYSTEMS:
DOS

MORE DOS For Dummies®	by Dan Gookin	ISBN: 1-56884-046-2	$19.95 USA/$26.95 Canada
OS/2® Warp For Dummies®, 2nd Edition	by Andy Rathbone	ISBN: 1-56884-205-8	$19.95 USA/$26.99 Canada

UNIX

MORE UNIX® For Dummies®	by John R. Levine & Margaret Levine Young	ISBN: 1-56884-361-5	$19.99 USA/$26.99 Canada
UNIX® For Dummies®	by John R. Levine & Margaret Levine Young	ISBN: 1-878058-58-4	$19.95 USA/$26.95 Canada

WINDOWS

MORE Windows® For Dummies®, 2nd Edition	by Andy Rathbone	ISBN: 1-56884-048-9	$19.95 USA/$26.95 Canada
Windows® 95 For Dummies®	by Andy Rathbone	ISBN: 1-56884-240-6	$19.99 USA/$26.99 Canada

PCS/HARDWARE

Illustrated Computer Dictionary For Dummies®, 2nd Edition	by Dan Gookin & Wallace Wang	ISBN: 1-56884-218-X	$12.95 USA/$16.95 Canada
Upgrading and Fixing PCs For Dummies®, 2nd Edition	by Andy Rathbone	ISBN: 1-56884-903-6	$19.99 USA/$26.99 Canada

PRESENTATION/AUTOCAD

AutoCAD For Dummies®	by Bud Smith	ISBN: 1-56884-191-4	$19.95 USA/$26.95 Canada
PowerPoint 4 For Windows® For Dummies®	by Doug Lowe	ISBN: 1-56884-161-2	$16.99 USA/$22.99 Canada

PROGRAMMING

Borland C++ For Dummies®	by Michael Hyman	ISBN: 1-56884-162-0	$19.95 USA/$26.95 Canada
C For Dummies®, Volume 1	by Dan Gookin	ISBN: 1-878058-78-9	$19.95 USA/$26.95 Canada
C++ For Dummies®	by Stephen R. Davis	ISBN: 1-56884-163-9	$19.95 USA/$26.95 Canada
Delphi Programming For Dummies®	by Neil Rubenking	ISBN: 1-56884-200-7	$19.99 USA/$26.99 Canada
Mac® Programming For Dummies®	by Dan Parks Sydow	ISBN: 1-56884-173-6	$19.95 USA/$26.95 Canada
PowerBuilder 4 Programming For Dummies®	by Ted Coombs & Jason Coombs	ISBN: 1-56884-325-9	$19.99 USA/$26.99 Canada
QBasic Programming For Dummies®	by Douglas Hergert	ISBN: 1-56884-093-4	$19.95 USA/$26.95 Canada
Visual Basic 3 For Dummies®	by Wallace Wang	ISBN: 1-56884-076-4	$19.95 USA/$26.95 Canada
Visual Basic "X" For Dummies®	by Wallace Wang	ISBN: 1-56884-230-9	$19.99 USA/$26.99 Canada
Visual C++ 2 For Dummies®	by Michael Hyman & Bob Arnson	ISBN: 1-56884-328-3	$19.99 USA/$26.99 Canada
Windows® 95 Programming For Dummies®	by S. Randy Davis	ISBN: 1-56884-327-5	$19.99 USA/$26.99 Canada

SPREADSHEET

1-2-3 For Dummies®	by Greg Harvey	ISBN: 1-878058-60-6	$16.95 USA/$22.95 Canada
1-2-3 For Windows® 5 For Dummies®, 2nd Edition	by John Walkenbach	ISBN: 1-56884-216-3	$16.95 USA/$22.95 Canada
Excel 5 For Macs® For Dummies®	by Greg Harvey	ISBN: 1-56884-186-8	$19.95 USA/$26.95 Canada
Excel For Dummies®, 2nd Edition	by Greg Harvey	ISBN: 1-56884-050-0	$16.95 USA/$22.95 Canada
MORE 1-2-3 For DOS For Dummies®	by John Weingarten	ISBN: 1-56884-224-4	$19.99 USA/$26.99 Canada
MORE Excel 5 For Windows® For Dummies®	by Greg Harvey	ISBN: 1-56884-207-4	$19.95 USA/$26.95 Canada
Quattro Pro 6 For Windows® For Dummies®	by John Walkenbach	ISBN: 1-56884-174-4	$19.95 USA/$26.95 Canada
Quattro Pro For DOS For Dummies®	by John Walkenbach	ISBN: 1-56884-023-3	$16.95 USA/$22.95 Canada

UTILITIES

Norton Utilities 8 For Dummies®	by Beth Slick	ISBN: 1-56884-166-3	$19.95 USA/$26.95 Canada

VCRS/CAMCORDERS

VCRs & Camcorders For Dummies™	by Gordon McComb & Andy Rathbone	ISBN: 1-56884-229-5	$14.99 USA/$20.99 Canada

WORD PROCESSING

Ami Pro For Dummies®	by Jim Meade	ISBN: 1-56884-049-7	$19.95 USA/$26.95 Canada
MORE Word For Windows® 6 For Dummies®	by Doug Lowe	ISBN: 1-56884-165-5	$19.95 USA/$26.95 Canada
MORE WordPerfect® 6 For Windows® For Dummies®	by Margaret Levine Young & David C. Kay	ISBN: 1-56884-206-6	$19.95 USA/$26.95 Canada
MORE WordPerfect® 6 For DOS For Dummies®	by Wallace Wang, edited by Dan Gookin	ISBN: 1-56884-047-0	$19.95 USA/$26.95 Canada
Word 6 For Macs® For Dummies®	by Dan Gookin	ISBN: 1-56884-190-6	$19.95 USA/$26.95 Canada
Word For Windows® 6 For Dummies®	by Dan Gookin	ISBN: 1-56884-075-6	$16.95 USA/$22.95 Canada
Word For Windows® For Dummies®	by Dan Gookin & Ray Werner	ISBN: 1-878058-86-X	$16.95 USA/$22.95 Canada
WordPerfect® 6 For DOS For Dummies®	by Dan Gookin	ISBN: 1-878058-77-0	$16.95 USA/$22.95 Canada
WordPerfect® 6.1 For Windows® For Dummies®, 2nd Edition	by Margaret Levine Young & David Kay	ISBN: 1-56884-243-0	$16.95 USA/$22.95 Canada
WordPerfect® For Dummies®		ISBN: 1-878058-52-5	$16.95 USA/$22.95 Canada

Windows is a registered trademark of Microsoft Corporation. Mac is a registered trademark of Apple Computer. OS/2 is a registered trademark of IBM. UNIX is a registered trademark of AT&T. WordPerfect is a registered trademark of Novell. The "...For Dummies Book Series" logo, the IDG Books Worldwide logos, Dummies Press, and The Fun & Easy Way are trademarks, and ---- For Dummies and ... For Dummies are registered trademarks under exclusive license to IDG Books Worldwide, Inc., from International Data Group, Inc.

For scholastic requests & educational orders please call Educational Sales at 1. 800. 434. 2086

FOR MORE INFO OR TO ORDER, PLEASE CALL ▶ 800 762 2974

For volume discounts & special orders please call Tony Real, Special Sales, at 415. 655. 3048

DUMMIES PRESS™ QUICK REFERENCES

Fun, Fast, & Cheap!™

The Internet For Macs® For Dummies® Quick Reference — NEW!
by Charles Seiter
ISBN:1-56884-967-2
$9.99 USA/$12.99 Canada

Windows® 95 For Dummies® Quick Reference — NEW!
by Greg Harvey
ISBN: 1-56884-964-8
$9.99 USA/$12.99 Canada

Photoshop 3 For Macs For Dummies® Quick Reference — SUPER STAR
by Deke McClelland
ISBN: 1-56884-968-0
$9.99 USA/$12.99 Canada

WordPerfect® For DOS For Dummies® Quick Reference — SUPER STAR
by Greg Harvey
ISBN: 1-56884-009-8
$8.95 USA/$12.95 Canada

Title	Author	ISBN	Price
DATABASE			
Access 2 For Dummies® Quick Reference	by Stuart J. Stuple	ISBN: 1-56884-167-1	$8.95 USA/$11.95 Canada
dBASE 5 For DOS For Dummies® Quick Reference	by Barrie Sosinsky	ISBN: 1-56884-954-0	$9.99 USA/$12.99 Canada
dBASE 5 For Windows® For Dummies® Quick Reference	by Stuart J. Stuple	ISBN: 1-56884-953-2	$9.99 USA/$12.99 Canada
Paradox 5 For Windows® For Dummies® Quick Reference	by Scott Palmer	ISBN: 1-56884-960-5	$9.99 USA/$12.99 Canada
DESKTOP PUBLISHING/ILLUSTRATION/GRAPHICS			
CorelDRAW! 5 For Dummies® Quick Reference	by Raymond E. Werner	ISBN: 1-56884-952-4	$9.99 USA/$12.99 Canada
Harvard Graphics For Windows® For Dummies® Quick Reference	by Raymond E. Werner	ISBN: 1-56884-962-1	$9.99 USA/$12.99 Canada
Photoshop 3 For Macs® For Dummies® Quick Reference	by Deke McClelland	ISBN: 1-56884-968-0	$9.99 USA/$12.99 Canada
FINANCE/PERSONAL FINANCE			
Quicken 4 For Windows® For Dummies® Quick Reference	by Stephen L. Nelson	ISBN: 1-56884-950-8	$9.95 USA/$12.95 Canada
GROUPWARE/INTEGRATED			
Microsoft® Office 4 For Windows® For Dummies® Quick Reference	by Doug Lowe	ISBN: 1-56884-958-3	$9.99 USA/$12.99 Canada
Microsoft® Works 3 For Windows® For Dummies® Quick Reference	by Michael Partington	ISBN: 1-56884-959-1	$9.99 USA/$12.99 Canada
INTERNET/COMMUNICATIONS/NETWORKING			
The Internet For Dummies® Quick Reference	by John R. Levine & Margaret Levine Young	ISBN: 1-56884-168-X	$8.95 USA/$11.95 Canada
MACINTOSH			
Macintosh® System 7.5 For Dummies® Quick Reference	by Stuart J. Stuple	ISBN: 1-56884-956-7	$9.99 USA/$12.99 Canada
OPERATING SYSTEMS:			
DOS			
DOS For Dummies® Quick Reference	by Greg Harvey	ISBN: 1-56884-007-1	$8.95 USA/$11.95 Canada
UNIX			
UNIX® For Dummies® Quick Reference	by John R. Levine & Margaret Levine Young	ISBN: 1-56884-094-2	$8.95 USA/$11.95 Canada
WINDOWS			
Windows® 3.1 For Dummies® Quick Reference, 2nd Edition	by Greg Harvey	ISBN: 1-56884-951-6	$8.95 USA/$11.95 Canada
PCs/HARDWARE			
Memory Management For Dummies® Quick Reference	by Doug Lowe	ISBN: 1-56884-362-3	$9.99 USA/$12.99 Canada
PRESENTATION/AUTOCAD			
AutoCAD For Dummies® Quick Reference	by Ellen Finkelstein	ISBN: 1-56884-198-1	$9.95 USA/$12.95 Canada
SPREADSHEET			
1-2-3 For Dummies® Quick Reference	by John Walkenbach	ISBN: 1-56884-027-6	$8.95 USA/$11.95 Canada
1-2-3 For Windows® 5 For Dummies® Quick Reference	by John Walkenbach	ISBN: 1-56884-957-5	$9.95 USA/$12.95 Canada
Excel For Windows® For Dummies® Quick Reference, 2nd Edition	by John Walkenbach	ISBN: 1-56884-096-9	$8.95 USA/$11.95 Canada
Quattro Pro 6 For Windows® For Dummies® Quick Reference	by Stuart J. Stuple	ISBN: 1-56884-172-8	$9.95 USA/$12.95 Canada
WORD PROCESSING			
Word For Windows® 6 For Dummies® Quick Reference	by George Lynch	ISBN: 1-56884-095-0	$8.95 USA/$11.95 Canada
Word For Windows® For Dummies® Quick Reference	by George Lynch	ISBN: 1-56884-029-2	$8.95 USA/$11.95 Canada
WordPerfect® 6.1 For Windows® For Dummies® Quick Reference, 2nd Edition	by Greg Harvey	ISBN: 1-56884-966-4	$9.99 USA/$12.99/Canada

Microsoft and Windows are registered trademarks of Microsoft Corporation. Mac and Macintosh are registered trademarks of Apple Computer. UNIX is a registered trademark of AT&T. WordPerfect is a registered trademark of Novell. The "...For Dummies Book Series" logo, the IDG Books Worldwide logos, Dummies Press, The Fun & Easy Way, and Fun, Fast, & Cheap! are trademarks, and ---- For Dummies and ... For Dummies are registered trademarks under exclusive license to IDG Books Worldwide, Inc., from International Data Group, Inc.

For scholastic requests & educational orders please call Educational Sales at 1. 800. 434. 2086

FOR MORE INFO OR TO ORDER, PLEASE CALL ▶ 800. 762. 2974

For volume discounts & special orders please call Tony Real, Special Sales, at 415. 655. 3048

PC PRESS

IDG BOOKS WORLDWIDE

10/31/95

Windows® 3.1 SECRETS™
by Brian Livingston
ISBN: 1-878058-43-6
$39.95 USA/$52.95 Canada
Includes software.

MORE Windows® 3.1 SECRETS™
by Brian Livingston
ISBN: 1-56884-019-5
$39.95 USA/$52.95 Canada
Includes software.

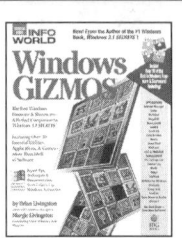

Windows® GIZMOS™
by Brian Livingston
& Margie Livingston
ISBN: 1-878058-66-5
$39.95 USA/$52.95 Canada
Includes software.

Windows® 3.1 Connectivity SECRETS™
by Runnoe Connally, David Rorabaugh, & Sheldon Hall
ISBN: 1-56884-030-6
$49.95 USA/$64.95 Canada
Includes software.

Windows® 3.1 Configuration SECRETS™
by Valda Hilley & James Blakely
ISBN: 1-56884-026-8
$49.95 USA/$64.95 Canada
Includes software.

Internet SECRETS™
by John Levine & Carol Baroudi
ISBN: 1-56884-452-2
$39.99 USA/$54.99 Canada
Includes software.

Internet GIZMOS™ For Windows®
by Joel Diamond, Howard Sobel, & Valda Hilley
ISBN: 1-56884-451-4
$39.99 USA/$54.99 Canada
Includes software.

Network Security SECRETS™
by David Stang & Sylvia Moon
ISBN: 1-56884-021-7
Int'l. ISBN: 1-56884-151-5
$49.95 USA/$64.95 Canada
Includes software.

PC SECRETS™
by Caroline M. Halliday
ISBN: 1-878058-49-5
$39.95 USA/$52.95 Canada
Includes software.

WordPerfect® 6 SECRETS™
by Roger C. Parker & David A. Holzgang
ISBN: 1-56884-040-3
$39.95 USA/$52.95 Canada
Includes software.

DOS 6 SECRETS™
by Robert D. Ainsbury
ISBN: 1-878058-70-3
$39.95 USA/$52.95 Canada
Includes software.

Paradox 4 Power Programming SECRETS™ 2nd Edition
by Gregory B. Salcedo & Martin W. Rudy
ISBN: 1-878058-54-1
$44.95 USA/$59.95 Canada
Includes software.

Paradox 5 For Windows® Power Programming SECRETS™
by Gregory B. Salcedo & Martin W. Rudy
ISBN: 1-56884-083-3
$44.95 USA/$59.95 Canada
Includes software.

Hard Disk SECRETS™
by John M. Goodman, Ph.D.
ISBN: 1-878058-64-9
$39.95 USA/$52.95 Canada
Includes software.

WordPerfect® 6 For Windows® Tips & Techniques Revealed
by David A. Holzgang & Roger C. Parker
ISBN: 1-56884-202-3
$39.95 USA/$52.95 Canada
Includes software.

Excel 5 For Windows® Power Programming Techniques
by John Walkenbach
ISBN: 1-56884-303-8
$39.95 USA/$52.95 Canada
Includes software.

...SECRETS®

INFO WORLD TECHNICAL BOOKS

Windows is a registered trademark of Microsoft Corporation. WordPerfect is a registered trademark of Novell. ----SECRETS, ----GIZMOS, and the IDG Books Worldwide logos are trademarks, and ...SECRETS is a registered trademark under exclusive license to IDG Books Worldwide, Inc., from International Data Group, Inc.

For scholastic requests & educational orders please call Educational Sales, at 1. 800. 434. 2086

FOR MORE INFO OR TO ORDER, PLEASE CALL ▶ 800. 762. 2974

For volume discounts & special orders please call Tony Real, Special Sales, at 415. 655. 3048

PC PRESS

IDG BOOKS WORLDWIDE

10/31/95

"A lot easier to use than the book Excel gives you!"

Lisa Schmeckpeper, New Berlin, WI, on PC World Excel 5 For Windows Handbook

Official Hayes Modem Communications Companion
by Caroline M. Halliday
ISBN: 1-56884-072-1
$29.95 USA/$39.95 Canada
Includes software.

1,001 Komputer Answers from Kim Komando
by Kim Komando
ISBN: 1-56884-460-3
$29.99 USA/$39.99 Canada
Includes software.

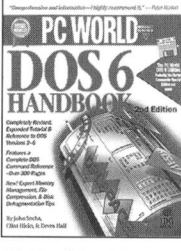

PC World DOS 6 Handbook, 2nd Edition
by John Socha, Clint Hicks, & Devra Hall
ISBN: 1-878058-79-7
$34.95 USA/$44.95 Canada
Includes software.

PC World Word For Windows 6 Handbook
by Brent Heslop & David Angell
ISBN: 1-56884-054-3
$34.95 USA/$44.95 Canada
Includes software.

PC World Microsoft Access 2 Bible, 2nd Edition
by Cary N. Prague & Michael R. Irwin
ISBN: 1-56884-086-1
$39.95 USA/$52.95 Canada
Includes software.

PC World Excel 5 For Windows Handbook, 2nd Edition
by John Walkenbach & Dave Maguiness
ISBN: 1-56884-056-X
$34.95 USA/$44.95 Canada
Includes software.

PC World WordPerfect 6 Handbook
by Greg Harvey
ISBN: 1-878058-80-0
$34.95 USA/$44.95 Canada
Includes software.

QuarkXPress For Windows Designer Handbook
by Barbara Assadi & Galen Gruman
ISBN: 1-878058-45-2
$29.95 USA/$39.95 Canada

Official XTree Companion, 3rd Edition
by Beth Slick
ISBN: 1-878058-57-6
$19.95 USA/$26.95 Canada

PC World DOS 6 Command Reference and Problem Solver
by John Socha & Devra Hall
ISBN: 1-56884-055-1
$24.95 USA/$32.95 Canada

Client/Server Strategies: A Survival Guide for Corporate Reengineers
by David Vaskevitch
ISBN: 1-56884-064-0
$29.95 USA/$39.95 Canada

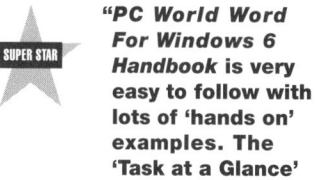

"PC World Word For Windows 6 Handbook is very easy to follow with lots of 'hands on' examples. The 'Task at a Glance' is very helpful!"

Jacqueline Martens, Tacoma, WA

"Thanks for publishing this book! It's the best money I've spent this year!"

Robert D. Templeton, Ft. Worth, TX, on MORE Windows 3.1 SECRETS

Microsoft and Windows are registered trademarks of Microsoft Corporation. WordPerfect is a registered trademark of Novell. ----STRATEGIES and the IDG Books Worldwide logos are trademarks under exclusive license to IDG Books Worldwide, Inc., from International Data Group, Inc.

For scholastic requests & educational orders please call Educational Sales, at 1. 800. 434. 2086

FOR MORE INFO OR TO ORDER, PLEASE CALL ▶ 800 762 2974

For volume discounts & special orders please call Tony Real, Special Sales, at 415. 655. 3048

MACWORLD® PRESS

10/31/95

Macworld® Mac & Power Mac SECRETS,™ 2nd Edition
by David Pogue & Joseph Schorr

This is the definitive Mac reference for those who want to become power users! Includes three disks with 9MB of software!

ISBN: 1-56884-175-2
$39.95 USA/$54.95 Canada

Includes 3 disks chock full of software.

WINNERS 1994-95 TECHNICAL PUBLICATIONS AND ART COMPETITIONS OF THE SOCIETY FOR TECHNICAL COMMUNICATION

NEWBRIDGE BOOK CLUB SELECTION

Macworld® Mac® FAQs™
by David Pogue

Written by the hottest Macintosh author around, David Pogue, *Macworld Mac FAQs* gives users the ultimate Mac reference. Hundreds of Mac questions and answers side-by-side, right at your fingertips, and organized into six easy-to-reference sections with lots of sidebars and diagrams.

ISBN: 1-56884-480-8
$19.99 USA/$26.99 Canada

Macworld® System 7.5 Bible, 3rd Edition
by Lon Poole

ISBN: 1-56884-098-5
$29.95 USA/$39.95 Canada

NATIONAL BESTSELLER!

Macworld® ClarisWorks 3.0 Companion, 3rd Edition
by Steven A. Schwartz

ISBN: 1-56884-481-6
$24.99 USA/$34.99 Canada

NATIONAL BESTSELLER!

Macworld® Complete Mac® Handbook Plus Interactive CD, 3rd Edition
by Jim Heid

ISBN: 1-56884-192-2
$39.95 USA/$54.95 Canada

Includes an interactive CD-ROM.

BMUG SPRING 1995 CHOICE PRODUCT

NEWBRIDGE BOOK CLUB SELECTION

Macworld® Ultimate Mac® CD-ROM
by Jim Heid

ISBN: 1-56884-477-8
$19.95 USA/$26.99 Canada

CD-ROM includes version 2.0 of QuickTime, and over 65 MB of the best shareware, freeware, fonts, sounds, and more!

Macworld® Networking Bible, 2nd Edition
by Dave Kosiur & Joel M. Snyder

ISBN: 1-56884-194-9
$29.95 USA/$39.95 Canada

Macworld® Photoshop 3 Bible, 2nd Edition
by Deke McClelland

ISBN: 1-56884-158-2
$39.95 USA/$54.95 Canada

Includes stunning CD-ROM with add-ons, digitized photos and more.

WINNERS 1994-95 TECHNICAL PUBLICATIONS AND ART COMPETITIONS OF THE SOCIETY FOR TECHNICAL COMMUNICATION

NEW!

Macworld® Photoshop 2.5 Bible
by Deke McClelland

ISBN: 1-56884-022-5
$29.95 USA/$39.95 Canada

NATIONAL BESTSELLER!

Macworld® FreeHand 4 Bible
by Deke McClelland

ISBN: 1-56884-170-1
$29.95 USA/$39.95 Canada

Macworld® Illustrator 5.0/5.5 Bible
by Ted Alspach

ISBN: 1-56884-097-7
$39.95 USA/$54.95 Canada

Includes CD-ROM with QuickTime tutorials.

Mac is a registered trademark of Apple Computer. Macworld is a registered trademark of International Data Group, Inc. ----SECRETS, and ----FAQs are trademarks under exclusive license to IDG Books Worldwide, Inc., from International Data Group, Inc.

For scholastic requests & educational orders please call Educational Sales, at 1. 800. 434. 2086

FOR MORE INFO TO ORDER, PLEASE CALL ▶ 800 762 2974

For volume discounts & special orders please call Tony Real, Special Sales, at 415. 655. 3048

MACWORLD® PRESS

"Macworld Complete Mac Handbook Plus CD covered everything I could think of and more!"

Peter Tsakiris, New York, NY

"Very useful for PageMaker beginners and veterans alike—contains a wealth of tips and tricks to make you a faster, more powerful PageMaker user."

Paul Brainerd, President and founder, Aldus Corporation

"Thanks for the best computer book I've ever read—Photoshop 2.5 Bible. Best $30 I ever spent. I love the detailed index....Yours blows them all out of the water. This is a great book. We must enlighten the masses!"

Kevin Lisankie, Chicago, Illinois

"Macworld Guide to ClarisWorks 2 is the easiest computer book to read that I have ever found!"

Steven Hanson, Lutz, FL

"...thanks to the Macworld Excel 5 Companion, 2nd Edition occupying a permanent position next to my computer, I'll be able to tap more of Excel's power."

Lauren Black, Lab Director, Macworld Magazine

Macworld® QuarkXPress 3.2/3.3 Bible
by Barbara Assadi & Galen Gruman
ISBN: 1-878058-85-1
$39.95 USA/$52.95 Canada
Includes disk with QuarkXPress XTensions and scripts.

Macworld® PageMaker 5 Bible
by Craig Danuloff
ISBN: 1-878058-84-3
$39.95 USA/$52.95 Canada
Includes 2 disks with PageMaker utilities, clip art, and more.

Macworld® FileMaker Pro 2.0/2.1 Bible
by Steven A. Schwartz
ISBN: 1-56884-201-5
$34.95 USA/$46.95 Canada
Includes disk with ready-to-run data bases.

Macworld® Word 6 Companion, 2nd Edition
by Jim Heid
ISBN: 1-56884-082-9
$24.95 USA/$34.95 Canada
NEWBRIDGE BOOK CLUB SELECTION

Macworld® Guide To Microsoft® Word 5/5.1
by Jim Heid
ISBN: 1-878058-39-8
$22.95 USA/$29.95 Canada

Macworld® ClarisWorks 2.0/2.1 Companion, 2nd Edition
by Steven A. Schwartz
ISBN: 1-56884-180-9
$24.95 USA/$34.95 Canada

Macworld® Guide To Microsoft® Works 3
by Barrie Sosinsky
ISBN: 1-878058-42-8
$22.95 USA/$29.95 Canada

Macworld® Excel 5 Companion, 2nd Edition
by Chris Van Buren & David Maguiness
ISBN: 1-56884-081-0
$24.95 USA/$34.95 Canada
NEWBRIDGE BOOK CLUB SELECTION

Macworld® Guide To Microsoft® Excel 4
by David Maguiness
ISBN: 1-878058-40-1
$22.95 USA/$29.95 Canada

Microsoft is a registered trademark of Microsoft Corporation. Macworld is a registered trademark of International Data Group, Inc.

For scholastic requests & educational orders please call Educational Sales, at 1. 800. 434. 2086 | **FOR MORE INFO OR TO ORDER, PLEASE CALL ▶ 800. 762. 2974** | For volume discounts & special orders please call Tony Real, Special Sales, at 415. 655. 3048

PROFESSIONAL PUBLISHING GROUP

10/31/95

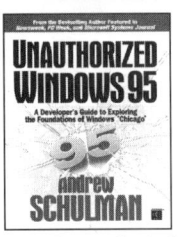

Unauthorized Windows® 95: A Developer's Guide to Exploring the Foundations of Windows "Chicago"
by Andrew Schulman
ISBN: 1-56884-169-8
$29.99 USA/$39.99 Canada

Unauthorized Windows® 95 Developer's Resource Kit
by Andrew Schulman
ISBN: 1-56884-305-4
$39.99 USA/$54.99 Canada

Best of the Net
by Seth Godin
ISBN: 1-56884-313-5
$22.99 USA/$32.99 Canada

Detour: The Truth About the Information Superhighway
by Michael Sullivan-Trainor
ISBN: 1-56884-307-0
$22.99 USA/$32.99 Canada

PowerPC Programming For Intel Programmers
by Kip McClanahan
ISBN: 1-56884-306-2
$49.99 USA/$64.99 Canada

Foundations™ of Visual C++ Programming For Windows® 95
by Paul Yao & Joseph Yao
ISBN: 1-56884-321-6
$39.99 USA/$54.99 Canada

Heavy Metal™ Visual C++ Programming
by Steve Holzner
ISBN: 1-56884-196-5
$39.95 USA/$54.95 Canada

Heavy Metal™ OLE 2.0 Programming
by Steve Holzner
ISBN: 1-56884-301-1
$39.95 USA/$54.95 Canada

Lotus Notes Application Development Handbook
by Erica Kerwien
ISBN: 1-56884-308-9
$39.99 USA/$54.99 Canada

The Internet Direct Connect Kit
by Peter John Harrison
ISBN: 1-56884-135-3
$29.95 USA/$39.95 Canada

Macworld® Ultimate Mac® Programming
by Dave Mark
ISBN: 1-56884-195-7
$39.95 USA/$54.95 Canada

The UNIX®-Haters Handbook
by Simson Garfinkel, Daniel Weise, & Steven Strassmann
ISBN: 1-56884-203-1
$16.95 USA/$22.95 Canada

Learn C++ Today!
by Martin Rinehart
ISBN: 1-56884-310-0
34.99 USA/$44.99 Canada

Type & Learn™ C
by Tom Swan
ISBN: 1-56884-073-X
34.95 USA/$44.95 Canada

Type & Learn™ Windows® Programming
by Tom Swan
ISBN: 1-56884-071-3
34.95 USA/$44.95 Canada

Windows is a registered trademark of Microsoft Corporation. Mac is a registered trademark of Apple Computer. UNIX is a registered trademark of AT&T. Macworld is a registered trademark of International Data Group, Inc. Foundations of ----, Heavy Metal, Type & Learn, and the IDG Books Worldwide logos are trademarks used under exclusive license to IDG Books Worldwide, Inc., from International Data Group, Inc.

For scholastic requests & educational orders please call Educational Sales, at 1. 800. 434. 2086

FOR MORE INFO OR TO ORDER, PLEASE CALL ▶ 800. 762. 2974

For volume discounts & special orders please call Tony Real, Special Sales, at 415. 655. 3048

DUMMIES PRESS™ PROGRAMMING BOOKS

COMPUTER BOOK SERIES FROM IDG

For Dummies who want to program...

Delphi Programming For Dummies®
by Neil Rubenking
ISBN: 1-56884-200-7
$19.99 USA/$26.99 Canada

Access Programming For Dummies®
by Rob Krumm
ISBN: 1-56884-091-8
$19.95 USA/$26.95 Canada

TCP/IP For Dummies®
by Marshall Wilensky & Candace Leiden
ISBN: 1-56884-241-4
$19.99 USA/$26.99 Canada

HTML For Dummies®
by Ed Tittel & Carl de Cordova
ISBN: 1-56884-330-5
$29.99 USA/$39.99 Canada

Windows® 95 Programming For Dummies®
by S. Randy Davis
ISBN: 1-56884-327-5
$19.99 USA/$26.99 Canada

Mac® Programming For Dummies®
by Dan Parks Sydow
ISBN: 1-56884-173-6
$19.95 USA/$26.95 Canada

PowerBuilder 4 Programming For Dummies®
by Ted Coombs & Jason Coombs
ISBN: 1-56884-325-9
$19.99 USA/$26.99 Canada

Visual Basic 3 For Dummies®
by Wallace Wang
ISBN: 1-56884-076-4
$19.95 USA/$26.95 Canada
Covers version 3.

ISDN For Dummies®
by David Angell
ISBN: 1-56884-331-3
$19.99 USA/$26.99 Canada

Visual C++ "2" For Dummies®
by Michael Hyman & Bob Arnson
ISBN: 1-56884-328-3
$19.99 USA/$26.99 Canada

Borland C++ For Dummies®
by Michael Hyman
ISBN: 1-56884-162-0
$19.95 USA/$26.95 Canada

C For Dummies® Volume I
by Dan Gookin
ISBN: 1-878058-78-9
$19.95 USA/$26.95 Canada

C++ For Dummies®
by Stephen R. Davis
ISBN: 1-56884-163-9
$19.95 USA/$26.95 Canada

QBasic Programming For Dummies®
by Douglas Hergert
ISBN: 1-56884-093-4
$19.95 USA/$26.95 Canada

dBase 5 For Windows® Programming For Dummies®
by Ted Coombs & Jason Coombs
ISBN: 1-56884-215-5
$19.99 USA/$26.99 Canada

Windows is a registered trademark of Microsoft Corporation. Mac is a registered trademark of Apple Computer. Dummies Press, the "...For Dummies Book Series" logo and the IDG Books Worldwide logos are trademarks, and ----For Dummies, ... For Dummies and the "...For Dummies Computer Book Series" logo are registered trademarks under exclusive license to IDG Books Worldwide, Inc., from International Data Group, Inc.

For scholastic requests & educational orders please call Educational Sales, at 1. 800. 434. 2086

FOR MORE INFO OR TO ORDER, PLEASE CALL ▶ 800. 762. 2974

For volume discounts & special orders please call Tony Real, Special Sales, at 415. 655. 3048

ORDER FORM

9/19/95

IDG BOOKS WORLDWIDE

Order Center: **(800) 762-2974** (8 a.m.–6 p.m., EST, weekdays)

Quantity	ISBN	Title	Price	Total

Shipping & Handling Charges

	Description	First book	Each additional book	Total
Domestic	Normal	$4.50	$1.50	$
	Two Day Air	$8.50	$2.50	$
	Overnight	$18.00	$3.00	$
International	Surface	$8.00	$8.00	$
	Airmail	$16.00	$16.00	$
	DHL Air	$17.00	$17.00	$

*For large quantities call for shipping & handling charges.
**Prices are subject to change without notice.

Ship to:
Name _____
Company _____
Address _____
City/State/Zip _____
Daytime Phone _____

Payment: ☐ Check to IDG Books Worldwide (US Funds Only)
☐ VISA ☐ MasterCard ☐ American Express
Card # _____ Expires _____
Signature _____

Subtotal _____
CA residents add applicable sales tax _____
IN, MA, and MD residents add 5% sales tax _____
IL residents add 6.25% sales tax _____
RI residents add 7% sales tax _____
TX residents add 8.25% sales tax _____

Shipping _____

Total _____

Please send this order form to:
IDG Books Worldwide, Inc.
7260 Shadeland Station, Suite 100
Indianapolis, IN 46256

*Allow up to 3 weeks for delivery.
Thank you!*

IDG BOOKS WORLDWIDE REGISTRATION CARD

RETURN THIS REGISTRATION CARD FOR FREE CATALOG

Title of this book: Discover Intranets

My overall rating of this book: ❏ Very good [1] ❏ Good [2] ❏ Satisfactory [3] ❏ Fair [4] ❏ Poor [5]

How I first heard about this book:

❏ Found in bookstore; name: [6] ❏ Book review: [7]
❏ Advertisement: [8] ❏ Catalog: [9]
❏ Word of mouth; heard about book from friend, co-worker, etc.: [10] ❏ Other: [11]

What I liked most about this book:

What I would change, add, delete, etc., in future editions of this book:

Other comments:

Number of computer books I purchase in a year: ❏ 1 [12] ❏ 2-5 [13] ❏ 6-10 [14] ❏ More than 10 [15]

I would characterize my computer skills as: ❏ Beginner [16] ❏ Intermediate [17] ❏ Advanced [18] ❏ Professional [19]

I use ❏ DOS [20] ❏ Windows [21] ❏ OS/2 [22] ❏ Unix [23] ❏ Macintosh [24] ❏ Other: [25] _____
(please specify)

I would be interested in new books on the following subjects:
(please check all that apply, and use the spaces provided to identify specific software)

❏ Word processing: [26] ❏ Spreadsheets: [27]
❏ Data bases: [28] ❏ Desktop publishing: [29]
❏ File Utilities: [30] ❏ Money management: [31]
❏ Networking: [32] ❏ Programming languages: [33]
❏ Other: [34]

I use a PC at (please check all that apply): ❏ home [35] ❏ work [36] ❏ school [37] ❏ other: [38] _____

The disks I prefer to use are ❏ 5.25 [39] ❏ 3.5 [40] ❏ other: [41] _____

I have a CD ROM: ❏ yes [42] ❏ no [43]

I plan to buy or upgrade computer hardware this year: ❏ yes [44] ❏ no [45]

I plan to buy or upgrade computer software this year: ❏ yes [46] ❏ no [47]

Name: _____ Business title: [48] _____ Type of Business: [49] _____

Address (❏ home [50] ❏ work [51]/Company name: _____)

Street/Suite# _____

City [52]/State [53]/Zipcode [54]: _____ Country [55] _____

❏ **I liked this book!** You may quote me by name in future IDG Books Worldwide promotional materials.

My daytime phone number is _____

IDG BOOKS
THE WORLD OF COMPUTER KNOWLEDGE

❑ **YES!**
Please keep me informed about IDG's World of Computer Knowledge. Send me the latest IDG Books catalog.

BUSINESS REPLY MAIL
FIRST CLASS MAIL   PERMIT NO. 2605   FOSTER CITY, CALIFORNIA

IDG Books Worldwide
919 E Hillsdale Blvd, STE 400
Foster City, CA 94404-9691

NO POSTAGE
NECESSARY
IF MAILED
IN THE
UNITED STATES